CICS for the COBOL Programmer

Part 2: An Advanced Course

CICS for the COBOL Programmer

Part 2: An Advanced Course

Second Edition

Doug Lowe

Mike Murach & Associates, Inc.

4697 W. Jacquelyn Avenue, Fresno, California, 93722, (209) 275-3335

Acknowledgements

Thanks to Marjorie Robertson and Mike Fidel of Micro Focus Inc. and Kathy Magenheim of XDB Systems, Inc. for providing technical assistance and the software used to develop the application programs in this book.

Editorial team: Steve Eckols
                                 Anne Prince

Production/Design: Steve Ehlers

Related books

CICS for the COBOL Programmer, Part 1: An Introductory Course, Doug Lowe

Structured ANS COBOL, Part 1: A Course for Novices, Mike Murach & Paul Noll
Structured ANS COBOL, Part 2: An Advanced Course, Mike Murach & Paul Noll

VS COBOL II: A Guide for Programmers and Managers, Anne Prince

VSAM: Access Method Services and Application Programming, Doug Lowe

DB2 for the COBOL Programmer, Part 1: An Introductory Course, Steve Eckols
DB2 for the COBOL Programmer, Part 2: An Advanced Course, Steve Eckols

IMS for the COBOL Programmer, Part 1: Data Base Processing with IMS/VS and DL/I DOS/VSE, Steve Eckols
IMS for the COBOL Programmer, Part 2: Data Communications and Message Format Service, Steve Eckols

MVS TSO, Part 1: Concepts and ISPF, Doug Lowe
MVS TSO, Part 2: Commands and Procedures, Doug Lowe

How to Design and Develop Business Systems, Steve Eckols

20 19 18 17 16 15 14 13 12 11 10 9 8 7 6 5 4 3 2

ISBN: 0-91165-67-4

Library of Congress Cataloging-in-Publication Data

Lowe, Doug.
  CICS for the COBOL programmer.

  Includes index.
  Contents: Pt. 1. An introductory course —
Pt. 2. An advanced course
  1. COBOL (Computer program language)
2. CICS (Computer system). I. Title.
QA76.73.C25L67 1992 005.4'3   92-17814
ISBN 0-911625-60-7 (pbk. : v. 1 : alk. paper)
ISBN 0-911625-67-4 (pbk. : v. 2 : alk. paper)

Contents

■   **V**

Preface

CICS is a complex system that provides many powerful features. For any given programming problem, there are probably half a dozen different CICS facilities you can choose from to solve that problem in slightly different ways. Because CICS provides so much flexibility, it's crucial that programmers and analysts have a broad understanding of what its facilities are, how they're used, and how they interact.

Too often, though, a programmer's training ends before he or she has mastered all of the important elements of CICS. Consider, for example, the typical CICS programming course: one week of intensive training where just about every CICS command and facility is presented. As part of this course, the student codes three or four simple programs that use the basic CICS elements. With luck, one or two of them work. But there just isn't enough time to learn anything more than the basics in that one short week. As a result, most trainees get just part of a CICS education. They're expected to figure out the rest on the job.

What this book does

This is the second of a two-part series of CICS training. In *Part 1, An Introductory Course*, I presented a basic subset of CICS command-level programming that included programming for 3270-type display terminals and direct access to VSAM files. This book presents the advanced features of CICS—features like file browsing, transient data control, temporary storage control, logical message building, and much more.

Although I designed this book to stand on its own, it also works well when used with other training programs. In particular, if you attend a CICS training course, this book will help you both before and after the course. If you read through the book before hand, you'll be that much better prepared for the intensity of the week-long course. And after the course, you can turn to this book to gain a more complete understanding of the CICS facilities there just wasn't time for in that short week of training.

Why this book is effective

I believe this book is effective for three reasons. First, I spent much time selecting the content of this book. It would be easy to go through the IBM manual and cover every available CICS command. I'm sure you've seen, as I have, books that do...almost verbatim sometimes. Unfortunately,

You should be able to do the following:

1. Design, code, and test simple interactive programs using pseudo-conversational programming techniques.
2. Define mapsets, use the SEND MAP, SEND TEXT, and RECEIVE MAP commands, position the cursor on the screen, and detect the use of PF keys, PA keys, and the Clear key.
3. Use the following file control commands:

   READ   DELETE
   WRITE   UNLOCK
   REWRITE

4. Use the XCTL and LINK commands to manage the execution of programs within a task.
5. Use the RESP option for response code checking.

Table 1   What you should be able to do before studying this book

many of those commands just aren't that useful in a command-level environment.

Second, I emphasize a solid understanding of how CICS works so you can use it more effectively. Learning advanced features of CICS means more than learning the syntax of a few commands. It means understanding how those commands work and how they relate to other CICS and operating system elements. So this book goes beyond presenting command syntax: It shows you what happens inside CICS when you issue a command.

Third, I've included extensive illustrations to show you how to use various CICS elements in COBOL programs. You'll find 12 complete program listings, plus several shorter program segments. These examples not only illustrate CICS language elements, but also serve as models for similar programs you'll write on the job.

Who this book is for

This book is for CICS programmers who want to learn how to use more than the basic elements of CICS. In particular, this book is meant to follow *CICS for the COBOL Programmer, Part 1: An Introductory Course.* Table 1 shows the essential CICS programming skills *Part 1* teaches. Any course that teaches these minimum skills will serve as a prerequisite to this book.

Section	Chapters	Title	Subjects
1	1-3	Advanced file processing features	Browsing, alternate indexes, generic keys, MASSINSERT, data tables
2	4-5	Data base processing features	DB2 and DL/I data base processing
3	6-7	Advanced terminal processing features	BMS logical message building, terminal control
4	8-12	Other advanced CICS features	Temporary storage control, transient data control, interval control, task control, program control, storage control, abend processing, recovery processing, journal control, distributed processing

Table 2   How this book is organized

A note about CICS versions

As I write this book, IBM supports five versions of CICS for MVS users: 1.7, 2.1, 3.1.1, 3.2.1, and 3.3. For VSE users, two versions are supported: 1.7 and 2.1. (Service for CICS 1.7 under MVS will be discontinued in December of 1992, but support for 1.7 under VSE will continue.) For OS/2 users, the current version is 1.2. The CICS elements presented in this book will work for any of these CICS versions.

All of the programming examples in this book were tested on a PC using CICS OS/2. The programs were developed to be compatible with Release 3 of the VS COBOL II compiler. However, it should be easy to adapt them to work with other COBOL compilers.

How to use this book

Table 2 shows the general plan of this book. With one exception, the chapters are self-contained, so you can study the CICS facilities this book presents in almost any sequence you choose. The only exception is chapter 2: It builds on information presented in chapter 1. In a few cases, a chapter will make a minor reference to a subject presented earlier in the book. So if you read the chapters in order, those references will make perfect sense. But because they are minor references, I don't think they'll cause any problems if you read the chapters out of order. And feel free to skip topics or entire chapters that present CICS facilities your installation doesn't use.

Conclusion

I'm confident that this book will make you a more effective CICS programmer. But I'd love to hear any comments or suggestions you might have. So please use the postage-paid comment form at the back of this book. With your help, we'll be able to improve not only this product, but future products as well.

Doug Lowe
Fresno, California
July, 1992

Section 1

Advanced file processing features

In *Part 1: An Introductory Course,* you learned how to use basic file control commands to process VSAM files randomly. The chapters in this section show you how to use advanced file handling features. In chapter 1, you'll learn how to process a file sequentially using browse commands. In chapter 2, you'll learn how to process VSAM files using alternate indexes. Then, in chapter 3, you'll learn how to use three advanced file handling techniques: generic keys, MASSINSERT, and data tables.

Chapter 1

Sequential processing using browse commands

Most on-line applications process files using the random file processing elements you learned in *Part 1: An Introductory Course*. Still, some on-line applications need to access files sequentially. Under CICS, accessing a file sequentially is called *browsing*. That's just what you'll learn how to do in this chapter. After I show you the commands you use for sequential processing (called *browse commands*), I'll illustrate how they're used with two program examples.

The two browse commands you'll use most are STARTBR and READNEXT. The STARTBR command initiates a browse operation, and the READNEXT command retrieves records sequentially. Other browse commands are READPREV (read a record in *reverse* order), ENDBR (end a browse operation), and RESETBR (change the current position during a browse operation).

You can issue browse commands for all three types of VSAM data sets: key-sequenced data sets (KSDS), relative record data sets (RRDS), and entry-sequenced data sets (ESDS). Sequential processing of a KSDS is usually based on the file's key values. For an RRDS, browse operations use relative record numbers. And for an ESDS, browse operations are based on relative byte addresses.

■ **3**

The STARTBR command

The STARTBR command, shown in figure 1-1, initiates a browse operation and identifies the location within the data set where the browse begins. The STARTBR command doesn't retrieve a record from the file. Instead, it just establishes a position in the file so subsequent READNEXT or READPREV commands can retrieve records.

You can think of a STARTBR command like a standard COBOL START statement—its function is similar. The main difference is that a STARTBR command is *always* required when you want to browse a data set, even if you want to begin with the first record in the file. In contrast, standard batch COBOL requires a START statement only when you want to begin sequential retrieval at a point other than the first record in the file.

In its simplest form, you code the STARTBR command like this:

```
EXEC CICS
    STARTBR DATASET('CUSTMAS')
            RIDFLD(CM-CUSTOMER-NUMBER)
            RESP(RESPONSE-CODE)
END-EXEC.
```

This STARTBR command initiates a browse operation for the KSDS named CUSTMAS. The browse begins at the record identified by the value of CM-CUSTOMER-NUMBER. For example, if the value of CM-CUSTOMER-NUMBER is 10000, the browse begins at the record in CUSTMAS whose key is 10000. If there's no record with that key, processing starts with the first record whose key is greater than 10000. That's because the GTEQ option is in effect by default for this STARTBR command.

Notice that I also coded the RESP option on this command. If there's no record in the KSDS whose key is greater than or equal to the value you specify in the RIDFLD field, the RESP field will indicate that the NOTFND condition was raised. The default action for the NOTFND condition is to terminate your task. So you should always provide for it by coding the RESP option and testing its value following the execution of the command or by using a HANDLE CONDITION command.

(If you're not familiar with using the RESP option for response code checking, you should realize that it's available on every CICS command, even though I don't include it in the syntax diagrams in this book. The RESP option specifies a binary fullword item (PIC S9(8) COMP) where CICS places a response code that corresponds to exceptional conditions. The RESP option lets you test for exceptional conditions without coding HANDLE CONDITION commands. You'll see examples of testing response code values in the programming examples throughout this book.)

So far, I've assumed you're processing a VSAM key-sequenced data set. You can also use the STARTBR command (and any of the other

The STARTBR command

```
EXEC CICS
    STARTBR   DATASET(filename)
              RIDFLD(data-area)
          [ RRN | RBA ]
          [ GTEQ | EQUAL ]
          [ GENERIC ]
          [ KEYLENGTH(data-value) ]
END-EXEC
```

Explanation

DATASET	Specifies the file name from the File Control Table.
RIDFLD	Specifies the field identifying the record where the browse operation will start. For VSAM key-sequenced files (KSDS), the value is the key of the record. For relative record files (RRDS), the value is the relative record number. And for entry-sequenced files (ESDS), the value is a relative byte address. For an RRDS or ESDS, the data area must be a binary fullword field (PIC S9(8) COMP).
RRN	Specifies that the file is a relative record file, and the RIDFLD option should be interpreted as a relative record number.
RBA	Specifies that the file is an entry-sequenced file, and the RIDFLD option should be interpreted as a relative byte address.
GTEQ	Specifies that the browse operation will start at the first record whose key is greater than or equal to the value in RIDFLD.
EQUAL	Specifies that the browse operation will start at the record whose key is equal to the value in RIDFLD. If there is no such record, the NOTFND condition is raised.
GENERIC	Specifies that only a part of the key in the RIDFLD field should be used. Positioning is established at the first record with a key whose leftmost character positions, as specified by the KEYLENGTH option, match the RIDFLD field. Valid only for KSDS files.
KEYLENGTH	Specifies a binary halfword (PIC S9(4) COMP) or literal value that indicates the length of the key, which must be less than the file's defined key length. Used with the GENERIC option.

Figure 1-1   The STARTBR command

browse commands) to process a relative record data set or an entry-sequenced data set. For a relative record data set, the value of the RIDFLD field is a relative record number within the file, and you must specify the RRN parameter in the STARTBR command. For an entry-sequenced data set, the RIDFLD is a relative byte address, and you must code RBA in the STARTBR command. For an RRDS or ESDS, the RIDFLD field must be a fullword binary field (PIC S9(8) COMP).

The last two options you can code on the STARTBR command, GENERIC and KEYLENGTH, let you specify a RIDFLD key whose length is less than the full length of the key defined for the file. You'll learn how these two options work in chapter 3.

How to start a browse at the beginning of a file   You can start processing with the first record in a KSDS by moving LOW-VALUE to the RIDFLD field before you issue the STARTBR command. That way, processing begins at the first record whose key is greater than or equal to hexadecimal zeros—and that's always the first record in the file. If a KSDS has a numeric key, though, you must move ZERO rather than LOW-VALUE to the key field to start a browse at the first record. That's because the COBOL compiler won't let you move LOW-VALUE to a numeric field.

To start a browse at the beginning of an ESDS, move ZERO to the RIDFLD field. That way, the browse starts at the record whose RBA is zero—the first record in the file. And to browse an RRDS from the beginning, move 1 to the RIDFLD field.

How to start a browse at a specific record   You can start a browse at a specific record that *must* exist in the file by coding the EQUAL option on the STARTBR command, like this:

```
EXEC CICS
    STARTBR DATASET('CUSTMAS')
            RIDFLD(CM-CUSTOMER-NUMBER)
            EQUAL
            RESP(RESPONSE-CODE)
END-EXEC
```

Suppose CM-CUSTOMER-NUMBER contains 10000. Then, processing will start only with record 10000. If there's no record in the file with the key value you specify, the NOTFND condition will be indicated by the RESPONSE-CODE field.

How to start a browse at the end of a file   In some cases, you might want to start processing with the last record in a file. For a KSDS, you can do that by moving HIGH-VALUE (hexadecimal FFs) to the RIDFLD field. Issuing the STARTBR command when the RIDFLD field contains HIGH-VALUE is a special case—it doesn't cause the NOTFND condition to be raised, as you might expect. Instead, it establishes the position in the file at the last record.

Unfortunately, you can't move all 9's to a numeric RIDFLD field to start processing at the last record. That's because the NOTFND condition will be raised if there isn't a record with that key in the file. Since the compiler won't let you move HIGH-VALUE to a numeric field, you'll have to redefine the RIDFLD as alphanumeric to be able to move HIGH-VALUE to it.

To begin a browse at the end of a relative record or entry-sequenced file, simply move HIGH-VALUE to the RIDFLD field.

```
2100-START-ACCOUNT-BROWSE.
*
     MOVE LOW-VALUE TO AR-ACCOUNT-NUMBER.
     EXEC CICS
         STARTBR DATASET('ACCOUNT')
                 RIDFLD(AR-ACCOUNT-NUMBER)
                 RESP(RESPONSE-CODE)
     END-EXEC.
     IF RESPONSE-CODE = DFHRESP(NOTFND)
         MOVE 'Y' TO ACCOUNT-EOF-SW
     ELSE IF RESPONSE-CODE NOT = DFHRESP(NORMAL)
         GO TO 9999-TERMINATE-PROGRAM.
```

Figure 1-2   Typical coding for a start-browse module

A typical STARTBR module   Figure 1-2 shows the coding for a typical start-browse module. First, I move LOW-VALUE to the file's RIDFLD field. That way, the STARTBR command positions the file at the first record. After the STARTBR command, I test the response code field with an IF statement. If the NOTFND condition occurs, I set a switch (ACCOUNT-EOF-SW) that indicates the end of the file has been reached. Then, I can test that switch to determine if the STARTBR command executed normally. If a serious error occurs, I branch to a paragraph named 9999-TERMINATE-PROGRAM to end the program.

The READNEXT command

After you've used the STARTBR command to initiate a browse operation, you can retrieve records sequentially using the READNEXT command. Figure 1-3 shows the READNEXT command's format. Each time you issue a READNEXT command, the next record in the file identified by the DATASET parameter is retrieved and stored in the INTO field. When there are no more records in the file, the ENDFILE condition is raised. So be sure to test the response code field immediately after the READNEXT command.

The data name you specify in the RIDFLD parameter in a READNEXT command must be the same as the one you've already specified in the STARTBR command. Normally, your program shouldn't alter the contents of this field during the browse. Instead, the READNEXT command updates it to indicate the key, RRN, or RBA value of the record it retrieved. That way, subsequent READNEXT commands continue to retrieve records in sequence.

If you do change the RIDFLD field, you must change it to a value that's greater than the value returned by the last READNEXT command that was issued. Then, CICS skips ahead to the specified record. This is called *skip sequential processing*. If you specified GTEQ on the STARTBR command, the browse skips forward to the next record whose key is greater than or equal to the new RIDFLD value. However, if you

The READNEXT command

```
EXEC CICS
     READNEXT    DATASET(filename)
                 INTO(data-area)
                 RIDFLD(data-area)
              [ RRN | RBA ]
              [ GENERIC ]
              [ KEYLENGTH(data-value) ]
END-EXEC
```

Explanation

DATASET   Specifies the file name from the File Control Table.

INTO   Specifies the area that will contain the record being read.

RIDFLD   Must specify the same data name specified in the STARTBR command. After
                   completion of the READNEXT command, this field is updated so it contains the key,
                   RRN, or RBA of the record read.

RRN   Specifies that the file is a relative record file.

RBA   Specifies that the file is an entry-sequenced file.

GENERIC   Specifies that only a part of the key in the RIDFLD field should be used. Positioning is
                   established at the first record with a key whose leftmost character positions, as
                   specified by the KEYLENGTH option, match the RIDFLD field. Valid only for KSDS files.

KEYLENGTH   Specifies a binary halfword (PIC S9(4) COMP) or literal value that indicates the length of
                   the key, which must be less than the file's defined key length. Used with the GENERIC
                   option.

Figure 1-3   The READNEXT command

specified EQUAL on the STARTBR command, the NOTFND condition is raised if the new RIDFLD value doesn't exist in the file.

To retrieve records sequentially from an RRDS, you code RRN on the READNEXT command. Similarly, to retrieve records sequentially from an ESDS, specify RBA. If you omit both RRN and RBA, CICS assumes you're processing a KSDS.

Figure 1-4 shows the coding for a typical READNEXT module that's executed repeatedly by a PERFORM UNTIL statement. Here, module 2000 is performed until the ENDFILE condition is detected. Following the PERFORM statement in module 2000 would be statements that process the record retrieved by module 2100. What those statements would be depends on the requirements of the application. For the sake of clarity, I omitted them in figure 1-4.

```
        .
        .
        .
    PERFORM 2000-PROCESS-ACCOUNT-RECORD
        UNTIL ACCOUNT-EOF.
        .
        .
        .
*
 2000-PROCESS-ACCOUNT-RECORD.
*
    PERFORM 2100-READ-NEXT-ACCOUNT.
    IF NOT ACCOUNT-EOF
            .
            .
            .
*
 2100-READ-NEXT-ACCOUNT.
*
    EXEC CICS
        READNEXT DATASET('ACCOUNT')
                 INTO(ACCOUNT-RECORD)
                 RIDFLD(AR-ACCOUNT-NUMBER)
                 RESP(RESPONSE-CODE)
    END-EXEC.
    IF RESPONSE-CODE = DFHRESP(ENDFILE)
        MOVE 'Y' TO ACCOUNT-EOF-SW
    ELSE IF RESPONSE-CODE NOT = DFHRESP(NORMAL)
        GO TO 9999-TERMINATE-PROGRAM.
```

Figure 1-4   Typical coding for a read-next module.

The READPREV command

The READPREV command, shown in figure 1-5, is similar to the READNEXT command except that it retrieves records in reverse order. In short, the READPREV command lets you read a file backwards, from the current position toward the beginning of the file. When a READPREV command tries to retrieve a record that would be beyond the beginning of the file, the ENDFILE condition is raised. You should provide for it just as you do for the READNEXT command.

The READPREV command has two peculiarities you should know about. First, if you issue a READPREV command following a READNEXT command, the same record is retrieved twice. For example, suppose a file contains three records with keys 1000, 1001, and 1002. You issue a READNEXT command that retrieves record 1001. If you then issue a READPREV command, it too retrieves record 1001. To retrieve record 1000, you must issue *two* READPREV commands: the first retrieves record 1001, the second record 1000. The opposite is true as well: If you issue a READNEXT command following a READPREV command, the same record is retrieved.

The second peculiarity of READPREV has to do with issuing the command immediately after a STARTBR command. If the STARTBR

The READPREV command

```
EXEC CICS
    READPREV    DATASET(filename)
                INTO(data-area)
                RIDFLD(data-area)
            [ RRN | RBA ]
            [ GENERIC ]
            [ KEYLENGTH(data-value) ]
END-EXEC
```

Explanation

DATASET	Specifies the file name from the File Control Table.
INTO	Specifies the area that will contain the record being read.
RIDFLD	Must specify the same data name specified in the STARTBR command. After completion of the READPREV command, this field is updated to indicate the key, RRN, or RBA of the record read.
RRN	Specifies that the file is a relative record file.
RBA	Specifies that the file is an entry-sequenced file.
GENERIC	Specifies that only a part of the key in the RIDFLD field should be used. Positioning is established at the first record with a key whose leftmost character positions, as specified by the KEYLENGTH option, match the RIDFLD field. Valid only for KSDS files.
KEYLENGTH	Specifies a binary halfword (PIC S9(4) COMP) or literal value that indicates the length of the key, which must be less than the file's defined key length. Used with the GENERIC option.

Figure 1-5   The READPREV command

command establishes positioning for the file at the last record because the RIDFLD field contains HIGH-VALUE, it's safe to issue a READPREV command. But if the RIDFLD field for the STARTBR command doesn't contain HIGH-VALUE, you shouldn't follow it with a READPREV command. That's because READPREV raises the NOTFND condition if the STARTBR command refers to a record that isn't in the file—even if the GTEQ option on the STARTBR command positions the file to the next record in sequence. So as a rule, don't code a READPREV command right after a STARTBR command unless the STARTBR command's RIDFLD field contains HIGH-VALUE.

How can you achieve the effect of a STARTBR command with a RIDFLD field that doesn't contain HIGH-VALUE followed by a READPREV? You must issue four commands: STARTBR, READNEXT, READPREV, and READPREV. The STARTBR command positions the

The ENDBR command

```
EXEC CICS
    ENDBR DATASET(filename)
END-EXEC
```

Explanation

DATASET   Specifies the file name from the File Control Table.

Figure 1-6   The ENDBR command

file to the record you specify. Then, the READNEXT command retrieves the record. Next, the READPREV command changes the direction of the browse. But since it retrieves the same record as the READNEXT command, another READPREV command is required to read the previous record. You'll see an example of this coding later in this chapter, so don't worry if this seems confusing. I think it will make sense when you see the example. And frankly, it's a function you won't have to code often.

Because the READPREV command is so similar to the READNEXT command, I don't provide an example of a typical READPREV module. If you wish, you can use the coding in figure 1-4 as a model. Just change the READNEXT command to a READPREV command.

The ENDBR command

Figure 1-6 gives the format of the ENDBR command, used to terminate a browse operation. Normally, you don't need to issue an ENDBR command, since your browse is terminated automatically when your task ends. However, if your program does extensive processing after it completes a browse operation, you should issue an ENDBR command for efficiency's sake. As long as your browse is active, VSAM resources are allocated to your task. Releasing those resources by terminating your browse frees them for other users.

The RESETBR command

Figure 1-7 shows the RESETBR command. As you can see, its format is similar to the format of the STARTBR command. You use the RESETBR command to restart a browse operation at a new position in a file. It has the same effect as issuing an ENDBR command followed by a STARTBR command, but it's more efficient. That's because when you issue an ENDBR command, the VSAM resources allocated to your task are released and a subsequent STARTBR command must reallocate them. In

The RESETBR command

```
EXEC CICS
    RESETBR    DATASET(filename)
               RIDFLD(data-area)
           [ RRN | RBA ]
           [ GTEQ | EQUAL ]
           [ GENERIC ]
           [ KEYLENGTH(data-value) ]
END-EXEC
```

Explanation

DATASET	Specifies the file name from the File Control Table.
RIDFLD	Specifies the field identifying the record where the browse operation will be repositioned. For VSAM key-sequenced files (KSDS), the value is the key of the record. For relative record files (RRDS), the value is the relative record number. And for entry-sequenced files (ESDS), the value is a relative byte address. For an RRDS or ESDS, the data area must be a binary fullword field (PIC S9(8) COMP).
RRN	Specifies that the file is a relative record file, and the RIDFLD option should be interpreted as a relative record number.
RBA	Specifies that the file is an entry-sequenced file, and the RIDFLD option should be interpreted as a relative byte address.
GTEQ	Specifies that the browse operation will be repositioned at the first record whose key is greater than or equal to the value in RIDFLD.
EQUAL	Specifies that the browse operation will be repositioned at the record whose key is equal to the value in RIDFLD. If there is no such record, the NOTFND condition is raised.
GENERIC	Specifies that only a part of the key in the RIDFLD field should be used. Positioning is established at the first record with a key whose leftmost character positions, as specified by the KEYLENGTH option, match the RIDFLD field. Valid only for KSDS files.
KEYLENGTH	Specifies a binary halfword (PIC S9(4) COMP) or literal value that indicates the length of the key, which must be less than the file's defined key length. Used with the GENERIC option.

Figure 1-7   The RESETBR command

contrast, if you issue a RESETBR command, VSAM resources are not released, so they don't need to be reallocated.

Browse exceptional conditions

Besides the NOTFND and ENDFILE conditions I've already mentioned, a number of other conditions might be raised during a browse operation. Figure 1-8 summarizes those conditions, including NOTFND and ENDFILE. Most of them are caused by programming errors or CICS problems, so there's usually no need to provide for them in production programs. Still, you should find out your shop's standards for handling these conditions and follow them.

Condition	Cause
DSIDERR	The data set isn't defined in the FCT.
ENDFILE	There are no more records to be read.
ILLOGIC	A VSAM error has occurred.
INVREQ	The browse request is invalid. Usually, this is because you didn't issue a successful STARTBR command before a READNEXT or READPREV command.
IOERR	An I/O error has occurred.
LENGERR	A length error has occurred.
NOTFND	The record specified in a STARTBR command doesn't exist.
NOTOPEN	The data set isn't open.

Figure 1-8   File control exceptional conditions that might be raised during browse operations

An invoice summary program

Figures 1-9 through 1-13 present a simple, non-interactive program that browses a file of invoice records and displays information summarized from the file. You can see from the specifications in figure 1-9 that the summary display shows the number of invoices in the file, the first and last invoice numbers, and the sum of the values in the invoice total fields of the records in the file. To accumulate this summary information, the program browses through the entire file.

Because the invoice summary program doesn't interact with a user, its processing is done at computer system speed rather than operator speed. As a result, it's not pseudo-conversational—its structure is more like what you'd expect for a batch COBOL report-preparation program than for a CICS program. Keep in mind, however, that the invoice summary program is not typical; most CICS programs have to be pseudo-conversational.

Figure 1-10 shows the structure chart for this program. Here, module 0000 is the main processing module. It performs module 1000 to start the browse. Then, it invokes module 2000 repeatedly to read records sequentially from the invoice file. When the end of the file has been reached, module 0000 calls module 3000 to send the summary display to the terminal.

Figure 1-11 gives the mapset listing for the invoice summary program, and figure 1-12 gives the symbolic map. There's nothing unusual about the invoice summary program's mapset, so you shouldn't have any trouble understanding it.

Figure 1-13 gives the complete source listing for this program. Module 0000 controls the execution of modules 1000, 2000, and 3000,

Program INVSUM1

Overview Reads the records in the invoice file and displays a summary screen showing a count of the invoices, the beginning and ending invoice number, and the sum of the invoice total fields.

Input/output specifications

SUMMAP1	Invoice summary map
INVOICE	Invoice file

Processing specifications

1. Control is transferred to this program via XCTL from a menu program with no communication area. The user can also start the program by entering the trans-id SUM1.

2. The program processes the invoice records using CICS browse commands, then displays the summary map and terminates with a RETURN command. The TRANSID should specify that the MENU transaction is invoked when the user presses the Enter key (or any other attention key).

3. If an unrecoverable error occurs, the program invokes SYSERR by issuing an XCTL command, passing appropriate data in the ERRPARM parameter group.

Figure 1-9 Specifications for the invoice summary program (part 1 of 3)

Map name ___SUMMAP1___ Date ___07/01/92___
Program name ___INVSUM1___ Designer ___Doug Lowe___

```
 1  SUMMAP1              Invoice summary.
 2
 3  Press Enter to return to menu.
 4
 5  Invoices in file. . . . . . :  ZZ,ZZ9
 6  First invoice number. . . . :  999999
 7  Last invoice number . . . . :  999999
 8
 9  Total value of invoices . . :  $$,$$$,$$9.99
10
11
12
13
14
15
16
17
18
19
20
21
22
23  XXXXXXXXXXXXXXXXXXXXXXXXXXXXXXXXXXXXXXXXXXXXXXXXXXXXXXXXXXXXXXXXXXXXXXXXXXXXXXXX
24  F3=Exit   F12=Cancel                                                          X
```

Figure 1-9 Specifications for the invoice summary program (part 2 of 3)

The INVOICE copy member

```
01   INVOICE-RECORD.
*
     05   INV-INVOICE-NUMBER          PIC 9(6).
     05   INV-INVOICE-DATE            PIC X(6).
     05   INV-CUSTOMER-NUMBER         PIC X(6).
     05   INV-PO-NUMBER               PIC X(10).
     05   INV-LINE-ITEM               OCCURS 10.
          10   INV-PRODUCT-CODE       PIC X(10).
          10   INV-QUANTITY           PIC S9(7)      COMP-3.
          10   INV-UNIT-PRICE         PIC S9(7)V99   COMP-3.
          10   INV-AMOUNT             PIC S9(7)V99   COMP-3.
     05   INV-INVOICE-TOTAL           PIC S9(7)V99   COMP-3.
*
```

The ERRPARM copy member

```
01   ERROR-PARAMETERS.
*
     05   ERR-RESP        PIC S9(8)   COMP.
     05   ERR-RESP2       PIC S9(8)   COMP.
     05   ERR-TRNID       PIC X(4).
     05   ERR-RSRCE       PIC X(8).
*
```

Figure 1-9 Specifications for the invoice summary program (part 3 of 3)

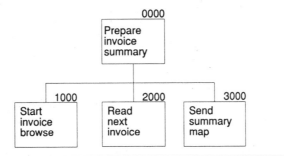

Figure 1-10 Structure chart for the invoice summary program

just as the structure chart shows. After module 3000 sends the summary map to the terminal, a RETURN command terminates the program. When the operator presses an attention key after looking at the summary display, the MENU transaction is started because of the TRANSID specification on the RETURN command.

Notice that Y is moved to INVOICE-EOF-SW if the NOTFND condition is raised by the STARTBR command or if the ENDFILE condition is raised by the READNEXT command. Since module 2000 is performed until INVOICE-EOF, records are read until the end of the file

```
           PRINT NOGEN
SUMSET1    DFHMSD TYPE=&SYSPARM,                                          X
                  LANG=COBOL,                                            X
                  MODE=INOUT,                                            X
                  TERM=3270-2,                                          X
                  CTRL=FREEKB,                                           X
                  STORAGE=AUTO,                                          X
                  TIOAPFX=YES
***********************************************************************
SUMMAP1    DFHMDI SIZE=(24,80),                                         X
                  LINE=1,                                               X
                  COLUMN=1
***********************************************************************
           DFHMDF POS=(1,1),                                            X
                  LENGTH=8,                                             X
                  ATTRB=(NORM,PROT),                                    X
                  COLOR=BLUE,                                           X
                  INITIAL='SUMMAP1'
           DFHMDF POS=(1,20),                                           X
                  LENGTH=15,                                            X
                  ATTRB=(NORM,PROT),                                    X
                  COLOR=BLUE,                                           X
                  INITIAL='Invoice summary'
***********************************************************************
           DFHMDF POS=(3,1),                                            X
                  LENGTH=29,                                            X
                  ATTRB=(NORM,PROT),                                    X
                  COLOR=GREEN,                                          X
                  INITIAL='Press Enter to return to menu.'
           DFHMDF POS=(5,1),                                            X
                  LENGTH=29,                                            X
                  ATTRB=(NORM,PROT),                                    X
                  COLOR=GREEN,                                          X
                  INITIAL='Invoices in file. . . . . . :'
COUNT      DFHMDF POS=(5,31),                                           X
                  LENGTH=6,                                             X
                  ATTRB=(NORM,PROT),                                    X
                  COLOR=TURQUOISE,                                      X
                  PICOUT='ZZ,ZZ9'
           DFHMDF POS=(6,1),                                            X
                  LENGTH=29,                                            X
                  ATTRB=(NORM,PROT),                                    X
                  COLOR=GREEN,                                          X
                  INITIAL='First invoice number. . . . :'
FIRST      DFHMDF POS=(6,31),                                           X
                  LENGTH=6,                                             X
                  COLOR=TURQUOISE,                                      X
                  ATTRB=(NORM,PROT),                                    X
                  PICOUT='999999'
           DFHMDF POS=(7,1),                                            X
                  LENGTH=29,                                            X
                  ATTRB=(NORM,PROT),                                    X
                  COLOR=GREEN,                                          X
                  INITIAL='Last invoice number . . . . :'
LAST       DFHMDF POS=(7,31),                                           X
                  LENGTH=6,                                             X
                  COLOR=TURQUOISE,                                      X
                  ATTRB=(NORM,PROT),                                    X
                  PICOUT='999999'
```

Figure 1-11 Mapset listing for the invoice summary program (part 1 of 2)

```
          DFHMDF POS=(9,1),                                                  X
                 LENGTH=29,                                                  X
                 ATTRB=(NORM,PROT),                                          X
                 COLOR=GREEN,                                                X
                 INITIAL='Total value of invoices . . :'
TOTAL     DFHMDF POS=(9,31),                                                 X
                 LENGTH=13,                                                  X
                 COLOR=TURQUOISE,                                            X
                 ATTRB=(NORM,PROT),                                          X
                 PICOUT='$$,$$$,$$9.99'
*******************************************************************************
MESSAGE   DFHMDF POS=(23,1),                                                 X
                 LENGTH=79,                                                  X
                 ATTRB=(BRT,PROT),                                           X
                 COLOR=YELLOW
          DFHMDF POS=(24,1),                                                 X
                 LENGTH=19,                                                  X
                 ATTRB=(NORM,PROT),                                          X
                 COLOR=BLUE,                                                 X
                 INITIAL='F3=Exit   F12=Cancel'
DUMMY     DFHMDF POS=(24,79),                                                X
                 LENGTH=1,                                                   X
                 ATTRB=(DRK,PROT,FSET),                                      X
                 INITIAL=' '
*******************************************************************************
          DFHMSD TYPE=FINAL
          END
```

Figure 1-11 Mapset listing for the invoice summary program (part 2 of 2)

is reached. And since a COBOL PERFORM UNTIL test is done *before* the specified paragraph is performed, module 2000 isn't performed at all if the NOTFND condition is raised on the STARTBR command. As a result, this program works properly even if the invoice file is empty: The invoice count and total value fields will contain zero, and the first and last invoice number fields will be blank.

If a more serious error occurs during the STARTBR or READNEXT commands, control is transferred to 9999-TERMINATE-PROGRAM. This paragraph moves some useful diagnostic information to fields in the ERROR-PARAMETERS group, which I copied into the program from the ERRPARM copy member. Then, it transfers control to a generalized error handling program called SYSERR. This simple program sends an error message to the terminal, then issues an ABEND command to terminate the task. You'll see this program used in all of the programs in this book. However, I didn't include its source listing here because it doesn't affect the operation of any of the programs. (If you want to see the source listing for SYSERR, it's in *CICS for the COBOL Programmer, Part 1.*) I also didn't include the module that calls SYSERR on any of the program structure charts, because I don't think it's necessary.

```
01   SUMMAP1I.
     02    FILLER    PIC X(12).
     02    COUNTL    PIC S9(4) COMP.
     02    COUNTF    PIC X.
     02    FILLER REDEFINES COUNTF.
      03   COUNTA    PIC X.
     02    COUNTI    PIC X(0006).
     02    FIRSTL    PIC S9(4) COMP.
     02    FIRSTF    PIC X.
     02    FILLER REDEFINES FIRSTF.
      03   FIRSTA    PIC X.
     02    FIRSTI    PIC X(0006).
     02    LASTL     PIC S9(4) COMP.
     02    LASTF     PIC X.
     02    FILLER REDEFINES LASTF.
      03   LASTA     PIC X.
     02    LASTI     PIC X(0006).
     02    TOTALL    PIC S9(4) COMP.
     02    TOTALF    PIC X.
     02    FILLER REDEFINES TOTALF.
      03   TOTALA    PIC X.
     02    TOTALI    PIC X(0013).
     02    MESSAGEL  PIC S9(4) COMP.
     02    MESSAGEF  PIC X.
     02    FILLER REDEFINES MESSAGEF.
      03   MESSAGEA  PIC X.
     02    MESSAGEI  PIC X(0079).
     02    DUMMYL    PIC S9(4) COMP.
     02    DUMMYF    PIC X.
     02    FILLER REDEFINES DUMMYF.
      03   DUMMYA    PIC X.
     02    DUMMYI    PIC X(0001).
01   SUMMAP1O REDEFINES SUMMAP1I.
     02    FILLER    PIC X(12).
     02    FILLER    PIC X(3).
     02    COUNTO    PIC ZZ,ZZ9.
     02    FILLER    PIC X(3).
     02    FIRSTO    PIC 999999.
     02    FILLER    PIC X(3).
     02    LASTO     PIC 999999.
     02    FILLER    PIC X(3).
     02    TOTALO    PIC $$,$$$,$$9.99.
     02    FILLER    PIC X(3).
     02    MESSAGEO  PIC X(0079).
     02    FILLER    PIC X(3).
     02    DUMMYO    PIC X(0001).
```

Figure 1-12   Symbolic map for the invoice summary program

```
IDENTIFICATION DIVISION.
*
PROGRAM-ID. INVSUM1.
*
ENVIRONMENT DIVISION.
*
DATA DIVISION.
*
WORKING-STORAGE SECTION.
*
01  SWITCHES.
*
    05   INVOICE-EOF-SW          PIC X          VALUE 'N'.
         88   INVOICE-EOF                        VALUE 'Y'.
    05   FIRST-RECORD-SW         PIC X          VALUE 'Y'.
         88   FIRST-RECORD                       VALUE 'Y'.
*
01  WORK-FIELDS.
*
    05   INVOICE-COUNT           PIC S9(5)      COMP-3   VALUE ZERO.
    05   INVOICE-TOTAL           PIC S9(7)V99   COMP-3   VALUE ZERO.
    05   STARTBR-KEY             PIC X(6).
*
01  RESPONSE-CODE               PIC S9(8)      COMP.
*
COPY SUMSET1.
*
COPY INVOICE.
*
COPY ERRPARM.
*
PROCEDURE DIVISION.
*
0000-PREPARE-INVOICE-SUMMARY.
*
    MOVE LOW-VALUE TO SUMMAP10.
    PERFORM 1000-START-INVOICE-BROWSE.
    PERFORM 2000-READ-NEXT-INVOICE
        UNTIL INVOICE-EOF.
    PERFORM 3000-SEND-SUMMARY-MAP.
    EXEC CICS
        RETURN TRANSID('MENU')
    END-EXEC.
*
1000-START-INVOICE-BROWSE.
*
    MOVE LOW-VALUE TO STARTBR-KEY.
    EXEC CICS
        STARTBR DATASET('INVOICE')
                RIDFLD(STARTBR-KEY)
                RESP(RESPONSE-CODE)
    END-EXEC.
    IF RESPONSE-CODE = DFHRESP(NOTFND)
        MOVE 'Y' TO INVOICE-EOF-SW
    ELSE IF RESPONSE-CODE NOT = DFHRESP(NORMAL)
        GO TO 9999-TERMINATE-PROGRAM.
*
```

Figure 1-13 Source listing for the invoice summary program (part 1 of 2)

```
/
 2000-READ-NEXT-INVOICE.
*
     EXEC CICS
          READNEXT DATASET('INVOICE')
                   INTO(INVOICE-RECORD)
                   RIDFLD(INV-INVOICE-NUMBER)
                   RESP(RESPONSE-CODE)
     END-EXEC.
     IF RESPONSE-CODE = DFHRESP(NORMAL)
          MOVE INV-INVOICE-NUMBER TO LASTO
          ADD 1 TO INVOICE-COUNT
          ADD INV-INVOICE-TOTAL TO INVOICE-TOTAL
          IF FIRST-RECORD
               MOVE INV-INVOICE-NUMBER TO FIRSTO
               MOVE 'N' TO FIRST-RECORD-SW
          END-IF
     ELSE IF RESPONSE-CODE = DFHRESP(ENDFILE)
          MOVE 'Y' TO INVOICE-EOF-SW
     ELSE
          GO TO 9999-TERMINATE-PROGRAM.
*
 3000-SEND-SUMMARY-MAP.
*
     MOVE INVOICE-COUNT TO COUNTO.
     MOVE INVOICE-TOTAL TO TOTALO.
     EXEC CICS
          SEND MAP('SUMMAP1')
               MAPSET('SUMSET1')
               FROM(SUMMAP1O)
               ERASE
     END-EXEC.
*
 9999-TERMINATE-PROGRAM.
*
     MOVE EIBRESP  TO ERR-RESP.
     MOVE EIBRESP2 TO ERR-RESP2.
     MOVE EIBTRNID TO ERR-TRNID.
     MOVE EIBRSRCE TO ERR-RSRCE.
     EXEC CICS
          XCTL PROGRAM('SYSERR')
               COMMAREA(ERROR-PARAMETERS)
     END-EXEC.
```

Figure 1-13 Source listing for the invoice summary program (part 2 of 2)

Program CUSTINQ2

Overview Displays records from the customer file, allowing the user to scroll forwards or backwards using PF keys.

Input/output
specifications

INQMAP1 Customer inquiry map
CUSTMAS Customer master file

Processing
specifications

1. Control is transferred to this program via XCTL from the menu program INVMENU with no communication area. The user can also start the program by entering the trans-id INQ2. In either case, the program should respond by displaying the inquiry map.

2. The user selects a customer record display by pressing an attention key, as follows:

   Enter   Display the customer indicated by the entry in the customer number field.
   PF5   Display the first customer in the file.
   PF6   Display the last customer in the file.
   PF7   Display the previous customer.
   PF8   Display the next customer.

   The program then reads and displays the appropriate customer record.

3. Use the pseudo-conversational programming technique. To restart the browse at the correct record during the next program execution, save the key of the customer currently displayed in the communication area.

4. If the user presses PF3 or PF12, return to the menu program INVMENU by issuing an XCTL command.

Figure 1-14 Specifications for the customer inquiry program (part 1 of 3)

A customer inquiry program

Figures 1-14 through 1-19 present a customer inquiry program that lets a terminal user display records from a file of customer records. As you can see in the specifications in figure 1-14, the user presses various attention keys to indicate which record to display. The user types a customer number and presses the Enter key to display a particular customer record. To display the first record in the file, the user presses PF5. To display the last record in the file, the user presses PF6. And to display the previous customer or the next customer, the user presses PF7 or PF8.

Bear in mind, however, that this is a pseudo-conversational program. As a result, even though the entire terminal session might appear to the user to be a single browse session, it isn't. Each pseudo-conversational execution of the program that performs a browse requires one STARTBR command and one or more READNEXT or READPREV commands. Between executions, the program keeps track

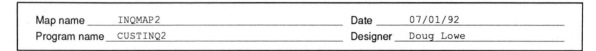

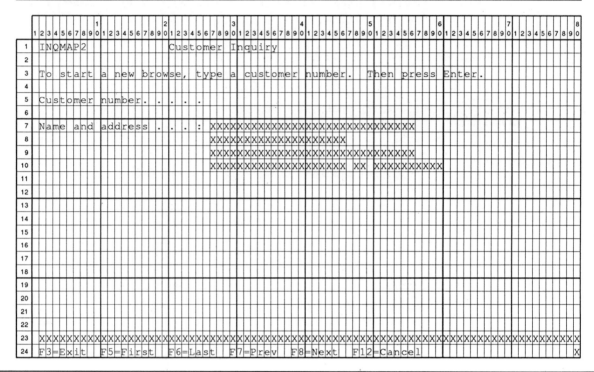

Figure 1-14 Specifications for the customer inquiry program (part 2 of 3)

The CUSTMAS copy member

```
01    CUSTOMER-MASTER-RECORD.
*
      05    CM-CUSTOMER-NUMBER      PIC X(6).
      05    CM-FIRST-NAME           PIC X(20).
      05    CM-LAST-NAME            PIC X(30).
      05    CM-ADDRESS              PIC X(30).
      05    CM-CITY                 PIC X(20).
      05    CM-STATE                PIC X(2).
      05    CM-ZIP-CODE             PIC X(10).
*
```

The ERRPARM copy member

```
01    ERROR-PARAMETERS.
*
      05    ERR-RESP        PIC S9(8)    COMP.
      05    ERR-RESP2       PIC S9(8)    COMP.
      05    ERR-TRNID       PIC X(4).
      05    ERR-RSRCE       PIC X(8).
*
```

Figure 1-14 Specifications for the customer inquiry program (part 3 of 3)

Event	Response
Start the program	Display the inquiry map.
PF3 PF12	Transfer control to the menu program.
Enter	Read and display the customer record indicated by the customer number entered by the user using this sequence of commands: RECEIVE MAP READ SEND MAP
PF5	Read and display the first record in the file using this sequence of commands: STARTBR RIDFLD(low-values) READNEXT SEND MAP
PF6	Read and display the last record in the file using this sequence of commands: STARTBR RIDFLD(high-values) READPREV SEND MAP
PF7	Read and display the previous record using this sequence of commands: STARTBR RIDFLD(commarea key) READNEXT READPREV READPREV SEND MAP
PF8	Read and display the next record using this sequence of commands: STARTBR RIDFLD(commarea key) READNEXT SEND MAP
Clear	Redisplay the current map.
PA1, PA2, or PA3	Ignore the key.
Any other key	Display an appropriate error message.

Figure 1-15 An event/response chart for the customer inquiry program

of the position in the customer file by storing the customer number in the communication area.

Figure 1-15 shows an event/response chart for the inquiry program. If you haven't read *Part 1: An Introductory Course,* you may not be familiar with this type of chart. Basically, it lists each event that can

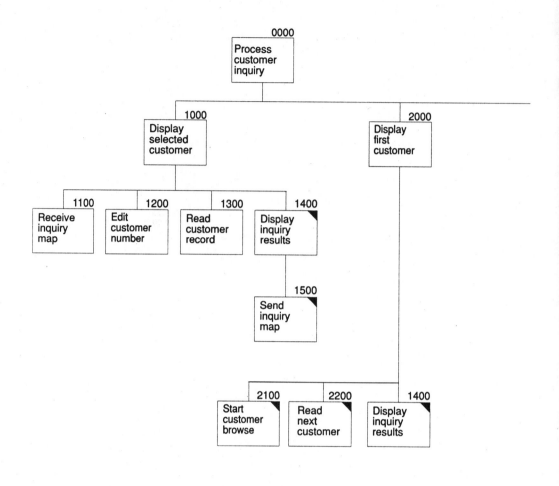

Figure 1-16 Structure chart for the customer inquiry program

trigger the execution of the program. For each event, it summarizes the program's response. For example, if the user invokes the program by pressing PF5, the program responds by starting the browse at the beginning of the file, reading the first record, and displaying it at the terminal.

Figure 1-16 gives the structure chart for this program. Although module 0000 is the main control module, the key to understanding this program's sequential processing lies in modules 2000, 3000, 4000, and 5000. These are the modules that retrieve the first, last, previous, and next record based on the user's input. Notice that these modules do not invoke a module to receive map input. Because these modules obtain the starting customer number from the communication area, they have no need to receive data from the terminal.

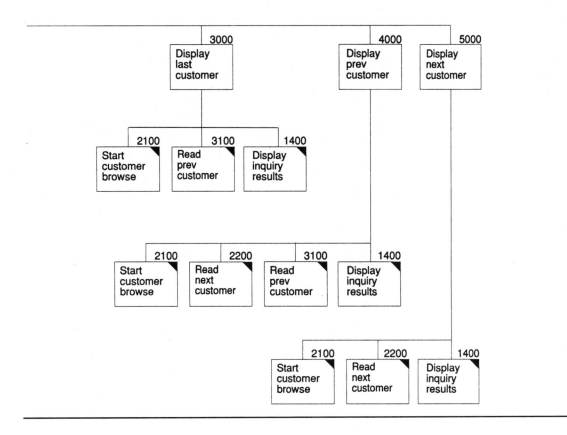

Figures 1-17 and 1-18 present the BMS mapset and symbolic map listings for this program. They're similar to the listings for the customer inquiry program I presented in *Part 1: An Introductory Course.*

Figure 1-19 gives the complete source listing for the customer inquiry program. Here, module 0000 handles the pseudo-conversational processing requirements much like the programs in *Part 1: An Introductory Course.* Quite simply, an EVALUATE statement determines what user event triggered the execution of the program. If EIBCALEN is zero or if the user pressed the Clear key, a fresh map is sent to the terminal. The PA keys are ignored. If the user pressed PF3 or PF12, the program ends by issuing an XCTL command to transfer control to a menu program. If the user pressed the Enter key, PF5, PF6, PF7, or PF8, module 1000, 2000, 3000, 4000, or 5000 is invoked to

```
         PRINT NOGEN
INQSET2  DFHMSD TYPE=&SYSPARM,                                            X
                LANG=COBOL,                                               X
                MODE=INOUT,                                               X
                TERM=3270-2,                                              X
                CTRL=FREEKB,                                              X
                STORAGE=AUTO,                                             X
                TIOAPFX=YES
*****************************************************************
INQMAP2  DFHMDI SIZE=(24,80),                                            X
                LINE=1,                                                  X
                COLUMN=1
*****************************************************************
         DFHMDF POS=(1,1),                                              X
                LENGTH=8,                                               X
                ATTRB=(NORM,PROT),                                      X
                COLOR=BLUE,                                             X
                INITIAL='INQMAP2'
         DFHMDF POS=(1,20),                                            X
                LENGTH=16,                                              X
                ATTRB=(NORM,PROT),                                      X
                COLOR=BLUE,                                             X
                INITIAL='Customer Inquiry'
*****************************************************************
         DFHMDF POS=(3,1),                                             X
                LENGTH=65,                                              X
                ATTRB=(NORM,PROT),                                      X
                COLOR=GREEN,                                            X
                INITIAL='To start a new browse, type a customer number. X
                Then press Enter.'
         DFHMDF POS=(5,1),                                             X
                LENGTH=24,                                              X
                ATTRB=(NORM,PROT),                                      X
                COLOR=GREEN,                                            X
                INITIAL='Customer number. . . . .'
CUSTNO   DFHMDF POS=(5,26),                                            X
                LENGTH=6,                                               X
                ATTRB=(NORM,UNPROT,IC),                                 X
                COLOR=TURQUOISE,                                        X
                INITIAL='_____'
         DFHMDF POS=(5,33),                                            X
                LENGTH=1,                                               X
                ATTRB=ASKIP
*****************************************************************
         DFHMDF POS=(7,1),                                             X
                LENGTH=24,                                              X
                ATTRB=(NORM,PROT),                                      X
                COLOR=GREEN,                                            X
                INITIAL='Name and address . . . :'
LNAME    DFHMDF POS=(7,26),                                            X
                LENGTH=30,                                              X
                COLOR=TURQUOISE,                                        X
                ATTRB=(NORM,PROT)
FNAME    DFHMDF POS=(8,26),                                            X
                LENGTH=20,                                              X
                COLOR=TURQUOISE,                                        X
                ATTRB=(NORM,PROT)
ADDR     DFHMDF POS=(9,26),                                            X
                LENGTH=30,                                              X
                COLOR=TURQUOISE,                                        X
                ATTRB=(NORM,PROT)
CITY     DFHMDF POS=(10,26),                                           X
                LENGTH=20,                                              X
                COLOR=TURQUOISE,                                        X
                ATTRB=(NORM,PROT)
```

Figure 1-17   Mapset listing for the customer inquiry program (part 1 of 2)

```
STATE      DFHMDF POS=(10,47),                                          X
                  LENGTH=2,                                             X
                  COLOR=TURQUOISE,                                      X
                  ATTRB=(NORM,PROT)
ZIPCODE    DFHMDF POS=(10,50),                                         X
                  LENGTH=10,                                            X
                  COLOR=TURQUOISE,                                      X
                  ATTRB=(NORM,PROT)
***********************************************************************
MESSAGE    DFHMDF POS=(23,1),                                          X
                  LENGTH=79,                                            X
                  ATTRB=(BRT,PROT),                                     X
                  COLOR=YELLOW
           DFHMDF POS=(24,1),                                          X
                  LENGTH=34,                                            X
                  ATTRB=(NORM,PROT),                                    X
                  COLOR=BLUE,                                           X
                  INITIAL='F3=Exit   F5=First   F6=Last   F7=Prev'
           DFHMDF POS=(24,38),                                         X
                  LENGTH=19,                                            X
                  ATTRB=(NORM,PROT),                                    X
                  COLOR=BLUE,                                           X
                  INITIAL='F8=Next   F12=Cancel'
DUMMY      DFHMDF POS=(24,79),                                         X
                  LENGTH=1,                                             X
                  ATTRB=(DRK,PROT,FSET),                                X
                  INITIAL=' '
***********************************************************************
           DFHMSD TYPE=FINAL
           END
```

Figure 1-17 Mapset listing for the customer inquiry program (part 2 of 2)

retrieve and display the appropriate customer record. If any other key was pressed, an error message is displayed.

Module 1000 is invoked when the user requests a specific customer record by pressing the Enter key. It invokes module 1100 to receive the inquiry map, then invokes module 1200 to edit the input data. (In this program, the only editing requirement is that the user enters something in the customer number field.) Then, it invokes module 1300 to read the customer record and module 1400 to display the query results.

I coded module 1400 so that it can be called from various places in the inquiry program to format and display the result of each query. Notice how module 1400 uses the flag, DISPLAY-FLAG, to determine how to display the query result. The first of DISPLAY-FLAG's three possible settings, DISPLAY-NEW-CUSTOMER, is used to display data for a successful inquiry. It moves data from the customer record to the output map, then calls module 1500 to send the map.

The DISPLAY-SPACES and DISPLAY-LOW-VALUES settings are used when the inquiry is unsuccessful...that is, when the requested customer record isn't in the file. DISPLAY-SPACES is used when an inquiry for a specific customer number, the first customer, or the last customer is unsuccessful. It moves spaces to the data fields in the output map, then calls module 1500 to send the map. So, data that was previously on the screen will be erased. DISPLAY-LOW-VALUES is

```
01  INQMAP2I.
    02    FILLER     PIC X(12).
    02    CUSTNOL    PIC S9(4) COMP.
    02    CUSTNOF    PIC X.
    02    FILLER REDEFINES CUSTNOF.
     03   CUSTNOA    PIC X.
    02    CUSTNOI    PIC X(0006).
    02    LNAMEL     PIC S9(4) COMP.
    02    LNAMEF     PIC X.
    02    FILLER REDEFINES LNAMEF.
     03   LNAMEA     PIC X.
    02    LNAMEI     PIC X(0030).
    02    FNAMEL     PIC S9(4) COMP.
    02    FNAMEF     PIC X.
    02    FILLER REDEFINES FNAMEF.
     03   FNAMEA     PIC X.
    02    FNAMEI     PIC X(0020).
    02    ADDRL      PIC S9(4) COMP.
    02    ADDRF      PIC X.
    02    FILLER REDEFINES ADDRF.
     03   ADDRA      PIC X.
    02    ADDRI      PIC X(0030).
    02    CITYL      PIC S9(4) COMP.
    02    CITYF      PIC X.
    02    FILLER REDEFINES CITYF.
     03   CITYA      PIC X.
    02    CITYI      PIC X(0020).
    02    STATEL     PIC S9(4) COMP.
    02    STATEF     PIC X.
    02    FILLER REDEFINES STATEF.
     03   STATEA     PIC X.
    02    STATEI     PIC X(0002).
    02    ZIPCODEL   PIC S9(4) COMP.
    02    ZIPCODEF   PIC X.
    02    FILLER REDEFINES ZIPCODEF.
     03   ZIPCODEA   PIC X.
    02    ZIPCODEI   PIC X(0010).
    02    MESSAGEL   PIC S9(4) COMP.
    02    MESSAGEF   PIC X.
    02    FILLER REDEFINES MESSAGEF.
     03   MESSAGEA   PIC X.
    02    MESSAGEI   PIC X(0079).
    02    DUMMYL     PIC S9(4) COMP.
    02    DUMMYF     PIC X.
    02    FILLER REDEFINES DUMMYF.
     03   DUMMYA     PIC X.
    02    DUMMYI     PIC X(0001).
```

Figure 1-18 Symbolic map for the customer inquiry program (part 1 of 2)

used when an inquiry for the previous or next customer is unsuccessful. It calls module 1500 without changing the symbolic map contents. Since LOW-VALUE is moved to the map elsewhere in the program, the data currently displayed on the screen will be unchanged.

Module 2000 is invoked when the user presses PF5 to display the first record in the file. It starts by moving LOW-VALUE to CM-CUSTOMER-NUMBER, then it invokes module 2100 to start a browse operation. If the STARTBR command is successful, module 2000

```
01  INQMAP2O REDEFINES INQMAP2I.
    02    FILLER     PIC X(12).
    02    FILLER     PIC X(3).
    02    CUSTNOO    PIC X(0006).
    02    FILLER     PIC X(3).
    02    LNAMEO     PIC X(0030).
    02    FILLER     PIC X(3).
    02    FNAMEO     PIC X(0020).
    02    FILLER     PIC X(3).
    02    ADDRO      PIC X(0030).
    02    FILLER     PIC X(3).
    02    CITYO      PIC X(0020).
    02    FILLER     PIC X(3).
    02    STATEO     PIC X(0002).
    02    FILLER     PIC X(3).
    02    ZIPCODEO   PIC X(0010).
    02    FILLER     PIC X(3).
    02    MESSAGEO   PIC X(0079).
    02    FILLER     PIC X(3).
    02    DUMMYO     PIC X(0001).
```

Figure 1-18 Symbolic map for the customer inquiry program (part 2 of 2)

invokes module 2200 to read the first record in the file. Then, it invokes modules 1400 to display the new customer data.

Module 3000 displays the last record in the file. It is similar to module 2000, but begins by moving HIGH-VALUE to the customer number. After starting the browse, it invokes module 3100, which issues a READPREV command. Then, it calls module 1400 to display the new customer data.

Module 4000 displays the previous record in sequence by calling modules to (1) issue a STARTBR command, (2) issue a READNEXT command, (3) issue a READPREV command to retrieve the same record retrieved in step 2, and (4) issue another READPREV command to retrieve the previous record. Notice how it uses the customer number from the communication area to establish position in the customer file. Notice also that if the beginning of the file has been reached, module 1400 is called with DISPLAY-LOW-VALUE set. That way, the previous customer data will remain on the screen.

Module 5000 displays the next record in sequence by calling modules to issue a STARTBR command followed by a READNEXT command. It too uses the customer number stored in the communication area to establish position in the customer file.

Terms

browse
browse command
skip sequential processing

```
IDENTIFICATION DIVISION.
*
PROGRAM-ID.  CUSTINQ2.
*
ENVIRONMENT DIVISION.
*
DATA DIVISION.
*
WORKING-STORAGE SECTION.
*
01   SWITCHES.
*
     05   VALID-DATA-SW            PIC X      VALUE 'Y'.
          88   VALID-DATA                     VALUE 'Y'.
     05   CUSTOMER-FOUND-SW        PIC X      VALUE 'Y'.
          88   CUSTOMER-FOUND                 VALUE 'Y'.
*
01   FLAGS.
*
     05   DISPLAY-FLAG             PIC X.
          88   DISPLAY-NEW-CUSTOMER           VALUE '1'.
          88   DISPLAY-SPACES                 VALUE '2'.
          88   DISPLAY-LOW-VALUES             VALUE '3'.
     05   SEND-FLAG               PIC X.
          88   SEND-ERASE                     VALUE '1'.
          88   SEND-DATAONLY                  VALUE '2'.
          88   SEND-DATAONLY-ALARM            VALUE '3'.
*
01   COMMUNICATION-AREA.
*
     05   CA-CUSTOMER-NUMBER       PIC X(6).
*
01   RESPONSE-CODE                PIC S9(8)  COMP.
*
COPY CUSTMAS.
*
COPY INQSET2.
*
COPY DFHAID.
*
COPY ERRPARM.
*
LINKAGE SECTION.
*
01   DFHCOMMAREA                  PIC X(6).
```

Figure 1-19 Source listing for the customer inquiry program (part 1 of 6)

Objective

Given specifications for a CICS program that retrieves records from a file sequentially, code an acceptable program using the browse commands this chapter presents.

```
/
 PROCEDURE DIVISION.
*
 0000-PROCESS-CUSTOMER-INQUIRY.
*
     MOVE DFHCOMMAREA TO COMMUNICATION-AREA.

     EVALUATE TRUE

         WHEN EIBCALEN = ZERO
             MOVE LOW-VALUE TO CA-CUSTOMER-NUMBER
             MOVE LOW-VALUE TO INQMAP2O
             SET SEND-ERASE TO TRUE
             PERFORM 1500-SEND-INQUIRY-MAP

         WHEN EIBAID = DFHCLEAR
             MOVE LOW-VALUE TO CA-CUSTOMER-NUMBER
             MOVE LOW-VALUE TO INQMAP2O
             SET SEND-ERASE TO TRUE
             PERFORM 1500-SEND-INQUIRY-MAP

         WHEN EIBAID = DFHPA1 OR DFHPA2 OR DFHPA3
             CONTINUE

         WHEN EIBAID = DFHPF3 OR DFHPF12
             EXEC CICS
                 XCTL PROGRAM('INVMENU')
             END-EXEC

         WHEN EIBAID = DFHENTER
             PERFORM 1000-DISPLAY-SELECTED-CUSTOMER

         WHEN EIBAID = DFHPF5
             PERFORM 2000-DISPLAY-FIRST-CUSTOMER

         WHEN EIBAID = DFHPF6
             PERFORM 3000-DISPLAY-LAST-CUSTOMER

         WHEN EIBAID = DFHPF7
             PERFORM 4000-DISPLAY-PREV-CUSTOMER

         WHEN EIBAID = DFHPF8
             PERFORM 5000-DISPLAY-NEXT-CUSTOMER

         WHEN OTHER
             MOVE LOW-VALUE TO INQMAP2O
             MOVE 'Invalid key pressed.' TO MESSAGEO
             SET SEND-DATAONLY-ALARM TO TRUE
             PERFORM 1500-SEND-INQUIRY-MAP

     END-EVALUATE.

     EXEC CICS
         RETURN TRANSID('INQ2')
                 COMMAREA(COMMUNICATION-AREA)
     END-EXEC.
```

Figure 1-19 Source listing for the customer inquiry program (part 2 of 6)

```
/
 1000-DISPLAY-SELECTED-CUSTOMER.
*
     PERFORM 1100-RECEIVE-INQUIRY-MAP.
     PERFORM 1200-EDIT-CUSTOMER-NUMBER.
     IF VALID-DATA
         PERFORM 1300-READ-CUSTOMER-RECORD
         IF CUSTOMER-FOUND
             SET DISPLAY-NEW-CUSTOMER TO TRUE
             PERFORM 1400-DISPLAY-INQUIRY-RESULTS
             MOVE CM-CUSTOMER-NUMBER TO CA-CUSTOMER-NUMBER
         ELSE
             SET DISPLAY-SPACES TO TRUE
             PERFORM 1400-DISPLAY-INQUIRY-RESULTS
     ELSE
         SET DISPLAY-LOW-VALUES TO TRUE
         PERFORM 1400-DISPLAY-INQUIRY-RESULTS.
*
 1100-RECEIVE-INQUIRY-MAP.
*
     EXEC CICS
         RECEIVE MAP('INQMAP2')
                 MAPSET('INQSET2')
                 INTO(INQMAP2I)
     END-EXEC.
     INSPECT INQMAP2I
         REPLACING ALL '_' BY SPACE.
*
 1200-EDIT-CUSTOMER-NUMBER.
*
     IF        CUSTNOL = ZERO
          OR CUSTNOI = SPACE
         MOVE 'N' TO VALID-DATA-SW
         MOVE 'You must enter a customer number.' TO MESSAGEO.
*
 1300-READ-CUSTOMER-RECORD.
*
     EXEC CICS
         READ DATASET('CUSTMAS')
              INTO(CUSTOMER-MASTER-RECORD)
              RIDFLD(CUSTNOI)
              RESP(RESPONSE-CODE)
     END-EXEC.
     IF RESPONSE-CODE = DFHRESP(NOTFND)
         MOVE 'N' TO CUSTOMER-FOUND-SW
         MOVE 'That customer does not exist.' TO MESSAGEO
     ELSE IF RESPONSE-CODE NOT = DFHRESP(NORMAL)
         GO TO 9999-TERMINATE-PROGRAM.
*
 1400-DISPLAY-INQUIRY-RESULTS.
*
     IF DISPLAY-NEW-CUSTOMER
         MOVE CM-CUSTOMER-NUMBER TO CUSTNOO
         MOVE CM-LAST-NAME       TO LNAMEO
         MOVE CM-FIRST-NAME      TO FNAMEO
         MOVE CM-ADDRESS         TO ADDRO
         MOVE CM-CITY            TO CITYO
         MOVE CM-STATE           TO STATEO
         MOVE CM-ZIP-CODE        TO ZIPCODEO
         SET SEND-DATAONLY       TO TRUE
```

Figure 1-19 Source listing for the customer inquiry program (part 3 of 6)

```
/
        ELSE IF DISPLAY-SPACES
            MOVE LOW-VALUE TO CUSTNOO
            MOVE SPACE     TO LNAMEO
                              FNAMEO
                              ADDRO
                              CITYO
                              STATEO
                              ZIPCODEO
            SET SEND-DATAONLY-ALARM TO TRUE
        ELSE IF DISPLAY-LOW-VALUES
            SET SEND-DATAONLY-ALARM TO TRUE.
        PERFORM 1500-SEND-INQUIRY-MAP.
*
 1500-SEND-INQUIRY-MAP.
*
        IF SEND-ERASE
            EXEC CICS
                SEND MAP('INQMAP2')
                     MAPSET('INQSET2')
                     FROM(INQMAP2O)
                     ERASE
            END-EXEC
        ELSE IF SEND-DATAONLY
            EXEC CICS
                SEND MAP('INQMAP2')
                     MAPSET('INQSET2')
                     FROM(INQMAP2O)
                     DATAONLY
            END-EXEC
        ELSE IF SEND-DATAONLY-ALARM
            EXEC CICS
                SEND MAP('INQMAP2')
                     MAPSET('INQSET2')
                     FROM(INQMAP2O)
                     DATAONLY
                     ALARM
            END-EXEC.
*
 2000-DISPLAY-FIRST-CUSTOMER.
*
        MOVE LOW-VALUE TO CM-CUSTOMER-NUMBER
                          INQMAP2O.
        PERFORM 2100-START-CUSTOMER-BROWSE.
        IF CUSTOMER-FOUND
            PERFORM 2200-READ-NEXT-CUSTOMER.
        IF CUSTOMER-FOUND
            SET DISPLAY-NEW-CUSTOMER TO TRUE
            PERFORM 1400-DISPLAY-INQUIRY-RESULTS
            MOVE CM-CUSTOMER-NUMBER TO CA-CUSTOMER-NUMBER
        ELSE
            SET DISPLAY-SPACES TO TRUE
            PERFORM 1400-DISPLAY-INQUIRY-RESULTS.
*
 2100-START-CUSTOMER-BROWSE.
*
        EXEC CICS
            STARTBR DATASET('CUSTMAS')
                    RIDFLD(CM-CUSTOMER-NUMBER)
                    RESP(RESPONSE-CODE)
        END-EXEC.
        IF RESPONSE-CODE = DFHRESP(NORMAL)
            MOVE 'Y' TO CUSTOMER-FOUND-SW
            MOVE SPACE TO MESSAGEO
        ELSE IF RESPONSE-CODE = DFHRESP(NOTFND)
            MOVE 'N' TO CUSTOMER-FOUND-SW
            MOVE 'There are no customers in the file.' TO MESSAGEO
        ELSE
            GO TO 9999-TERMINATE-PROGRAM.
```

Figure 1-19 Source listing for the customer inquiry program (part 4 of 6)

```
/
 2200-READ-NEXT-CUSTOMER.
*
     EXEC CICS
         READNEXT DATASET('CUSTMAS')
                  INTO(CUSTOMER-MASTER-RECORD)
                  RIDFLD(CM-CUSTOMER-NUMBER)
                  RESP(RESPONSE-CODE)
     END-EXEC.
     IF RESPONSE-CODE = DFHRESP(NORMAL)
         MOVE 'Y' TO CUSTOMER-FOUND-SW
     ELSE IF RESPONSE-CODE = DFHRESP(ENDFILE)
         MOVE 'N' TO CUSTOMER-FOUND-SW
         MOVE 'There are no more records in the file.'
             TO MESSAGEO
     ELSE
         GO TO 9999-TERMINATE-PROGRAM.
*
 3000-DISPLAY-LAST-CUSTOMER.
*
     MOVE HIGH-VALUE TO CM-CUSTOMER-NUMBER.
     MOVE LOW-VALUE  TO INQMAP2O.
     PERFORM 2100-START-CUSTOMER-BROWSE.
     IF CUSTOMER-FOUND
         PERFORM 3100-READ-PREV-CUSTOMER.
     IF CUSTOMER-FOUND
         SET DISPLAY-NEW-CUSTOMER TO TRUE
         PERFORM 1400-DISPLAY-INQUIRY-RESULTS
         MOVE CM-CUSTOMER-NUMBER TO CA-CUSTOMER-NUMBER
     ELSE
         SET DISPLAY-SPACES TO TRUE
         PERFORM 1400-DISPLAY-INQUIRY-RESULTS.
*
 3100-READ-PREV-CUSTOMER.
*
     EXEC CICS
         READPREV DATASET('CUSTMAS')
                  INTO(CUSTOMER-MASTER-RECORD)
                  RIDFLD(CM-CUSTOMER-NUMBER)
                  RESP(RESPONSE-CODE)
     END-EXEC.
     IF RESPONSE-CODE = DFHRESP(NORMAL)
         MOVE 'Y' TO CUSTOMER-FOUND-SW
     ELSE IF RESPONSE-CODE = DFHRESP(ENDFILE)
         MOVE 'N' TO CUSTOMER-FOUND-SW
         MOVE 'There are no more records in the file.'
             TO MESSAGEO
     ELSE
         GO TO 9999-TERMINATE-PROGRAM.
*
 4000-DISPLAY-PREV-CUSTOMER.
*
     MOVE CA-CUSTOMER-NUMBER TO CM-CUSTOMER-NUMBER.
     MOVE LOW-VALUE              TO INQMAP2O.
     PERFORM 2100-START-CUSTOMER-BROWSE.
     IF CUSTOMER-FOUND
         PERFORM 2200-READ-NEXT-CUSTOMER
         PERFORM 3100-READ-PREV-CUSTOMER
         PERFORM 3100-READ-PREV-CUSTOMER.
     IF CUSTOMER-FOUND
         SET DISPLAY-NEW-CUSTOMER TO TRUE
         PERFORM 1400-DISPLAY-INQUIRY-RESULTS
         MOVE CM-CUSTOMER-NUMBER TO CA-CUSTOMER-NUMBER
     ELSE
         SET DISPLAY-LOW-VALUES TO TRUE
         PERFORM 1400-DISPLAY-INQUIRY-RESULTS.
```

Figure 1-19 Source listing for the customer inquiry program (part 5 of 6)

```
/
 5000-DISPLAY-NEXT-CUSTOMER.
*
     MOVE CA-CUSTOMER-NUMBER TO CM-CUSTOMER-NUMBER.
     MOVE LOW-VALUE          TO INQMAP20.
     PERFORM 2100-START-CUSTOMER-BROWSE.
     IF CUSTOMER-FOUND
         PERFORM 2200-READ-NEXT-CUSTOMER
         PERFORM 2200-READ-NEXT-CUSTOMER.
     IF CUSTOMER-FOUND
         SET DISPLAY-NEW-CUSTOMER TO TRUE
         PERFORM 1400-DISPLAY-INQUIRY-RESULTS
         MOVE CM-CUSTOMER-NUMBER TO CA-CUSTOMER-NUMBER
     ELSE
         SET DISPLAY-LOW-VALUES TO TRUE
         PERFORM 1400-DISPLAY-INQUIRY-RESULTS.
*
 9999-TERMINATE-PROGRAM.
*
     MOVE EIBRESP  TO ERR-RESP.
     MOVE EIBRESP2 TO ERR-RESP2.
     MOVE EIBTRNID TO ERR-TRNID.
     MOVE EIBRSRCE TO ERR-RSRCE.
     EXEC CICS
         XCTL PROGRAM('SYSERR')
              COMMAREA(ERROR-PARAMETERS)
     END-EXEC.
```

Figure 1-19 Source listing for the customer inquiry program (part 6 of 6)

Chapter 2

VSAM alternate index processing

When you use a simple VSAM key-sequenced file, you can retrieve specific records directly using basic file control commands or in key sequence using browse commands. In either case, each record in the file is identified by a key value that's maintained in the file's index. Many on-line applications, however, require that you access the records of a key-sequenced file in other sequences as well. When you use key-sequenced files with alternate indexes, you can do just that.

In this chapter, you'll learn how to write CICS programs that process VSAM files using alternate indexes. First, you'll learn some important concepts about alternate indexing. Then, you'll see a sample program that processes a file using an alternate index.

Before I go on, I should point out that this chapter shows you how to process an existing alternate index in a CICS program. To create an alternate index, you use the VSAM Access Method Services (AMS) program. However, AMS is outside the scope of this book. If you want to learn how to use AMS, I recommend my book, *VSAM: Access Method Services and Application Programming*, available from Mike Murach & Associates, Inc.

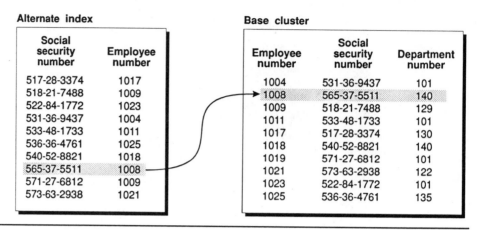

Figure 2-1   An alternate index with unique keys

Alternate indexes

A VSAM *alternate index* lets you access the records of a key-sequenced data set in an order other than that provided by the data set's *primary key* (or *base key*). The data set over which an alternate index exists is called a *base cluster*.

To understand the concept of an alternate index, consider figure 2-1. Here, the base cluster is a KSDS containing employee records. Each record of the base cluster contains three fields: employee number, social security number, and department number. The primary key for the base cluster is employee number. As a result, you can access the base cluster sequentially by employee number using the browse commands you learned in chapter 1. Or, you can read any record directly if you know the record's employee number.

The alternate index in figure 2-1 lets you process the base cluster in social security number sequence by relating each *alternate key* value to a primary key value. So, as the shading indicates, when you tell VSAM to retrieve the record for the employee whose social security number is 565-37-5511, VSAM searches the alternate index, retrieves the primary key (1008), and uses that value to locate the correct record in the base cluster.

In figure 2-1, each alternate key is associated with one primary key. This type of alternate key is called a *unique key*. In contrast, figure 2-2 illustrates an alternate index with *nonunique*, or *duplicate*, *keys*. Here, the alternate key is department number.

To illustrate, consider the alternate index record for department number 101. Here, four employee numbers are specified: 1004, 1011, 1019, and 1023. When you use browse commands to process this alternate index sequentially, all four of these employee records are retrieved in order. However, when an alternate index with duplicate

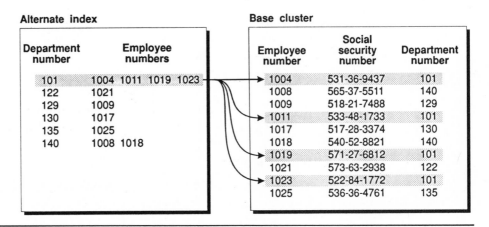

Figure 2-2   An alternate index with duplicate keys

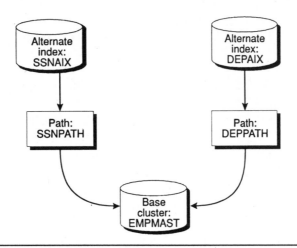

Figure 2-3   The relationships among alternate indexes, paths, and a base cluster

keys is processed directly, only the *first* base cluster record for each alternate key value is available.

Path

Before you can process a base cluster using an alternate index, you must define a VSAM catalog entry called a *path* to establish a relationship between the alternate index and its base cluster. Figure 2-3 illustrates this relationship for the alternate indexes in figures 2-1 and 2-2. Here, two alternate indexes (SSNAIX and DEPAIX) are defined for a single base cluster (EMPMAST). Each alternate index is related to the base cluster through a path (SSNPATH and DEPPATH).

To process a base cluster through an alternate index, you actually process the path. So, as you'll see in the program example later in this chapter, you specify a path name rather than a file name in the DATASET option of file control commands you issue to access a file using an alternate index. Otherwise, the CICS commands you code to process a file using an alternate index are the same as those you'd code to process a file without using an alternate index.

Upgrade set

You would expect that changes you make to the base cluster would be reflected not only in the base cluster but also in any associated alternate indexes. For example, consider figure 2-4. Here, a record for employee 1013 is added to the base cluster. As the shading indicates, both alternate indexes are updated as well: A new entry is made in the social security number alternate index, and the entry for department 101 in the department number alternate index is extended.

In VSAM, the process of updating an alternate index is called *upgrading*. VSAM doesn't require that an alternate index be upgraded each time its base cluster is changed. An alternate index is an *upgradable index* if you specify (via AMS) that it should be automatically upgraded by VSAM whenever changes are made to the base cluster. The collection of upgradable alternate indexes for a base cluster is called the base cluster's *upgrade set*. Every time a change is made to the base cluster that affects the alternate indexes, each affected alternate index in the upgrade set is automatically updated by VSAM.

Whether an alternate index is upgradable has no effect on how you code your CICS programs. But you should realize that if an alternate index is not upgradable, some changes made to the base cluster won't be reflected in the alternate index until the alternate index is recreated. Normally, alternate indexes—both upgradable and non-upgradable—are recreated on a regular basis, perhaps nightly.

It may surprise you that upgradable alternate indexes need to be recreated regularly. That's because VSAM maintains upgrades to an alternate index in the order they're made, and that's usually not in primary key sequence. Notice in figure 2-4 that the alternate index entry for employee 1013 was made after all of the existing entries for department 101, not between the entries for employees 1011 and 1019 where you'd expect it. So, if you try to process the employee master file sequentially using the department number alternate index shown in figure 2-4, you will *not* receive records in employee number within department number sequence.

As a result, to return the alternate index entries to primary key sequence, alternate indexes are generally rebuilt during off hours, even if they are upgradable. Since making an index upgradable doesn't

Base cluster

Employee number	Social security number	Department number
1004	531-36-9437	101
1008	565-37-5511	140
1009	518-21-7488	129
1011	533-48-1733	101
1013	552-57-2735	101
1017	517-28-3374	130
1018	540-52-8821	140
1019	571-27-6812	101
1021	573-63-2938	122
1023	522-84-1772	101
1025	536-36-4761	135

Alternate index (social security number)

Social security number	Employee number
517-28-3374	1017
518-21-7488	1009
522-84-1772	1023
531-36-9437	1004
533-48-1733	1011
536-36-4761	1025
540-52-8821	1018
552-57-2735	1013
565-37-5511	1008
571-27-6812	1009
573-63-2938	1021

Alternate index (department number)

Department number	Employee numbers
101	1004 1011 1019 1023 1013
122	1021
129	1009
130	1017
135	1025
140	1008 1018

Figure 2-4   Base cluster and alternate indexes after insertion of employee number 1013

always save additional processing, alternate indexes are generally *not* upgradable unless they really need to be.

An enhanced customer inquiry program

Now that you understand what an alternate index is, you're ready to learn how to write programs that process files using an alternate index. Figures 2-5 through 2-10 present a customer inquiry program that lets a user display customer information retrieved from two files: a customer master file and an invoice file. This program is an enhancement of the inquiry program in chapter 1, which retrieved data from the customer master file only. The program in this chapter displays not just customer

Figure 2-5   The invoice file and its alternate index and path

information, but related invoices for each displayed customer as well. To do this, it uses an alternate index that's based on the customer number field contained in the invoice records.

Figure 2-5 shows the relationship of the invoice file's base cluster to its alternate index and path. To access the invoice file via its alternate index, you specify the path name (INVPATH) in the DATASET parameter of any file control commands for the file.

Figure 2-6 presents the specifications for this program. As you can see, the screen layout is similar to the screen layout for the inquiry program in chapter 1. However, it provides an area for displaying information for up to ten invoices for each customer.

Before I go on, I want to point out that an actual production program like this would provide for displaying more invoices than will fit on one screen. Although that's a reasonable requirement for a production program, it makes the program's logic more complicated without illustrating any additional CICS elements related to alternate indexing. So, to help you focus more on the coding requirements for alternate indexes, this program displays a maximum of ten invoices for each customer—that's just enough to fit on one screen.

Figure 2-7 presents the event/response chart for the customer inquiry program. It's similar to the event/response chart for the inquiry program I presented in chapter 1, so I won't review it in detail.

Figure 2-8 presents the structure chart for this program. Again, it's similar to the structure chart for the inquiry program in chapter 1. In fact, the only difference is that I've added three modules (1410, 1420, and 1430). Module 1410 is invoked by module 1400 to start a browse operation on the invoice file. Then, module 1400 invokes module 1420 to format each invoice line. Module 1420, in turn, invokes module 1430 to read the invoice records.

Program   CUSTINQ3

Overview   Displays records from the customer and invoice files, allowing the user to scroll forwards or backwards using PF keys.

Input/output   INQMAP3   Customer inquiry map
specifications   CUSTMAS   Customer master file
                      INVPATH   Customer number path to invoice file

Processing   1. Control is transferred to this program via XCTL from the menu program INVMENU
specifications   with no communication area. The user can also start the program by entering the
                         trans-id INQ3. In either case, the program should respond by displaying the
                         customer inquiry map.

                 2. The user selects a customer record display by pressing an attention key, as follows:

                    Enter   Display the customer indicated by the entry in the customer number field.
                    PF5   Display the first customer in the file.
                    PF6   Display the last customer in the file.
                    PF7   Display the previous customer.
                    PF8   Display the next customer.

                    The program then reads and displays the appropriate customer record.

                 3. For each customer record selected, display the first 10 invoice records from the
                    invoice file. Use the INVPATH path to access the invoice records via the customer
                    number alternate key.

                 4. Use the pseudo-conversational programming technique. To restart the browse during
                    each program execution, save the key of the customer currently displayed in the
                    communication area.

                 5. If the user presses PF3 or PF12, return to the menu program INVMENU by issuing an
                    XCTL command.

Figure 2-6   Specifications for the enhanced customer inquiry program (part 1 of 3)

Figure 2-9 presents the BMS mapset for this program. Notice that I defined each invoice line as a single 42-byte field. To make it easier to manipulate these fields in the COBOL program, I created my own symbolic map, shown in figure 2-10. Here, I used an OCCURS clause to make it easier to process the invoice lines.

Figure 2-11 is the complete source listing for this program. If you need a refresher on its basic operation, refer to chapter 1. I want to concentrate here on the elements required to access the invoice file via its path. In other words, I'm going to focus on modules 1410, 1420, and 1430.

You may recall from chapter 1 that module 1400 is invoked to format and display the results of each inquiry. Before module 1400 is called, the program must set DISPLAY-FLAG to indicate how module 1400 is to operate. If DISPLAY-NEW-CUSTOMER is set, module 1400

| Map name | INQMAP3 | | Date | 07/01/92 |
| Program name | CUSTINQ3 | | Designer | Doug Lowe |

```
    1         1         2         3         4         5         6         7         8
    1234567890123456789012345678901234567890123456789012345678901234567890123456789 0
 1  INQMAP3              Customer Inquiry
 2
 3  Type a customer number.   Then press Enter.
 4
 5  Customer number. . . . .
 6
 7  Name and address . . . :  XXXXXXXXXXXXXXXXXXXXXXXXXXXXXX
 8                            XXXXXXXXXXXXXXXXXXXXX
 9                            XXXXXXXXXXXXXXXXXXXXXXXXXXXXXX
10                            XXXXXXXXXXXXXXXXXXX XX XXXXXXXXXX
11
12  Invoice   PO Number      Date            Total
13   999999   XXXXXXXXXX   Z9/99/99    Z,ZZZ,ZZ9.99
14   999999   XXXXXXXXXX   Z9/99/99    Z,ZZZ,ZZ9.99
15   999999   XXXXXXXXXX   Z9/99/99    Z,ZZZ,ZZ9.99
16   999999   XXXXXXXXXX   Z9/99/99    Z,ZZZ,ZZ9.99
17   999999   XXXXXXXXXX   Z9/99/99    Z,ZZZ,ZZ9.99
18   999999   XXXXXXXXXX   Z9/99/99    Z,ZZZ,ZZ9.99
19   999999   XXXXXXXXXX   Z9/99/99    Z,ZZZ,ZZ9.99
20   999999   XXXXXXXXXX   Z9/99/99    Z,ZZZ,ZZ9.99
21   999999   XXXXXXXXXX   Z9/99/99    Z,ZZZ,ZZ9.99
22   999999   XXXXXXXXXX   Z9/99/99    Z,ZZZ,ZZ9.99
23  XXXXXXXXXXXXXXXXXXXXXXXXXXXXXXXXXXXXXXXXXXXXXXXXXXXXXXXXXXXXXXXXXXXXXXXXXXXXXXXXX
24  F3=Exit   F5=First   F6=Last   F7=Prev   F8=Next   F12=Cancel                   X
```

Figure 2-6   Specifications for the enhanced customer inquiry program (part 2 of 3)

moves data from the customer record to the output map and calls module 1500 to send the map. If DISPLAY-SPACES is set, module 1400 moves spaces to the data fields in the output map and calls module 1500. And if DISPLAY-LOW-VALUES is set, module 1400 calls module 1500 without moving any data to the output map.

For this version of the inquiry program, I've enhanced the function of module 1400 to include formatting the invoice lines if data for a new customer is to be displayed. Thus, if DISPLAY-NEW-CUSTOMER is set, module 1400 invokes module 1410, which initiates a browse operation with this command:

```
EXEC CICS
    STARTBR DATASET('INVPATH')
            RIDFLD(CM-CUSTOMER-NUMBER)
            EQUAL
            RESP(RESPONSE-CODE)
END-EXEC.
```

The CUSTMAS copy member

```
01    CUSTOMER-MASTER-RECORD.
*
      05    CM-CUSTOMER-NUMBER      PIC  X(6).
      05    CM-FIRST-NAME          PIC  X(20).
      05    CM-LAST-NAME           PIC  X(30).
      05    CM-ADDRESS             PIC  X(30).
      05    CM-CITY                PIC  X(20).
      05    CM-STATE               PIC  X(2).
      05    CM-ZIP-CODE            PIC  X(10).
*
```

The INVOICE copy member

```
01    INVOICE-RECORD.
*
      05    INV-INVOICE-NUMBER           PIC  9(6).
      05    INV-INVOICE-DATE             PIC  X(6).
      05    INV-CUSTOMER-NUMBER          PIC  X(6).
      05    INV-PO-NUMBER                PIC  X(10).
      05    INV-LINE-ITEM                OCCURS  10.
      10    INV-PRODUCT-CODE             PIC  X(10).
      10    INV-QUANTITY                 PIC  S9(7)        COMP-3.
      10    INV-UNIT-PRICE               PIC  S9(7)V99     COMP-3.
      10    INV-AMOUNT                   PIC  S9(7)V99     COMP-3.
      05    INV-INVOICE-TOTAL            PIC  S9(7)V99     COMP-3.
*
```

The ERRPARM copy member

```
01    ERROR-PARAMETERS.
*
      05    ERR-RESP       PIC  S9(8)    COMP.
      05    ERR-RESP2      PIC  S9(8)    COMP.
      05    ERR-TRNID      PIC  X(4).
      05    ERR-RSRCE      PIC  X(8).
*
```

Figure 2-6   Specifications for the enhanced customer inquiry program (part 3 of 3)

Here, the DATASET parameter specifies INVPATH, not INVOICE, as the input file. As a result, this command begins a browse operation using the file's alternate key, not it's primary key. The RIDFLD parameter specifies CM-CUSTOMER-NUMBER, which contains the primary key of the customer record to be displayed. Note that CM-CUSTOMER-NUMBER is a field within the customer record, not the invoice record. That makes good sense: The program is retrieving all of the invoice records that relate to a particular customer record.

Because I specify EQUAL on the STARTBR command, the NOTFND condition is raised if there are no records in the invoice file for the specified customer. If this condition is detected, I move N to a switch named MORE-INVOICES-SW. As you'll see in a moment, I use this

Event	Response
Start the program	Display the inquiry map.
PF3 PF12	Transfer control to the menu program.
Enter	Read and display the customer and related invoice records indicated by the customer number entered by the user.
PF5	Read and display the first customer record and related invoice records.
PF6	Read and display the last customer record and related invoice records.
PF7	Read and display the previous customer record and related invoice records.
PF8	Read and display the next customer record and related invoice records.
Clear	Redisplay the current map.
PA1, PA2, or PA3	Ignore the key.
Any other key	Display an appropriate error message.

Figure 2-7 An event/response chart for the enhanced customer inquiry program

switch to control how many invoice records should be read. If you'll check in the Working-Storage Section, you'll see that the initial value of this switch is Y. And since this is a pseudo-conversational program, the switch value is restored to Y each time the program is invoked. Module 1410 changes the switch to N only if the STARTBR command doesn't find a record.

If the STARTBR command in module 1410 finds an invoice record for the customer, module 1400 invokes module 1420 with this statement:

```
PERFORM 1420-FORMAT-INVOICE-LINE
    VARYING INVOICE-SUB FROM 1 BY 1
    UNTIL INVOICE-SUB > 10
```

As a result, module 1420 is performed ten times.

Module 1420's job is to format each of the ten invoice lines. It does that in one of two ways. If there are more invoice records for the customer, module 1420 invokes module 1430 to read an invoice record. Then, it moves data from the invoice record to the working-storage area, INVOICE-LINE. Finally, it moves INVOICE-LINE to the appropriate CIM-D-INVOICE-LINE field in the symbolic map. On the other hand, if there are no more invoice records to be read, module 1420 simply moves SPACE to the appropriate CIM-D-INVOICE-LINE field. That way, any invoice data from a previous inquiry will be erased. (This probably isn't the most efficient way to erase existing invoice data on the screen, but it's sufficient for this example.)

In module 1430, you can see the one significant CICS variation for processing files using an alternate index: the DUPKEY condition. The DUPKEY condition is raised whenever you issue a READ, READNEXT, or READPREV command and at least one *more* record—*not* counting the one currently being read—exists with the same alternate key value.

To illustrate, suppose the program is reading invoice records for customer 10000. If there's just one invoice record for customer 10000, the DUPKEY condition is never raised, because when the program reads the first invoice record, there aren't any additional invoice records with the same alternate key. If there are two invoices for customer 10000, DUPKEY is raised when the program reads the first record. But when the program reads the second (and last) record, DUPKEY isn't raised. If there are three invoices for the customer, DUPKEY is raised for the first two but not for the third, and so on. In short, the DUPKEY condition is not raised when you read the last record with a given alternate key value.

Look now to see how module 1430 deals with the DUPKEY condition. The IF statement that tests the response code for the READNEXT command is this:

```
IF RESPONSE-CODE = DFHRESP(NORMAL)
    MOVE 'N' TO MORE-INVOICES-SW
ELSE IF RESPONSE-CODE NOT = DFHRESP(DUPKEY)
    GO TO 9999-TERMINATE-PROGRAM.
```

Here, the only two allowable response codes are NORMAL and DUPKEY; if any other response code is encountered, control is transferred to 9999-TERMINATE-PROGRAM. If the response code is NORMAL, it means the READNEXT command has read the last invoice record for a given customer. So, MORE-INVOICES-SW is turned off. If the response code is DUPKEY, MORE-INVOICES-SW is left on so the READNEXT command will be issued again on the next iteration of module 1420.

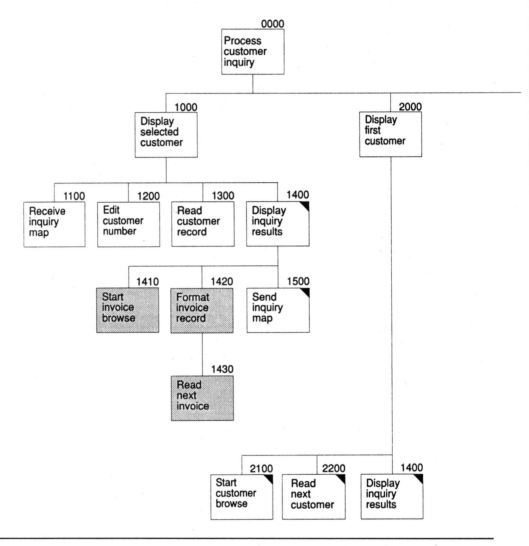

Figure 2-8   Structure chart for the enhanced customer inquiry program

Discussion

As you probably realize, alternate indexes introduce considerable overhead into the processing of VSAM files. Depending on factors such as how many alternate indexes are associated with the file, how many of those alternate indexes are upgradable, and how much free space is available within the file's control intervals, a single WRITE command for

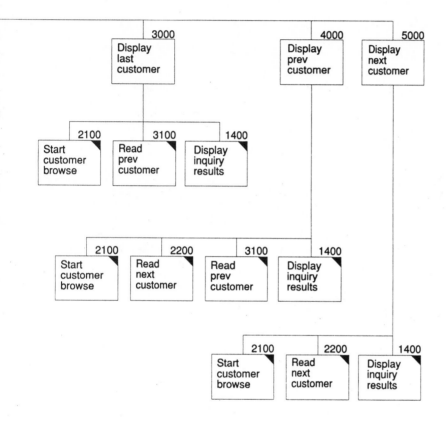

a file with alternate indexes can cause dozens of physical I/O operations. And that can result in considerable performance degradation, especially if many users are updating the same file at once. As a result, alternate indexes—particularly upgradable alternate indexes—are used only when their advantages outweigh their disadvantages.

```
          PRINT NOGEN
INQSET3   DFHMSD TYPE=&SYSPARM,                                          X
                 LANG=COBOL,                                             X
                 MODE=INOUT,                                             X
                 TERM=3270-2,                                            X
                 CTRL=FREEKB,                                            X
                 STORAGE=AUTO,                                           X
                 TIOAPFX=YES
*****************************************************************
INQMAP3   DFHMDI SIZE=(24,80),                                          X
                 LINE=1,                                                 X
                 COLUMN=1
*****************************************************************
          DFHMDF POS=(1,1),                                             X
                 LENGTH=8,                                               X
                 ATTRB=(NORM,PROT),                                      X
                 COLOR=BLUE,                                             X
                 INITIAL='INQMAP3'
          DFHMDF POS=(1,20),                                            X
                 LENGTH=16,                                              X
                 ATTRB=(NORM,PROT),                                      X
                 COLOR=BLUE,                                             X
                 INITIAL='Customer Inquiry'
*****************************************************************
          DFHMDF POS=(3,1),                                             X
                 LENGTH=42,                                              X
                 ATTRB=(NORM,PROT),                                      X
                 COLOR=GREEN,                                            X
                 INITIAL='Type a customer number.  Then press Enter.'
          DFHMDF POS=(5,1),                                             X
                 LENGTH=24,                                              X
                 ATTRB=(NORM,PROT),                                      X
                 COLOR=GREEN,                                            X
                 INITIAL='Customer number. . . . .'
CUSTNO    DFHMDF POS=(5,26),                                            X
                 LENGTH=6,                                               X
                 ATTRB=(NORM,UNPROT,IC),                                 X
                 COLOR=TURQUOISE,                                        X
                 INITIAL='_____'
          DFHMDF POS=(5,33),                                            X
                 LENGTH=1,                                               X
                 ATTRB=ASKIP
*****************************************************************
          DFHMDF POS=(7,1),                                             X
                 LENGTH=24,                                              X
                 ATTRB=(NORM,PROT),                                      X
                 COLOR=GREEN,                                            X
                 INITIAL='Name and address . . . :'
LNAME     DFHMDF POS=(7,26),                                            X
                 LENGTH=30,                                              X
                 COLOR=TURQUOISE,                                        X
                 ATTRB=(NORM,PROT)
FNAME     DFHMDF POS=(8,26),                                            X
                 LENGTH=20,                                              X
                 COLOR=TURQUOISE,                                        X
                 ATTRB=(NORM,PROT)
```

Figure 2-9   Mapset listing for the enhanced customer inquiry program (part 1 of 3)

```
ADDR       DFHMDF POS=(9,26),                                              X
               LENGTH=30,                                                 X
               COLOR=TURQUOISE,                                           X
               ATTRB=(NORM,PROT)
CITY       DFHMDF POS=(10,26),                                             X
               LENGTH=20,                                                 X
               COLOR=TURQUOISE,                                           X
               ATTRB=(NORM,PROT)
STATE      DFHMDF POS=(10,47),                                             X
               LENGTH=2,                                                  X
               COLOR=TURQUOISE,                                           X
               ATTRB=(NORM,PROT)
ZIPCODE    DFHMDF POS=(10,50),                                             X
               LENGTH=10,                                                 X
               COLOR=TURQUOISE,                                           X
               ATTRB=(NORM,PROT)
*********************************************************************
           DFHMDF POS=(12,1),                                             X
               LENGTH=43,                                                 X
               COLOR=GREEN,                                               X
               ATTRB=(NORM,PROT),                                         X
               INITIAL='Invoice  PO Number    Date         Total'
INV1       DFHMDF POS=(13,2),                                             X
               LENGTH=42,                                                 X
               COLOR=TURQUOISE,                                           X
               ATTRB=(NORM,PROT)
INV2       DFHMDF POS=(14,2),                                             X
               LENGTH=42,                                                 X
               COLOR=TURQUOISE,                                           X
               ATTRB=(NORM,PROT)
INV3       DFHMDF POS=(15,2),                                             X
               LENGTH=42,                                                 X
               COLOR=TURQUOISE,                                           X
               ATTRB=(NORM,PROT)
INV4       DFHMDF POS=(16,2),                                             X
               LENGTH=42,                                                 X
               COLOR=TURQUOISE,                                           X
               ATTRB=(NORM,PROT)
INV5       DFHMDF POS=(17,2),                                             X
               LENGTH=42,                                                 X
               COLOR=TURQUOISE,                                           X
               ATTRB=(NORM,PROT)
INV6       DFHMDF POS=(18,2),                                             X
               LENGTH=42,                                                 X
               COLOR=TURQUOISE,                                           X
               ATTRB=(NORM,PROT)
INV7       DFHMDF POS=(19,2),                                             X
               LENGTH=42,                                                 X
               COLOR=TURQUOISE,                                           X
               ATTRB=(NORM,PROT)
INV8       DFHMDF POS=(20,2),                                             X
               LENGTH=42,                                                 X
               COLOR=TURQUOISE,                                           X
               ATTRB=(NORM,PROT)
```

Figure 2-9 Mapset listing for the enhanced customer inquiry program (part 2 of 3)

```
INV9       DFHMDF POS=(21,2),                                               X
                  LENGTH=42,                                                X
                  COLOR=TURQUOISE,                                          X
                  ATTRB=(NORM,PROT)
INV10      DFHMDF POS=(22,2),                                               X
                  LENGTH=42,                                                X
                  COLOR=TURQUOISE,                                          X
                  ATTRB=(NORM,PROT)
***********************************************************************
MESSAGE    DFHMDF POS=(23,1),                                               X
                  LENGTH=79,                                                X
                  ATTRB=(BRT,PROT),                                         X
                  COLOR=YELLOW
           DFHMDF POS=(24,1),                                               X
                  LENGTH=34,                                                X
                  ATTRB=(NORM,PROT),                                        X
                  COLOR=BLUE,                                               X
                  INITIAL='F3=Exit   F5=First   F6=Last   F7=Prev'
           DFHMDF POS=(24,38),                                              X
                  LENGTH=19,                                                X
                  ATTRB=(NORM,PROT),                                        X
                  COLOR=BLUE,                                               X
                  INITIAL='F8=Next   F12=Cancel'
DUMMY      DFHMDF POS=(24,79),                                              X
                  LENGTH=1,                                                 X
                  ATTRB=(DRK,PROT,FSET),                                    X
                  INITIAL=' '
***********************************************************************
           DFHMSD TYPE=FINAL
           END
```

Figure 2-9   Mapset listing for the enhanced customer inquiry program (part 3 of 3)

Terms

alternate index	nonunique key
primary key	duplicate key
base key	path
base cluster	upgrading
alternate key	upgradable index
unique key	upgrade set

Objectives

1. Briefly explain the meaning of the following terms:

   alternate index
   path
   upgrade set

2. Given a programming problem involving a file with an alternate index, code an acceptable program for its solution.

```
01    CUSTOMER-INQUIRY-MAP.
*
      05   FILLER                      PIC  X(12).
*
      05   CIM-L-CUSTNO                PIC  S9(4)    COMP.
      05   CIM-A-CUSTNO                PIC  X.
      05   CIM-D-CUSTNO                PIC  X(6).
*
      05   CIM-L-LNAME                 PIC  S9(4)    COMP.
      05   CIM-A-LNAME                 PIC  X.
      05   CIM-D-LNAME                 PIC  X(30).
*
      05   CIM-L-FNAME                 PIC  S9(4)    COMP.
      05   CIM-A-FNAME                 PIC  X.
      05   CIM-D-FNAME                 PIC  X(20).
*
      05   CIM-L-ADDR                  PIC  S9(4)    COMP.
      05   CIM-A-ADDR                  PIC  X.
      05   CIM-D-ADDR                  PIC  X(30).
*
      05   CIM-L-CITY                  PIC  S9(4)    COMP.
      05   CIM-A-CITY                  PIC  X.
      05   CIM-D-CITY                  PIC  X(20).
*
      05   CIM-L-STATE                 PIC  S9(4)    COMP.
      05   CIM-A-STATE                 PIC  X.
      05   CIM-D-STATE                 PIC  XX.
*
      05   CIM-L-ZIPCODE               PIC  S9(4)    COMP.
      05   CIM-A-ZIPCODE               PIC  X.
      05   CIM-D-ZIPCODE               PIC  X(10).
*
      05   CIM-INVOICE-LINE            OCCURS 10.
*
           10   CIM-L-INVOICE-LINE     PIC  S9(4)    COMP.
           10   CIM-A-INVOICE-LINE     PIC  X.
           10   CIM-D-INVOICE-LINE     PIC  X(42).
*
      05   CIM-L-MESSAGE               PIC  S9(4)    COMP.
      05   CIM-A-MESSAGE               PIC  X.
      05   CIM-D-MESSAGE               PIC  X(79).
*
      05   CIM-L-DUMMY                 PIC  S9(4)    COMP.
      05   CIM-A-DUMMY                 PIC  X.
      05   CIM-D-DUMMY                 PIC  X.
*
```

Figure 2-10 Programmer-generated symbolic map for the enhanced customer inquiry program

```
       IDENTIFICATION DIVISION.
      *
       PROGRAM-ID.  CUSTINQ3.
      *
       ENVIRONMENT DIVISION.
      *
       DATA DIVISION.
      *
       WORKING-STORAGE SECTION.
      *
       01  SWITCHES.
      *
           05   VALID-DATA-SW            PIC X       VALUE 'Y'.
               88   VALID-DATA                       VALUE 'Y'.
           05   CUSTOMER-FOUND-SW        PIC X       VALUE 'Y'.
               88   CUSTOMER-FOUND                   VALUE 'Y'.
           05   MORE-INVOICES-SW         PIC X       VALUE 'Y'.
               88   MORE-INVOICES                    VALUE 'Y'.
      *
       01  FLAGS.
      *
           05   DISPLAY-FLAG             PIC X.
               88   DISPLAY-NEW-CUSTOMER             VALUE '1'.
               88   DISPLAY-SPACES                   VALUE '2'.
               88   DISPLAY-LOW-VALUES               VALUE '3'.
           05   SEND-FLAG               PIC X.
               88   SEND-ERASE                       VALUE '1'.
               88   SEND-DATAONLY                    VALUE '2'.
               88   SEND-DATAONLY-ALARM              VALUE '3'.
      *
       01  WORK-FIELDS.
      *
           05   INVOICE-SUB             PIC S9(4) COMP.
      *
       01  INVOICE-LINE.
      *
           05   IL-INVOICE-NUMBER       PIC 9(6).
           05   FILLER                  PIC XX    VALUE SPACE.
           05   IL-PO-NUMBER            PIC X(10).
           05   FILLER                  PIC XX    VALUE SPACE.
           05   IL-INVOICE-DATE         PIC Z9/99/99.
           05   FILLER                  PIC XX    VALUE SPACE.
           05   IL-INVOICE-TOTAL        PIC Z,ZZZ,ZZ9.99.
      *
       01  COMMUNICATION-AREA.
      *
           05   CA-CUSTOMER-NUMBER      PIC X(6).
      *
       01  RESPONSE-CODE               PIC S9(8)  COMP.
      *
       COPY CUSTMAS.
      *
       COPY INVOICE.
      *
       COPY INQSET3.
      *
       COPY DFHAID.
      *
       COPY ERRPARM.
      *
       LINKAGE SECTION.
      *
       01  DFHCOMMAREA                 PIC X(6).
```

Figure 2-11 Source listing for the enhanced customer inquiry program (part 1 of 7)

```
/
 PROCEDURE DIVISION.
*
 0000-PROCESS-CUSTOMER-INQUIRY.
*
     MOVE DFHCOMMAREA TO COMMUNICATION-AREA.

     EVALUATE TRUE

         WHEN EIBCALEN = ZERO
             MOVE LOW-VALUE TO CA-CUSTOMER-NUMBER
             MOVE LOW-VALUE TO CUSTOMER-INQUIRY-MAP
             SET SEND-ERASE TO TRUE
             PERFORM 1500-SEND-INQUIRY-MAP

         WHEN EIBAID = DFHCLEAR
             MOVE LOW-VALUE TO CA-CUSTOMER-NUMBER
             MOVE LOW-VALUE TO CUSTOMER-INQUIRY-MAP
             SET SEND-ERASE TO TRUE
             PERFORM 1500-SEND-INQUIRY-MAP

         WHEN EIBAID = DFHPA1 OR DFHPA2 OR DFHPA3
             CONTINUE

         WHEN EIBAID = DFHPF3 OR DFHPF12
             EXEC CICS
                 XCTL PROGRAM('INVMENU')
             END-EXEC

         WHEN EIBAID = DFHENTER
             PERFORM 1000-DISPLAY-SELECTED-CUSTOMER

         WHEN EIBAID = DFHPF5
             PERFORM 2000-DISPLAY-FIRST-CUSTOMER

         WHEN EIBAID = DFHPF6
             PERFORM 3000-DISPLAY-LAST-CUSTOMER

         WHEN EIBAID = DFHPF7
             PERFORM 4000-DISPLAY-PREV-CUSTOMER

         WHEN EIBAID = DFHPF8
             PERFORM 5000-DISPLAY-NEXT-CUSTOMER

         WHEN OTHER
             MOVE LOW-VALUE TO CUSTOMER-INQUIRY-MAP
             MOVE 'Invalid key pressed.' TO CIM-D-MESSAGE
             SET SEND-DATAONLY-ALARM TO TRUE
             PERFORM 1500-SEND-INQUIRY-MAP

     END-EVALUATE.

     EXEC CICS
         RETURN TRANSID('INQ3')
                COMMAREA(COMMUNICATION-AREA)
     END-EXEC.
```

Figure 2-11 Source listing for the enhanced customer inquiry program (part 2 of 7)

```
/
 1000-DISPLAY-SELECTED-CUSTOMER.
*
     PERFORM 1100-RECEIVE-INQUIRY-MAP.
     PERFORM 1200-EDIT-CUSTOMER-NUMBER.
     IF VALID-DATA
         PERFORM 1300-READ-CUSTOMER-RECORD
         IF CUSTOMER-FOUND
             SET DISPLAY-NEW-CUSTOMER TO TRUE
             PERFORM 1400-DISPLAY-INQUIRY-RESULTS
             MOVE CM-CUSTOMER-NUMBER TO CA-CUSTOMER-NUMBER
         ELSE
             SET DISPLAY-SPACES TO TRUE
             PERFORM 1400-DISPLAY-INQUIRY-RESULTS
     ELSE
         SET DISPLAY-LOW-VALUES TO TRUE
         PERFORM 1400-DISPLAY-INQUIRY-RESULTS.
*
 1100-RECEIVE-INQUIRY-MAP.
*
     EXEC CICS
         RECEIVE MAP('INQMAP3')
                 MAPSET('INQSET3')
                 INTO(CUSTOMER-INQUIRY-MAP)
     END-EXEC.
     INSPECT CUSTOMER-INQUIRY-MAP
         REPLACING ALL '_' BY SPACE.
*
 1200-EDIT-CUSTOMER-NUMBER.
*
     IF       CIM-L-CUSTNO = ZERO
         OR CIM-D-CUSTNO = SPACE
         MOVE 'N' TO VALID-DATA-SW
         MOVE 'You must enter a customer number.'
             TO CIM-D-MESSAGE.
*
 1300-READ-CUSTOMER-RECORD.
*
     EXEC CICS
         READ DATASET('CUSTMAS')
             INTO(CUSTOMER-MASTER-RECORD)
             RIDFLD(CIM-D-CUSTNO)
             RESP(RESPONSE-CODE)
     END-EXEC.
     IF RESPONSE-CODE = DFHRESP(NOTFND)
         MOVE 'N' TO CUSTOMER-FOUND-SW
         MOVE 'That customer does not exist.' TO CIM-D-MESSAGE
     ELSE IF RESPONSE-CODE NOT = DFHRESP(NORMAL)
         GO TO 9999-TERMINATE-PROGRAM.
*
 1400-DISPLAY-INQUIRY-RESULTS.
*
     IF DISPLAY-NEW-CUSTOMER
         MOVE CM-CUSTOMER-NUMBER TO CIM-D-CUSTNO
         MOVE CM-LAST-NAME       TO CIM-D-LNAME
         MOVE CM-FIRST-NAME      TO CIM-D-FNAME
         MOVE CM-ADDRESS         TO CIM-D-ADDR
         MOVE CM-CITY            TO CIM-D-CITY
         MOVE CM-STATE           TO CIM-D-STATE
         MOVE CM-ZIP-CODE        TO CIM-D-ZIPCODE
         PERFORM 1410-START-INVOICE-BROWSE
         PERFORM 1420-FORMAT-INVOICE-LINE
             VARYING INVOICE-SUB FROM 1 BY 1
             UNTIL INVOICE-SUB > 10
         SET SEND-DATAONLY TO TRUE
```

Figure 2-11   Source listing for the enhanced customer inquiry program (part 3 of 7)

```
/
        ELSE IF DISPLAY-SPACES
            MOVE LOW-VALUE TO CIM-D-CUSTNO
            MOVE SPACE      TO CIM-D-LNAME
                               CIM-D-FNAME
                               CIM-D-ADDR
                               CIM-D-CITY
                               CIM-D-STATE
                               CIM-D-ZIPCODE
            PERFORM VARYING INVOICE-SUB FROM 1 BY 1
                    UNTIL INVOICE-SUB > 10
                MOVE SPACE TO CIM-D-INVOICE-LINE(INVOICE-SUB)
            END-PERFORM
            SET SEND-DATAONLY-ALARM TO TRUE
        ELSE IF DISPLAY-LOW-VALUES
            SET SEND-DATAONLY-ALARM TO TRUE.
        PERFORM 1500-SEND-INQUIRY-MAP.
*
 1410-START-INVOICE-BROWSE.
*
        EXEC CICS
            STARTBR DATASET('INVPATH')
                    RIDFLD(CM-CUSTOMER-NUMBER)
                    EQUAL
                    RESP(RESPONSE-CODE)
        END-EXEC.
        IF RESPONSE-CODE = DFHRESP(NOTFND)
            MOVE 'N' TO MORE-INVOICES-SW
        ELSE IF RESPONSE-CODE NOT = DFHRESP(NORMAL)
            GO TO 9999-TERMINATE-PROGRAM.
*
 1420-FORMAT-INVOICE-LINE.
*
        IF MORE-INVOICES
            PERFORM 1430-READ-NEXT-INVOICE
            MOVE INV-INVOICE-NUMBER TO IL-INVOICE-NUMBER
            MOVE INV-PO-NUMBER      TO IL-PO-NUMBER
            MOVE INV-INVOICE-DATE   TO IL-INVOICE-DATE
            MOVE INV-INVOICE-TOTAL  TO IL-INVOICE-TOTAL
            MOVE INVOICE-LINE TO CIM-D-INVOICE-LINE(INVOICE-SUB)
        ELSE
            MOVE SPACE TO CIM-D-INVOICE-LINE(INVOICE-SUB).
*
 1430-READ-NEXT-INVOICE.
*
        EXEC CICS
            READNEXT DATASET('INVPATH')
                     RIDFLD(CM-CUSTOMER-NUMBER)
                     INTO(INVOICE-RECORD)
                     RESP(RESPONSE-CODE)
        END-EXEC.
        IF RESPONSE-CODE = DFHRESP(NORMAL)
            MOVE 'N' TO MORE-INVOICES-SW
        ELSE IF RESPONSE-CODE NOT = DFHRESP(DUPKEY)
            GO TO 9999-TERMINATE-PROGRAM.
*
 1500-SEND-INQUIRY-MAP.
*
        IF SEND-ERASE
            EXEC CICS
                SEND MAP('INQMAP3')
                     MAPSET('INQSET3')
                     FROM(CUSTOMER-INQUIRY-MAP)
                     ERASE
            END-EXEC
```

Figure 2-11 Source listing for the enhanced customer inquiry program (part 4 of 7)

```
/
          ELSE IF SEND-DATAONLY
              EXEC CICS
                  SEND MAP('INQMAP3')
                      MAPSET('INQSET3')
                      FROM(CUSTOMER-INQUIRY-MAP)
                      DATAONLY
              END-EXEC
          ELSE IF SEND-DATAONLY-ALARM
              EXEC CICS
                  SEND MAP('INQMAP3')
                      MAPSET('INQSET3')
                      FROM(CUSTOMER-INQUIRY-MAP)
                      DATAONLY
                      ALARM
              END-EXEC.
     *
      2000-DISPLAY-FIRST-CUSTOMER.
     *
          MOVE LOW-VALUE TO CM-CUSTOMER-NUMBER
                            CUSTOMER-INQUIRY-MAP.
          PERFORM 2100-START-CUSTOMER-BROWSE.
          IF CUSTOMER-FOUND
              PERFORM 2200-READ-NEXT-CUSTOMER.
          IF CUSTOMER-FOUND
              SET DISPLAY-NEW-CUSTOMER TO TRUE
              PERFORM 1400-DISPLAY-INQUIRY-RESULTS
              MOVE CM-CUSTOMER-NUMBER TO CA-CUSTOMER-NUMBER
          ELSE
              SET DISPLAY-SPACES TO TRUE
              PERFORM 1400-DISPLAY-INQUIRY-RESULTS.
     *
      2100-START-CUSTOMER-BROWSE.
     *
          EXEC CICS
              STARTBR DATASET('CUSTMAS')
                      RIDFLD(CM-CUSTOMER-NUMBER)
                      RESP(RESPONSE-CODE)
          END-EXEC.
          IF RESPONSE-CODE = DFHRESP(NORMAL)
              MOVE 'Y' TO CUSTOMER-FOUND-SW
              MOVE SPACE TO CIM-D-MESSAGE
          ELSE IF RESPONSE-CODE = DFHRESP(NOTFND)
              MOVE 'N' TO CUSTOMER-FOUND-SW
              MOVE 'There are no customers in the file.'
                  TO CIM-D-MESSAGE
          ELSE
              GO TO 9999-TERMINATE-PROGRAM.
     *
      2200-READ-NEXT-CUSTOMER.
     *
          EXEC CICS
              READNEXT DATASET('CUSTMAS')
                      INTO(CUSTOMER-MASTER-RECORD)
                      RIDFLD(CM-CUSTOMER-NUMBER)
                      RESP(RESPONSE-CODE)
          END-EXEC.
          IF RESPONSE-CODE = DFHRESP(NORMAL)
              MOVE 'Y' TO CUSTOMER-FOUND-SW
          ELSE IF RESPONSE-CODE = DFHRESP(ENDFILE)
              MOVE 'N' TO CUSTOMER-FOUND-SW
              MOVE 'There are no more records in the file.'
                  TO CIM-D-MESSAGE
          ELSE
              GO TO 9999-TERMINATE-PROGRAM.
```

Figure 2-11   Source listing for the enhanced customer inquiry program (part 5 of 7)

```
/
 3000-DISPLAY-LAST-CUSTOMER.
*
     MOVE HIGH-VALUE TO CM-CUSTOMER-NUMBER.
     MOVE LOW-VALUE   TO CUSTOMER-INQUIRY-MAP.
     PERFORM 2100-START-CUSTOMER-BROWSE.
     IF CUSTOMER-FOUND
         PERFORM 3100-READ-PREV-CUSTOMER.
     IF CUSTOMER-FOUND
         SET DISPLAY-NEW-CUSTOMER TO TRUE
         PERFORM 1400-DISPLAY-INQUIRY-RESULTS
         MOVE CM-CUSTOMER-NUMBER TO CA-CUSTOMER-NUMBER
     ELSE
         SET DISPLAY-SPACES TO TRUE
         PERFORM 1400-DISPLAY-INQUIRY-RESULTS.
*
 3100-READ-PREV-CUSTOMER.
*
     EXEC CICS
         READPREV DATASET('CUSTMAS')
                  INTO(CUSTOMER-MASTER-RECORD)
                  RIDFLD(CM-CUSTOMER-NUMBER)
                  RESP(RESPONSE-CODE)
     END-EXEC.
     IF RESPONSE-CODE = DFHRESP(NORMAL)
         MOVE 'Y' TO CUSTOMER-FOUND-SW
     ELSE IF RESPONSE-CODE = DFHRESP(ENDFILE)
         MOVE 'N' TO CUSTOMER-FOUND-SW
         MOVE 'There are no more records in the file.'
             TO CIM-D-MESSAGE
     ELSE
         GO TO 9999-TERMINATE-PROGRAM.
*
 4000-DISPLAY-PREV-CUSTOMER.
*
     MOVE CA-CUSTOMER-NUMBER TO CM-CUSTOMER-NUMBER.
     MOVE LOW-VALUE           TO CUSTOMER-INQUIRY-MAP.
     PERFORM 2100-START-CUSTOMER-BROWSE.
     IF CUSTOMER-FOUND
         PERFORM 2200-READ-NEXT-CUSTOMER
         PERFORM 3100-READ-PREV-CUSTOMER
         PERFORM 3100-READ-PREV-CUSTOMER.
     IF CUSTOMER-FOUND
         SET DISPLAY-NEW-CUSTOMER TO TRUE
         PERFORM 1400-DISPLAY-INQUIRY-RESULTS
         MOVE CM-CUSTOMER-NUMBER TO CA-CUSTOMER-NUMBER
     ELSE
         SET DISPLAY-LOW-VALUES TO TRUE
         PERFORM 1400-DISPLAY-INQUIRY-RESULTS.
*
 5000-DISPLAY-NEXT-CUSTOMER.
*
     MOVE CA-CUSTOMER-NUMBER TO CM-CUSTOMER-NUMBER.
     MOVE LOW-VALUE           TO CUSTOMER-INQUIRY-MAP.
     PERFORM 2100-START-CUSTOMER-BROWSE.
     IF CUSTOMER-FOUND
         PERFORM 2200-READ-NEXT-CUSTOMER
         PERFORM 2200-READ-NEXT-CUSTOMER.
     IF CUSTOMER-FOUND
         SET DISPLAY-NEW-CUSTOMER TO TRUE
         PERFORM 1400-DISPLAY-INQUIRY-RESULTS
         MOVE CM-CUSTOMER-NUMBER TO CA-CUSTOMER-NUMBER
     ELSE
         SET DISPLAY-LOW-VALUES TO TRUE
         PERFORM 1400-DISPLAY-INQUIRY-RESULTS.
```

Figure 2-11 Source listing for the enhanced customer inquiry program (part 6 of 7)

```
/
 9999-TERMINATE-PROGRAM.
*
     MOVE EIBRESP  TO ERR-RESP.
     MOVE EIBRESP2 TO ERR-RESP2.
     MOVE EIBTRNID TO ERR-TRNID.
     MOVE EIBRSRCE TO ERR-RSRCE.
     EXEC CICS
         XCTL PROGRAM('SYSERR')
              COMMAREA(ERROR-PARAMETERS)
     END-EXEC.
```

Figure 2-11 Source listing for the enhanced customer inquiry program (part 7 of 7)

Chapter 3

Other advanced file processing features

In this chapter, I'll present a variety of CICS file handling features you may need to use on occasion. Here, you'll learn how to use generic keys, the MASSINSERT option, and CICS data tables. Although you probably won't need to use these features often, it's good to know about them should the need arise.

How to use generic keys

A *generic key* is a portion of a primary or alternate key used to identify records in a key-sequenced data set. The generic key can be any length that's shorter than the full length of the file's key, but it always begins at the first byte of the key. For example, suppose an inventory parts file is indexed by a ten-byte key that's made up of a vendor number (four bytes) and an item number (six bytes). In this example, you could use a four-byte generic key to access part records based on vendor number alone. However, you couldn't use the item number portion of the inventory file's key as a generic key because it doesn't begin at the first byte of the complete key.

You can use generic keys with browse commands (STARTBR, READNEXT, READPREV, and RESETBR), the READ command, and the DELETE command. To use generic keys with these commands, you must specify two options: GENERIC and KEYLENGTH. The GENERIC option tells CICS to treat the key specified in the RIDFLD option as a generic key. Although only part of a file's key is used when you specify this option, the data area you specify in the RIDFLD option must still be large enough to hold the record's entire key.

The KEYLENGTH option provides the length of the generic key. It should be a numeric literal or a binary halfword field (PIC S9(4) COMP). It's value must be less than the full length of the file's key. If it isn't, the INVREQ condition will result.

When you use generic keys with the STARTBR command, the effect is similar to using the GTEQ option. To illustrate, figure 3-1 shows two STARTBR routines designed to start a browse operation at the first inventory parts record for a particular vendor. The first example uses the GTEQ option to start the browse. It moves a vendor number to the vendor number portion of the key and low-values to the part number portion of the key, then issues a STARTBR command with the GTEQ option specified. As a result, the browse will be positioned to the first record for the specified vendor.

Example 2 in figure 3-1 uses the GENERIC option to achieve a similar result. Here, I moved the vendor number to the vendor number portion of the key. Then, I issued this STARTBR command:

```
EXEC CICS
    STARTBR  DATASET('INVPART')
             RIDFLD(IP-RECORD-KEY)
             GENERIC
             KEYLENGTH(4)
             EQUAL
             RESP(RESPONSE-CODE)
END-EXEC.
```

Here, the GENERIC option specifies that the STARTBR command is using a generic key, and the KEYLENGTH option tells CICS that the generic key is four bytes in length. As a result, this STARTBR command will use only the vendor number portion of the record key.

Notice in example 2 that I specified the EQUAL option. So, although the coding in examples 1 and 2 have similar results, they operate differently when there are no records in the parts file for the specified vendor. In example 1, the STARTBR command will position the browse at the first record for the next vendor in sequence. In contrast, the STARTBR command in example 2 will generate a NOTFND condition if there are no records for the vendor.

You can also use a generic key on a READ command. When you do, CICS retrieves the first record in the file whose key begins with characters matching the generic key you supply. Figure 3-2 shows a module that reads the first inventory part record for a particular vendor. Because this command does not establish position for subsequent READNEXT commands, it is useful only when you need just the first record for a particular generic key value. Since that's an

Inventory parts record

```
01  INVENTORY-PARTS-RECORD.
*
    05  IP-RECORD-KEY.
        10  IP-VENDOR-NUMBER       PIC X(4).
        10  IP-ITEM-NUMBER         PIC X(6).
    05  IP-INVENTORY-DATA.
        .
        .
        .
```

Example 1

```
2100-START-INVENTORY-BROWSE.
*
    MOVE VENDNOI   TO IP-VENDOR-NUMBER.
    MOVE LOW-VALUE TO IP-ITEM-NUMBER.
    EXEC CICS
        STARTBR DATASET('INVPART')
                RIDFLD(IP-RECORD-KEY)
                GTEQ
                RESP(RESPONSE-CODE)
    END-EXEC.
*
```

Example 2

```
2100-START-INVENTORY-BROWSE.
*
    MOVE VENDNOI TO IP-VENDOR-NUMBER.
    EXEC CICS
        STARTBR DATASET('INVPART')
                RIDFLD(IP-RECORD-KEY)
                GENERIC
                KEYLENGTH(4)
                EQUAL
                RESP(RESPONSE-CODE)
    END-EXEC.
*
```

Figure 3-1   Using a generic key in a STARTBR command

unlikely application, you'll probably rarely use generic keys on the READ command.

You can use the GENERIC option on a DELETE command to delete all of the records whose keys begin with the generic key value you supply. For example, figure 3-3 shows a DELETE command that deletes all of the inventory part records for a particular vendor. As you can imagine, a DELETE command like this can be potentially dangerous. So be careful about how you use it.

When you use a generic key with a DELETE command, you can also use an additional option: NUMREC. It returns a count of the number of

```
 3200-READ-FIRST-INVENTORY-RECORD.
*
     MOVE VENDNOI TO IP-VENDOR-NUMBER.
     EXEC CICS
         READ DATASET('INVPART')
              INTO(INVENTORY-PARTS-RECORD)
              RIDFLD(IP-RECORD-KEY)
              GENERIC
              KEYLENGTH(4)
              EQUAL
              RESP(RESPONSE-CODE)
     END-EXEC.
*
```

Figure 3-2   Using a generic key in a READ command

records that matched the generic key and were deleted. On this option, you specify a working-storage field that's defined as a binary halfword item (PIC S9(4) COMP). In figure 3-3, I named this field WS-DELETE-COUNT.

Incidentally, you might suspect that you could delete all of the records in a file by specifying a generic key length of zero. This isn't the case, however. The IBM manuals list the effect of such an operation as "undefined." So you shouldn't attempt it.

How to use the MASSINSERT option

Some CICS applications require that more than one record be written to the same point in a file. For example, suppose a customer file is set up with three types of records: customers, invoices, and line items. For each customer record, there may be one or more invoice records. And for each invoice record, there may be one or more line item records. The file's primary key is arranged so that line item records follow their related invoice record, and invoice records follow their related customer record. A CICS data entry program creates the invoice and line item records for an existing customer by inserting them after the customer record. On average, each new invoice requires a total of six records: one invoice record and five line item records.

The MASSINSERT option can make the insertion of these records more efficient. To understand why, you need to know that VSAM stores records in blocks called *control intervals*. Whenever you write a record to a control interval that's full, a *control interval split* occurs. To do a control interval split, VSAM normally moves half the records in the control interval to another control interval. Then, it inserts the new record.

When you use the MASSINSERT option on a WRITE command, VSAM changes the way it splits control intervals. Rather than split the control interval at the middle, it splits it at the point of insertion, whether its at the beginning, middle, or end of the control interval. That

```
4200-DELETE-INVENTORY-RECORDS.
*
    MOVE VENDNOI TO IP-VENDOR-NUMBER.
    EXEC CICS
        DELETE DATASET('INVPART')
               RIDFLD(IP-RECORD-KEY)
               GENERIC
               KEYLENGTH(4)
               EQUAL
               NUMREC(WS-DELETE-COUNT)
               RESP(RESPONSE-CODE)
    END-EXEC.
*
```

Figure 3-3 Using a generic key in a DELETE command

leaves free space after the inserted record, so subsequent records can be inserted without unnecessary control interval splits.

Figure 3-4 shows a portion of a program that uses a MASSINSERT operation to write invoice and line item records. Notice that both WRITE commands contain the MASSINSERT option. The MASSINSERT operation begins when the program issues its first WRITE command with the MASSINSERT option. Then, any subsequent WRITE commands you want to include in the MASSINSERT operation must also contain the MASSINSERT option. If they don't, the results will be unpredictable. In fact, you shouldn't issue any other file control command against a file undergoing a MASSINSERT operation unless you first end the MASSINSERT.

To end a MASSINSERT operation so you can issue other commands against the file, you use the UNLOCK command. Then, the control intervals involved in the insertion and the additional VSAM resources necessary to process the operation are released. You should also use the UNLOCK command if your program does any significant processing after the MASSINSERT operation. That way, the resources it was using can be used by other programs. If you don't issue an UNLOCK command, the MASSINSERT operation continues, and the resources remain held, until the task ends.

How to use CICS data tables

With CICS/MVS version 2.1, IBM introduced a new feature called *data tables* that can dramatically improve the performance of files that are accessed frequently. Simply put, a data table is a virtual storage copy of a VSAM key-sequenced file. When CICS starts up, it copies records from the VSAM file (called the *source data set*) into the data table. Then, whenever an application program performs an I/O operation against the file, CICS uses the data in the data table instead of accessing the file on disk. The result, as you can imagine, is much faster file access.

```
          .
          .
          .
     PERFORM 3200-WRITE-INVOICE-RECORD.
     PERFORM 3300-WRITE-LINE-ITEM-RECORD
         VARYING LINE-ITEM-SUB FROM 1 BY 1
         UNTIL LINE-ITEM-SUB > LINE-ITEM-COUNT.
          .
          .
          .
*
 3200-WRITE-INVOICE-RECORD.
*
     EXEC CICS
         WRITE DATASET('CUSTINV')
               FROM(INVOICE-RECORD)
               RIDFLD(INV-RECORD-KEY)
               MASSINSERT
               RESP(RESPONSE-CODE)
     END-EXEC.
     IF RESPONSE-CODE NOT = DFHRESP(NORMAL)
         GO TO 9999-TERMINATE-PROGRAM.
*
 3300-WRITE-LINE-ITEM-RECORD.
*
     MOVE LINE-ITEM-DATA(LINE-ITEM-SUB) TO LINE-ITEM-RECORD.
     EXEC CICS
         WRITE DATASET('CUSTINV')
               FROM(LINE-ITEM-RECORD)
               RIDFLD(LI-RECORD-KEY)
               MASSINSERT
               RESP(RESPONSE-CODE)
     END-EXEC.
     IF RESPONSE-CODE NOT = DFHRESP(NORMAL)
         GO TO 9999-TERMINATE-PROGRAM.
*
```

Figure 3-4   Using the MASSINSERT option

What happens when an application program updates data in a data table by writing, rewriting, or deleting records? That depends on whether the data table is defined as a CICS-maintained table or a user-maintained table. For a *CICS-maintained table* (or *CMT*), CICS automatically updates records in the source data set. However, your application program doesn't have to wait until the disk update has completed before it can continue. Instead, control returns to your application program as soon as the update has been reflected in the data table.

In a *user-maintained table* (or *UMT*), CICS does not automatically update the source data set when the table is updated. So if you want to make sure that updates to the data table are reflected in the source data set, you must provide a program that periodically updates the source data set. Because of that, UMT's are typically used for read-only files.

With CICS/ESA version 3.3, IBM introduced a new type of data table: *shared data tables*. A shared data table works much like a CMT or UMT, but it can be accessed by more than one CICS system. It does this by placing the shared data table in a separate address space that can be accessed by each CICS region that needs the table. The only restriction is that each CICS region that accesses the table must be run under the same MVS system. In other words, you can't share a data table across MVS systems.

No matter what type of data table you're using, the fact that your program is accessing a data table rather than a disk file is completely transparent to you. In other words, the use of data tables doesn't affect how you code CICS file control commands. Instead, whether or not a data set is accessed from disk or from virtual storage as a data table depends on how the systems programmer sets up the resource definition for the file.

Terms

generic key
control interval
control interval split
data table
source data set
CICS-maintained table
CMT
user-maintained table
UMT
shared data table

Objectives

1. Use generic keys on a STARTBR, READ, and DELETE command to access records using only a portion of the full key.

2. Explain how a MASSINSERT operation differs from a standard WRITE operation, and identify when MASSINSERT is appropriate.

3. Explain the difference between a CMT and a UMT, and describe how the use of data tables affects application programming.

Section 2

Data base processing features

So far in this book (and in *Part 1: An Introductory Course*), all of the file handling examples have used VSAM data sets. That's appropriate because most CICS file processing uses VSAM files. Even so, for some applications, you need to be able to use more complex data structures than VSAM provides. For those applications, data base packages are often used.

This section shows you how to write CICS programs to process data stored by IBM's two most popular IBM mainframe data base packages: DB2 and IMS. To process DB2 data through CICS, you code statements in DB2's Structured Query Language (SQL) in your application programs. Chapter 4 introduces DB2, describes SQL, and shows you how to use it in a CICS program. To process IMS data through CICS, you code requests in IMS's Data Language/I (DL/I) in your application programs. Chapter 5 introduces you to DL/I data bases and shows you how to code DL/I requests.

Chapter 4

DB2 (SQL) data base processing

This chapter introduces DB2 and describes how to process DB2 data in CICS programs. If you're already familiar with DB2, this chapter will present all you need to know to write CICS programs that process DB2 data. If DB2 is new to you, you'll find that although this chapter introduces DB2 concepts, terms, and operations, it doesn't present everything you need to know to work at a professional level as a CICS/DB2 programmer. In many ways, DB2 is as complicated as CICS, and one chapter in this book can't cover it completely. For more information, I recommend *DB2 for the COBOL Programmer, Part 1* and *Part 2*, by Steve Eckols, available from Mike Murach & Associates, Inc.

This chapter has two topics. Topic 1 introduces DB2 terms and concepts and describes DB2 programming considerations. If you have DB2 experience, most of the material in topic 1 will be familiar. Topic 2 illustrates the special programming requirements for accessing DB2 data through CICS with a sample CICS/DB2 inquiry program.

DB2 data base concepts and terms

This topic introduces IBM's current strategic data base management system: *DB2*. The complete, official name of the program is *Database 2*, but you'll almost always see it referred to as DB2. In this topic, I'll present the basic concepts you need to understand before you try to process DB2 data from an application program. Then, I'll describe how you request DB2 services from an application program. Finally, I'll describe the steps you need to go through to compile a CICS/DB2 program.

Before I go on, you should know that DB2 runs only under MVS. However, it has a parallel product that runs under the VSE and VM operating systems: SQL/DS. As a result, if you're using SQL/DS (instead of DB2), you can apply what you learn in this topic and the next.

How DB2 organizes and processes data

Tables   DB2 is a *relational data base management system*. *Relation* is a mathematical term for a *table*, a two dimensional array that consists of horizontal *rows* and vertical *columns*. DB2 stores and processes data as tables. For example, figure 4-1 shows a small customer table. It contains 16 rows and 7 columns.

At a superficial level, a table is much like a standard file. In fact, there's little to distinguish the table in figure 4-1 from the customer file you've seen in examples in this book and *Part 1: An Introductory Course*. A table row corresponds to a file record, and a table column corresponds to a field in a file's record description. Each row in a table contains the same columns as all of the other rows in the table. Of course, the values in a given column vary from one row to another in a table, just as the contents of a field vary from one record to another in a standard file.

In practice, the DB2 data for an application is rarely stored in a single table. Instead, data base designers use a rigorous procedure called *normalization* to organize the data elements for an application into a collection of interrelated tables. Related elements in different tables are tied to each other through *keys*.

For example, suppose you want to create a DB2 data base that stores invoice information. You could store all the information for a single invoice in a single table. But you'd be more likely to create four separate but interrelated tables, like the ones in figure 4-2.

CUSTNO	FNAME	LNAME	ADDR	CITY	STATE	ZIPCODE
400001	KEITH	MCDONALD	4501 W MOCKINGBIRD	DALLAS	TX	75209
400002	ARREN	ANELLI	40 FORD RD	DENVILLE	NJ	07834
400003	SUSAN	HOWARD	1107 SECOND AVE #312	REDWOOD CITY	CA	94063
400004	CAROL ANN	EVANS	74 SUTTON CT	GREAT LAKES	IL	60088
400005	ELAINE	ROBERTS	12914 BRACKNELL	CERRITOS	CA	90701
400006	PAT	HONG	73 HIGH ST	SAN FRANCISCO	CA	94114
400007	PHIL	ROACH	25680 ORCHARD	DEARBORN HTS	MI	48125
400008	TIM	JOHNSON	145 W 27TH ST	SO CHICAGO HTS	IL	60411
400009	MARIANNE	BUSBEE	3920 BERWYN DR S #199	MOBILE	AL	36608
400010	ENRIQUE	OTHON	BOX 26729	RICHMOND	VA	23261
400011	WILLIAM C	FERGUSON	BOX 1283	MIAMI	FL	34002-1283
400012	S D	HOEHN	PO BOX 27	RIDDLE	OR	97469
400013	DAVID R	KEITH	BOX 1266	MAGNOLIA	AR	71757-1266
400014	R	BINDER	3425 WALDEN AVE	DEPEW	NY	14043
400015	VIVIAN	GEORGE	229 S 18TH ST	PHILADELPHIA	PA	19103
400016	J	NOETHLICH	11 KINGSTON CT	MERRIMACK	NH	03054

Figure 4-1   A customer table

One rule of normalization is that all of the data elements in a table row should depend only on the key value that identifies that row. For example, although each invoice has an associated name and address, that information depends on the customer number rather than on the invoice number. That's why the name and address information is stored in the customer table rather than in the invoice table. Then, each invoice row contains a customer number that relates the invoice to a particular customer.

Another normalization rule is that a table row can't contain repeating groups. That's why I didn't include line item data in the invoice table in figure 4-2. Instead, I created a separate table for line items. Each row in the line item table contains an invoice number that identifies the related invoice row.

A relationship like invoice/line item is called a *parent/child relationship*. The parent, invoice, "owns" one or more line items, which are the children. Although you can implement data structures like this with standard VSAM files, VSAM can't maintain the parent/child relationships for you. In other words, VSAM can't check every invoice number field in the line item file to make sure there's a corresponding record in the invoice file. DB2, in contrast, can automatically insure *referential integrity* between tables that are defined with parent/child relationships.

Another advantage DB2 has over standard VSAM is that a single DB2 request can often accomplish complicated data base operations

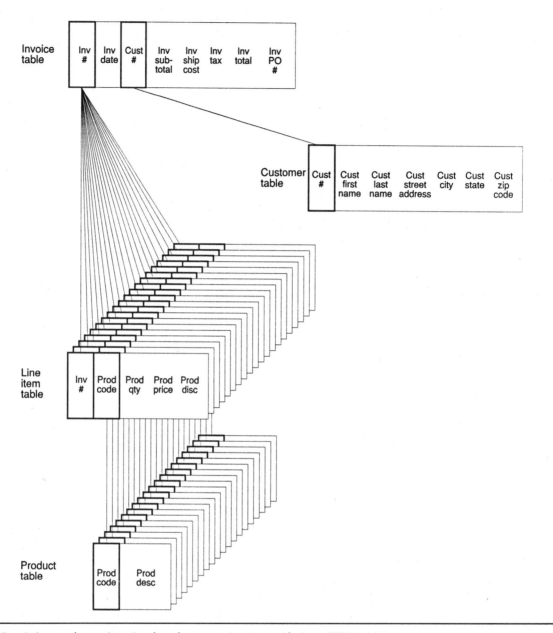

Figure 4-2 Information related to invoices can be stored in four DB2 tables

that would require many statements with VSAM files. For example, a single DB2 statement can combine data from the invoice, customer, line item, and product tables in figure 4-2 to retrieve all of the information necessary to generate a complete invoice. To do that with VSAM files, you'd have to code separate CICS commands to retrieve records from the customer, invoice, line item, and product files.

SQL To understand how DB2 processes data, you need to be familiar with the language you use to request DB2 services: SQL. *SQL*, short for *Structured Query Language*, is an ANSI standard language that many data base management packages use. For example, if you learn SQL for processing DB2 data (under MVS), you can transfer that knowledge directly to processing SQL/DS data (under VSE and VM).

As its name suggests, SQL was designed for interactive use to let users do queries against stored tables. A *query* is a selection of specific DB2 data. In fact, the SQL statement you use to do a query is SELECT. Other SQL statements that are commonly used are INSERT (to add new information to a table), UPDATE (to change existing information), and DELETE (to delete information). SQL statements can be entered interactively by a terminal user using a product called *QMF*, which stands for *Query Management Facility*. Alternately, they can be coded directly in application programs.

DB2 and its SQL statements can be complicated. However, I'm sure you'll be able to understand the examples I'll present in this chapter. For example, figure 4-3 illustrates a simple interactive SELECT statement:

```
SELECT *
    FROM MMADBV.CUST
    WHERE CUSTNO = '400001'
```

This statement directs DB2 to retrieve the data in all columns from the row in the customer table where the value of the customer number column is 400001. The asterisk after SELECT specifies "all columns," and MMADBV.CUST is the name of the table. CUSTNO is the name of the customer number column.

This interactive SELECT statement works much like a CICS READ command would work in a COBOL program: It retrieves one row from the customer table. However, the SELECT statement is much more flexible than the READ command. First, it doesn't force you to retrieve all the columns that make up a table. So rather than retrieve all the columns from the customer table, you might retrieve just the first and last name columns. In contrast, when you read a record from a standard file, you always get the entire record even if you need only a few of its fields.

Second, a single SQL statement can retrieve data based on the contents of any column, not just one defined as a key. In contrast, to retrieve data based on a non-key column from a standard data set, you have to examine all the records to identify the ones you're interested in. That can involve many statements.

Third, DB2 can return more than one row in response to a single SELECT statement. In fact, the result of a SELECT statement is itself a table. The number of rows in a *results table* depends on the request. It may be one row, as in the example in figure 4-3, or thousands or rows.

SELECT
statement

```
SELECT *
    FROM MMADBV.CUST
    WHERE CUSTNO = '400011'
```

Customer table
(MMADBV.CUST)

CUSTNO	FNAME	LNAME	ADDR	CITY	STATE	ZIPCODE
400001	KEITH	MCDONALD	4501 W MOCKINGBIRD	DALLAS	TX	75209
400002	ARREN	ANELLI	40 FORD RD	DENVILLE	NJ	07834
400003	SUSAN	HOWARD	1107 SECOND AVE #312	REDWOOD CITY	CA	94063
400004	CAROL ANN	EVANS	74 SUTTON CT	GREAT LAKES	IL	60088
400005	ELAINE	ROBERTS	12914 BRACKNELL	CERRITOS	CA	90701
400006	PAT	HONG	73 HIGH ST	SAN FRANCISCO	CA	94114
400007	PHIL	ROACH	25680 ORCHARD	DEARBORN HTS	MI	48125
400008	TIM	JOHNSON	145 W 27TH ST	SO CHICAGO HTS	IL	60411
400009	MARIANNE	BUSBEE	3920 BERWYN DR S #199	MOBILE	AL	36608
400010	ENRIQUE	OTHON	BOX 26729	RICHMOND	VA	23261
400011	WILLIAM C	FERGUSON	BOX 1283	MIAMI	FL	34002-1283
400012	S D	HOEHN	PO BOX 27	RIDDLE	OR	97469
400013	DAVID R	KEITH	BOX 1266	MAGNOLIA	AR	71757-1266
400014	R	BINDER	3425 WALDEN AVE	DEPEW	NY	14043
400015	VIVIAN	GEORGE	229 S 18TH ST	PHILADELPHIA	PA	19103
400016	J	NOETHLICH	11 KINGSTON CT	MERRIMACK	NH	03054

Results table

CUSTNO	FNAME	LNAME	ADDR	CITY	STATE	ZIPCODE
400011	WILLIAM C	FERGUSON	BOX 1283	MIAMI	FL	34002-1283

Figure 4-3   A SELECT statement can simulate standard file operations

To understand these three differences, consider the example in figure 4-4. It's a simple variation of the SELECT statement I just showed you:

```
SELECT FNAME, LNAME
    FROM MMADBV.CUST
    WHERE STATE = 'CA'
```

This statement requests data from the customer table. However, instead of requesting data from all columns, it requests data from just two: first name and last name. So, even though the stored table contains address information, it won't be returned in the results table this statement produces. Also, the WHERE clause of this statement names a different column in its selection condition: State. This statement works, even though State wasn't defined as a key column. The WHERE clause

SELECT
statement

```
SELECT FNAME, LNAME
    FROM MMADBV.CUST
    WHERE STATE = 'CA'
```

Customer table
(MMADBV.CUST)

CUSTNO	FNAME	LNAME	ADDR	CITY	STATE	ZIPCODE
400001	KEITH	MCDONALD	4501 W MOCKINGBIRD	DALLAS	TX	75209
400002	ARREN	ANELLI	40 FORD RD	DENVILLE	NJ	07834
400003	SUSAN	HOWARD	1107 SECOND AVE #312	REDWOOD CITY	CA	94063
400004	CAROL ANN	EVANS	74 SUTTON CT	GREAT LAKES	IL	60088
400005	ELAINE	ROBERTS	12914 BRACKNELL	CERRITOS	CA	90701
400006	PAT	HONG	73 HIGH ST	SAN FRANCISCO	CA	94114
400007	PHIL	ROACH	25680 ORCHARD	DEARBORN HTS	MI	48125
400008	TIM	JOHNSON	145 W 27TH ST	SO CHICAGO HTS	IL	60411
400009	MARIANNE	BUSBEE	3920 BERWYN DR S #199	MOBILE	AL	36608
400010	ENRIQUE	OTHON	BOX 26729	RICHMOND	VA	23261
400011	WILLIAM C	FERGUSON	BOX 1283	MIAMI	FL	34002-1283
400012	S D	HOEHN	PO BOX 27	RIDDLE	OR	97469
400013	DAVID R	KEITH	BOX 1266	MAGNOLIA	AR	71757-1266
400014	R	BINDER	3425 WALDEN AVE	DEPEW	NY	14043
400015	VIVIAN	GEORGE	229 S 18TH ST	PHILADELPHIA	PA	19103
400016	J	NOETHLICH	11 KINGSTON CT	MERRIMACK	NH	03054

Results table

FNAME	LNAME
SUSAN	HOWARD
ELAINE	ROBERTS
PAT	HONG

Figure 4-4   A SELECT statement can retrieve a subset of the rows and columns from a stored table

specifies that data only for customers from California should be returned. Because the source table contains three rows for California customers, the results table contains three rows, as you can see in the figure.

There's also a fourth difference between DB2 and standard file processing. DB2 can combine, or *join*, data from two or more tables when it creates a results table. For example, figure 4-5 shows a SELECT statement that joins name information (from the customer table) with sales information (from the invoice table). You might use a SELECT statement like this one to retrieve data to prepare a sales report. This one SELECT statement returns a results table that contains one row for each row in the invoice table that's associated with a California

**SELECT
statement**

```
SELECT CUSTNO, INVNO, INVDATE, FNAME, LNAME, CITY, INVTOTAL
     FROM MMADBV.CUST, MMADBV.INV
   WHERE STATE = 'CA' AND
       CUSTNO = INVCUST
```

**Customer table
(MMADBV.CUST)**

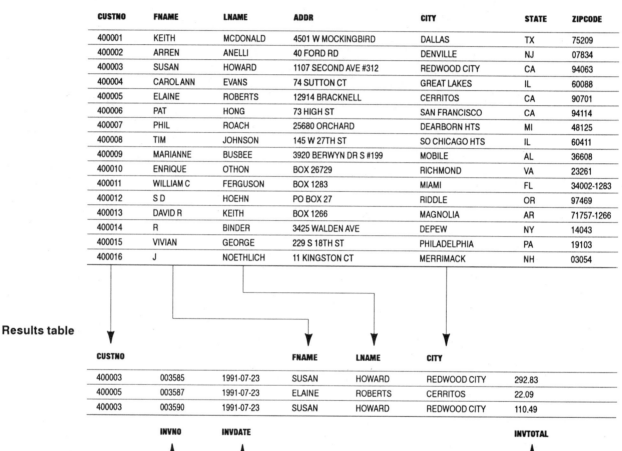

CUSTNO	FNAME	LNAME	ADDR	CITY	STATE	ZIPCODE
400001	KEITH	MCDONALD	4501 W MOCKINGBIRD	DALLAS	TX	75209
400002	ARREN	ANELLI	40 FORD RD	DENVILLE	NJ	07834
400003	SUSAN	HOWARD	1107 SECOND AVE #312	REDWOOD CITY	CA	94063
400004	CAROL ANN	EVANS	74 SUTTON CT	GREAT LAKES	IL	60088
400005	ELAINE	ROBERTS	12914 BRACKNELL	CERRITOS	CA	90701
400006	PAT	HONG	73 HIGH ST	SAN FRANCISCO	CA	94114
400007	PHIL	ROACH	25680 ORCHARD	DEARBORN HTS	MI	48125
400008	TIM	JOHNSON	145 W 27TH ST	SO CHICAGO HTS	IL	60411
400009	MARIANNE	BUSBEE	3920 BERWYN DR S #199	MOBILE	AL	36608
400010	ENRIQUE	OTHON	BOX 26729	RICHMOND	VA	23261
400011	WILLIAM C	FERGUSON	BOX 1283	MIAMI	FL	34002-1283
400012	S D	HOEHN	PO BOX 27	RIDDLE	OR	97469
400013	DAVID R	KEITH	BOX 1266	MAGNOLIA	AR	71757-1266
400014	R	BINDER	3425 WALDEN AVE	DEPEW	NY	14043
400015	VIVIAN	GEORGE	229 S 18TH ST	PHILADELPHIA	PA	19103
400016	J	NOETHLICH	11 KINGSTON CT	MERRIMACK	NH	03054

Results table

CUSTNO			FNAME	LNAME	CITY	
400003	003585	1991-07-23	SUSAN	HOWARD	REDWOOD CITY	292.83
400005	003587	1991-07-23	ELAINE	ROBERTS	CERRITOS	22.09
400003	003590	1991-07-23	SUSAN	HOWARD	REDWOOD CITY	110.49

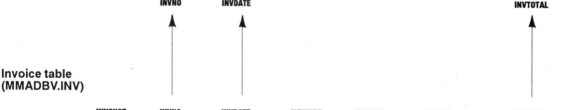

**Invoice table
(MMADBV.INV)**

INVCUST	INVNO	INVDATE	INVSUBT	INVSHIP	INVTAX	INVTOTAL	INVPO
400015	003584	1991-07-23	50.00	1.75	0.00	51.75	PROM1
400003	003585	1991-07-23	265.00	9.28	18.55	292.83	PROM1
400007	003586	1991-07-23	66.54	2.33	0.00	68.87	PROM1
400005	003587	1991-07-23	19.99	0.70	1.40	22.09	PROM1
400004	003588	1991-07-23	55.68	1.95	0.00	57.63	PROM1
400016	003589	1991-07-23	687.00	24.05	0.00	711.05	PROM1
400003	003590	1991-07-23	99.99	3.50	7.00	110.49	PROM1

Figure 4-5   A single SELECT statement can join data from two or more tables

customer. In each, data from the parent table, customer, is joined with data from the child table, invoice.

Multi-row results tables, like the ones in figures 4-4 and 4-5, are fine for interactive query applications, but they present a real problem for COBOL programs. That's because COBOL is based on record-at-a-time operations. A COBOL program can deal well with a CICS READ command that can return either one or no record from a standard file, but it can't deal directly with an SQL SELECT statement that may return one row, no rows, a dozen rows, or a thousand rows. Fortunately, DB2 includes a feature that bridges the gap between these two approaches to processing: cursors.

Cursors A *cursor* is a pointer that identifies one row in a results table as the *current row*. When a results table is processed with a cursor, a program can retrieve (or *fetch*) one row at a time. With each fetch operation, DB2 advances the cursor to the next row. Retrieving data using a cursor works much like browsing data in a sequential data set. However, remember that the results table contains only the rows and columns you requested. Thus, this type of sequential processing is relatively efficient.

To process DB2 data through a cursor-controlled results table, a program must define the table with an SQL DECLARE CURSOR statement. The DECLARE CURSOR statement contains a SELECT component that defines the contents of the results table. The program issues an SQL OPEN statement to generate the results table, then it retrieves one row after another with the SQL FETCH statement. After the program has retrieved the last row from the results table, it releases the cursor-controlled results table by issuing an SQL CLOSE statement.

Actually, it's not necessary to issue a CLOSE statement explicitly. That's because when a program ends, any DB2 resources it was using, including cursor-controlled results tables, are released. Unfortunately, this means that browses of DB2 data can't be done efficiently with pseudo-conversational CICS programs. There are different strategies you can use to implement DB2 browses in CICS; I'll describe them in the next topic. But for now, just realize that browsing DB2 data in a CICS program can be costly, regardless of how it's implemented.

How CICS and DB2 work together

DB2 executes as an MVS subsystem. When a CICS program issues an SQL statement, CICS passes the statement to the DB2 subsystem. DB2 then processes the statement and returns the result to CICS, which passes it along to the program. At the least, that means that the program receives a DB2 status code value that reports the success or failure of the statement. Often, it also means the program will receive data selected from one or more DB2 tables.

CICS manages its communications with DB2 with special interface modules called the *CICS/DB2 attachment facility*. These modules are loaded into storage with the other CICS modules. When a CICS program issues an SQL statement, CICS requests that the attachment facility establish a connection with DB2 called a *thread*. Figure 4-6 illustrates this connection.

Although there are some systems programming considerations for controlling the CICS/DB2 interface, as an application programmer, you don't have to worry about them. You simply include the appropriate SQL statements in your program. The CICS systems programmer defines the connection between your program's CICS transaction and DB2. That's done by making an entry in the CICS *Resource Control Table* (*RCT*).

The RCT contains the names of all CICS transactions that request DB2 services. For each transaction, the RCT contains the name of the DB2 application plan that's used with it. (I'll describe application plans in a moment.) The RCT also specifies the DB2 authorizations for CICS transactions. (DB2 has its own security system that has to be coordinated with CICS's.) And the RCT specifies the total number of threads that will be available to connect CICS and DB2. Because the number of threads is a limited resource, contention for threads can affect overall system performance.

DB2 programming under CICS

To issue an SQL statement from an application program you have to follow the rules listed in figure 4-7. First, you have to code the SQL statement between EXEC SQL and END-EXEC delimiters. This is much like you code a CICS command.

Second, to use program variables in an SQL statement, you must precede their names with colons. A program variable you code in an SQL statement is called a *host variable*. One reason you'll use host variables is to provide variable control information for an SQL statement, such as a key value that varies from one program execution to another. You also use host variables for input and output areas.

For example, to retrieve a single row from the customer table in an application program, you'd code

```
EXEC SQL
     SELECT *
          INTO :CUSTOMER-ROW
          FROM MMADBV.CUST
          WHERE CUSTNO = :CUSTNOI
END-EXEC
```

Notice in this example that the statement specifies an INTO clause that names a program data structure called CUSTOMER-ROW. DB2 will return the data this SELECT retrieves to that data area. This SELECT statement also includes a host variable in the WHERE clause. It specifies that the results table should contain the base table row whose CUSTNO

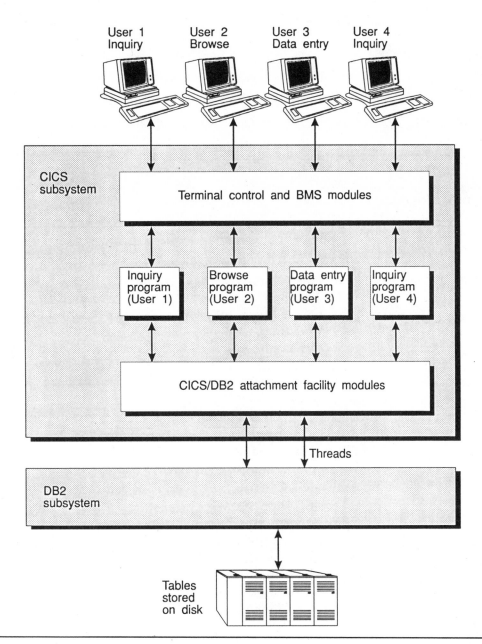

Figure 4-6 Attachment facility modules within CICS manage threads through which CICS and DB2 communicate

column contains the value currently in the program host variable CUSTNOI.

Third, to copy definitions for input/output data areas into your program, you use the SQL INCLUDE statement. Although you can code your own input/output data areas, if you do, you must make sure that

Code SQL statements between EXEC SQL and END-EXEC delimiters.

Precede a host variable name with a colon.

Use SQL INCLUDE statements rather than COBOL COPY statements to copy definitions of host variable data areas into a program.

Don't code a SELECT statement that can return more than one row.

Check the value of SQLCODE after each SQL statement to determine whether it executed successfully.

Figure 4-7   Rules for coding SQL in COBOL

the field definitions you use have the same lengths, data types, and sequence as the columns that DB2 will return. So most DB2 shops that process DB2 data use a DB2 utility procedure called *DCLGEN* (Declarations Generator) to create host variable definitions. DCLGEN accesses DB2's cataloged definitions of the tables it manages. As a result, you can be sure that current DCLGEN definitions are correct. Figure 4-8 shows DCLGEN output for the customer table. As you can see, it includes a COBOL group item that includes a field for each column in the table.

Fourth, when you code a SELECT statement in an application program, be sure that it won't return more than one row. If you issue a SELECT statement that generates a multi-row results table, your SQL statement will fail. To process a multi-row results table in a COBOL program, you have to use the cursor feature. The program example in the next topic shows you how to do that.

Finally, just as your CICS programs must check the completion status of the CICS commands they issue, they must also check the completion status of SQL statements they issue. The simplest way to do that is to evaluate the contents of a field in the *SQL communication area*, or *SQLCA*, named SQLCODE. Every program that processes DB2 data must contain an SQL INCLUDE statement to include the SQLCA definition. You'll see the definition of the SQLCA and how to check SQLCODE in the program example in the next topic.

How to prepare a CICS DB2 program for execution

Figure 4-9 presents the steps in the preparation of a CICS/DB2 program. As you can see, the process includes all the steps required for any CICS program. However, programming for the DB2 environment requires you to add two steps to the process: precompilation and binding. In addition, the link-edit step has a special requirement.

Precompiling the program   Before you translate and compile a CICS COBOL program that will access DB2 data, you first must process your source code with the *DB2 precompiler* (often called just the

```
************************************************************************
* DCLGEN TABLE(MMADBV.CUST)                                           *
*        LIBRARY(MMA002.DCLGENS.COBOL(CUST))                          *
*        ACTION(REPLACE)                                              *
*        STRUCTURE(CUSTOMER-ROW)                                      *
*        APOST                                                        *
* ... IS THE DCLGEN COMMAND THAT MADE THE FOLLOWING STATEMENTS        *
************************************************************************
     EXEC SQL DECLARE MMADBV.CUST TABLE
      ( CUSTNO                          CHAR(6) NOT NULL,
        FNAME                           CHAR(20) NOT NULL,
        LNAME                           CHAR(30) NOT NULL,
        ADDR                            CHAR(30) NOT NULL,
        CITY                            CHAR(20) NOT NULL,
        STATE                           CHAR(2) NOT NULL,
        ZIPCODE                         CHAR(10) NOT NULL
      ) END-EXEC.
************************************************************************
* COBOL DECLARATION FOR TABLE MMADBV.CUST                             *
************************************************************************
  01   CUSTOMER-ROW.
       10 CUSTNO              PIC X(6).
       10 FNAME               PIC X(20).
       10 LNAME               PIC X(30).
       10 ADDR                PIC X(30).
       10 CITY                PIC X(20).
       10 STATE               PIC X(2).
       10 ZIPCODE             PIC X(10).
************************************************************************
* THE NUMBER OF COLUMNS DESCRIBED BY THIS DECLARATION IS 7            *
************************************************************************
```

Figure 4-8   DCLGEN output for the CUST table

precompiler). The precompiler processes some SQL statements, like INCLUDE, and converts other SQL statements to a form that's meaningful to the COBOL compiler. In other words, the DB2 precompiler does for SQL statements what the CICS translator does for CICS commands. It also includes the source code for the original commands as comments in the precompiled version of the source program. These comments can help you read the precompiled program.

Note in figure 4-9 that you run the DB2 precompiler before you run the CICS translator. If you don't, the CICS translator will return a series of diagnostic messages because it doesn't recognize SQL statements. In contrast, the DB2 precompiler recognizes CICS commands and ignores them.

When you precompile your program, you need to be careful to specify the same delimiter character (quote or apostrophe) for the precompiler as you do for the CICS translator and the COBOL compiler. The defaults for the SQL precompiler and the COBOL compiler are different from the default for the CICS translator.

In addition to translating your program's SQL statements into COBOL, the precompiler also creates a *data base request module*, or *DBRM*. DB2 uses the DBRM as input to the binding step of program preparation.

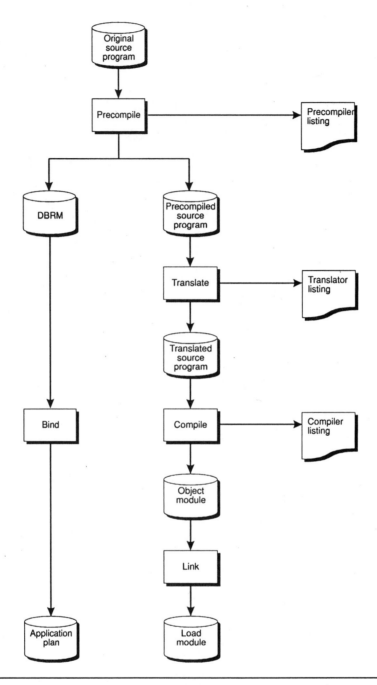

Figure 4-9 The steps required to prepare a CICS/DB2 program for execution

Binding the program   The *bind* process uses the data base request module (DBRM) the precompiler produces and creates an *application plan*. The application plan specifies which techniques DB2 should use to process the program's SQL statements in the most efficient manner. In some cases, there's a separate application plan for each application program. However, because CICS applications are often designed as sets of related programs, the bind process can create an application plan that services several programs.

When you bind a program, you can specify a number of options that affect DB2 performance. Among the most important are options that control how DB2 locks the resources programs use. Because locking can prevent other users from accessing stored data, data base and CICS administrators need to make careful decisions about these options. Then, they need to monitor system performance and make adjustments as necessary. Your shop's CICS and DB2 systems programmers can suggest which bind option values you should use.

Link-editing the program   The link-edit step of the CICS/DB2 program development process has a special requirement. To issue SQL statements from a CICS program, you must link-edit the program so it includes an interface to the CICS/DB2 attachment facility. The module that provides that interface is DSNCLI. If your shop uses a cataloged procedure for CICS/DB2 program development, it almost certainly contains the link-edit INCLUDE directive for this module.

Terms

DB2
Database 2
relational data base management system
relation
table
row
column
normalization
key
parent/child relationship
referential integrity
SQL
Structured Query Language
query
QMF
Query Management Facility
results table
join
cursor
current row

fetch
CICS/DB2 attachment facility
thread
Resource Control Table (RCT)
host variable
DCLGEN
SQL communication area
SQLCA
DB2 precompiler
precompiler
data base request module
DBRM
bind
application plan

Objectives

1. Describe the similarities and differences between the structures and processing of DB2 tables and standard files.

2. Describe how to request DB2 services from a COBOL program.

3. Explain how the fact that a results table can contain more than one row presents problems for application programs.

4. Describe the mechanism DB2 uses to provide access to one row at a time from a multi-row results table.

5. Describe how a CICS and DB2 subsystem work together to allow an interactive application to access data stored in DB2 tables.

6. List the rules for coding SQL statements in a COBOL program.

7. List and describe the steps required to prepare a CICS/DB2 program for execution.

How to access a DB2 data base

Now that you've seen how DB2 stores and processes data, you're ready to learn how to code a CICS program to access DB2 data. In this topic, I'll present a DB2 version of the CICS customer inquiry program. After I've presented the sample program, I'll offer three strategies you can use to deal with the inefficiencies of browsing cursor-controlled results tables in a CICS program. Finally, I'll mention some additional considerations you should keep in mind as you code programs that process DB2 data.

The DB2 version of the customer inquiry program

Figures 4-10 through 4-15 present the DB2 version of the customer inquiry program. This program is similar to the customer inquiry program I presented in chapter 2. One difference is that the data it processes is stored in DB2 tables rather than VSAM data sets. So, the program uses a SELECT statement to retrieve data for a specific customer, then uses a cursor to retrieve that customer's invoices. Another difference is that customer data can be displayed only by entering a customer number. You can't use PF keys to display the first, last, previous, or next customer like you could in the program in chapter 2. As I describe this program, I'll focus on the DB2 programming implications. The rest of the program is simple enough that you should have little trouble understanding it.

The specifications

Figure 4-10 presents the specifications for the DB2 version of the customer inquiry program. As you can see in the program overview in part 1 of the figure, the program retrieves data from two DB2 tables: CUST and INV. After accepting a customer number and retrieving the customer row from the CUST table, the program retrieves the most recent invoice rows associated with the customer from the INV table. As the screen layout in part 2 of figure 4-10 indicates, information is displayed for up to eight invoices.

Even though the program may not display details for all the invoices for a customer, it does display the total number of invoices present in the INV table for the customer and the total dollar amount billed on them. To determine these values, the program uses another SQL feature: column functions. I'll describe column functions when I

Program   DB2INQ1

Overview   Displays data from a selected row in the customer table, along with the total number of invoices issued to that customer, their total dollar value, and detail information for up to the first eight invoices.

Input/output specifications

DLIMAP1	Customer inquiry map
CUST	Customer table
INV	Invoice table

Processing specifications

1. Control is transferred to the program via XCTL from the menu program INVMENU with no communication area. The user can also start the program by entering the trans-id DIN1. In either case, the program should respond by displaying the customer inquiry map.

2. If the user enters a customer number, select the corresponding row from the customer table.

3. If the requested customer row was selected successfully, retrieve and display data from the most recent rows in the invoice table for that customer. If more than eight related invoices are present, display only the first eight. Also, determine and display the total number of related rows in the invoice table and the sum of the invoice amounts billed on all of them.

4. If the user presses PF3 or PF12, return to the menu program INVMENU by issuing an XCTL command.

Figure 4-10   Specifications for the DB2 version of the customer inquiry program (part 1 of 4)

present the program code. Note that the message "The most recent 8 are shown." appears only if more than eight invoices for the customer are present.

Part 3 of figure 4-10 shows output from DB2's DCLGEN process for the CUST and INV tables. These are copy members that are included in your source program, much like a standard COBOL copy member. However, unlike standard file record descriptions, you don't use the COBOL COPY statement to combine DCLGEN output with your source code. Instead, you must use the SQL INCLUDE statement. (You'll see examples of INCLUDE in the program source code later in this topic.)

Map name	DB2MAP1	Date	07/01/92
Program name	DB2INQ1	Designer	Doug Lowe

```
     1         1         2         3         4         5         6         7         8
     1234567890123456789012345678901234567890123456789012345678901234567890123456789 0
 1   DB2MAP1            Customer Inquiry
 2
 3   Type a customer number.  Then press Enter.
 4
 5   Customer number. . . . .
 6
 7   Name and address . . . : XXXXXXXXXXXXXXXXXXXXXXXXXXXXXX
 8                            XXXXXXXXXXXXXXXXXXXXX
 9                            XXXXXXXXXXXXXXXXXXXXXXXXXXXXX
10                            XXXXXXXXXXXXXXXXXXX XX XXXXXXXXXX
11
12   Z,ZZZ,ZZ9 invoices total $$,$$$,$$9.99.  The most recent 8 are shown.
13
14   Invoice  PO Number    Date              Total
15    999999  XXXXXXXXXX   XXXXXXXXXX   Z,ZZZ,ZZ9.99
16    999999  XXXXXXXXXX   XXXXXXXXXX   Z,ZZZ,ZZ9.99
17    999999  XXXXXXXXXX   XXXXXXXXXX   Z,ZZZ,ZZ9.99
18    999999  XXXXXXXXXX   XXXXXXXXXX   Z,ZZZ,ZZ9.99
19    999999  XXXXXXXXXX   XXXXXXXXXX   Z,ZZZ,ZZ9.99
20    999999  XXXXXXXXXX   XXXXXXXXXX   Z,ZZZ,ZZ9.99
21    999999  XXXXXXXXXX   XXXXXXXXXX   Z,ZZZ,ZZ9.99
22    999999  XXXXXXXXXX   XXXXXXXXXX   Z,ZZZ,ZZ9.99
23   XXXXXXXXXXXXXXXXXXXXXXXXXXXXXXXXXXXXXXXXXXXXXXXXXXXXXXXXXXXXXXXXXXXXXXXXXXXXXXXXX
24   F3=Exit  F12=Cancel                                                            X
```

Figure 4-10 Specifications for the DB2 version of the customer inquiry program (part 2 of 4)

As you can see, a DCLGEN member contains a COBOL data structure that is similar to a file's record description. You can use the fields in these data structures as host variables in your SQL statements.

In addition to DCLGEN output, you need to specify an INCLUDE statement for one other data structure: SQLCA. Part 4 of figure 4-10 presents its format. It's a set of fields that describes the data elements that make up the SQL communication area. DB2 reports the success or failure of the SQL statements your program issues through one of the SQLCA fields, SQLCODE. You'll see how the sample program evaluates SQLCODE later in this topic.

DCLGEN INCLUDE copy member for the customer table (CUST)

```
*******************************************************************
* DCLGEN TABLE(MMADBV.CUST)                                       *
*         LIBRARY(MMA002.DCLGENS.COBOL(CUST))                     *
*         ACTION(REPLACE)                                         *
*         STRUCTURE(CUSTOMER-ROW)                                 *
*         APOST                                                   *
* ... IS THE DCLGEN COMMAND THAT MADE THE FOLLOWING STATEMENTS    *
*******************************************************************
      EXEC SQL DECLARE MMADBV.CUST TABLE
      (   CUSTNO                    CHAR (6) NOT NULL,
          FNAME                     CHAR (20) NOT NULL,
          LNAME                     CHAR (30) NOT NULL,
          ADDR                      CHAR (30) NOT NULL,
          CITY                      CHAR (20) NOT NULL,
          STATE                     CHAR (2) NOT NULL,
          ZIPCODE                   CHAR (10) NOT NULL
      ) END-EXEC.
*******************************************************************
* COBOL DECLARATION FOR TABLE MMADBV.CUST                         *
*******************************************************************
  01 CUSTOMER-ROW.
      10 CUSTNO              PIC X(6).
      10 FNAME               PIC X(20).
      10 LNAME               PIC X(30).
      10 ADDR                PIC X(30).
      10 CITY                PIC X(20).
      10 STATE               PIC X(2).
      10 ZIPCODE             PIC X(10).
*******************************************************************
* THE NUMBER OF COLUMNS DESCRIBED BY THIS DECLARATION IS 7        *
*******************************************************************
```

DCLGEN INCLUDE copy member for the invoice table (INV)

```
*******************************************************************
* DCLGEN TABLE(MMADBV.INV)                                        *
*         LIBRARY(MMA002.DCLGENS.COBOL(INV))                      *
*         ACTION(REPLACE)                                         *
*         STRUCTURE(INVOICE-ROW)                                  *
*         APOST                                                   *
* ... IS THE DCLGEN COMMAND THAT MADE THE FOLLOWING STATEMENTS    *
*******************************************************************
      EXEC SQL DECLARE MMADBV.INV TABLE
      (   INVCUST                   CHAR (6) NOT NULL,
          INVNO                     CHAR (6) NOT NULL,
          INVDATE                   DATE NOT NULL,
          INVSUBT                   DECIMAL (9, 2) NOT NULL
          INVSHIP                   DECIMAL (7, 2) NOT NULL,
          INVTAX                    DECIMAL (7, 2) NOT NULL,
          INVTOTAL                  DECIMAL (9, 2) NOT NULL,
          INVPO                     CHAR (10) NOT NULL
      ) END-EXEC.
*******************************************************************
* COBOL DECLARATION FOR TABLE MMADBV.INV                          *
*******************************************************************
  01  INVOICE-ROW.
      10 INVCUST             PIC X(6).
      10 INVNO               PIC X(6).
      10 INVDATE             PIC X(10).
      10 INVSUBT             PIC S9999999V99 USAGE COMP-3.
      10 INVSHIP             PIC S99999V99 USAGE COMP-3.
      10 INVTAX              PIC S99999V99 USAGE COMP-3.
      10 INVTOTAL            PIC S9999999V99 USAGE COMP-3.
      10 INVPO               PIC X(10).
*******************************************************************
* THE NUMBER OF COLUMNS DESCRIBED BY THIS DECLARATION IS 8        *
*******************************************************************
```

Figure 4-10   Specifications for the DB2 version of the customer inquiry program (part 3 of 4)

INCLUDE copy member for the SQL communication area (SQLCA)

```
01 SQLCA.
   05 SQLCAID     PIC X(8).
   05 SQLCABC     PIC S9(4) COMP-4.
   05 SQLCODE     PIC S9(4) COMP-4.
   05 SQLERRM.
      49 SQLERRML PIC S9(4) COMP-4.
      49 SQLERRMC PIC X(70).
   05 SQLERRP     PIC X(8).
   05 SQLERRD     OCCURS 6 TIMES
                  PIC S9(9) COMP-4.
   05 SQLWARN.
      10 SQLWARN0 PIC X.
      10 SQLWARN1 PIC X.
      10 SQLWARN2 PIC X.
      10 SQLWARN3 PIC X.
      10 SQLWARN4 PIC X.
      10 SQLWARN5 PIC X.
      10 SQLWARN6 PIC X.
      10 SQLWARN7 PIC X.
   05 SQLEXT      PIC X(8).
```

The ERRPARM copy member

```
*
 01   ERROR-PARAMETERS.
*
      05   ERR-RESP        PIC S9(8)    COMP.
      05   ERR-RESP2       PIC S9(8)    COMP.
      05   ERR-TRNID       PIC X(4).
      05   ERR-RSRCE       PIC X(4).
```

Figure 4-10 Specifications for the DB2 version of the customer inquiry program (part 4 of 4)

The design

Figures 4-11 and 4-12 present the event/response chart and structure chart for this program. Because the event/response chart is simple and so much like those for other programs I've presented, I won't discuss it in detail. However, the structure chart has some differences I want to point out.

As you can see, module 1300 retrieves a row from the customer table. Then, modules 1410, 1420, 1430, and 1440 retrieve data for the invoice detail lines the program displays. Module 1410 creates a cursor-controlled results table that contains invoices only for the current customer. Module 1420 is performed repeatedly to format the eight invoice detail lines. It performs module 1430 to retrieve the next invoice row from the cursor-controlled results table module 1410 generated. After the last invoice has been retrieved, module 1440 is invoked to release the cursor-controlled results table.

Finally, the program executes module 1450 to retrieve the summary information that appears in the total line on line 12 of the screen. It, in turn, invokes module 1460 to get the total information the program needs.

Event	Response
Start the program	Display the customer inquiry map.
PF3 PF12	Transfer control to the menu program.
Enter	Select and display the customer row and the eight most recent invoice rows for the customer number entered by the user. Determine the total number of invoices billed and their total dollar value.
Clear	Redisplay the customer inquiry map.
PA1, PA2, or PA3	Ignore the key.
Any other key	Display an appropriate error message.

Figure 4-11 An event/response chart for the DB2 version of the customer inquiry program

The mapset and symbolic map

Figures 4-13 and 4-14 present the BMS mapset and the programmer-generated symbolic map for this program. Except for the total line displayed on line 12, they're almost identical to the mapset and symbolic map for the inquiry program in chapter 2. So, you shouldn't have any problem understanding them.

The source listing

Figure 4-15 presents the COBOL source code for the DB2 version of the customer inquiry program. Before I describe the Procedure Division code, I want you to notice several things in the Working-Storage Section. First, I included a field named INVOICE-COUNT, which is used with the SQL function that returns the total number of invoices for a specific customer. I also included a group item named TOTAL-LINE, which is used to prepare the summary that appears in line 12 of the screen.

The last four items in the Working-Storage Section are SQL statements. The first two are INCLUDE statements that include the DCLGEN descriptions for the CUST and INV tables. The third item is an INCLUDE statement that includes the description for the SQLCA.

The last item in the Working-Storage Section is an SQL DECLARE CURSOR statement. It supplies the SELECT that will be used to generate a cursor-controlled results table containing the invoices for a selected customer. I'll describe this statement when I show you how the program retrieves the appropriate invoices. For now, you should realize that, as its name suggests, DECLARE CURSOR is a "declarative"

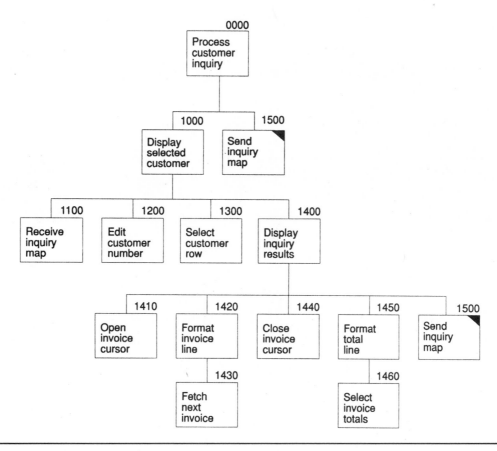

Figure 4-12 Structure chart for the DB2 version of the customer inquiry program

statement, not an action statement. It simply "declares" what the results table should contain; it doesn't actually create the results table. That's why it appears in the program's Working-Storage Section, not in its Procedure Division.

How the program retrieves a customer row   After the program receives a customer number from the user and edits it, module 1300 retrieves data from the CUST table. As you'd expect, it does that by issuing a SELECT statement:

```
EXEC SQL
    SELECT      FNAME,            LNAME,
                ADDR,             CITY,
                STATE,            ZIPCODE
         INTO  :CIM-D-FNAME,  :CIM-D-LNAME,
               :CIM-D-ADDR,   :CIM-D-CITY,
               :CIM-D-STATE,  :CIM-D-ZIPCODE
         FROM  MMADBV.CUST
         WHERE CUSTNO = :CIM-D-CUSTNO
END-EXEC.
```

```
           PRINT NOGEN
DB2SET1 DFHMSD TYPE=&SYSPARM,                                          X
               LANG=COBOL,                                             X
               MODE=INOUT,                                             X
               TERM=3270-2,                                            X
               CTRL=FREEKB,                                            X
               STORAGE=AUTO,                                           X
               TIOAPFX=YES
*****************************************************************************
DB2MAP1 DFHMDI SIZE=(24,80),                                          X
               LINE=1,                                                X
               COLUMN=1
*****************************************************************************
        DFHMDF POS=(1,1),                                             X
               LENGTH=7,                                              X
               ATTRB=(NORM,PROT),                                     X
               COLOR=BLUE,                                            X
               INITIAL='DB2MAP1'
        DFHMDF POS=(1,20),                                           X
               LENGTH=16,                                            X
               ATTRB=(NORM,PROT),                                    X
               COLOR=BLUE,                                           X
               INITIAL='Customer Inquiry'
*****************************************************************************
        DFHMDF POS=(3,1),                                            X
               LENGTH=42,                                           X
               ATTRB=(NORM,PROT),                                   X
               COLOR=GREEN,                                         X
               INITIAL='Type a customer number.  Then press Enter.'
        DFHMDF POS=(5,1),                                            X
               LENGTH=24,                                           X
               ATTRB=(NORM,PROT),                                   X
               COLOR=GREEN,                                         X
               INITIAL='Customer number. . . . .'
CUSTNO  DFHMDF POS=(5,26),                                           X
               LENGTH=6,                                            X
               ATTRB=(NORM,UNPROT,IC),                              X
               COLOR=TURQUOISE,                                     X
               INITIAL='_____'
        DFHMDF POS=(5,33),                                           X
               LENGTH=1,                                            X
               ATTRB=ASKIP
*****************************************************************************
        DFHMDF POS=(7,1),                                            X
               LENGTH=24,                                           X
               ATTRB=(NORM,PROT),                                   X
               COLOR=GREEN,                                         X
               INITIAL='Name and address . . . .:'
LNAME   DFHMDF POS=(7,26),                                           X
               LENGTH=30,                                           X
               COLOR=TURQUOISE,                                     X
               ATTRB=(NORM,PROT)
FNAME   DFHMDF POS=(8,26),                                           X
               LENGTH=20,                                           X
               COLOR=TURQUOISE,                                     X
               ATTRB=(NORM,PROT)
```

Figure 4-13   Mapset listing for the DB2 version of the customer inquiry program (part 1 of 3)

```
ADDR        DFHMDF POS=(9,26),                                           X
                   LENGTH=30,                                            X
                   COLOR=TURQUOISE,                                      X
                   ATTRB=(NORM,PROT)
CITY        DFHMDF POS=(10,26),                                          X
                   LENGTH=20,                                            X
                   COLOR=TURQUOISE,                                      X
                   ATTRB=(NORM,PROT)
STATE       DFHMDF POS=(10,47),                                          X
                   LENGTH=2,                                             X
                   COLOR=TURQUOISE,                                      X
                   ATTRB=(NORM,PROT)
ZIPCODE     DFHMDF POS=(10,50),                                          X
                   LENGTH=10,                                            X
                   COLOR=TURQUOISE,                                      X
                   ATTRB=(NORM,PROT)
***********************************************************************
TOTAL       DFHMDF POS=(12,1),                                           X
                   LENGTH=69,                                            X
                   COLOR=TURQUOISE,                                      X
                   ATTRB=(NORM,PROT)
            DFHMDF POS=(14,1),                                           X
                   LENGTH=45,                                            X
                   COLOR=GREEN,                                          X
                   ATTRB=(NORM,PROT),                                    X
                   INITIAL='Invoice  PO Number   Date           Total'
INV1        DFHMDF POS=(15,2),                                           X
                   LENGTH=44,                                            X
                   COLOR=TURQUOISE,                                      X
                   ATTRB=(NORM,PROT)
INV2        DFHMDF POS=(16,2),                                           X
                   LENGTH=44,                                            X
                   COLOR=TURQUOISE,                                      X
                   ATTRB=(NORM,PROT)
INV3        DFHMDF POS=(17,2),                                           X
                   LENGTH=44,                                            X
                   COLOR=TURQUOISE,                                      X
                   ATTRB=(NORM,PROT)
INV4        DFHMDF POS=(18,2),                                           X
                   LENGTH=44,                                            X
                   COLOR=TURQUOISE,                                      X
                   ATTRB=(NORM,PROT)
INV5        DFHMDF POS=(19,2),                                           X
                   LENGTH=44,                                            X
                   COLOR=TURQUOISE,                                      X
                   ATTRB=(NORM,PROT)
INV6        DFHMDF POS=(20,2),                                           X
                   LENGTH=44,                                            X
                   COLOR=TURQUOISE,                                      X
                   ATTRB=(NORM,PROT)
INV7        DFHMDF POS=(21,2),                                           X
                   LENGTH=44,                                            X
                   COLOR=TURQUOISE,                                      X
                   ATTRB=(NORM,PROT)
INV8        DFHMDF POS=(22,2),                                           X
                   LENGTH=44,                                            X
                   COLOR=TURQUOISE,                                      X
                   ATTRB=(NORM,PROT)
```

Figure 4-13 Mapset listing for the DB2 version of the customer inquiry program (part 2 of 3)

```
*********************************************************************
MESSAGE    DFHMDF POS=(23,1),                                       X
                  LENGTH=79,                                        X
                  ATTRB=(BRT,PROT),                                 X
                  COLOR=YELLOW
           DFHMDF POS=(24,1),                                       X
                  LENGTH=18,                                        X
                  ATTRB=(NORM,PROT),                                X
                  COLOR=BLUE,                                       X
                  INITIAL='F3=Exit   F12=Cancel'
DUMMY      DFHMDF POS=(24,79),                                      X
                  LENGTH=1,                                         X
                  ATTRB=(DRK,PROT,FSET),                            X
                  INITIAL=' '
*********************************************************************
           DFHMSD TYPE=FINAL
           END
```

Figure 4-13 Mapset listing for the DB2 version of the customer inquiry program (part 3 of 3)

Because the customer table was designed so the CUSTNO column is a unique key, this statement will never return a results table with more than one row. As a result, I was able to code this SELECT statement directly in the program's Procedure Division.

This SELECT statement will return a results table with six columns: all of the columns that comprise the customer table, except CUSTNO. The INTO clause specifies that the DB2 data will be placed in fields from the symbolic map rather than fields from the DCLGEN structure. If I had specified fields from the DCLGEN structure in the SELECT statement, I would have followed the SELECT statement with MOVE statements that move the data from the DCLGEN structure to the symbolic map fields. By specifying the map fields on the SELECT statement, I avoided having to code the MOVE statements.

I didn't specify the customer number in the INTO clause because the current value is already present in the host variable named CIM-D-CUSTNO. This field is from the symbolic map, and contains the customer number entered by the user. You can see that I used this field in the SELECT statement's WHERE clause.

As I've already mentioned, DB2 returns a status code value to report the success or failure of each SQL statement through the SQLCODE field in the SQL communication area (part 5 of figure 4-10). Although DB2 can return many different SQLCODE values to report different error conditions, you only need to deal with a few.

For the SELECT statement in module 1300, I tested the SQLCODE value with these statements:

```
IF SQLCODE = 100
    MOVE 'N' TO CUSTOMER-FOUND-SW
    MOVE 'That customer does not exist." to CIM-D-MESSAGE
ELSE IF SQLCODE NOT = 0
    GO TO 9999-TERMINATE-PROGRAM.
```

```
*
 01    CUSTOMER-INQUIRY-MAP.
*
       05    FILLER                    PIC X(12).
*
       05    CIM-L-CUSTNO              PIC S9(4)    COMP.
       05    CIM-A-CUSTNO              PIC X.
       05    CIM-D-CUSTNO              PIC X(6).
*
       05    CIM-L-LNAME               PIC S9(4)    COMP.
       05    CIM-A-LNAME               PIC X.
       05    CIM-D-LNAME               PIC X(30).
*
       05    CIM-L-FLAME               PIC S9(4)    COMP.
       05    CIM-A-FNAME               PIC X.
       05    CIM-D-FNAME               PIC X(20).
*
       05    CIM-L-ADDR                PIC S9(4)    COMP.
       05    CIM-A-ADDR                PIC X.
       05    CIM-D-ADDR                PIC X(30).
*
       05    CIM-L-CITY                PIC S9(4)    COMP.
       05    CIM-A-CITY                PIC X.
       05    CIM-D-CITY                PIC X(20).
*
       05    CIM-L-STATE               PIC S9(4)    COMP.
       05    CIM-A-STATE               PIC X.
       05    CIM-D-STATE               PIC XX.
*
       05    CIM-L-ZIPCODE             PIC S9(4)    COMP.
       05    CIM-A-ZIPCODE             PIC X.
       05    CIM-D-ZIPCODE             PIC X(10).
*
       05    CIM-L-TOTAL               PIC S9(4)    COMP.
       05    CIM-A-TOTAL               PIC X.
       05    CIM-D-TOTAL               PIC X(69).
*
       05    CIM-INVOICE-LINE          OCCURS 8.
*
          10    CIM-L-INVOICE-LINE     PIC S9(4)    COMP.
          10    CIM-A-INVOICE-LINE     PIC X.
          10    CIM-D-INVOICE-LINE     PIC X(44).
*
       05    CIM-L-MESSAGE             PIC S9(4)    COMP.
       05    CIM-A-MESSAGE             PIC X.
       05    CIM-D-MESSAGE             PIC X(79).
*
       05    CIM-L-DUMMY               PIC S9(4)    COMP.
       05    CIM-A-DUMMY               PIC X.
       05    CIM-D-DUMMY               PIC X.
```

Figure 4-14 Programmer-generated symbolic map for the DB2 version of the customer inquiry program

If the value of SQLCODE is 100, it means that the requested customer row doesn't exist. (This is the equivalent of the NOTFND condition for a CICS READ command.) In that case, the program moves N to CUSTOMER-FOUND-SW and moves an error message to CIM-D-MESSAGE. If the SQLCODE is some other non-zero value, it means that a serious error has occurred. So, the program branches to

```
       IDENTIFICATION DIVISION.
     *
       PROGRAM-ID.  DB2INQ1.
     *
       ENVIRONMENT DIVISION.
     *
       DATA DIVISION.
     *
       WORKING-STORAGE SECTION.
     *
       01  SWITCHES.
     *
           05   VALID-DATA-SW         PIC X            VALUE 'Y'.
               88   VALID-DATA                         VALUE 'Y'.
           05   CUSTOMER-FOUND-SW     PIC X            VALUE 'Y'.
               88   CUSTOMER-FOUND                     VALUE 'Y'.
           05   MORE-INVOICES-SW      PIC X            VALUE 'Y'.
               88   MORE-INVOICES                      VALUE 'Y'.
     *
       01  FLAGS.
     *
           05   DISPLAY-FLAG          PIC X.
               88   DISPLAY-NEW-CUSTOMER               VALUE '1'.
               88   DISPLAY-SPACES                     VALUE '2'.
               88   DISPLAY-LOW-VALUES                 VALUE '3'.
           05   SEND-FLAG             PIC X.
               88   SEND-ERASE                         VALUE '1'.
               88   SEND-DATAONLY                      VALUE '2'.
               88   SEND-DATAONLY-ALARM                VALUE '3'.
     *
       01  WORK-FIELDS.
     *
           05   INVOICE-SUB           PIC S9(4)        COMP.
           05   INVOICE-COUNT         PIC S9(9)        COMP.
     *
       01  INVOICE-LINE.
     *
           05   IL-INVOICE-NUMBER     PIC X(6).
           05   FILLER                PIC XX           VALUE SPACE.
           05   IL-PO-NUMBER          PIC X(10).
           05   FILLER                PIC XX           VALUE SPACE.
           05   IL-INVOICE-DATE       PIC X(10).
           05   FILLER                PIC XX           VALUE SPACE.
           05   IL-INVOICE-TOTAL      PIC Z,ZZZ,ZZ9.99.
     *
       01  TOTAL-LINE.
     *
           05   TL-COUNT              PIC Z,ZZZ,ZZ9.
           05   FILLER                PIC X(16) VALUE ' invoices total '.
           05   TL-TOTAL              PIC $$,$$$,$$9.99.
           05   FILLER                PIC X      VALUE '.'.
           05   TL-MESSAGE            PIC X(30).
     *
       01  COMMUNICATION-AREA.
     *
           05   CA-CUSTOMER-NUMBER    PIC X(6).
     *
       COPY DB2SET1.
     *
       COPY DFHAID.
     *
       COPY ERRPARM.
```

Figure 4-15 Source listing for the DB2 version of the customer inquiry program (part 1 of 5)

```
/
      EXEC SQL
          INCLUDE CUST
      END-EXEC.
*
      EXEC SQL
          INCLUDE INV
      END-EXEC.
*
      EXEC SQL
          INCLUDE SQLCA
      END-EXEC.
*
      EXEC SQL
          DECLARE CUSTINV CURSOR FOR
              SELECT INVNO, INVPO, CHAR(INVDATE,USA), INVTOTAL
                  FROM MMADBV.INV
                  WHERE INVCUST = :CIM-D-CUSTNO
                  ORDER BY 1 DESC
      END-EXEC.
*
  LINKAGE SECTION.
*
  01  DFHCOMMAREA              PIC X(6).
*
  PROCEDURE DIVISION.
*
  0000-PROCESS-CUSTOMER-INQUIRY.
*
      MOVE DFHCOMMAREA TO COMMUNICATION-AREA.

      EVALUATE TRUE

          WHEN EIBCALEN = ZERO
              MOVE LOW-VALUE TO CA-CUSTOMER-NUMBER
              MOVE LOW-VALUE TO CUSTOMER-INQUIRY-MAP
              SET SEND-ERASE TO TRUE
              PERFORM 1500-SEND-INQUIRY-MAP

          WHEN EIBAID = DFHCLEAR
              MOVE LOW-VALUE TO CA-CUSTOMER-NUMBER
              MOVE LOW-VALUE TO CUSTOMER-INQUIRY-MAP
              SET SEND-ERASE TO TRUE
              PERFORM 1500-SEND-INQUIRY-MAP

          WHEN EIBAID = DFHPA1 OR DFHPA2 OR DFHPA3
              CONTINUE

          WHEN EIBAID = DFHPF3 OR DFHPF12
              EXEC CICS
                  XCTL PROGRAM('INVMENU')
              END-EXEC

          WHEN EIBAID = DFHENTER
              PERFORM 1000-DISPLAY-SELECTED-CUSTOMER

          WHEN OTHER
              MOVE LOW-VALUE TO CUSTOMER-INQUIRY-MAP
              MOVE 'Invalid key pressed.' TO CIM-D-MESSAGE
              SET SEND-DATAONLY-ALARM TO TRUE
              PERFORM 1500-SEND-INQUIRY-MAP

      END-EVALUATE.

      EXEC CICS
          RETURN TRANSID('DIN1')
                  COMMAREA(COMMUNICATION-AREA)
      END-EXEC.
```

Figure 4-15 Source listing for the DB2 version of the customer inquiry program (part 2 of 5)

```
/
 1000-DISPLAY-SELECTED-CUSTOMER.
*
     PERFORM 1100-RECEIVE-INQUIRY-MAP.
     PERFORM 1200-EDIT-CUSTOMER-NUMBER.
     IF VALID-DATA
         PERFORM 1300-SELECT-CUSTOMER-ROW
         IF CUSTOMER-FOUND
             SET DISPLAY-NEW-CUSTOMER TO TRUE
             PERFORM 1400-DISPLAY-INQUIRY-RESULTS
             MOVE CUSTNO TO CA-CUSTOMER-NUMBER
         ELSE
             SET DISPLAY-SPACES TO TRUE
             PERFORM 1400-DISPLAY-INQUIRY-RESULTS
     ELSE
         SET DISPLAY-LOW-VALUES TO TRUE
         PERFORM 1400-DISPLAY-INQUIRY-RESULTS.
*
 1100-RECEIVE-INQUIRY-MAP.
*
     EXEC CICS
         RECEIVE MAP('DB2MAP1')
                 MAPSET('DB2SET1')
                 INTO(CUSTOMER-INQUIRY-MAP)
     END-EXEC.
     INSPECT CUSTOMER-INQUIRY-MAP
         REPLACING ALL '_' BY SPACE.
*
 1200-EDIT-CUSTOMER-NUMBER.
*
     IF        CIM-L-CUSTNO = ZERO
         OR CIM-D-CUSTNO = SPACE
         MOVE 'N' TO VALID-DATA-SW
         MOVE 'You must enter a customer number.'
             TO CIM-D-MESSAGE.
*
 1300-SELECT-CUSTOMER-ROW.
*
     EXEC SQL
         SELECT     FNAME,        LNAME,
                    ADDR,         CITY,
                    STATE,        ZIPCODE
             INTO :CIM-D-FNAME, :CIM-D-LNAME,
                  :CIM-D-ADDR,  :CIM-D-CITY,
                  :CIM-D-STATE, :CIM-D-ZIPCODE
             FROM  MMADBV.CUST
             WHERE CUSTNO = :CIM-D-CUSTNO
     END-EXEC.
     IF SQLCODE = 100
         MOVE 'N' TO CUSTOMER-FOUND-SW
         MOVE 'That customer does not exist.' TO CIM-D-MESSAGE
     ELSE IF SQLCODE NOT = 0
         GO TO 9999-TERMINATE-PROGRAM.
```

Figure 4-15 Source listing for the DB2 version of the customer inquiry program (part 3 of 5)

```
/
 1400-DISPLAY-INQUIRY-RESULTS.
*
     IF DISPLAY-NEW-CUSTOMER
         PERFORM 1410-OPEN-INVOICE-CURSOR
         PERFORM 1420-FORMAT-INVOICE-LINE
             VARYING INVOICE-SUB FROM 1 BY 1
             UNTIL INVOICE-SUB > 8
         PERFORM 1440-CLOSE-INVOICE-CURSOR
         PERFORM 1450-FORMAT-TOTAL-LINE
         MOVE SPACE TO CIM-D-MESSAGE
         SET SEND-DATAONLY TO TRUE
     ELSE IF DISPLAY-SPACES
         MOVE LOW-VALUE TO CIM-D-CUSTNO
         MOVE SPACE          TO CIM-D-LNAME
                                CIM-D-FNAME
                                CIM-D-ADDR
                                CIM-D-CITY
                                CIM-D-STATE
                                CIM-D-ZIPCODE
                                CIM-D-TOTAL
         PERFORM VARYING INVOICE-SUB FROM 1 BY 1
                 UNTIL INVOICE-SUB > 8
             MOVE SPACE TO CIM-D-INVOICE-LINE(INVOICE-SUB)
         END-PERFORM
         SET SEND-DATAONLY-ALARM TO TRUE
     ELSE IF DISPLAY-LOW-VALUES
         SET SEND-DATAONLY-ALARM TO TRUE.
     PERFORM 1500-SEND-INQUIRY-MAP.
*
 1410-OPEN-INVOICE-CURSOR.
*
     EXEC SQL
         OPEN CUSTINV
     END-EXEC.
     IF SQLCODE NOT = 0
         GO TO 9999-TERMINATE-PROGRAM.
*
 1420-FORMAT-INVOICE-LINE.
*
     IF MORE-INVOICES
         PERFORM 1430-FETCH-NEXT-INVOICE
         IF MORE-INVOICES
             MOVE INVOICE-LINE TO CIM-D-INVOICE-LINE(INVOICE-SUB)
         ELSE
             MOVE SPACE TO CIM-D-INVOICE-LINE(INVOICE-SUB)
     ELSE
         MOVE SPACE TO CIM-D-INVOICE-LINE(INVOICE-SUB).
*
 1430-FETCH-NEXT-INVOICE.
*
     EXEC SQL
         FETCH CUSTINV
             INTO :INVNO, :INVPO, :INVDATE, :INVTOTAL
     END-EXEC.
     IF SQLCODE = 0
         MOVE INVNO      TO IL-INVOICE-NUMBER
         MOVE INVPO      TO IL-PO-NUMBER
         MOVE INVDATE    TO IL-INVOICE-DATE
         MOVE INVTOTAL   TO IL-INVOICE-TOTAL
     ELSE IF SQLCODE = 100
         MOVE 'N' TO MORE-INVOICES-SW
     ELSE
         GO TO 9999-TERMINATE-PROGRAM.
*
 1440-CLOSE-INVOICE-CURSOR.
*
     EXEC SQL
         CLOSE CUSTINV
     END-EXEC.
     IF SQLCODE NOT = 0
         GO TO 9999-TERMINATE-PROGRAM.
```

Figure 4-15 Source listing for the DB2 version of the customer inquiry program (part 4 of 5)

```
/
 1450-FORMAT-TOTAL-LINE.
*
     PERFORM 1460-SELECT-INVOICE-TOTALS.
     MOVE INVOICE-COUNT TO TL-COUNT.
     MOVE INVTOTAL      TO TL-TOTAL.
     IF INVOICE-COUNT > 8
         MOVE '  The most recent 8 are shown.' TO TL-MESSAGE
     ELSE
         MOVE SPACE TO TL-MESSAGE.
     MOVE TOTAL-LINE TO CIM-D-TOTAL.

 1460-SELECT-INVOICE-TOTALS.
*
     EXEC SQL
         SELECT COUNT(*), VALUE(SUM(INVTOTAL),0)
             INTO :INVOICE-COUNT, :INVTOTAL
             FROM MMADBV.INV
             WHERE INVCUST = :CIM-D-CUSTNO
     END-EXEC.
     IF SQLCODE NOT = 0
         GO TO 9999-TERMINATE-PROGRAM.
*
 1500-SEND-INQUIRY-MAP.
*
     IF SEND-ERASE
         EXEC CICS
             SEND MAP('DB2MAP1')
                  MAPSET('DB2SET1')
                  FROM(CUSTOMER-INQUIRY-MAP)
                  ERASE
         END-EXEC
     ELSE IF SEND-DATAONLY
         EXEC CICS
             SEND MAP('DB2MAP1')
                  MAPSET('DB2SET1')
                  FROM(CUSTOMER-INQUIRY-MAP)
                  DATAONLY
         END-EXEC
     ELSE IF SEND-DATAONLY-ALARM
         EXEC CICS
             SEND MAP('DB2MAP1')
                  MAPSET('DB2SET1')
                  FROM(CUSTOMER-INQUIRY-MAP)
                  DATAONLY
                  ALARM
         END-EXEC.
*
 9999-TERMINATE-PROGRAM.
*
     MOVE EIBRESP  TO ERR-RESP.
     MOVE EIBRESP2 TO ERR-RESP2.
     MOVE EIBTRNID TO ERR-TRNID.
     MOVE EIBRSRCE TO ERR-RSRCE.
     EXEC CICS
         XCTL PROGRAM('SYSERR')
              COMMAREA(ERROR-PARAMETERS)
     END-EXEC.
```

Figure 4-15 Source listing for the DB2 version of the customer inquiry program (part 5 of 5)

9999-TERMINATE-PROGRAM. The only other possibility is that the SQLCODE value is zero. This means that the SELECT statement successfully retrieved the requested customer row.

How the program retrieves rows from the invoice table   If the
SELECT statement in module 1300 successfully retrieves a customer row,
module 1400 is invoked with DISPLAY-NEW-CUSTOMER set to true.
Then, module 1400 invokes modules 1410, 1420, and 1440 to retrieve the
first eight invoices for the customer.

Module 1410 is called first to issue an SQL OPEN statement. This is
the statement that actually generates a cursor-controlled results table
with invoice rows for the current customer. The rows that are retrieved
are based on the SELECT component of the DECLARE CURSOR
statement in the Working-Storage Section:

```
EXEC SQL
    DECLARE CUSTINV CURSOR FOR
        SELECT INVNO, INVPO, CHAR(INVDATE,USA), INVTOTAL
            FROM MMADBV.INV
            WHERE INVCUST = :CIM-D-CUSTNO
            ORDER BY 1 DESC
END-EXEC.
```

Take a close look at this statement. First, notice that it supplies a
name for the cursor: CUSTINV. This is the name that's specified in the
OPEN statement. Then, it includes a SELECT component. This SELECT
component specifies that the cursor-controlled results table will consist
of four columns, all drawn from the base table MMADBV.INV. The first
two column specifications (INVNO and INVPO) and the last
(INVTOTAL) are easy to understand: They specify that the data from
those columns in the base table should be made available through the
cursor-controlled results table.

The third column specification, CHAR(INVDATE,USA), is a little
more complicated. It uses a DB2 function, CHAR, to modify the
contents of the base table's INVDATE column before they're presented
to the program through the cursor-controlled results table. CHAR
directs DB2 to format the date according to a pattern called USA, which
is MM/DD/YYYY.

The WHERE clause specifies that data should be returned from the
INV table only from rows where the contents of the customer number
column (INVCUST) are equal to the value in the program host variable
CIM-D-CUSTNO. Again, this field contains the customer number
entered by the user.

Finally, the ORDER BY clause directs DB2 to sort the rows that are
selected. The number "1" in the clause specifies that the sort key should
be column 1, the INVNO column. DESC directs DB2 to sort the rows
into descending sequence. As a result, the rows will be presented to the
program starting with the one with the largest value in the invoice
number column. This insures that the first rows that the program
retrieves will be most recent. If I hadn't included the ORDER BY clause,
the sequence of rows would be unpredictable.

Although the OPEN statement generates an appropriate results table, it doesn't return data to the program. Instead, it sets a pointer at the start of the table that identifies the position of the cursor. Then, to build the invoice detail lines for the display, module 1400 invokes module 1420 eight times. This module either retrieves a row from the results table or, if no more rows are available, moves space to the display line.

To retrieve a row from the results table, module 1420 performs module 1430, which issues this FETCH statement:

```
EXEC SQL
    FETCH CUSTINV
        INTO :INVNO, :INVPO, :INVDATE, :INVTOTAL
END-EXEC.
```

Notice that the FETCH statement names the cursor (CUSTINV) and provides the INTO clause that was missing from the SELECT component of the DECLARE CURSOR statement. As a result, data from each row will be returned into the INVNO, INVPO, INVDATE, and INVTOTAL fields.

Each time it's executed, this FETCH statement moves the position of the cursor forward in the results table so it identifies the next row. The first time it's executed, this statement returns data from the first row in the results table; the second time it's executed, it returns data from the second row in the results table, and so on.

The next statements in module 1430 evaluate SQLCODE to determine the results of the FETCH statement. If the value of SQLCODE is 0, the FETCH successfully retrieved a row from the results table. In that case, the program moves the contents of the host variables INVNO, INVPO, INVDATE, and INVTOTAL into corresponding fields in the Working-Storage group item INVOICE-LINE to construct a complete text string for an invoice detail line. (If you look back to module 1420, you'll see that the program moves INVOICE-LINE to the appropriate CIM-D-INVOICE-LINE item in the symbolic map.)

If the results table contains fewer than eight rows, the program will fetch all of them. Then, when it tries to fetch a row after it has already retrieved the last one, DB2 will return 100 as the SQLCODE value. So, the code in module 1430 checks for this value and, when it's encountered, sets the value of MORE-INVOICES-SW to N. After that, module 1420 will not invoke 1430 again. Instead, it simply moves spaces to the remaining invoice line data fields in the symbolic map. (Because module 1420 is performed only eight times, an SQLCODE value of 100 will never be encountered if the results table contains eight or more rows.)

As with the SELECT for the CUST table in module 1300, an SQLCODE value other than 0 or 100 in module 1430 means the FETCH statement encountered a serious error. In that case, the program branches to module 9999, the generalized error handling module.

After the program has prepared the eight invoice detail lines, it performs module 1440. Module 1440 issues an SQL CLOSE statement to release the cursor-controlled results table. Although any cursor-controlled results tables a CICS program creates are automatically released when the program ends, it can result in slightly greater system throughput if your program explicitly issues a CLOSE statement.

How the program formats the total line Next, module 1400 executes module 1450 to retrieve data for the totals that appear on line 12 of the screen. The SELECT statement that performs this function is in module 1460:

```
EXEC SQL
    SELECT COUNT(*), VALUE(SUM(INVTOTAL),0)
        INTO :INVOICE-COUNT, :INVTOTAL
        FROM MMADBV.INV
        WHERE INVCUST = :CIM-D-CUSTNO
END-EXEC.
```

This statement uses two SQL *column functions*: COUNT and SUM. Both return single results that represent aggregate values for all of the rows that meet the selection condition. As a result, SQL column functions are sometimes called *aggregate functions*. Because this statement returns a one-row results table, I was able to code it directly in the Procedure Division.

The first column specification in this statement, COUNT(*), returns the total number of rows in the results table. This statement specifies that the count value should be stored in the program host variable INVOICE-COUNT. This is one of the two fields I defined under the group item WORK-FIELDS in the Working-Storage Section; its picture (S9(9)) and usage (COMP) are appropriate for the result the function returns.

The second column specification in this SELECT statement, VALUE(SUM(INVTOTAL),0), combines two DB2 functions and returns its result in the numeric host variable INVTOTAL. The inner function, SUM, directs DB2 to sum the contents of the INVTOTAL column for all rows that meet the selection condition. As long as there's at least one row for the customer in the invoice table, the inner function will return a value. However, for customers who have made no purchases (and, as a result, for whom there are no rows in the invoice table), this function doesn't return 0, as you might expect. Instead, it returns a null indicator. To handle null indicators, I nested the SUM function within a VALUE function. The VALUE function specifies that if the SUM function returns a null value, DB2 should substitute zero for it.

Programming strategies for browsing DB2 data

In the program example in this topic, I restricted the number of invoices displayed for a customer to only the eight most recent. That's because this program's screen only has room for eight. You might expect that this application would let the user browse all of the invoices related to the customer by using PF7 and PF8 as scrolling keys. In other words, if the customer had more than eight invoices, the user could press PF8 to display the next eight invoices after the initial display. Unfortunately, providing this seemingly simple function in a CICS program significantly complicates the program's code.

The problem with browsing DB2 data in a CICS program stems from the simple fact that DB2 and CICS were designed with different objectives in mind. DB2 was designed to provide the most flexible methods of retrieving information, while CICS was designed to allow the most efficient execution of on-line transactions. These design objectives come into conflict when you're browsing DB2 data under CICS. That's because when a pseudo-conversational CICS program ends, DB2 drops any results tables it was using. When the program restarts after the user presses an attention key, it must somehow recreate the results table and reestablish position within it. Unfortunately, there's no easy way to do that.

The conflict between the operating modes of CICS and DB2 is so severe that some shops prohibit CICS/DB2 browse programs altogether or strictly limit their use. For applications that could involve huge numbers of rows, limiting CICS/DB2 browses is certainly reasonable. For example, if an on-line table contains millions of rows, it would be unreasonable *not* to prohibit browses. However, for results tables that contain modest numbers of rows, browsing with a CICS program may be reasonable if you adopt an appropriate programming strategy.

Here, I'll present three programming strategies you can use for CICS/DB2 browse programs. Figure 4-16 lists them. As you'll see, none of these programming strategies is ideal. They all involve trade-offs of processing efficiencies and additional coding.

Although I'll discuss these strategies separately, you should realize that you can use them together and in different combinations to meet your specific application requirements. And, you can reduce the impact of DB2 browse operations by following two general guidelines regardless of which programming strategy you adopt. First, you should minimize the number of rows DB2 includes in the results tables it produces. That means that if you know the limiting key values for the rows you want to select, you should specify them through host variables in the WHERE clause of the DECLARE CURSOR statement. Second, you should display as much data on each screen as you can. Doing that reduces the number of screen interactions required for a browse program.

Strategy 1	Do a separate query for each execution of the program.
Strategy 2	Do a single query and browse in a conversational program.
Strategy 3	Do a single query and save the results in:

- a DB2 work table
- a VSAM data set
- CICS temporary storage

Figure 4-16   Strategies you can use to browse DB2 table data in a CICS program

Strategy 1: Do a single query and browse in a conversational program   One way to address the CICS/DB2 conflict is to avoid pseudo-conversational programming altogether. In other words, implement the inquiry program using conversational processing. A conversational program doesn't end and pass control back to CICS with each user interaction. Instead, it continues to run (and occupy CICS storage and use CICS resources) while it waits for a user to make a terminal entry. The program doesn't end until the user specifically tells it to.

By coding the program in conversational style, you don't have to worry about recreating the results table or reestablishing your position within it. The downside, of course, is that conversational programs are an unacceptable burden in CICS systems. They hold on to CICS resources such as main storage for unreasonably long periods, and they may impose DB2 locks and tie up DB2 threads for unacceptably long periods as well. So this strategy is rarely used.

Strategy 2: Do a separate query for each execution of the program   If the number of rows that will be browsed is small, it may be best to recreate the results table each time the CICS program executes. To implement this strategy, the CICS program would need to store values between executions to indicate the current position within the results table. An execution of the program would use that data to determine which rows to fetch, format, and display. In effect, that means that the CICS program starts the browse from scratch each time it runs.

This strategy provides the best initial performance for each inquiry, but does not provide very good performance for subsequent scrolling requests. In other words, if it takes three seconds to retrieve and display the data for the first eight invoices, it will also take three seconds to retrieve the customer's next eight invoices. That's because the program must rebuild the complete results table for each execution.

Strategy 3: Do a single query and save the results   A third way
to implement DB2 browsing under CICS is to create the results table only
once, then save the results table in some form for subsequent browsing.
The bulleted list under Strategy 3 in figure 4-16 presents three
approaches you can take to use this strategy. All of the approaches
impose a similar performance trade-off on the transaction. They result in
a longer waiting time for the initial query, as the program creates the
results table and copies it to some other location. But they offer faster
response for subsequent browsing, because DB2 doesn't have to process
the complete base table each time.

The first approach is to save the initial results table in a DB2 work
table. To use this approach, your program would perform a DB2 mass
insert at the beginning of a browse operation to construct the work
table. A mass insert simply directs DB2 to copy all of the rows from the
results table created by a SELECT to the work table.

To scroll through the data in the work table, each execution of the
program could create a cursor-controlled results table from the work
table, not the base table. Then, the program would fetch the appropriate
rows from that cursor-controlled results table. When the browse was
completed, the program would delete the data from the temporary
work table.

By itself, this strategy doesn't reduce the number of SQL operations
the program performs. However, it can improve efficiency because it
reduces access to the base tables that many other users may be
accessing. Also, the DB2 locks your program's SQL statements generate
won't block other programs' requests. Your program is the only one
that will access your temporary work table.

The disadvantage of this approach is the extra overhead it requires,
both in terms of disk space and processor time. And, it still doesn't
eliminate the fundamental conflict between CICS and DB2. Browsing
data in a temporary work table still requires the program to create a
cursor-controlled results table each time it's executed.

Two other approaches to this strategy involve creating a working set
of the selected table data outside DB2. To do this, your program would
fetch each row from a cursor-controlled results table at the start of a
browse operation, then write its contents at another location that's
accessible to CICS. One option is to use a VSAM data set. Then, after
you transfer the data into the VSAM data set, you can use CICS's
browse commands (STARTBR, READNEXT, READPREV, ENDBR, and
RESETBR) to retrieve the data for display. This approach is much more
efficient in terms of processor time because it's less costly to browse
VSAM data than it is to browse DB2 data. Still, this approach may be
unacceptable for performance reasons.

A variation of this approach is to store the contents of the results
table in a CICS storage area called temporary storage. CICS provides
temporary storage for your programs through a VSAM data set it

manages for you. CICS also provides special commands for saving and retrieving data from temporary storage. I'll show you how to use temporary storage facilities in chapter 8.

Additional CICS/DB2 programming considerations

On-line transaction-processing programs need to be small and quick in their execution. Because of that, it makes sense to minimize the number of different SQL statements you use, to code the simplest statements you can, and to minimize the number of different tables a program processes. That leads to more efficient program execution.

You may also be able to improve performance by grouping SQL statements as closely as you can and deferring them to near the end of the execution of a program. Doing that can reduce the amount of time a program controls a thread, since the CICS/DB2 attachment facility doesn't create a thread for a transaction until the program makes its first DB2 request.

Just as with programs that process DB2 data in batch or under TSO, CICS/DB2 programs should commit their work often. Doing so reduces the amount of data DB2 has to maintain during a unit of work, and it makes the data available to other programs sooner. In addition, under CICS, committing a unit of work causes threads to be released and made available to other users. You'll learn about units of work and how to commit them in chapter 11.

Discussion

DB2 programming is a complicated subject. Frankly, if this is your first exposure to DB2, you're not ready to start writing DB2/CICS programs. However, this chapter should put you in a good position to start learning DB2 in the context of CICS. And if you're experienced with SQL, this chapter should enable you to apply your SQL skills in a CICS environment.

Terms

column function
aggregate function

Objectives

1. Given program specifications, design and code a CICS/DB2 inquiry program that processes a cursor-controlled results table.

2. Describe programming strategies you can use to perform CICS/DB2 browse operations.

Chapter 5

DL/I data base processing

This chapter shows you how to develop CICS programs that access DL/I data bases. However, this chapter won't show you all you need to know about DL/I to process DL/I data bases. So if you're not already familiar with DL/I, you can expand on the basics presented in this chapter by studying other DL/I training materials. I recommend *IMS for the COBOL Programmer, Part 1: Data Base Processing with IMS/VS and DL/I DOS/VSE*, by Steve Eckols, available from Mike Murach & Associates, Inc.

This chapter has two topics. The first introduces you to DL/I data base organization and programming concepts. If you've worked with DL/I before, feel free to skip topic 1. Topic 2 shows you the special programming requirements for processing a DL/I data base under CICS and presents a sample CICS DL/I program.

DL/I data base concepts and terminology

This topic presents a basic introduction to one of IBM's most popular data base management systems: *DL/I (Data Language/I)*. First, I present the basics of how a DL/I data base is organized. Then, I describe in general terms the DL/I considerations for batch COBOL programs that process DL/I data bases.

The DL/I concepts in this topic apply to both MVS and VSE systems. However, the software products that let you implement DL/I data bases differ under the two groups of operating systems. On MVS systems, DL/I is part of a larger product called *IMS (Information Management System)*. IMS provides not only data base management services through DL/I, but data communications services as well. In that respect, it's similar to CICS. In this chapter, I cover just the DL/I facilities of IMS.

Although the complete IMS implementation isn't available on VSE systems, VSE can support DL/I compatible data bases. The programming requirements to access DL/I databases are the same whether you're using MVS or VSE.

How a DL/I data base is organized

DL/I data bases are organized hierarchically. Simply put, that means the entire data base is organized as a structure of related data elements, some of which are subordinate to others. By using this organizational form, DL/I maintains a high degree of control over the relationships among data elements in a data base.

Hierarchical data relationships

The idea of hierarchical data organization isn't unique to DL/I. In fact, many applications use ordinary VSAM files with hierarchical relationships. For example, the enhanced customer inquiry program in chapter 2 used a simple hierarchical data structure, shown in figure 5-1. Here, one customer record can have many invoice records subordinate to it. This structure was implemented using two separate VSAM data sets (CUSTMAS and INVOICE) related to one another by an alternate index. The alternate index's key was the customer number field in the invoice record.

Although figure 5-1 doesn't show it, there's another hierarchical relationship in the CUSTMAS/INVOICE pair of files. Each record in INVOICE has ten line items (not all of which have to be used), as figure

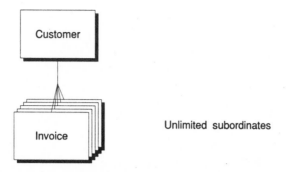

Figure 5-1 The hierarchical data relationship between the customer and invoice files

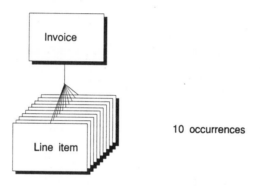

Figure 5-2 The hierarchical data relationship between the invoice data and line item data within the invoice file

5-2 shows. They're stored in a ten-element table within the invoice record.

The physical implementations of the hierarchical relationships illustrated in figures 5-1 and 5-2 differ. One is implemented by alternate indexing, the other by a table within a record. But each still represents a hierarchical organization of data. It's just such organizations of data that DL/I is designed to support. Figure 5-3 shows how the data elements from the customer and invoice files might be combined in one DL/I hierarchy. Of course, DL/I can support data groupings much more complex than the one in figure 5-3. But figure 5-3 illustrates the concepts you need to understand before you can use DL/I.

How DL/I implements hierarchical data structures

The data elements in the hierarchy in figure 5-3 would probably be implemented under DL/I as a single *data base*. Don't confuse this DL/I term with the more general use of "data base" to mean an organization's

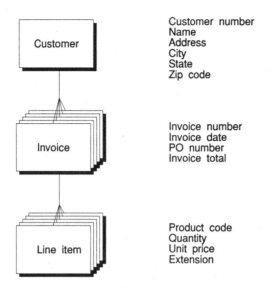

Figure 5-3   How the hierarchical data relationship among the data elements in the customer and invoice files can be represented in a DL/I data base

complete "base of data." A DL/I data base is a set of related data elements stored together to meet the requirements of one or more applications. If you'd like, you can think of a DL/I data base as a single complex file. An organization's complete base of data might consist of dozens of DL/I data bases, as well as VSAM and other files.

Segments   Within a DL/I data base, data is organized in *segments*. A segment is the unit of data DL/I can access for you. The different kinds of segments that make up a data base are called *segment types*. The three segment types in the structure in figure 5-3 are customer, invoice, and line item. Each segment type contains one or more fields, much like a record in a standard file.

I want you to distinguish between the terms segment type and *segment occurrence*. Within a data base, there may be many occurrences of one segment type. For example, the data base structure in figure 5-3 has only one customer segment type. However, the actual data base may contain thousands of customer segment occurrences.

The customer segment in figure 5-3 is at the top of the hierarchy—it's called the *root segment*. A single occurrence of one root segment plus all of the occurrences of all segments subordinate to it comprise one *data base record*. Figure 5-4 illustrates what might be a data base record for one customer segment occurrence in the data base in figure 5-3. As you can see, three occurrences of the invoice segment are subordinate to the customer segment in this record. And each invoice segment occurrence can have a variable number of line item occurrences subordinate to it.

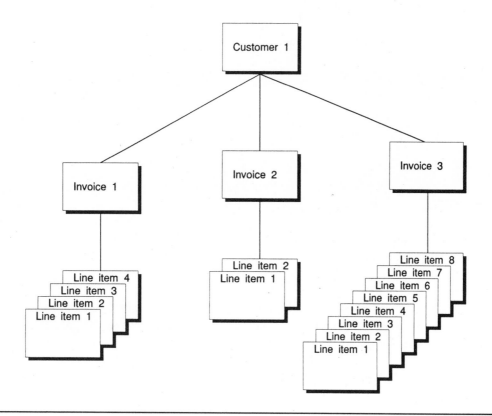

Figure 5-4   One data base record

Obviously, a data base record isn't fixed-length. It can be as long as necessary to accommodate all the segment occurrences subordinate to a particular occurrence of the root segment.

Don't let the term data base record confuse you. In standard file processing, you retrieve and process records. Not so in data base processing. The closest thing to a file record in DL/I is a segment—that's the unit of information you receive and process in a DL/I program. The idea of data base records just helps you understand the hierarchical nature of a DL/I data base.

Segment dependence and parentage   Some of the terminology you're likely to come across as you work with DL/I has to do with *segment dependence*. Within a DL/I data base, a particular segment is dependent on the segments that are above it. In figure 5-3, the invoice segment type is dependent on the customer segment type, and the line item segment type is dependent on both invoice and customer.

The relationships among dependent segments can be described in terms of *parentage*. For example, invoice is dependent on customer. Therefore, invoice is the *child segment* of the *parent segment* customer. A segment that is a child can also be a parent. For example, invoice is the parent segment of line item. The segments at the bottom of the hierarchy cannot be parents and the segment at the top of the hierarchy (the root segment) cannot be a child.

How applications view a DL/I data base

One of the advantages of using DL/I is that each application program that accesses a data base can have a unique view of it. Simply put, a *view* (sometimes called an *application data structure*) is a subset of the segments and fields that make up a complete data base. The particular segments and fields that make up a view depend on the requirements of the application program.

Even a simple data base like the one in figure 5-3 can have different views for different application programs. For example, imagine the requirements of two programs: an inquiry program that displays a customer's name and address and an order entry program that adds invoices and line items to the data base. The inquiry program needs to access only the data in the customer segment. What's in the invoice and line item segments subordinate to a given occurrence of the customer segment doesn't matter to the inquiry program. As a result, the inquiry program's view of the data base includes only the customer segment. In contrast, the order entry program needs to be able to access segments of all three types. Accordingly, it's view of the data base must be complete.

Besides restricting a program's access to specific data, a view also specifies the type of processing a program can do for each segment or field. For example, the inquiry program is allowed to retrieve customer segments, but not to modify or delete them. The order entry program can not only retrieve customer segments, but it can also create new invoice and line item segments.

Program specification block   The way the data base administrator specifies an application program's view of a data base is by coding and assembling a *Program Specification Block* (or *PSB*) for it. Each application program has its own PSB. For each different data base a program accesses, the program's PSB contains one *Program Communication Block* (or *PCB*). So if a program accesses three different data bases, its PSB contains three PCBs.

Within the PCB, the data base administrator specifies which segments in the data base are in the program's view. These are called *sensitive segments*. And within the sensitive segments, the data base administrator may specify the fields that are in the program's view, called *sensitive fields*. As you can tell, the data base administrator has much control over what application programs can and cannot do with DL/I data bases.

```
CALL 'CBLTDLI' USING DLI-GET-UNIQUE
                     CUSTOMER-PCB
                     CUSTOMER-SEGMENT
                     CUSTOMER-SSA.
```

Figure 5-5   A typical DL/I call

The DL/I CALL interface

Now that you have a general idea of how a DL/I data base is organized, I want you to learn a little of how a batch COBOL program processes a DL/I data base. Because a CICS program uses many of the same techniques as a batch program, this material will help you understand topic 2. Note, however, that this section won't teach you everything you need to know to write a DL/I program. Instead, it just introduces you to the most important concepts.

COBOL itself doesn't provide for processing DL/I data bases. To process a DL/I data base in COBOL, you use the *CALL interface*. Basically, that means you code CALL statements to invoke DL/I functions. With the CALL interface, you invoke an interface routine named *CBLTDLI* to process DL/I requests. The relationship of CBLTDLI to your COBOL program is complex, but it's useful from a coding perspective to think of CBLTDLI as a simple subprogram.

Although there are a number of ways you can code a DL/I call, the example in figure 5-5 is typical. Here, I specify four parameters on the CALL statement. They identify (1) the DL/I function to be performed, (2) the PCB of the data base that's to be processed, (3) the segment I/O area, and (4) any required segment search arguments. In some cases, you can specify additional parameters. But most DL/I calls use just these four.

DL/I function

The *DL/I function* parameter is a four-byte alphanumeric field whose value indicates which DL/I function is to be performed. Figure 5-6 lists nine commonly used DL/I functions. I'm not going to describe them in detail here, but the information in figure 5-6 should give you a general idea of what each function does.

PCB mask

As you know, each PCB within your program's PSB identifies a data base your program can process. To tell DL/I which data base to process, you must specify a PCB name in a DL/I call, just as you must specify a file name in each standard file control command. Actually, you don't specify a PCB name directly in a DL/I call. Instead, you specify a Linkage Section field called a *PCB mask*. Figure 5-7 shows the coding for a complete PCB mask.

Code	Function
GU	Get a unique segment.
GHU	Get a unique segment and hold it for subsequent update.
GN	Get the next segment in sequence.
GHN	Get the next segment in sequence and hold it for subsequent update.
GNP	Get the next segment in sequence within the established parent.
GHNP	Get the next segment in sequence within the established parent and hold it for subsequent update.
ISRT	Insert a segment.
REPL	Replace a segment.
DLET	Delete a segment.

Figure 5-6   Nine commonly used DL/I functions

In most cases, you won't need to code the complete PCB description in your program. Instead, you'll include only the fields your program references and any fields that precede them. You'll see an example of that in the next chapter. For now, just realize that for each data base your program processes, the program's Linkage Section contains one PCB mask group item.

The only field in the PCB mask you need to know about is the status code field (STATUS-CODE in figure 5-7). After each DL/I operation on a particular data base has completed, the status code field in that data base's PCB mask contains an indication of any errors that may have occurred during the operation. Because most DL/I error conditions don't cause application programs to abend, application programs should test the PCB mask's status code field to detect errors that occur.

Segment I/O area

The *segment I/O area* is like a record I/O area for standard file processing. For input, DL/I places the retrieved segment in this area. For output, your program must place the segment data in this area before it issues the DL/I call.

Segment search argument

The *segment search argument*, or *SSA*, is the most complicated part of a DL/I call. It identifies which segment in a data base is to be processed. In the simplest case, an *unqualified SSA* supplies the eight-byte name of a

```
LINKAGE SECTION.
    .
    .
    .
01  CUSTOMER-PCB.
*
    05  DBD-NAME                 PIC  X(8).
    05  SEGMENT-LEVEL            PIC  XX.
    05  STATUS-CODE              PIC  XX.
    05  PROCESSING-OPTIONS       PIC  X(4).
    05  RESERVE-DLI              PIC  S9(5)      COMP.
    05  SEGMENT-NAME-FEEDBACK    PIC  X(8).
    05  KEY-LENGTH               PIC  S9(5)      COMP.
    05  NUMB-SENS-SEGMENTS       PIC  S9(5)      COMP.
    05  KEY-FEEDBACK-AREA        PIC  X(10).
```

Figure 5-7   A PCB mask description

segment type. For example, to insert an INVOICE segment, you could supply an unqualified SSA containing the segment name INVOICE.

A *qualified SSA* specifies not only a segment name, but a search value as well. Its function is similar to that of the RIDFLD parameter required in a CICS file control command. For example, a qualified SSA might indicate that an invoice segment whose invoice number field (named INVNO) is 10030 should be retrieved. That SSA would look like this:

```
INVOICE (INVNO    =10030)
```

Since DL/I segment and field names must be eight characters long in an SSA, blanks are required when the actual names are shorter. Also, one blank must separate the eight-character field name from the equal sign in a qualified SSA.

When you code a DL/I call, you don't code an SSA directly. Instead, you specify a data name that contains the SSA. Figure 5-8 gives an example of a typical working-storage definition of an SSA. Here, the customer number field is given its own data name. That way, you can move any value you wish to it before you issue the DL/I call. For example, the MOVE statement

```
MOVE WS-CUSTOMER-NUMBER TO CUSTNO-SSA.
```

formats the SSA so that it specifies the value in the field WS-CUSTOMER-NUMBER.

Discussion   Quite frankly, DL/I is much more complicated than this topic might indicate. So if you feel confused about DL/I at this point, don't worry. The main point of this topic is to help you better understand the CICS

```
 01  CUSTOMER-SSA.
 *
     05  FILLER            PIC X(19)  VALUE 'CUSTOMER(CUSTNO   ='.
     05  CUSTNO-SSA        PIC X(5).
     05  FILLER            PIC X      VALUE ')'.
```

Figure 5-8   A typical segment search argument description

material that's in the next topic. But a complete discussion of DL/I concepts and programming is a subject for another book.

Terms

DL/I
Data Language/I
IMS
Information Management System
data base
segment
segment type
segment occurrence
root segment
data base record
segment dependence
parentage
child segment
parent segment
view
application data structure
Program Specification Block
PSB
Program Communication Block
PCB
sensitive segment
sensitive field
CALL interface
CBLTDLI
DL/I function
PCB mask
segment I/O area
segment search argument
SSA
unqualified SSA
qualified SSA

Objectives

1. Compare the hierarchical organization of a DL/I data base with a similarly organized structure of VSAM files.

2. Explain the distinction between the following pairs of terms:

    data base and base of data
    segment type and segment occurrence
    file record and data base record
    child segment and parent segment

3. Describe the function of the four basic parameters required on a DL/I call.

How to process a DL/I data base

In this topic, you'll learn how to code a CICS program that processes a DL/I data base. At the outset, I assume you're somewhat familiar with DL/I batch programming. If your only experience with DL/I is having read the last topic, you may not understand everything this topic presents. Nevertheless, this topic will give you a basic understanding of how DL/I relates to CICS. If you're familiar with DL/I through a previous course or job experience, you should be able to write DL/I programs for execution under CICS when you complete this topic.

DL/I programming for CICS

If you've developed batch DL/I programs, you'll have little trouble learning how to code a DL/I program for execution under CICS. In fact, DL/I calls in a CICS program are identical to those in a batch program. But there are two differences you need to know about before you write a CICS DL/I program. First, your program must issue a special DL/I call—the *scheduling call*—before it can issue any other DL/I call. And second, DL/I error processing under CICS is a little different than it is in batch mode.

How to schedule a PSB

Before your program can issue a DL/I call to process a data base, it must issue a scheduling call to connect your program with DL/I. Among other things, this call creates the two areas of main storage shown in figure 5-9. The first, called the *User Interface Block*, or *UIB*, is an interface area between your program and the CICS routines that communicate with DL/I. Each DL/I program requires a single UIB. The second storage area is the Program Communication Block (PCB), an interface area directly between your program and DL/I. There may be more than one PCB, depending on how many data base views are defined in the program's PSB. (Remember that each program has one PSB, which contains one or more PCBs that define data base views.)

As Figure 5-9 indicates, the UIB and PCB are data areas that exist outside of your program's storage. In other words, the UIB and PCB are in storage that's owned by CICS rather than by your application program. As a result, you must define them in the Linkage Section rather than in the Working-Storage Section. When you do that, the entries act as masks for the actual storage areas associated with them. In fact, as you learned in the last topic, the Linkage Section description of a PCB is often called a PCB mask.

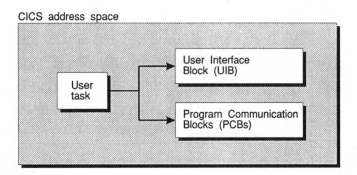

Figure 5-9   A DL/I task must establish addressability to the User Interface Block and one or more Program Communication Blocks (PCBs)

Figure 5-10 shows an IBM-supplied copy book named DLIUIB you can include in your program to define the UIB. If you'll study it for a moment, you'll see that the User Interface Block consists of just two fields. They're the 02-level items shaded in figure 5-10: UIBPCBAL and UIBRCODE. You'll see how both of these fields are used later in this topic.

Before you can access fields defined in the Linkage Section, you must establish addressability to them. How you do that depends on whether you're using the VS COBOL II compiler or the OS/VS COBOL compiler. Under VS COBOL II, you use the ADDRESS special register along with POINTER fields. With OS/VS COBOL, you use BLL cells. Either way, you need the addresses of the UIB and PCBs. The question is, how do you obtain these addresses?

Figure 5-11 gives part of the answer. Here, you can see that one of the UIB fields (UIBPCBAL) points indirectly to the PCBs. I say indirectly because rather than containing the address of a PCB, UIBPCBAL contains the address of another data area that contains a list of PCB addresses. In other words, the UIB points to a PCB address list. And the PCB address list, in turn, points to all of the PCBs.

Why does PCB addressing work that way? To provide for a variable number of PCBs within a PSB. Although the User Interface Block is a fixed-length area, it needs to point to a variable number of PCBs. That's why the PCB address list is used. The PCB address list is variable-length: It contains one pointer for each PCB in the program's PSB. In figure 5-11, two PCBs are defined. So the PCB address list contains two pointers.

An implication of the addressing scheme in figure 5-11 is that you must define an additional Linkage Section field for the PCB address list. In fact, for the example shown in figure 5-11, you would define four Linkage Section fields: one for the UIB, one for the PCB address list, and one for each of the two PCBs.

```
**********************************************************************
*                                                                    *
*         MODULE-NAME = DLIUIB                                        *
*                                                                    *
*         DESCRIPTIVE NAME = STRUCTURE FOR USER INTERFACE BLOCK      *
*                                                                    *
*         STATUS = 2.1.0                                             *
*                                                                    *
*         FUNCTION = DESCRIBE USER INTERFACE BLOCK FIELDS.           *
*                    THE UIB CONTAINS SCHEDULING AND SYSTEM CALL     *
*                    STATUS INFORMATION RETURNED TO THE USER.        *
*                                                                    *
*         MODULE-TYPE = STRUCTURE                                    *
*                                                                    *
*         CHANGE ACTIVITY = @BCAC80A                                 *
*                                                                    *
**********************************************************************
 01     DLIUIB.
 *      DLIUIB      EXTENDED CALL USER INTERFACE BLOCK
        02 UIBPCBAL PICTURE S9(8) USAGE IS COMPUTATIONAL.
 *      UIBPCBAL       PCB ADDRESS LIST
        02 UIBRCODE.
 *      UIBRCODE       DL/I RETURN CODES
          03 UIBFCTR PICTURE X.
 *          UIBFCTR      RETURN CODES
            88  FCNORESP    VALUE ' '.
            88  FCNOTOPEN   VALUE ' '.
            88  FCINVREQ    VALUE ' '.
            88  FCINVPCB    VALUE ' '.
          03 UIBDLTR PICTURE X.
 *          UIBDLTR      ADDITIONAL INFORMATION
            88  DLPSBNF     VALUE ' '.
            88  DLTASKNA    VALUE ' '.
            88  DLPSBSCH    VALUE ' '.
            88  DLLANGCON   VALUE ' '.
            88  DLPSBFAIL   VALUE ' '.
            88  DLPSBNA     VALUE ' '.
            88  DLTERMNS    VALUE ' '.
            88  DLFUNCNS    VALUE ' '.
            88  DLINA       VALUE ' '.
```

Figure 5-10 The DLIUIB copy member

Figure 5-11 shows that if you know the address of the UIB, you can establish addressability to the PCBs by using the pointer addresses in the PCB address list. The part of the addressing question left unanswered by figure 5-11 is how you get the address of the UIB itself. That's where the scheduling call comes in: Its function is to acquire storage for these areas and return the address of the UIB to your program. So once you've issued a scheduling call, you can address the UIB, the PCB address list, and the PCBs themselves.

Because I want to be sure you understand how PCB scheduling works, look at figure 5-12. The four parts of this figure show how your program establishes addressability to the required DL/I areas. The top section of each part shows the COBOL statement issued by the

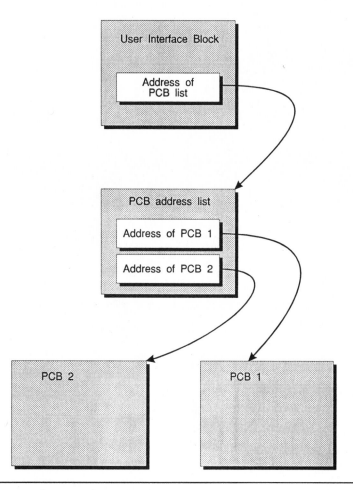

Figure 5-11 A field in the UIB points to a list of PCB addresses

program. The bottom section shows the relationship of Linkage Section entries to the actual storage areas for DL/I control blocks. The areas that are addressable after the COBOL statement executes are highlighted.

Part 1 of figure 5-12 shows the scheduling call. DLI-SCHEDULE is the name of a four-character field defined in the Working-Storage Section. It contains the function code required to perform a scheduling call: PCB. PSB-NAME is an eight-character field that contains the name of the PSB this program uses. For the sake of the illustration, assume the PSB contains two PCBs, called PCB-1 and PCB-2. The scheduling call returns the address of the UIB in the third parameter, specified here as ADDRESS OF DLIUIB. Thus, this call establishes addressability to DLIUIB.

The program issues the scheduling call:

```
CALL 'CBLTDLI' USING DLI-SCHEDULE
                     PSB-NAME
                     ADDRESS OF DLIUIB.
```

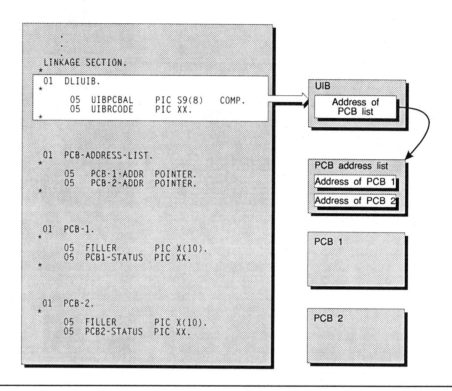

Figure 5-12 Addressing DL/I control blocks (part 1 of 4)

Part 2 shows how you establish addressability to the PCB address list by using the pointer (UIBPCBAL) to the address list in a SET statement, like this:

```
SET ADDRESS OF PCB-ADDRESS-LIST TO UIBPCBAL.
```

As a result of this statement, PCB-ADDRESS-LIST now masks the actual address list.

Part 3 shows how to establish addressability to the first PCB: A SET statement sets the address of PCB-1 to the first pointer in the PCB address list. After this SET statement executes, PCB-1 is addressable. In a similar manner, part 4 shows how addressability is established for the second PCB.

To summarize, the scheduling call establishes addressability to the UIB. Then, it's just a matter of setting the other addresses using the pointers. The COBOL coding required to establish addressability to all

The program establishes addressability to the PCB address list:

```
SET ADDRESS OF PCB-ADDRESS-LIST TO UIBPCBAL.
```

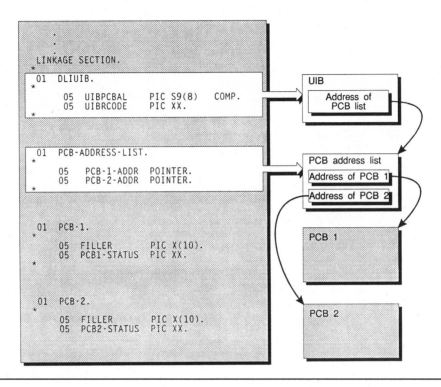

Figure 5-12 Addressing DL/I control blocks (part 2 of 4)

of the DL/I areas is simple. All you do is issue a CALL statement
followed by a series of SET statements, like this:

```
CALL 'CBLTDLI' USING DLI-SCHEDULE
                     PSB-NAME
                     ADDRESS OF DLIUIB.
SET ADDRESS OF PCB-LIST TO UIBPCBAL.
SET ADDRESS OF PCB-1    TO PCB-1-ADDR.
SET ADDRESS OF PCB-2    TO PCB-2-ADDR.
```

You'll see a complete example of how to schedule a PSB in the program
example in this topic. With this background, though, you'll better
understand what those simple COBOL elements really accomplish.

Considerations for the OS/VS COBOL compiler If you're still
using the OS/VS COBOL compiler, you must use BLL cells to establish
addressability to the UIB, PCB address list, and PCB's. In the example I

The program establishes addressability to PCB-1:

```
SET ADDRESS OF PCB-1 TO PCB-1-ADDR.
```

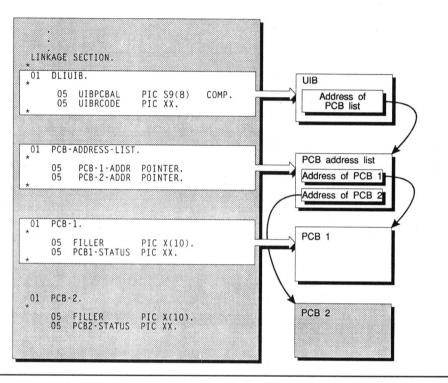

Figure 5-12 Addressing DL/I control blocks (part 3 of 4)

just explained, you would code the BLLs at the start of the Linkage Section, like this:

```
01  BLL-CELLS.
*
    05  FILLER          PIC S9(8)   COMP.
    05  BLL-UIB         PIC S9(8)   COMP.
    05  BLL-PCB-AL      PIC S9(8)   COMP.
    05  BLL-PCB-1       PIC S9(8)   COMP.
    05  BLL-PCB-2       PIC S9(8)   COMP.
```

Then, you would code these statements:

```
CALL 'CBLTDLI' USING DLI-SCHEDULE
                     PSB-NAME
                     BLL-UIB.
MOVE UIBPCBAL   TO BLL-PCB-AL.
MOVE PCB-1-ADDR TO BLL-PCB-1.
MOVE PCB-2-ADDR TO BLL-PCB-2.
```

The program establishes addressability to PCB-2:

```
SET ADDRESS OF PCB-2 TO PCB-2-ADDR.
```

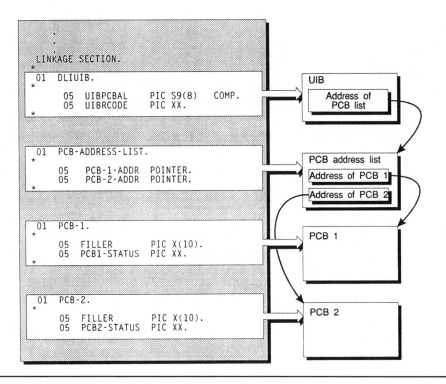

Figure 5-12 Addressing DL/I control blocks (part 4 of 4)

In addition, the address pointers in PCB-ADDRESS-LIST would be defined as binary fullwords (PIC S9(8) COMP) rather than as POINTER items.

How to handle DL/I errors

In a CICS DL/I program, as in a batch DL/I program, you are responsible for checking for error conditions after each DL/I call your program issues. To illustrate, consider the typical DL/I module shown in figure 5-13. Here, a DL/I call tries to retrieve a unique segment from a customer data base. The IF statements following the CALL statement provide the required error processing. To determine if a DL/I call is successful, your CICS program must test two status fields: one in the UIB, the other in the PCB.

How to test the UIB status code   The User Interface Block (figure 5-10) serves as an interface area between your program and the CICS

```
1300-GET-CUSTOMER-SEGMENT.
*
    MOVE CUSTNOI TO SSA-CUSTNO.
    CALL 'CBLTDLI' USING DLI-GET-UNIQUE
                         CUSTOMER-PCB
                         CUSTOMER-SEGMENT
                         CUSTOMER-SSA.
    IF UIBFCTR NOT = LOW-VALUE
        GO TO 9999-TERMINATE-PROGRAM.
    IF CUSTOMER-STATUS-CODE = SPACE
        MOVE 'Y' TO CUSTOMER-FOUND-SW
    ELSE IF CUSTOMER-STATUS-CODE = 'GE'
        MOVE 'N' TO CUSTOMER-FOUND-SW
    ELSE
        GO TO 9999-TERMINATE-PROGRAM.
```

Figure 5-13 A typical DL/I module

routines that communicate with DL/I. One of the fields in the UIB, UIBRCODE, contains a status code that indicates whether your DL/I call was successful. UIBRCODE contains two subfields: UIBFCTR and UIBDLTR. UIBFCTR contains a one-byte response code, while UIBDLTR contains a byte that provides additional error information if UIBFCTR indicates an error. Usually, you're only concerned with UIBFCTR.

UIBFCTR normally contains LOW-VALUE. If it does, there's no error. If it contains any other value, there was a serious error between your program and the CICS routine that handles DL/I calls. Usually, the cause of this type of error is that the scheduling call failed. An error indicated by UIBFCTR is always serious, so you should terminate your program if one occurs.

How to test the PCB status code   Following the test of UIBFCTR, the DL/I module in figure 5-13 tests the status code field in the PCB, CUSTOMER-STATUS-CODE. This error processing should be familiar to you if you've written DL/I batch programs. If the status code is GE, the requested customer segment doesn't exist, so a switch is set accordingly. Any other non-blank value indicates a serious error, so the program is terminated.

Depending on the DL/I function, you may need to check the PCB status code field for other values. At the very least, if you don't expect an operation to cause any return codes to be generated, you should test the status code field to make sure it contains blanks.

A sample program   Now that you know how to schedule a PSB for a CICS DL/I program and how to code DL/I requests under CICS, take a look at figures 5-14 through 5-19. Here, I present a DL/I version of the customer inquiry program I presented originally in *Part 1: An Introductory Course*. I'm not going to review all the details of this program; I'll just describe the DL/I

Program	DLIINQ1

Overview   Displays customer information from the customer data base based on customer numbers entered by the user.

Input/output specifications

CUSTOMER	Customer segment (DL/I)
INQMAP1	Customer inquiry map

Processing specifications

1. Control is transferred to this program via XCTL from the menu program INVMENU with no communication area. The user can also start the program by entering the trans-id DLI1. In either case, the program should respond by displaying the customer inquiry map.

2. If the user enters a customer number, retrieve the customer segment and display it. If the segment doesn't exist, display an error message.

3. If the user presses PF3 or PF12, return to the menu program INVMENU by issuing an XCTL command.

Figure 5-14 Specifications for the DL/I version of the customer inquiry program (part 1 of 3)

programming implications. The program is simple enough that you should have little trouble understanding it.

Figure 5-14 presents the specifications for this program. As you can see, the program receives a customer number from the user, gets the appropriate DL/I data, and displays it. In previous chapters of this book, I've presented more complicated versions of this program that let the user scroll forward or backward through the customer file or display invoices related to each customer. For the sake of illustrating how to use DL/I in a CICS program, however, this simple inquiry processing is sufficient.

Figure 5-15 shows an event/response chart for the program, and figure 5-16 shows the program structure chart. This program design is almost the same as the design I used for the customer inquiry program in *Part 1*. The differences are: (1) I've added module 0500 to schedule the PSB, and (2) module 1300 obtains data from a DL/I data base rather than from a VSAM file.

Figure 5-17 shows the BMS mapset for the inquiry program, and figure 5-18 shows the symbolic map. The complete source listing is shown in figure 5-19. I've shaded the parts that relate directly to DL/I processing. Now, I'll point out some of the highlights.

Module 0500 schedules the PSB. If you'll look to the Linkage Section, you'll see that the entries I coded are similar to those in figure 5-12. But since this program accesses only one segment type, I included just one PCB, named CUSTOMER-PCB.

Map name _____ INQMAP1 _____ Date _____ 07/01/92 _____

Program name _ DLIINQ1 _____ Designer __ Doug Lowe _____

```
      1         1         2         3         4         5         6         7         8
      1234567890123456789012345678901234567890123456789012345678901234567890123456789 0
  1   INQMAP1              Customer Inquiry
  2
  3   Type a customer number.  Then press Enter.
  4
  5   Customer number. . . . . XXXXXX
  6
  7   Name and address . . . : XXXXXXXXXXXXXXXXXXXXXXXXXXXXXXXXX
  8                            XXXXXXXXXXXXXXXXXXXXXXX
  9                            XXXXXXXXXXXXXXXXXXXXXXXXXXXXXXXXX
 10                            XXXXXXXXXXXXXXXXXXXX XX XXXXXXXXXX
 11
 12
 13
 14
 15
 16
 17
 18
 19
 20
 21
 22
 23   XXXXXXXXXXXXXXXXXXXXXXXXXXXXXXXXXXXXXXXXXXXXXXXXXXXXXXXXXXXXXXXXXXXXXXXXXXXXXXXXXXX X
 24   F3=Exit    F12=Cancel                                                              X
```

Figure 5-14 Specifications for the DL/I version of the customer inquiry program (part 2 of 3)

Notice that I coded an abbreviated version of the PCB mask. The status code field is the only one I reference in the program. As a result, I only had to account for it and the fields that precede it in the PCB. The subsequent fields in the PCB are irrelevant for this program.

Module 0500 first issues a scheduling call to get the address of the UIB. Then, it tests UIBFCTR to make sure the scheduling call worked. If it didn't, the program branches to 9999-TERMINATE-PROGRAM. Otherwise, two SET statements establish addressability to PCB-POINTERS and CUSTOMER-PCB.

Module 1300 retrieves a specific customer segment from the customer data base. Here, the DL/I function is get unique (GU), and CUSTOMER-SSA is used as a segment search argument to specify a particular customer. After issuing this statement, the program tests to make sure the call worked, and if it didn't, it branches to 9999-TERMINATE-PROGRAM. Otherwise, it tests the PCB status code field, CUSTOMER-STATUS-CODE. If no error was detected, the program formats the customer display. If the specified customer wasn't

The customer segment (CUSTSEG)

```
01   CUSTOMER-SEGMENT.
*
     05  CM-CUSTOMER-NUMBER      PIC  X(6).
     05  CM-FIRST-NAME           PIC  X(20).
     05  CM-LAST-NAME            PIC  X(30).
     05  CM-ADDRESS              PIC  X(30).
     05  CM-CITY                 PIC  X(20).
     05  CM-STATE                PIC  X(2).
     05  CM-ZIP-CODE             PIC  X(10).
*
```

The ERRPARM copy member

```
01   ERROR-PARAMETERS.
*
     05  ERR-RESP        PIC  S9(8)    COMP.
     05  ERR-RESP2       PIC  S9(8)    COMP.
     05  ERR-TRNID       PIC  X(4).
     05  ERR-RSRCE       PIC  X(8).
*
```

Figure 5-14 Specifications for the DL/I version of the customer inquiry program (part 3 of 3)

found, indicated by a CUSTOMER-STATUS-CODE of GE, the program sets a switch, formats an error message, and moves spaces to the fields in the customer display. If any other error occurred, the program branches to 9999-TERMINATE-PROGRAM.

Discussion DL/I programming is a complicated subject. Frankly, if this is your first exposure to DL/I, you're not ready to start writing DL/I programs. However, this chapter should put you in a good position to start learning DL/I in the context of CICS. And if you are an experienced DL/I programmer, this chapter should enable you to apply your DL/I batch programming skills in a CICS environment.

Terms

scheduling call   UIB
User Interface Block   mask

Objectives

1. Explain the function of the DL/I User Interface Block in a CICS DL/I program.

2. Explain how the scheduling call establishes addressability to the PCBs used by a CICS DL/I program.

3. Design, code, and test a CICS program that accesses a DL/I data base.

Event	Response
Start the program	Display the customer map.

Enter key	Receive the customer map.
	Edit the customer number.
	If valid
	    get the customer segment.
	If the segment exists
	    display it.
	If the number isn't valid or the segment doesn't exist
	    display an error message.

PF3 or PF12	Return to the menu program.
Clear key	Redisplay the customer map.
Any PA key	Ignore the key.
Any other key	Display an error message.

Figure 5-15 Event/response chart for the DL/I version of the customer inquiry program

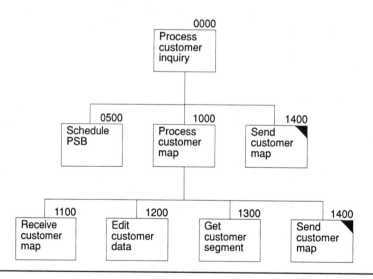

Figure 5-16 Structure chart for the customer inquiry program

```
          PRINT NOGEN
INQSET1   DFHMSD TYPE=&SYSPARM,                                         X
                 LANG=COBOL,                                            X
                 MODE=INOUT,                                            X
                 TERM=3270-2,                                           X
                 CTRL=FREEKB,                                           X
                 STORAGE=AUTO,                                          X
                 TIOAPFX=YES
***************************************************************************
INQMAP1   DFHMDI SIZE=(24,80),                                          X
                 LINE=1,                                                X
                 COLUMN=1
***************************************************************************
          DFHMDF POS=(1,1),                                            X
                 LENGTH=8,                                              X
                 ATTRB=(NORM,PROT),                                     X
                 COLOR=BLUE,                                            X
                 INITIAL='INQMAP1'
          DFHMDF POS=(1,20),                                           X
                 LENGTH=16,                                             X
                 ATTRB=(NORM,PROT),                                     X
                 COLOR=BLUE,                                            X
                 INITIAL='Customer Inquiry'
***************************************************************************
          DFHMDF POS=(3,1),                                            X
                 LENGTH=42,                                             X
                 ATTRB=(NORM,PROT),                                     X
                 COLOR=GREEN,                                           X
                 INITIAL='Type a customer number.  Then press Enter.'
          DFHMDF POS=(5,1),                                            X
                 LENGTH=24,                                             X
                 ATTRB=(NORM,PROT),                                     X
                 COLOR=GREEN,                                           X
                 INITIAL='Customer number. . . . .'
CUSTNO    DFHMDF POS=(5,26),                                           X
                 LENGTH=6,                                              X
                 ATTRB=(NORM,UNPROT,IC),                                X
                 COLOR=TURQUOISE,                                       X
                 INITIAL='_____'
          DFHMDF POS=(5,33),                                           X
                 LENGTH=1,                                              X
                 ATTRB=ASKIP
```

Figure 5-17 Mapset listing for the DL/I version of the customer inquiry program (part 1 of 2)

```
*********************************************************************
          DFHMDF POS=(7,1),                                          X
                 LENGTH=24,                                          X
                 ATTRB=(NORM,PROT),                                  X
                 COLOR=GREEN,                                        X
                 INITIAL='Name and address . . . . :'
LNAME     DFHMDF POS=(7,26),                                         X
                 LENGTH=30,                                          X
                 COLOR=TURQUOISE,                                    X
                 ATTRB=(NORM,PROT)
FNAME     DFHMDF POS=(8,26),                                         X
                 LENGTH=20,                                          X
                 COLOR=TURQUOISE,                                    X
                 ATTRB=(NORM,PROT)
ADDR      DFHMDF POS=(9,26),                                         X
                 LENGTH=30,                                          X
                 COLOR=TURQUOISE,                                    X
                 ATTRB=(NORM,PROT)
CITY      DFHMDF POS=(10,26),                                        X
                 LENGTH=20,                                          X
                 COLOR=TURQUOISE,                                    X
                 ATTRB=(NORM,PROT)
STATE     DFHMDF POS=(10,47),                                        X
                 LENGTH=2,                                           X
                 COLOR=TURQUOISE,                                    X
                 ATTRB=(NORM,PROT)
ZIPCODE   DFHMDF POS=(10,50),                                        X
                 LENGTH=10,                                          X
                 COLOR=TURQUOISE,                                    X
                 ATTRB=(NORM,PROT)
*********************************************************************
MESSAGE   DFHMDF POS=(23,1),                                         X
                 LENGTH=79,                                          X
                 ATTRB=(BRT,PROT),                                   X
                 COLOR=YELLOW
          DFHMDF POS=(24,1),                                         X
                 LENGTH=20,                                          X
                 ATTRB=(NORM,PROT),                                  X
                 COLOR=BLUE,                                         X
                 INITIAL='F3=Exit    F12=Cancel'
DUMMY     DFHMDF POS=(24,79),                                        X
                 LENGTH=1,                                           X
                 ATTRB=(DRK,PROT,FSET),                              X
                 INITIAL=' '
*********************************************************************
          DFHMSD TYPE=FINAL
          END
```

Figure 5-17 Mapset listing for the DL/I version of the customer inquiry program (part 2 of 2)

```
01   INQMAP1I.
     02   FILLER      PIC X(12).
     02   CUSTNOL     PIC S9(4) COMP.
     02   CUSTNOF     PIC X.
     02   FILLER REDEFINES CUSTNOF.
      03   CUSTNOA    PIC X.
     02   CUSTNOI     PIC X(0006).
     02   LNAMEL      PIC S9(4) COMP.
     02   LNAMEF      PIC X.
     02   FILLER REDEFINES LNAMEF.
      03   LNAMEA     PIC X.
     02   LNAMEI      PIC X(0030).
     02   FNAMEL      PIC S9(4) COMP.
     02   FNAMEF      PIC X.
     02   FILLER REDEFINES FNAMEF.
      03   FNAMEA     PIC X.
     02   FNAMEI      PIC X(0020).
     02   ADDRL       PIC S9(4) COMP.
     02   ADDRF       PIC X.
     02   FILLER REDEFINES ADDRF.
      03   ADDRA      PIC X.
     02   ADDRI       PIC X(0030).
     02   CITYL       PIC S9(4) COMP.
     02   CITYF       PIC X.
     02   FILLER REDEFINES CITYF.
      03   CITYA      PIC X.
     02   CITYI       PIC X(0020).
     02   STATEL      PIC S9(4) COMP.
     02   STATEF      PIC X.
     02   FILLER REDEFINES STATEF.
      03   STATEA     PIC X.
     02   STATEI      PIC X(0002).
     02   ZIPCODEL    PIC S9(4) COMP.
     02   ZIPCODEF    PIC X.
     02   FILLER REDEFINES ZIPCODEF.
      03   ZIPCODEA   PIC X.
     02   ZIPCODEI    PIC X(0010).
     02   MESSAGEL    PIC S9(4) COMP.
     02   MESSAGEF    PIC X.
     02   FILLER REDEFINES MESSAGEF.
      03   MESSAGEA   PIC X.
     02   MESSAGEI    PIC X(0079).
     02   DUMMYL      PIC S9(4) COMP.
     02   DUMMYF      PIC X.
     02   FILLER REDEFINES DUMMYF.
      03   DUMMYA     PIC X.
     02   DUMMYI      PIC X(0001).
01   INQMAP1O REDEFINES INQMAP1I.
     02   FILLER      PIC X(12).
     02   FILLER      PIC X(3).
     02   CUSTNOO     PIC X(0006).
     02   FILLER      PIC X(3).
     02   LNAMEO      PIC X(0030).
     02   FILLER      PIC X(3).
     02   FNAMEO      PIC X(0020).
     02   FILLER      PIC X(3).
     02   ADDRO       PIC X(0030).
     02   FILLER      PIC X(3).
     02   CITYO       PIC X(0020).
     02   FILLER      PIC X(3).
     02   STATEO      PIC X(0002).
     02   FILLER      PIC X(3).
     02   ZIPCODEO    PIC X(0010).
     02   FILLER      PIC X(3).
     02   MESSAGEO    PIC X(0079).
     02   FILLER      PIC X(3).
     02   DUMMYO      PIC X(0001).
```

Figure 5-18 Symbolic map for the DL/I version of the customer inquiry program

```
        IDENTIFICATION DIVISION.
       *
        PROGRAM-ID.  DLIINQ1.
       *
        ENVIRONMENT DIVISION.
       *
        DATA DIVISION.
       *
        WORKING-STORAGE SECTION.
       *
        01  SWITCHES.
       *
            05  VALID-DATA-SW              PIC X      VALUE 'Y'.
                88 VALID-DATA                          VALUE 'Y'.
       *
        01  FLAGS.
       *
            05  SEND-FLAG                  PIC X.
                88  SEND-ERASE                         VALUE '1'.
                88  SEND-DATAONLY                      VALUE '2'.
                88  SEND-DATAONLY-ALARM                VALUE '3'.
       *
        01  COMMUNICATION-AREA            PIC X.
       *
        01  DLI-FUNCTION-CODES.
       *
            05  DLI-SCHEDULE    PIC X(4) VALUE 'PSB '.
            05  DLI-GET-UNIQUE  PIC X(4) VALUE 'GU  '.
       *
        01  PSB-NAME          PIC X(8)  VALUE 'IQPSB   '.
       *
        01  CUSTOMER-SSA.
       *
            05  FILLER          PIC X(19) VALUE 'CUSTOMER(CUSTNO  ='.
            05  SSA-CUSTNO      PIC X(6).
            05  FILLER          PIC X     VALUE ')'.
       *
        COPY CUSTSEG.
       *
        COPY INQSET1.
       *
        COPY DFHAID.
       *
        COPY ERRPARM.
       *
        LINKAGE SECTION.
       *
        01  DFHCOMMAREA                   PIC X.
       *
        COPY DLIUIB.
       *
        01  PCB-POINTERS.
       *
            05  CUSTOMER-PCB-POINTER        POINTER.
       *
        01  CUSTOMER-PCB.
       *
            05  FILLER                      PIC X(10).
            05  CUSTOMER-STATUS-CODE        PIC XX.
```

Figure 5-19 Source listing for the DL/I version of the customer inquiry program (part 1 of 3)

```
/
 PROCEDURE DIVISION.
*
 0000-PROCESS-CUSTOMER-INQUIRY.
*
     EVALUATE TRUE

         WHEN EIBCALEN = ZERO
             MOVE LOW-VALUE TO INQMAP1O
             SET SEND-ERASE TO TRUE
             PERFORM 1400-SEND-CUSTOMER-MAP

         WHEN EIBAID = DFHCLEAR
             MOVE LOW-VALUE TO INQMAP1O
             SET SEND-ERASE TO TRUE
             PERFORM 1400-SEND-CUSTOMER-MAP

         WHEN EIBAID = DFHPA1 OR DFHPA2 OR DFHPA3
             CONTINUE

         WHEN EIBAID = DFHPF3 OR DFHPF12
             EXEC CICS
                 XCTL PROGRAM('INVMENU')
             END-EXEC

         WHEN EIBAID = DFHENTER
             PERFORM 0500-SCHEDULE-PSB
             PERFORM 1000-PROCESS-CUSTOMER-MAP

         WHEN OTHER
             MOVE LOW-VALUE TO INQMAP1O
             MOVE 'Invalid key pressed.' TO MESSAGEO
             SET SEND-DATAONLY-ALARM TO TRUE
             PERFORM 1400-SEND-CUSTOMER-MAP

     END-EVALUATE.

     EXEC CICS
         RETURN TRANSID('DLI1')
                 COMMAREA(COMMUNICATION-AREA)
     END-EXEC.
*
 0500-SCHEDULE-PSB.
*
     CALL 'CBLTDLI' USING DLI-SCHEDULE
                         PSB-NAME
                         ADDRESS OF DLIUIB.
     IF UIBFCTR NOT = LOW-VALUE
         GO TO 9999-TERMINATE-PROGRAM.
     SET ADDRESS OF PCB-POINTERS TO UIBPCBAL.
     SET ADDRESS OF CUSTOMER-PCB TO CUSTOMER-PCB-POINTER.
*
 1000-PROCESS-CUSTOMER-MAP.
*
     PERFORM 1100-RECEIVE-CUSTOMER-MAP.
     PERFORM 1200-EDIT-CUSTOMER-DATA.
     IF VALID-DATA
         PERFORM 1300-GET-CUSTOMER-SEGMENT.
     IF VALID-DATA
         SET SEND-DATAONLY TO TRUE
         PERFORM 1400-SEND-CUSTOMER-MAP
     ELSE
         SET SEND-DATAONLY-ALARM TO TRUE
         PERFORM 1400-SEND-CUSTOMER-MAP.
*
 1100-RECEIVE-CUSTOMER-MAP.
*
     EXEC CICS
         RECEIVE MAP('INQMAP1')
                 MAPSET('INQSET1')
                 INTO(INQMAP1I)
     END-EXEC.
```

Figure 5-19 Source listing for the DL/I version of the customer inquiry program (part 2 of 3)

```
/
 1200-EDIT-CUSTOMER-DATA.
*
     IF        CUSTNOL = ZERO
         OR CUSTNOI = SPACE
         MOVE 'N' TO VALID-DATA-SW
         MOVE 'You must enter a customer number.' TO MESSAGEO.
*
 1300-GET-CUSTOMER-SEGMENT.
*
     MOVE CUSTNOI TO SSA-CUSTNO.
     CALL 'CBLTDLI' USING DLI-GET-UNIQUE
                         CUSTOMER-PCB
                         CUSTOMER-SEGMENT
                         CUSTOMER-SSA.
     IF UIBFCTR NOT = LOW-VALUE
         GO TO 9999-TERMINATE-PROGRAM.
     IF CUSTOMER-STATUS-CODE = SPACE
         MOVE SPACE          TO MESSAGEO
         MOVE CM-LAST-NAME   TO LNAMEO
         MOVE CM-FIRST-NAME  TO FNAMEO
         MOVE CM-ADDRESS     TO ADDRO
         MOVE CM-CITY        TO CITYO
         MOVE CM-STATE       TO STATEO
         MOVE CM-ZIP-CODE    TO ZIPCODEO
     ELSE IF CUSTOMER-STATUS-CODE = 'GE'
         MOVE 'N' TO VALID-DATA-SW
         MOVE 'That customer does not exist.' TO MESSAGEO
         MOVE SPACE TO LNAMEO
                      FNAMEO
                      ADDRO
                      CITYO
                      STATEO
                      ZIPCODEO
     ELSE
         GO TO 9999-TERMINATE-PROGRAM.
*
 1400-SEND-CUSTOMER-MAP.
*
     IF SEND-ERASE
         EXEC CICS
             SEND MAP('INQMAP1')
                  MAPSET('INQSET1')
                  FROM(INQMAP1O)
                  ERASE
         END-EXEC
     ELSE IF SEND-DATAONLY
         EXEC CICS
             SEND MAP('INQMAP1')
                  MAPSET('INQSET1')
                  FROM(INQMAP1O)
                  DATAONLY
         END-EXEC
     ELSE IF SEND-DATAONLY-ALARM
         EXEC CICS
             SEND MAP('INQMAP1')
                  MAPSET('INQSET1')
                  FROM(INQMAP1O)
                  DATAONLY
                  ALARM
         END-EXEC.
*
 9999-TERMINATE-PROGRAM.
*
     MOVE EIBRESP  TO ERR-RESP.
     MOVE EIBRESP2 TO ERR-RESP2.
     MOVE EIBTRNID TO ERR-TRNID.
     MOVE EIBRSRCE TO ERR-RSRCE.
     EXEC CICS
         XCTL PROGRAM('SYSERR')
              COMMAREA(ERROR-PARAMETERS)
     END-EXEC.
```

Figure 5-19   Source listing for the DL/I version of the customer inquiry program (part 3 of 3)

Section 3

Advanced terminal processing features

In *Part 1: An Introductory Course,* you learned how to use basic mapping support (BMS) facilities to process simple terminal input and output. The chapters in this section show you how to use a variety of CICS facilities to process more complicated forms of terminal input and output. In chapter 6, you'll learn how to use BMS commands to create a logical message: a single unit of terminal output built by one or more SEND MAP or SEND TEXT commands that can be directed to one or more display or printer terminals. And in chapter 7, you'll learn how to use terminal control commands to bypass BMS so you can communicate directly with terminal devices.

BMS features for logical message building

In this chapter, you'll learn how to create logical messages. Logical messages are typically used for reports that are displayed or printed on 3270 terminal devices. For example, a terminal operator may want to display a listing of all items in a product file to see which ones need to be reordered. Or, the operator may need a printed copy of the listing. In this example, the product listing would be created as a logical message, then displayed or printed as necessary.

This chapter has three topics. Topic 1 presents the concepts and terms you need to know before you can code a program that creates a logical message. Then, topic 2 presents two techniques you can use to create a logical message; one uses the SEND TEXT command, the other uses SEND MAP. Finally, topic 3 shows you how to build a logical message that's intended for a printer.

As you study this chapter, I want you to understand that logical message building is one of the less commonly used facilities of CICS. In fact, many installations don't use it at all. Still, logical message building is a powerful facility that you should know about, even if you won't use it as often as other CICS facilities.

Logical message building concepts and terminology

A *logical message* is a single unit of output that's created from one or more SEND TEXT or SEND MAP commands. When you use SEND TEXT and SEND MAP commands for normal display output as I presented in *Part 1: An Introductory Course*, you do *not* create a logical message because the output from each SEND TEXT or SEND MAP command is treated separately. In contrast, when you use SEND TEXT or SEND MAP commands to build a logical message, BMS collects the output from one or more of those commands and treats it as a single logical unit.

Don't let the term "logical message" confuse you. Although the term implies that there's also a "physical message," there isn't. And in addition, the word "message" suggests that a logical message is brief—just one or two lines of information. Although logical messages can be that short, they more often contain many pages of information.

When you use logical message building, BMS automatically provides many features for you. For example, BMS handles the complex formatting requirements of different types of terminals, including 3270 printers. And BMS provides a set of message retrieval commands that you'll learn later in this topic.

I want you to realize, though, that logical message building does *not* provide many of the features of spooling systems like JES2, JES3, and VSE/POWER. As a result, many installations have either purchased a CICS-based spooling system or developed one of their own. If that's the case at your installation, some or all of the concepts this topic presents may not apply. So keep that in mind as you read on.

The process of creating a logical message is usually called *logical message building*, or just *message building*. Unfortunately, that term isn't clearly defined in the IBM literature. And you'll often encounter other terms, like *terminal paging* and *page building*, that mean the same thing. In any event, you code a *message building program* to create a logical message. In the message building program, you issue SEND TEXT or SEND MAP commands with special options to build the message. You'll learn how to do that in the next topic.

Once a message has been created, it must be delivered to a terminal. This process is called *message delivery.* Three factors affect how message building and message delivery work: message disposition, terminal status, and message routing. After I discuss these factors, I'll describe how the user retrieves logical messages.

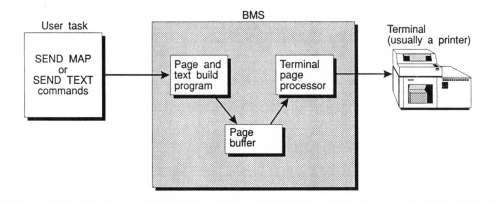

Figure 6-1 BMS sends logical messages with terminal disposition directly to the terminal

Message disposition

A logical message can have one of two *dispositions*: terminal or paging. You specify the disposition option you want with the SEND TEXT or SEND MAP commands that build the message, as you'll see in the next topic.

Terminal disposition When you specify *terminal disposition*, your logical message is sent directly to your terminal as it's created. You'll normally use terminal disposition when your task is attached directly to a printer. That way, your logical message is printed as it's created. To attach a task to a printer, you use the START command, which you'll learn in chapter 10.

Figure 6-1 shows how BMS handles logical messages with terminal disposition. Here, a user task issues multiple SEND TEXT or SEND MAP commands. The BMS module that processes those commands, the *page and text build program*, formats your data in an intermediate storage area called the *page buffer*. As you issue successive SEND TEXT or SEND MAP commands, data is added to the page buffer until the buffer is full. Then, another BMS module, the *terminal page processor*, transfers the data from the page buffer to the terminal and clears the page buffer so your program can continue. As a result, your logical message is built and delivered one *page* at a time.

Paging disposition When you specify *paging disposition*, your logical message isn't sent directly to a terminal. Instead, the entire message is held in temporary storage until an operator retrieves it. Typically, you use paging disposition when the output terminal is a display device.

A logical message with paging disposition is built much like one with terminal disposition, as figure 6-2 shows. Each time your program issues a SEND TEXT or SEND MAP command, data is formatted in the page buffer. However, when the page buffer is full, the page is written

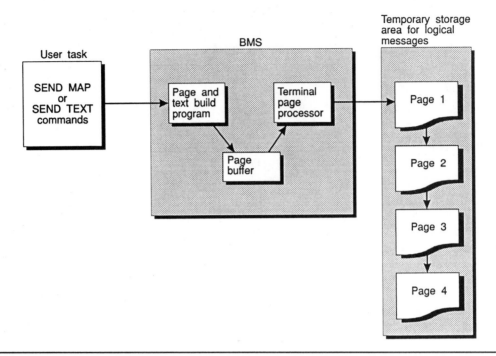

Figure 6-2   BMS stores logical messages with paging disposition in temporary storage

to temporary storage instead of the terminal. The result is that your logical message is stored as a collection of pages in temporary storage.

When you specify paging disposition, you can use *message routing* to direct a message to other terminals. I'll describe message routing in more detail in a moment. Whether or not you use message routing, though, a logical message in temporary storage is eventually delivered to one or more terminals. How a message is delivered to a terminal depends on that terminal's status.

Terminal status   Each terminal in a CICS system is assigned a *terminal status* that affects how messages with paging disposition are delivered to it. If a message is created with terminal disposition, terminal status doesn't affect how it's delivered. BMS provides two options for terminal status: paging and autopage.

Paging status   For a terminal with *paging status*, usually a display station, BMS delivers pages one at a time as an operator requests them. Figure 6-3 shows how BMS delivers a logical message with paging disposition to a terminal with paging status. To view a page of the logical message, the terminal operator enters a *message retrieval command*. Then, a BMS module called the *page retrieval program* retrieves the requested page from temporary storage and displays it at the terminal.

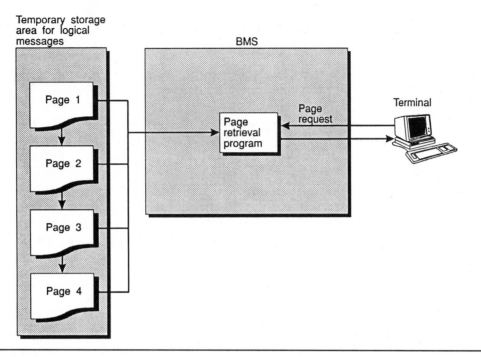

Figure 6-3   BMS retrieves pages from temporary storage under operator control

Don't confuse paging status with paging disposition. Paging status indicates that operators can request pages one at a time by issuing message retrieval commands. In contrast, paging disposition means a logical message is written to temporary storage for later delivery. Remember, paging status is meaningful only for output with paging disposition.

Autopage status   For a terminal with *autopage status*, usually a printer, the entire message is delivered automatically as soon as the terminal is ready. For an autopage terminal, BMS also uses the page retrieval program. But instead of processing message retrieval commands, the page retrieval program transfers pages one at a time, in order, to the autopage device. Although BMS lets any terminal have paging or autopage status, printer terminals almost always have autopage status. That way, logical messages sent to them are automatically printed.

The effect of paging disposition and autopage status together is similar to terminal disposition. The difference is that terminal disposition causes BMS to send your message directly to the terminal, while paging disposition and autopage status causes BMS to store the message in temporary storage before sending it to the terminal. Because terminal disposition is more efficient for printing applications, I recommend you use it unless you're directing a logical message to more than one printer by using message routing.

Message routing

So far, I've assumed that all logical messages are intended for the terminal where the message building task is attached. And that's normally the case: When an operator starts a message building program, its output is displayed at that operator's terminal. And for printer output, it's common to use an interval control START command to start a task attached to a particular printer.

It's not unusual, though, for a program to send a logical message to terminals other than the one the message building task is attached to. For example, consider an invoicing application that requires orders to be printed on two printers: one in the billing department, the other in the shipping department. In this case, the same logical message (an invoice) is routed to two terminals. You'll learn how to use message routing in topic 3.

Message retrieval

When a logical message with paging disposition is delivered to a terminal with paging status (a display terminal), only one page is displayed at a time. To tell BMS what page to display, you use message retrieval commands. Figure 6-4 shows the two most commonly used message retrieval commands: getpage and msgterm. You use getpage to retrieve pages, and you use msgterm to end a message retrieval session. Although there are other message retrieval commands, you're not likely to use them.

Each message retrieval command begins with a prefix that's assigned by your systems programmer. In figure 6-4, the prefix for the getpage command is P/, and the prefix for the msgterm command is T/. Although your installation may use different prefixes, the ones in figure 6-4 are common. And although the prefixes may vary, the values that follow them are always the same. As a result, you always code L on a getpage command to retrieve the last page of a message, regardless of what prefix is assigned to the getpage command.

Entering a message retrieval command is simple. When the first page of your message is displayed (that's automatic), press the Clear key, key in a message retrieval command, and press the Enter key. If you enter a valid message retrieval command prefix, CICS invokes the page retrieval program to process your command. In effect, CICS treats the prefix as shorthand for the transaction identifier CSPG, which starts the page retrieval program.

How to retrieve pages   You use the getpage command (prefix P/ in figure 6-4) to display a specific page. For example, to retrieve the third page of a message, you enter

P/3

The getpage command

P/*n*   Retrieve page *n*.
P/+*n*   Retrieve the page that's *n* pages past the current page.
P/-*n*   Retrieve the page that's *n* pages before the current page.
P/L   Retrieve the last page.
P/N   Retrieve the next page.
P/P   Retrieve the previous page.

The msgterm command

T/B   Terminate the page retrieval session and purge the message being displayed.

Figure 6-4   Message retrieval commands

You can move forward through a logical message by entering a command like this:

    P / + 2

Here, the page that's two pages beyond the current page is displayed. So if you enter that command when page 3 is displayed, the page retrieval program displays page 5. To display a page that's before the current page, use a minus sign, as in

    P / − 1

The effect of this command is to retrieve the previous page.

Three special forms of the getpage command let you retrieve the last page of a message, the next page, and the previous page. To display the last page, you enter P/L. To display the next page, you enter P/N (that's the same as P/+1). And to display the previous page, you enter P/P (that's the same as P/-1). Although there's no special option to retrieve the first page of a message, you can do that by entering P/1.

How to end a message retrieval session   When you've finished displaying a logical message, you must purge it before you can do other work on your terminal. To do that, you enter a msgterm command. Figure 6-4 shows the version of the msgterm command you're most likely to use: T/B. When you enter T/B, the message you're retrieving is deleted.

Single keystroke retrieval   Some installations use a feature called *single keystroke retrieval,* or *SKR,* to simplify message retrieval. When SKR is used, PF keys are associated with specific message retrieval commands. For example, suppose five PF keys are assigned like this:

    P F 5   P / 1
    P F 6   P / L
    P F 7   P / P
    P F 8   P / N
    P F 3   T / B

Then, you can display the first page of a logical message by pressing PF5 or the last page by pressing PF6. You can use PF7 and PF8 to move forward or backward through the message one page at a time. And you can purge the message by pressing PF3. These PF key assignments correspond to the CUA standards for function keys, so they should be easy to remember.

Note that you can still use PF keys in application programs when SKR is used. The PF keys take on their SKR meanings only during message retrieval.

Terms

logical message
logical message building
message building
terminal paging
page building
message building program
message delivery
disposition
terminal disposition
page and text build program
page buffer
terminal page processor
page
paging disposition
message routing
terminal status
paging status
message retrieval command
page retrieval program
autopage status
single keystroke retrieval
SKR

Objectives

1. Explain the meaning of the following terms:
   a. logical message
   b. message building
   c. message routing

2. Distinguish between:
   a. terminal and paging disposition
   b. paging and autopage status

3. Describe the function of the getpage and msgterm message retrieval commands.

Two techniques for building a logical message

In this topic, you'll learn two techniques for building a logical message. The first uses the SEND TEXT command and doesn't require a mapset; the second uses the SEND MAP command and *does* require a mapset. In most cases, I think it's easier to use the SEND TEXT technique, although there are cases where it's better to use the SEND MAP technique. So you need to know about both.

Throughout this topic, I assume that your logical message is delivered to a display terminal, not to a printer. In the next topic, you'll learn how directing a logical message to a printer affects the way you code the SEND TEXT and SEND MAP commands.

Figure 6-5 presents the specifications for a program that displays a listing of data from a file of product records. In this topic, I'll present two versions of this program. Although both produce identical output, they use different message building techniques. The first version uses the SEND TEXT command, and the other uses the SEND MAP command.

Notice the groupings of output lines I've marked in part 2 of figure 6-5. The first five lines of each output page are the *header*. Following the header are 17 occurrences of the product detail line. At the bottom of each output page except the last is a two-line *trailer* with a message that tells the user that the listing continues on the next page. And on the last page of the product listing, a total line shows the number of records in the product file. As you read on, you'll see that a significant difference between the SEND TEXT and SEND MAP techniques is in how you place headers and trailers on each page.

The product listing program: SEND TEXT version

The structure chart for the SEND TEXT version of the product listing program, shown in figure 6-6, is easy to understand. After module 1000 starts a browse operation on the product file, module 2000 is invoked repeatedly to produce product lines. It calls module 2100 to read a product record and module 2200 to add lines to the logical message. After all the product records have been processed, module 3000 is invoked to send the total line. (Because this program isn't pseudo-conversational, I didn't bother to create an event/response chart for it.)

As you've probably noticed, the structure chart in figure 6-6 provides no modules to format and send header or trailer lines, even

Program	PROLST1
Overview	Produces a listing of records in the product file.
Input/output specifications	PRODUCT Product file
Processing specifications	1. For each record in the product file, list the product code, description, unit price, and quantity on hand. At the end of the listing, list the number of products in the file.
	2. Create the listing using the BMS message building facility.

Figure 6-5   Specifications for the product listing program (part 1 of 3)

though the screen layout in figure 6-5 calls for both. There's no need for separate modules to handle those functions because BMS provides them automatically when you code the SEND TEXT command to build a logical message. That's one of the main advantages of using SEND TEXT rather than SEND MAP for message building. The SEND MAP command does *not* automatically format header and trailer lines.

Figure 6-7 gives the source listing for the SEND TEXT version of the product listing program. Because this program is easy to understand, I'll focus on those elements that relate directly to logical message building. In the Procedure Division, I've shaded three commands: the SEND TEXT commands in modules 2200 and 3000 and the SEND PAGE command in module 0000. Once you understand how those commands work, you'll have no trouble understanding this program.

The SEND TEXT command

In *Part 1: An Introductory Course*, you learned how to use the SEND TEXT command to send a short message to the terminal. Figure 6-8 gives a more complete format for the SEND TEXT command, showing the options you can code for message building. You already know about the FROM option: It supplies the data that's to be sent. (Under OS/VS COBOL, you must also specify the FROM field's length in the LENGTH option.) The ERASE option works the same way it does for a non-message building SEND TEXT command: It erases the previous contents of the screen. (You should always specify ERASE.) So the only new options are ACCUM, PAGING, HEADER, and TRAILER. After I describe the special formatting considerations for data you specify in the FROM option, I'll describe those options.

Output on all pages of the message except the last

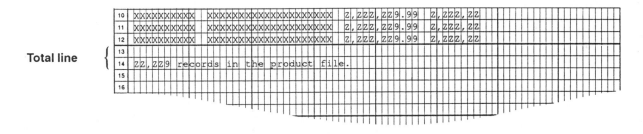

Figure 6-5 Specifications for the product listing program (part 2 of 3)

How to control vertical spacing in SEND TEXT output data

When you use a SEND TEXT command, the field you specify in the FROM option can provide one or more lines of output. To indicate where line endings fall in your output, you use *new-line characters*. To understand this, look at the coding for the product detail line

The PRODUCT copy member

```
01   PRODUCT-MASTER-RECORD.
*
     05   PRM-PRODUCT-CODE              PIC  X(10).
     05   PRM-PRODUCT-DESCRIPTION       PIC  X(20).
     05   PRM-UNIT-PRICE               PIC  S9(7)V99    COMP-3.
     05   PRM-QUANTITY-ON-HAND         PIC  S9(7)       COMP-3.
*
```

The ERRPARM copy member

```
01   ERROR-PARAMETERS.
*
     05   ERR-RESP        PIC  S9(8)    COMP.
     05   ERR-RESP2       PIC  S9(8)    COMP.
     05   ERR-TRNID       PIC  X(4).
     05   ERR-RSRCE       PIC  X(8).
*
```

Figure 6-5   Specifications for the product listing program (part 3 of 3)

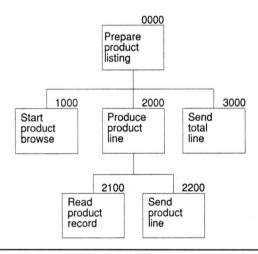

Figure 6-6   Structure chart for the product listing program (SEND TEXT)

(PRODUCT-LINE) in figure 6-7. Here, you can see that the last item in the group is this:

```
05   PL-NL        PIC  X     VALUE  X'15'.
```

Here, the VALUE clause supplies a new-line character—hex 15—for the PL-NL field. If you're using the OS/VS COBOL compiler, you can't specify a hexadecimal constant in the VALUE clause. So you'll have to

```
        IDENTIFICATION DIVISION.
       *
        PROGRAM-ID. PROLST1.
       *
        ENVIRONMENT DIVISION.
       *
        DATA DIVISION.
       *
        WORKING-STORAGE SECTION.
       *
        01  SWITCHES.
       *
            05  PRODUCT-EOF-SW    PIC X          VALUE 'N'.
                88  PRODUCT-EOF                  VALUE 'Y'.
       *
        01  WORK-FIELDS.
       *
            05  RECORD-COUNT     PIC S9(5)  VALUE ZERO   COMP-3.
       *
        01  RESPONSE-CODE        PIC S9(8)   COMP.
       *
        01  HEADER-AREA.
       *
            05  HA-PREFIX.
                10  HA-LENGTH     PIC S9(4) VALUE 176   COMP.
                10  HA-PAGE-CODE PIC X      VALUE '*'.
                10  FILLER        PIC X      VALUE SPACE.
            05  HEADER-LINE-1.
                10  FILLER        PIC X(20) VALUE '             Produ'.
                10  FILLER        PIC X(20) VALUE 'ct Listing          '.
                10  FILLER        PIC X(17) VALUE '        Page: ***'.
                10  HA1-NL        PIC XX    VALUE X'1515'.
            05  HEADER-LINE-2.
                10  FILLER        PIC X(20) VALUE 'Product             '.
                10  FILLER        PIC X(20) VALUE SPACE.
                10  FILLER        PIC X(17) VALUE ' Unit    Quantity'.
                10  HA2-NL        PIC X     VALUE X'15'.
            05  HEADER-LINE-3.
                10  FILLER        PIC X(20) VALUE 'Code         Descript'.
                10  FILLER        PIC X(20) VALUE 'ion                 '.
                10  FILLER        PIC X(17) VALUE ' Price     On Hand'.
                10  HA3-NL        PIC XX    VALUE X'1515'.
       *
        01  PRODUCT-LINE.
       *
            05  PL-PRODUCT-CODE PIC X(10).
            05  FILLER           PIC XX     VALUE SPACE.
            05  PL-DESCRIPTION  PIC X(20).
            05  FILLER           PIC XX     VALUE SPACE.
            05  PL-UNIT-PRICE   PIC Z,ZZZ,ZZZ.99.
            05  FILLER           PIC XX     VALUE SPACE.
            05  PL-QUANTITY     PIC Z,ZZZ,ZZ9.
            05  PL-NL           PIC X      VALUE X'15'.
       *
        01  TOTAL-LINE.
       *
            05  TL-NL           PIC X      VALUE X'15'.
            05  TL-RECORD-COUNT PIC ZZ,ZZ9.
            05  FILLER          PIC X(15) VALUE ' records in the'.
            05  FILLER          PIC X(15) VALUE ' product file. '.
```

Figure 6-7 Source listing for the product listing program (SEND TEXT) (part 1 of 3)

```
/
 01   TRAILER-AREA.
*
      05   TA-PREFIX.
           10  TA-LENGTH    PIC S9(4)    VALUE 26   COMP.
           10  FILLER       PIC XX       VALUE SPACE.
      05   TRAILER-LINE.
           10  TA-NL        PIC X        VALUE X'15'.
           10  FILLER       PIC X(20)    VALUE 'Continued on next pa'.
           10  FILLER       PIC X(5)     VALUE 'ge...'.
*
 COPY PRODUCT.
*
 COPY ERRPARM.
*
 PROCEDURE DIVISION.
*
 0000-PRODUCE-PRODUCT-LISTING.
*
      PERFORM 1000-START-PRODUCT-BROWSE.
      PERFORM 2000-PRODUCE-PRODUCT-LINE
          UNTIL PRODUCT-EOF.
      PERFORM 3000-SEND-TOTAL-LINE.
      EXEC CICS
          SEND PAGE
              OPERPURGE
      END-EXEC.
      EXEC CICS
          RETURN
      END-EXEC.
*
 1000-START-PRODUCT-BROWSE.
*
      MOVE LOW-VALUE TO PRM-PRODUCT-CODE.
      EXEC CICS
          STARTBR DATASET('PRODUCT')
                  RIDFLD(PRM-PRODUCT-CODE)
                  GTEQ
                  RESP(RESPONSE-CODE)
      END-EXEC.
      IF RESPONSE-CODE = DFHRESP(NOTFND)
          MOVE 'Y' TO PRODUCT-EOF-SW
      ELSE IF RESPONSE-CODE NOT = DFHRESP(NORMAL)
          GO TO 9999-TERMINATE-PROGRAM.
*
 2000-PRODUCE-PRODUCT-LINE.
*
      PERFORM 2100-READ-PRODUCT-RECORD.
      IF NOT PRODUCT-EOF
          PERFORM 2200-SEND-PRODUCT-LINE.
*
 2100-READ-PRODUCT-RECORD.
*
      EXEC CICS
          READNEXT DATASET('PRODUCT')
                   RIDFLD(PRM-PRODUCT-CODE)
                   INTO(PRODUCT-MASTER-RECORD)
                   RESP(RESPONSE-CODE)
      END-EXEC.
      IF RESPONSE-CODE = DFHRESP(NORMAL)
          ADD 1 TO RECORD-COUNT
      ELSE IF RESPONSE-CODE = DFHRESP(ENDFILE)
          MOVE 'Y' TO PRODUCT-EOF-SW
      ELSE
          GO TO 9999-TERMINATE-PROGRAM.
```

Figure 6-7   Source listing for the product listing program (SEND TEXT) (part 2 of 3)

```
/
 2200-SEND-PRODUCT-LINE.
*
     MOVE PRM-PRODUCT-CODE         TO PL-PRODUCT-CODE.
     MOVE PRM-PRODUCT-DESCRIPTION  TO PL-DESCRIPTION.
     MOVE PRM-UNIT-PRICE           TO PL-UNIT-PRICE.
     MOVE PRM-QUANTITY-ON-HAND     TO PL-QUANTITY.
     EXEC CICS
         SEND TEXT FROM(PRODUCT-LINE)
                   ACCUM
                   PAGING
                   ERASE
                   HEADER(HEADER-AREA)
                   TRAILER(TRAILER-AREA)
     END-EXEC.
*
 3000-SEND-TOTAL-LINE.
*
     MOVE RECORD-COUNT TO TL-RECORD-COUNT.
     EXEC CICS
         SEND TEXT FROM(TOTAL-LINE)
                   ACCUM
                   PAGING
                   ERASE
     END-EXEC.
*
 9999-TERMINATE-PROGRAM.
*
     MOVE EIBRESP  TO ERR-RESP.
     MOVE EIBTRNID TO ERR-TRNID.
     MOVE EIBRSRCE TO ERR-RSRCE.
     EXEC CICS
         XCTL PROGRAM('SYSERR')
              COMMAREA(ERROR-PARAMETERS)
     END-EXEC.
```

Figure 6-7   Source listing for the product listing program (SEND TEXT) (part 3 of 3)

use the hexadecimal editing feature of your text editor to enter a new-line character as a literal.

Figure 6-9 shows a more complex example of formatting data for a SEND TEXT command. Here, each SEND TEXT command will send the six lines in the screen layout. Of the six, two are blank, and four contain data showing a customer's number, name, address, city, state, and zip code. Notice how I coded two consecutive new-line characters at the end of CUSTOMER-LINE-1 and CUSTOMER-LINE-4 to force blank lines.

In the IBM-supplied copy member DFHBMSCA, there's an entry named DFHBMPNL that contains a new-line character. If you wish, you can use this entry by copying DFHBMSCA into your program. Then, near the start of your program, you can move DFHBMPNL to each field that should contain a new-line character like this:

```
MOVE DFHBMPNL TO IL-NL.
```

Frankly, I think it's easier to code the new-line characters directly in your program, especially if you're using VS COBOL II. But if you're using

The SEND TEXT command

```
EXEC CICS
    SEND TEXT    FROM(data-area)
               [ LENGTH(data-value) ]
               [ ACCUM ]
               [ PAGING ]
               [ ERASE ]
               [ HEADER(data-area) ]
               [ TRAILER(data-area) ].
END-EXEC
```

Explanation

FROM ·   Specifies the name of the field that contains the data to be added to the logical message.

LENGTH   Specifies the length of the FROM field. Must be numeric. If you use a data name, it must be a binary halfword (PIC S9(4) COMP). (Optional under VS COBOL II.)

ACCUM   Specifies that this SEND TEXT command is used to build a logical message.

PAGING   Specifies that output pages should be written to temporary storage for later retrieval under operator control.

ERASE   Specifies that the terminal's buffer should be erased as each page of the message is sent during page retrieval.

HEADER   Specifies the name of a field that contains header information to be placed at the top of each page.

TRAILER   Specifies the name of a field that contains trailer information to be placed at the bottom of each page.

Figure 6-8   The SEND TEXT command

OS/VS COBOL and your text editor doesn't provide a good hexadecimal editing facility, you may want to use DFHBMPNL.

Incidentally, if you know about hardware printer orders for 3270 printers, don't let the new-line character confuse you. Although the new-line character and the new-line printer order have the same hexadecimal value and similar functions, they're not the same. The new-line character I've just described is strictly a BMS facility: It tells BMS to format output data so that a line ending will fall wherever you place the character. In contrast, a new-line printer order is a hardware facility: It tells a 3270 printer to begin a new line. In the next topic, you'll learn that for printer output, BMS may or may not use new-line printer orders for line endings. But the BMS new-line character works for printer or display terminals and has nothing to do with the new-line printer order.

Sample screen layout

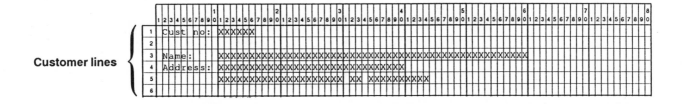

Working-storage definition using new-line characters

```
*
  01   CUSTOMER-LINES.
*
       05   CUSTOMER-LINE-1.
            10   FILLER          PIC X(9)    VALUE 'Cust no: '.
            10   CL1-CUST-NO     PIC X(6).
            10   CL1-NL          PIC XX      VALUE X'1515'.
       05   CUSTOMER-LINE-2.
            10   FILLER          PIC X(9)    VALUE 'Name:    '.
            10   CL2-NAME        PIC X(50).
            10   CL2-NL          PIC X       VALUE X'15'.
       05   CUSTOMER-LINE-3.
            10   FILLER          PIC X(9)    VALUE 'Address: '.
            10   CL3-ADDRESS     PIC X(30).
            10   CL3-NL          PIC X       VALUE X'15'.
       05   CUSTOMER-LINE-4.
            10   FILLER          PIC X(9)    VALUE SPACE.
            10   CL4-CITY        PIC X(20).
            10   FILLER          PIC X       VALUE SPACE.
            10   CL4-STATE       PIC XX.
            10   FILLER          PIC X       VALUE SPACE.
            10   CL4-ZIP-CODE    PIC X(10).
            10   CL4-NL          PIC XX      VALUE X'1515'.
*
```

Figure 6-9   Defining a multi-line output area

The ACCUM and PAGING options   You code the ACCUM and PAGING options on the SEND TEXT command to indicate that it's being used to build a logical message. Quite simply, ACCUM means that output from one or more SEND TEXT commands is accumulated in a page buffer rather than sent directly to the terminal. If you code the PAGING option, the message is created with paging disposition. Then, each page of the message is written to temporary storage. When the program ends, the terminal operator can display individual pages of the message using the message retrieval commands I described in the last topic. If you omit PAGING, the message is created with terminal disposition; as a result, it's written directly to the terminal.

The HEADER and TRAILER options   When you use the SEND TEXT command to build a logical message, BMS automatically formats header and trailer lines if you specify HEADER, TRAILER, or both. Simply put, the HEADER option identifies data that BMS places at the top of each page, and the TRAILER option identifies data that BMS places at the bottom of each page. When you use these options, you don't have to worry about counting the number of output lines to determine where to place header and trailer data. BMS handles that *overflow processing* for you.

To illustrate how overflow processing works, figure 6-10 shows the processing BMS does for a SEND TEXT command. First, BMS compares the number of output lines in your FROM area with the number of lines remaining on the page, allowing for the size of your trailer data. If there's enough room remaining on the page, BMS adds the FROM data to it and returns. However, if the FROM data won't fit, BMS adds the trailer data, writes the page to temporary storage, clears the page, and then adds the header data and the FROM data to the new page.

For BMS overflow processing to work, each header and trailer area must begin with a four-byte prefix that contains control information. In figure 6-7, the header area's prefix is HA-PREFIX and the trailer area's is TA-PREFIX.

As you can see in figure 6-7, HA-PREFIX contains three fields. The first is a two-byte length field (PIC S9(4) COMP) that defines the length of the header or trailer area, *not* including the four-byte prefix. The second is a one-byte field that's used for automatic page numbering. I'll explain how you use it in a moment. The third is a one-byte FILLER item that's reserved for use by BMS. Because page numbering isn't required in TA-PREFIX, I defined it with just two fields: the length field and a two-byte FILLER item.

After the four-byte prefix, you code the header or trailer data—as many bytes as you specify in the prefix's length field. To indicate line endings in a header or trailer, you use new-line characters just as you do in the FROM area.

Automatic page numbering   If you specify a non-blank value in the page-numbering field (byte 3) of a header or trailer prefix, BMS automatically numbers output pages for you. When an overflow situation occurs, BMS scans the header or trailer data until it finds one or more occurrences of the character you specify in byte 3 of the prefix. Then, it replaces those characters with the current page number.

In figure 6-7, I specified an asterisk (*) in the VALUE clause of HA-PAGE-CODE. Then, in the data portion of the header area, I coded three consecutive asterisks to indicate where the page numbers should go. As a result, BMS replaces those three asterisks with the page number. You can use any character that's part of the standard COBOL character set for a page code, other than HIGH-VALUE. And you can use up to five bytes for the page number. When you specify a page code

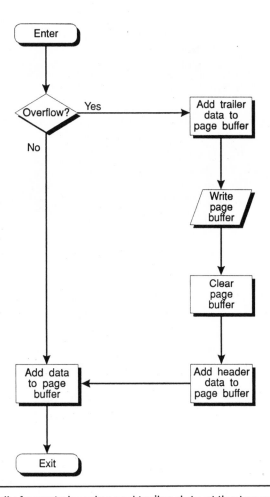

Figure 6-10 BMS automatically formats header and trailer data at the top and bottom of each page

in a header or trailer area, make sure that character doesn't appear anywhere in that area other than where you want the page number.

The SEND TEXT commands in modules 2200 and 3000   Now that you know how the SEND TEXT command works, you should have little trouble understanding modules 2200 and 3000 in figure 6-7. After module 2200 moves product data to the fields of PRODUCT-LINE, it issues this SEND TEXT command:

```
EXEC CICS
    SEND TEXT FROM(PRODUCT-LINE)
              ACCUM
              PAGING
              ERASE
              HEADER(HEADER-AREA)
              TRAILER(TRAILER-AREA)
END-EXEC.
```

This command adds a product line to the logical message. If the product line won't fit on the current page, the trailer data in TRAILER-AREA is added to the bottom of the page, the page is written to temporary storage, the header information in HEADER-AREA is added to the top of the next page, and the product line is added as the first detail line of that page. Because the prefix in HEADER-AREA specifies page numbering, BMS automatically numbers each page.

The SEND TEXT command in module 3000 is similar to the one in module 2200, but instead of sending a product line, it sends a total line. Notice that I omitted the HEADER and TRAILER options. That way, the final total line always appears on the same page as the last detail line. And, there's always enough room on that page for the total line because the SEND TEXT command in module 2200 reserves two lines for a trailer area, which isn't printed on the last page.

The SEND PAGE command

The SEND PAGE command serves two purposes. First, it insures that the last page of data is written to temporary storage even if it's not complete. And second, it lets you specify when the user can retrieve the message by issuing message retrieval commands. As a result, you should always code a SEND PAGE command after the last SEND TEXT command in your program. (The program in figure 6-7 issues a SEND PAGE command from module 0000 just before it ends.)

Figure 6-11 gives the format of the SEND PAGE command. You normally code it like this:

```
EXEC CICS
    SEND PAGE
        OPERPURGE
END-EXEC
```

The OPERPURGE option tells BMS that a user must explicitly purge the message by entering a termination command (like T/B). If you omit the OPERPURGE option, BMS purges the message as soon as the user enters anything that's not a valid message retrieval command. Since it's easy for a user to make a keying mistake, I recommend you always code OPERPURGE so the user doesn't accidentally purge your message.

Two other SEND PAGE command options determine when the user can view the message. If you specify the RETAIN option, the BMS page retrieval program is immediately invoked via the equivalent of a LINK command. Then, when the user has finished viewing the message, control returns to the statement that immediately follows the SEND PAGE command. If you specify RELEASE, the BMS page retrieval program is immediately invoked using the equivalent of an XCTL command. In that case, control never returns to your application program. If you omit both RETAIN and RELEASE, as I did in figure 6-7, the BMS page retrieval program is started as a separate task as soon as

The SEND PAGE command

```
EXEC CICS
    SEND PAGE [ OPERPURGE ]
              [ RETAIN | RELEASE ]
END-EXEC
```

Explanation

OPERPURGE   Specifies that the operator must issue a message termination command to delete the logical message. If you omit OPERPURGE, the message is automatically deleted when the operator enters anything that's not a message retrieval command.

RETAIN   Specifies that the page retrieval program is immediately invoked so the user can retrieve the pages. Control returns to the application program when the user finishes viewing the message.

RELEASE   Specifies that the page retrieval program is invoked immediately so the user can retrieve the pages. Control never returns to the application program.

Note: If both RETAIN and RELEASE are omitted, control returns immediately to the application program. Then, the page retrieval program is started automatically as a separate task as soon as the current task ends.

Figure 6-11 The SEND PAGE command

the current task finishes. So control returns to your program immediately after the SEND PAGE command is executed.

The product listing program: SEND MAP version

Now that you know how to use the SEND TEXT command to create a logical message, I'll present another version of the product listing program, this time using the SEND MAP command. To use the SEND MAP technique, you must do two things. First, you must create a BMS mapset that defines the maps that make up your logical message. You do that using the same BMS macro instructions you use for a non-message building program, with additional parameters on the DFHMDI macro. Second, you code your application program using the SEND MAP command to build the logical message and the SEND PAGE command to complete it.

The mapset: DFHMDI parameters for message building

Figure 6-12 shows the mapset I created for the product listing program. (The screen layout is in figure 6-5.) If you study this mapset for a moment, you'll see that it consists of four maps, each defined by a DFHMDI macro instruction. There's one map for the report's five-line header, one for the detail line, one for the two-line trailer, and one for the final total line.

The DFHMDI macros shaded in figure 6-12 present some new elements. Since none of the other macro instructions in this mapset require new coding elements, I'll concentrate on just the DFHMDI macro instruction.

Figure 6-13 shows the format of the DFHMDI macro and the parameters you code on it to produce a logical message. The label on the DFHMDI macro instruction is the name of the map (it must be unique within a mapset). If your installation has standards for forming map names, by all means follow them. In figure 6-12, I simply numbered the maps: LSTMAP1, LSTMAP2, LSTMAP3, and LSTMAP4.

The SIZE parameter   The SIZE parameter tells BMS the number of lines and columns in the map. The number of lines you specify depends on the number of lines required by your header, detail, or trailer area. For example, the header area in figure 6-5 requires five lines (lines 2 and 5 are blank). As a result, I specify SIZE=(5,80) in the DFHMDI macro for LSTMAP1 in figure 6-12.

The LINE, COLUMN, and JUSTIFY parameters   You use the next three parameters—LINE, COLUMN, and JUSTIFY—to specify the starting position within the current page for each map. For a non-message building program, you usually code a specific line number in the LINE parameter. Although you can do that in a mapset for a message building application, it's uncommon. You're more likely to use LINE=NEXT, JUSTIFY=FIRST, or JUSTIFY=LAST to position a map that's part of a logical message.

If you code LINE=NEXT, your map is positioned on the next line of the page. You usually code LINE=NEXT for a detail map. That way, detail maps are positioned on successive lines. In figure 6-12, I specified LINE=NEXT for the product detail map (LSTMAP2). I also coded LINE=NEXT for the final total map so it will follow the last detail map.

If you code JUSTIFY=FIRST, the map is placed at the beginning of the next page. You usually code JUSTIFY=FIRST for a header map, as I did for LSTMAP1 in figure 6-12. The effect of JUSTIFY=FIRST is similar to coding LINE=1 and COLUMN=1. The difference is that when you code JUSTIFY=FIRST, data in the page buffer is automatically written to temporary storage before any new data is added. In contrast, the combination LINE=1 and COLUMN=1 doesn't cause the page buffer to be automatically written to temporary storage. So always specify JUSTIFY=FIRST rather than LINE=1 and COLUMN=1 on your header maps.

As you might expect, JUSTIFY=LAST has the opposite effect of JUSTIFY=FIRST: It causes the map to be positioned at the bottom of the current page. Normally, you'll code JUSTIFY=LAST for trailer maps. In figure 6-12, I specified JUSTIFY=LAST for LSTMAP3.

Don't let the vertical orientation of the JUSTIFY parameter confuse you. If you're like me, you normally think of justification in horizontal

```
          PRINT NOGEN
LSTSET1   DFHMSD TYPE=&SYSPARM,                                          X
                 LANG=COBOL,                                             X
                 MODE=INOUT,                                             X
                 TERM=3270-2,                                            X
                 CTRL=FREEKB,                                            X
                 STORAGE=AUTO,                                           X
                 TIOAPFX=YES
***************************************************************************
***************************************************************************
LSTMAP1   DFHMDI SIZE=(5,80),                                            X
                 JUSTIFY=FIRST,                                          X
                 HEADER=YES
***************************************************************************
          DFHMDF POS=(1,16),                                            X
                 LENGTH=15,                                             X
                 ATTRB=(NORM,PROT),                                     X
                 INITIAL='Product Listing'
          DFHMDF POS=(1,49),                                            X
                 LENGTH=5,                                              X
                 ATTRB=(NORM,PROT),                                     X
                 INITIAL='Page:'
PAGENO    DFHMDF POS=(1,55),                                            X
                 LENGTH=3,                                              X
                 ATTRB=(NORM,PROT),                                     X
                 PICOUT='ZZ9'
          DFHMDF POS=(3,1),                                             X
                 LENGTH=7,                                              X
                 ATTRB=(NORM,PROT),                                     X
                 INITIAL='Product'
          DFHMDF POS=(3,43),                                            X
                 LENGTH=15,                                             X
                 ATTRB=(NORM,PROT),                                     X
                 INITIAL='Unit      Quantity'
          DFHMDF POS=(4,1),                                             X
                 LENGTH=23,                                             X
                 ATTRB=(NORM,PROT),                                     X
                 INITIAL='Code           Description'
          DFHMDF POS=(4,42),                                            X
                 LENGTH=16,                                             X
                 ATTRB=(NORM,PROT),                                     X
                 INITIAL='Price       On Hand'
***************************************************************************
***************************************************************************
LSTMAP2   DFHMDI SIZE=(1,80),                                            X
                 LINE=NEXT,                                              X
                 COLUMN=1
***************************************************************************
PCODE     DFHMDF POS=(1,1),                                             X
                 LENGTH=10,                                             X
                 ATTRB=(NORM,PROT)
DESCR     DFHMDF POS=(1,13),                                            X
                 LENGTH=20,                                             X
                 ATTRB=(NORM,PROT)
UPRICE    DFHMDF POS=(1,35),                                            X
                 LENGTH=12,                                             X
                 ATTRB=(NORM,PROT),                                     X
                 PICOUT='Z,ZZZ,ZZ9.99'
ONHAND    DFHMDF POS=(1,49),                                            X
                 LENGTH=9,                                              X
                 ATTRB=(NORM,PROT),                                     X
                 PICOUT='Z,ZZZ,ZZ9'
```

Figure 6-12 Mapset listing for the product listing program (SEND MAP) (part 1 of 2)

```
****************************************************************
****************************************************************
LSTMAP3   DFHMDI SIZE=(2,80),                                  X
                 JUSTIFY=LAST,                                 X
                 TRAILER=YES
****************************************************************
          DFHMDF POS=(2,1),                                    X
                 LENGTH=25,                                    X
                 ATTRB=(NORM,PROT),                            X
                 INITIAL='Continued on next page...'
****************************************************************
****************************************************************
LSTMAP4   DFHMDI SIZE=(2,80),                                  X
                 LINE=NEXT,                                    X
                 COLUMN=1,                                     X
                 TRAILER=YES
****************************************************************
COUNT     DFHMDF POS=(2,1),                                    X
                 LENGTH=6,                                     X
                 ATTRB=(NORM,PROT),                            X
                 PICOUT='ZZ,ZZ9'
          DFHMDF POS=(2,8),                                    X
                 LENGTH=28,                                    X
                 ATTRB=(NORM,PROT),                            X
                 INITIAL='records in the product file.'
****************************************************************
          DFHMSD TYPE=FINAL
          END
```

Figure 6-12 Mapset listing for the product listing program (SEND MAP) (part 2 of 2)

terms—that is, left or right justification. Although you can specify other values for the JUSTIFY parameter, you're most likely to use the vertical justification provided by JUSTIFY=FIRST and JUSTIFY=LAST.

Within a map, fields you define with a DFHMDF macro are positioned relative to the beginning of the map, without regard for how the map is positioned within the page. For example, suppose you define a field like this:

```
FIELD1      DFHMDF POS=(2,25),
                   LENGTH=5,
                   ATTRB=PROT
```

Then, if you specify JUSTIFY=FIRST in the DFHMDI macro, FIELD1 is displayed at column 25 of line 2. But if you specify LINE=NEXT and the next line is line 10, FIELD1 is displayed at column 25 of the line 11; that's position (2,25) relative to the start of the map.

The HEADER and TRAILER parameters   You use the HEADER and TRAILER parameters for header and trailer maps. For a header map, code HEADER=YES. And for a trailer map, code TRAILER=YES.

The HEADER and TRAILER parameters have nothing to do with map positioning. In other words, HEADER=YES doesn't mean that the map is automatically placed at the top of a new page. Nor does

The DFHMDI macro

```
name      DFHMDI    SIZE=(lines,columns),
          [ LINE= {line-number}, ]
                   {NEXT        }
          [ COLUMN=column-number, ]
          [ JUSTIFY= {FIRST}, ]
                     {LAST }
          [ {HEADER=YES }]
            {TRAILER=YES}
```

Explanation

SIZE	Specifies the size of the map in lines and columns.
LINE	Specifies the position of the first line of the map. If you code a line number, the map is positioned at the line you specify. If you code LINE=NEXT, the map is positioned starting at the next available line.
COLUMN	Specifies the starting column number for the map.
JUSTIFY	Specifies that the map should be aligned with one of the page margins. If you code JUSTIFY=FIRST, the map is placed at the top of a new page. If you code JUSTIFY=LAST, the map is placed at the bottom of the current page. If you use JUSTIFY, do not use LINE or COLUMN.
HEADER	If you code HEADER=YES, the map is treated as a header map.
TRAILER	If you code TRAILER=YES, the map is treated as a trailer map.

Figure 6-13 The DFHMDI macro

TRAILER=YES cause a map to be placed at the bottom of a page. It's the JUSTIFY parameter that controls positioning for header and trailer maps. The purpose of the HEADER and TRAILER parameters is to control overflow processing.

You'll learn the details of SEND MAP overflow processing in a moment. For now, though, I want you to understand two things. First, each time your program sends a detail map (one that doesn't specify HEADER=YES or TRAILER=YES), BMS makes sure there's enough room on the current page for both the map that's being sent *and* the largest trailer map (TRAILER=YES) in the mapset. If there is, the detail map is added to the page, but if there isn't, an overflow situation occurs.

When an overflow occurs, the detail map isn't added to the page. Instead, BMS raises the OVERFLOW condition, which you can detect using response code checking. It's then up to the program to send trailer and header maps to complete the current page and begin a new one; BMS doesn't automatically send those lines like it does when you use the SEND TEXT command. Then, after the new page has been started, the program must reissue the SEND MAP command for the detail line.

The second point I want you to understand is that the OVERFLOW condition is never raised when you send a header or trailer map. So once OVERFLOW occurs, you can send as many header or trailer maps as you wish without worrying about OVERFLOW occurring again. BMS begins checking again for page overflow as soon as you send a map that doesn't specify HEADER=YES or TRAILER=YES.

Incidentally, you don't have to code a trailer map at all if your program doesn't require a trailer area. In that case, the size of the trailer area is zero, so the OVERFLOW condition isn't raised until detail lines reach the bottom of the page.

The symbolic map

Figure 6-14 shows the symbolic map for the product listing mapset. There's nothing unusual about this symbolic map. However, notice that the only entry for LSTMAP3 is the 12-byte control field. That's because the trailer map doesn't contain data that's sent from the application program.

The program: SEND MAP options for message building

Figures 6-15 and 6-16 present the SEND MAP version of the product listing program. The structure chart, shown in figure 6-15, is similar to the structure chart for the SEND TEXT version presented earlier in this topic. The only difference is that I provided modules to send header and trailer information, since that's *not* done automatically when you use the SEND MAP command. Notice that module 2230 is invoked from module 0000 at the start of the program. That way, the header map for the first page of the logical message is sent before any detail maps are sent.

Figure 6-16 gives the source listing for the product listing program. Because most of this program is the same as the SEND TEXT version, I'll focus on module 2200 and its subordinates and on module 3000. Those are the modules that contain the program's message building functions.

This program uses four SEND MAP commands: one for each map in the program's mapset. The SEND MAP command in module 2210 sends a product detail map, the ones in modules 2220 and 2230 send trailer and header maps, and the one in module 3000 sends the total map.

Figure 6-17 gives the format of the SEND MAP command. It's similar to the format given in figure 6-16 of *Part 1: An Introductory Course*. But I've added two options (ACCUM and PAGING) that you

```
01  LSTMAP1I.
    02    FILLER    PIC X(12).
    02    PAGENOL   PIC S9(4) COMP.
    02    PAGENOF   PIC X.
    02    FILLER REDEFINES PAGENOF.
     03   PAGENOA   PIC X.
    02    PAGENOI   PIC X(0003).
01  LSTMAP1O REDEFINES LSTMAP1I.
    02    FILLER    PIC X(12).
    02    FILLER    PIC X(3).
    02    PAGENOO   PIC ZZ9.
01  LSTMAP2I.
    02    FILLER    PIC X(12).
    02    PCODEL    PIC S9(4) COMP.
    02    PCODEF    PIC X.
    02    FILLER REDEFINES PCODEF.
     03   PCODEA    PIC X.
    02    PCODEI    PIC X(0010).
    02    DESCRL    PIC S9(4) COMP.
    02    DESCRF    PIC X.
    02    FILLER REDEFINES DESCRF.
     03   DESCRA    PIC X.
    02    DESCRI    PIC X(0020).
    02    UPRICEL   PIC S9(4) COMP.
    02    UPRICEF   PIC X.
    02    FILLER REDEFINES UPRICEF.
     03   UPRICEA   PIC X.
    02    UPRICEI   PIC X(0012).
    02    ONHANDL   PIC S9(4) COMP.
    02    ONHANDF   PIC X.
    02    FILLER REDEFINES ONHANDF.
     03   ONHANDA   PIC X.
    02    ONHANDI   PIC X(0009).
01  LSTMAP2O REDEFINES LSTMAP2I.
    02    FILLER    PIC X(12).
    02    FILLER    PIC X(3).
    02    PCODEO    PIC X(0010).
    02    FILLER    PIC X(3).
    02    DESCRO    PIC X(0020).
    02    FILLER    PIC X(3).
    02    UPRICEO   PIC Z,ZZZ,ZZ9.99.
    02    FILLER    PIC X(3).
    02    ONHANDO   PIC Z,ZZZ,ZZ9.
01  LSTMAP3I.
    02    FILLER    PIC X(12).
01  LSTMAP3O REDEFINES LSTMAP3I.
    02    FILLER    PIC X(12).
01  LSTMAP4I.
    02    FILLER    PIC X(12).
    02    COUNTL    PIC S9(4) COMP.
    02    COUNTF    PIC X.
    02    FILLER REDEFINES COUNTF.
     03   COUNTA    PIC X.
    02    COUNTI    PIC X(0006).
01  LSTMAP4O REDEFINES LSTMAP4I.
    02    FILLER    PIC X(12).
    02    FILLER    PIC X(3).
    02    COUNTO    PIC ZZ,ZZ9.
```

Figure 6-14 Symbolic map for the product listing program (SEND MAP)

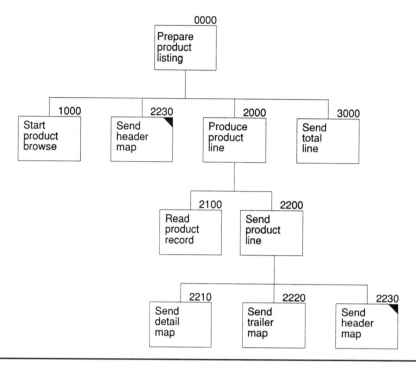

Figure 6-15 Structure chart for the product listing program (SEND MAP)

code to build messages. And I've dropped two (ERASEAUP and CURSOR) because they aren't used for message building.

The ACCUM and PAGING options You use the ACCUM and PAGING options together to indicate that a SEND MAP command is used to build a logical message. ACCUM means that data isn't sent immediately to the terminal; instead, it's accumulated in the page buffer until an entire page has been built. And PAGING means that when the page buffer is full, it's written to temporary storage rather than sent to the terminal. So the combined effect of ACCUM and PAGING is that pages of a logical message are built and stored in temporary storage.

Overflow processing As I've already mentioned, the SEND MAP command does *not* automatically format headers and trailers as the SEND TEXT command does. Instead, it raises the OVERFLOW condition whenever a map won't fit on the current page, allowing for the largest trailer map in the mapset.

By testing for the OVERFLOW condition, your program can detect page overflow and invoke an *overflow routine* to send trailer and header maps. As you can see in figure 6-16, I test for OVERFLOW immediately after issuing the SEND MAP command in module 2210.

When an OVERFLOW condition occurs, it means that just enough space remains in the page buffer for a trailer map. As a result, you

```
        IDENTIFICATION DIVISION.
    *
        PROGRAM-ID. PROLST2.
    *
        ENVIRONMENT DIVISION.
    *
        DATA DIVISION.
    *
        WORKING-STORAGE SECTION.
    *
        01  SWITCHES.
    *
            05  PRODUCT-EOF-SW       PIC X       VALUE 'N'.
                88  PRODUCT-EOF                  VALUE 'Y'.
            05  PAGE-OVERFLOW-SW      PIC X       VALUE 'N'.
                88  PAGE-OVERFLOW                VALUE 'Y'.
    *
        01  WORK-FIELDS.
    *
            05  RECORD-COUNT        PIC S9(5)  VALUE ZERO  COMP-3.
            05  PAGE-NO             PIC S9(3)  VALUE 1     COMP-3.
    *
        COPY LSTSET1.
    *
        COPY PRODUCT.
    *
        PROCEDURE DIVISION.
    *
        0000-PRODUCE-PRODUCT-LISTING.
    *
            MOVE LOW-VALUE TO LSTMAP10
                             LSTMAP20
                             LSTMAP40.
            PERFORM 1000-START-PRODUCT-BROWSE.
            PERFORM 2230-SEND-HEADER-MAP.
            PERFORM 2000-PRODUCE-PRODUCT-LINE
                UNTIL PRODUCT-EOF.
            PERFORM 3000-SEND-TOTAL-MAP.
            EXEC CICS
                SEND PAGE
                    OPERPURGE
            END-EXEC.
            EXEC CICS
                RETURN
            END-EXEC.
```

Figure 6-16 Source listing for the product listing program (SEND MAP) (part 1 of 4)

should issue a SEND MAP command for the trailer map to complete the page. Then, you should start a new page by issuing a SEND MAP command for your header map. That writes the old page to temporary storage, clears the page buffer, and adds your header map. Since the detail map specified in the original SEND MAP command was never actually sent, you should issue another SEND MAP command to place the detail map on the new page.

Look now at how the program in figure 6-16 provides for overflow processing. After moving fields to the symbolic map, module 2200

```
/
 1000-START-PRODUCT-BROWSE.
*
     MOVE LOW-VALUE TO PRM-PRODUCT-CODE.
     EXEC CICS
         STARTBR DATASET('PRODUCT')
                 RIDFLD(PRM-PRODUCT-CODE)
                 GTEQ
                 RESP(RESPONSE-CODE)
     END-EXEC.
     IF RESPONSE-CODE = DFHRESP(NOTFND)
         MOVE 'Y' TO PRODUCT-EOF-SW
     ELSE IF RESPONSE-CODE NOT = DFHRESP(NORMAL)
         GO TO 9999-TERMINATE-PROGRAM.
*
 2000-PRODUCE-PRODUCT-LINE.
*
     PERFORM 2100-READ-PRODUCT-RECORD.
     IF NOT PRODUCT-EOF
         PERFORM 2200-SEND-PRODUCT-LINE.
*
 2100-READ-PRODUCT-RECORD.
*
     EXEC CICS
         READNEXT DATASET('PRODUCT')
                  RIDFLD(PRM-PRODUCT-CODE)
                  INTO(PRODUCT-MASTER-RECORD)
                  RESP(RESPONSE-CODE)
     END-EXEC.
     IF RESPONSE-CODE = DFHRESP(NORMAL)
         ADD 1 TO RECORD-COUNT
     ELSE IF RESPONSE-CODE = DFHRESP(ENDFILE)
         MOVE 'Y' TO PRODUCT-EOF-SW
     ELSE
         GO TO 9999-TERMINATE-PROGRAM.
```

Figure 6-16   Source listing for the product listing program (SEND MAP) (part 2 of 4)

performs module 2210 to send a product detail map (LSTMAP2). Because the DFHMDI macro for LSTMAP2 specifies LINE=NEXT, detail maps are added to successive lines of each page. When a page becomes full, the overflow condition is raised. Then, the IF statement that follows the SEND MAP command sets PAGE-OVERFLOW-SW to Y to indicate that the OVERFLOW condition occurred. The real overflow processing happens in module 2200:

```
IF PAGE-OVERFLOW
    PERFORM 2220-SEND-TRAILER-MAP
    PERFORM 2230-SEND-HEADER-MAP
    PERFORM 2210-SEND-DETAIL-MAP
    MOVE 'N' TO PAGE-OVERFLOW-SW.
```

Here, three modules are invoked in sequence: module 2220 to send a trailer map, module 2230 to send a header map and start a new page, and module 2210 to send the detail map again, this time to the new page. Then, the program moves N to PAGE-OVERFLOW-SW so this

```
2200-SEND-PRODUCT-LINE.
*
    MOVE PRM-PRODUCT-CODE         TO PCODEO.
    MOVE PRM-PRODUCT-DESCRIPTION  TO DESCRO.
    MOVE PRM-UNIT-PRICE           TO UPRICEO.
    MOVE PRM-QUANTITY-ON-HAND     TO ONHANDO.
    PERFORM 2210-SEND-DETAIL-MAP.
    IF PAGE-OVERFLOW
        PERFORM 2220-SEND-TRAILER-MAP
        PERFORM 2230-SEND-HEADER-MAP
        PERFORM 2210-SEND-DETAIL-MAP
        MOVE 'N' TO PAGE-OVERFLOW-SW.
*
2210-SEND-DETAIL-MAP.
*
    EXEC CICS
        SEND MAP('LSTMAP2')
            MAPSET('LSTSET1')
            FROM(LSTMAP20)
            ACCUM
            PAGING
            ERASE
            RESP(RESPONSE-CODE)
    END-EXEC.
    IF RESPONSE-CODE = DFHRESP(OVERFLOW)
        MOVE 'Y' TO PAGE-OVERFLOW-SW
    ELSE IF RESPONSE-CODE NOT = DFHRESP(NORMAL)
        GO TO 9999-TERMINATE-PROGRAM.
*
2220-SEND-TRAILER-MAP.
*
    EXEC CICS
        SEND MAP('LSTMAP3')
            MAPSET('LSTSET1')
            MAPONLY
            ACCUM
            PAGING
            ERASE
    END-EXEC.
*
2230-SEND-HEADER-MAP.
*
    MOVE PAGE-NO TO PAGENOO.
    EXEC CICS
        SEND MAP('LSTMAP1')
            MAPSET('LSTSET1')
            FROM(LSTMAP10)
            ACCUM
            PAGING
            ERASE
    END-EXEC.
    ADD 1 TO PAGE-NO.
```

Figure 6-16 Source listing for the product listing program (SEND MAP) (Part 3 of 4)

```
    /
    3000-SEND-TOTAL-MAP.
*
        MOVE RECORD-COUNT TO COUNTO.
        EXEC CICS
            SEND MAP('LSTMAP4')
                 MAPSET('LSTSET1')
                 FROM(LSTMAP40)
                 ACCUM
                 PAGING
                 ERASE
        END-EXEC.
*
    9999-TERMINATE-PROGRAM.
*
        MOVE EIBRESP  TO ERR-RESP.
        MOVE EIBTRNID TO ERR-TRNID.
        MOVE EIBRSRCE TO ERR-RSRCE.
        EXEC CICS
            XCTL PROGRAM('SYSERR')
                 COMMAREA(ERROR-PARAMETERS)
        END-EXEC.
```

Figure 6-16   Source listing for the product listing program (SEND MAP) (part 4 of 4)

processing won't happen again until the OVERFLOW condition is raised when the new page is filled.

Modules 2220 and 2230 contain the SEND MAP commands for the trailer and header maps. Remember, though, that the OVERFLOW condition won't occur when you send a header or trailer map. So there's no reason to provide response code checking for these commands.

Module 2230 also provides the page-numbering logic for this program. In the Working-Storage Section, I provide a field named PAGE-NO whose initial value is 1. Then, in module 2230, I move PAGE-NO to the symbolic map before I send the header map. After I send the map, I add 1 to PAGE-NO.

In module 3000, a SEND MAP command sends the total map. Because the total map specifies TRAILER=YES, though, the OVERFLOW condition isn't raised even if the page is full. (The OVERFLOW condition is never raised when you send a header or trailer map.) As a result, the total map always appears on the same page as the last detail map—never on a page by itself. There's always enough room on the page for the total map because BMS considers its size when it determines the size of the trailer area.

Discussion   Now that you've seen both versions of the product listing program, take a moment to consider the difference between the two message building techniques. Apart from whether or not a mapset is required, I think you'll agree that the way overflow processing is handled is the most

The SEND MAP command

```
EXEC CICS
    SEND    MAP(name)
        [ MAPSET(name) ]
        [ FROM(data-area) ]
        [ MAPONLY | DATAONLY ]
        [ ACCUM ]
        [ PAGING ]
        [ ERASE  ]
END-EXEC
```

Explanation

MAP	Specifies the one- to seven-character name of the map to be used to map the output data.
MAPSET	Specifies the one- to eight-character name of the mapset that contains the map. If omitted, the map name is used. This name must be defined in the Processing Program Table (PPT).
FROM	Specifies the data area from which the data to be mapped is obtained (that is, the symbolic map).
MAPONLY	Specifies that only constant data from the BMS physical map is to be sent; no FROM area is used.
DATAONLY	Specifies that data from the FROM area is to be mapped; constant data from the physical map is not to be sent.
ACCUM	Specifies that this SEND MAP command is used to build a logical message.
PAGING	Specifies that output pages should be written to temporary storage for later retrieval under operator control.
ERASE	Specifies that the terminal's buffer should be erased as each page of the message is sent during page retrieval.

Figure 6-17 The SEND MAP command

significant programming difference between the SEND TEXT and SEND MAP techniques.

The advantage of the SEND TEXT method is that you don't have to worry about sending headers or trailers; they're sent automatically whenever necessary. Unfortunately, that's also a disadvantage of the SEND TEXT method: It provides little control of overflow processing. Consider, for example, a logical message that requires a page total at the bottom of each page. With the SEND MAP command, you accumulate the page total as you send detail maps. Then, when overflow occurs, you move the page total field to the trailer map, send the trailer map, and reset the page total field to zero so it's ready for the next page. Because the SEND TEXT command gives no indication of when overflow occurs, however, there's no easy way to provide page totals when you use it.

Terms

header
trailer
new-line character
overflow processing
overflow routine

Objective

Given the specifications for a message building program, code its solution using the either the SEND TEXT command or the SEND MAP command.

Printer output and message routing

In this topic, you'll learn how to code programs that produce printer output. You'll learn how to code special printing options in the SEND TEXT and SEND MAP commands and how to use two techniques to direct messages to a printer. The first technique lets you direct a message only to the terminal your program is attached to. The second technique, called message routing, lets you direct a logical message to other terminals.

Before I go on, I want to make sure you realize that many installations do *not* use the printing features this topic presents. Instead, they use transient data queues (as I'll describe in chapter 9) or a special printing subsystem they've developed themselves or purchased from a software vendor. If that's the case in your shop, feel free to skip this topic altogether.

3270 printer concepts

To code a message building program for printer output, you need to understand the basic concepts involved when you use a 3270 printer. To begin with, all 3270 printers contain a *buffer*. As a result, data you send to a printer isn't immediately printed. Instead, it's stored in the printer's buffer and printed later. The buffer acts as intermediate storage between the host system and the printer's print mechanism. Because the host system can write data to a printer's buffer much faster than the print mechanism can print it, buffers improve the overall efficiency of a system.

There's a close relationship between a 3270 printer's buffer and the page buffer BMS uses to build pages of a logical message. When the BMS page buffer is filled, the data in it is sent to the printer's buffer. As a result, the BMS page buffer can be no larger than the printer's buffer, which is typically 1920 bytes.

In fact, the BMS page buffer size is often specified as 11 lines of 132 columns each. That way, your program can use the full width of the printer's carriage. Since standard computer forms are 66 lines long, six 11x132 page buffers correspond to one printed page, as figure 6-18 illustrates.

It's important at this point that you don't confuse message pages with printed pages. Each page of a logical message is no larger than the size of the BMS page buffer (usually 11x132 for printer output). In contrast, the size of a printed page varies depending on the form being used, but usually it's 66x132.

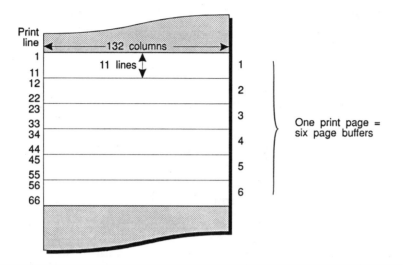

Figure 6-18　Six full 11x132 page buffers make up one printed page

As a result, you can't use the page overflow features of message building to place headers and trailers on printed pages. That's because page overflow occurs when the page buffer becomes full, without regard to when the printed page is full. Instead, you must count lines and format your own headers and trailers. The program examples in this topic show you how to do that.

Printer orders

You can control the format of printed data by inserting special control characters called *printer orders* at appropriate locations in the printer's buffer. Figure 6-19 shows the most commonly used printer orders and their hex values. To send a logical message to a printer, you need to understand how these printer orders work.

Form-feed　The *form-feed order* causes the printer to skip to the top of the next page. You use it to ensure that printed output is properly aligned on each page. In IBM literature, you'll often see the form-feed order abbreviated as *FF*. Don't confuse that with the hexadecimal value FF (decimal 256), though. It's just coincidental that the abbreviation FF is the same as a common hex value; the FF order's hex value is 0C.

The FF order actually prints as a space in position 1 of the first line of the page, so the first available print position on the page is position 2 of line 1. Form-feed is the only printer order that prints as a space, though. The other printer orders I'll describe do *not* occupy a space on the printed page.

Printer order	Abbreviation	Hex value
Form-feed	FF	0C
New-line	NL	15
Carriage-return	CR	0D
End-of-message	EM	19

Figure 6-19 Printer orders

New-line   The *new-line* (or *NL*) *order* indicates that printing should continue in the first position of the next print line. Normally, you use an NL order to mark the end of a print line. Don't confuse the new-line printer order with the BMS new-line character. You use the BMS new-line character when you build a logical message. Then, depending on how you code the commands to build the message, BMS may or may not use new-line printer orders to force line endings in the printer's buffer.

Carriage-return   The *carriage-return* (or *CR*) *order* is similar to the NL order, except that the paper doesn't advance to the next print line. Instead, the print mechanism returns to position 1 of the current line. One use of the CR order is to overprint a line. Another use is to reclaim the space printed by the FF order. If you follow an FF order with a CR order, the print mechanism returns to position 1 of line 1.

End-of-message   The *end-of-message* (or *EM*) *order* is used to mark the end of each page of data that's transmitted to the printer. Depending on how you code your message building commands, BMS may or may not add an EM order to the end of each page of your logical message. Either way, you don't need to worry about EM orders: BMS takes care of them for you.

How to send a message directly to a printer

One way to send a logical message to a printer is to attach the message building task directly to the printer. Then, the pages of your message are sent directly to the printer's buffer as they're completed. To attach a task to a printer, you use an interval control START command.

In chapter 10, I'll describe interval control and the START command in detail. For now, I just want you to know that a START command initiates a task much the same way as entering a transaction identifier at a display terminal does. When you enter a trans-id at a display terminal, a task is initiated and attached to that terminal. Then, any terminal output from the task is directed to the terminal that initiated

A SEND TEXT command with printer options

```
EXEC CICS
    SEND TEXT FROM(INVENTORY-LINE)
              LENGTH(51)
              ACCUM
              ERASE
              PRINT
              NLEOM
              FORMFEED
END-EXEC
```

A SEND MAP command with printer options

```
EXEC CICS
    SEND MAP('LSTMAP2')
         MAPSET('LSTSET1')
         ACCUM
         ERASE
         PRINT
         NLEOM
         FORMFEED
END-EXEC
```

Figure 6-20 Printer options on a SEND TEXT command and a SEND MAP command

the task. A START command also initiates a task, but the task is attached to whatever terminal you specify in the command. If you specify a printer terminal in a START command, the task is attached to that printer. Then, terminal output from the task is sent to the printer.

It's important to realize that the message building program itself doesn't issue the START command. Typically, a menu program issues a START command to initiate a message building program in response to an operator's selection. Because the message building program isn't attached to the operator's terminal, the operator can proceed with other work while the message building program executes.

Printer options of SEND MAP and SEND TEXT

BMS provides several options that affect the way a logical message is delivered to a printer. I'll describe just three of them here: PRINT, NLEOM, and FORMFEED. The others aren't used often. You can code any of them on a SEND TEXT or a SEND MAP command. There's nothing complex about the way you code these options, so I won't include another syntax diagram for the SEND TEXT or SEND MAP commands. Instead, figure 6-20 shows you how to code the PRINT, NLEOM and FORMFEED options.

The PRINT option   The PRINT option tells BMS to activate the printer's printing mechanism so the data you send will be printed. If you omit the PRINT option, data will be sent to the printer's buffer, but not

Program PROLST3

Overview Produces a printed listing of records in the product file.

Input/output specifications PRODUCT Product file

Processing specifications
1. For each record in the product file, print the product code, description, unit price, and quantity on hand. At the end of the listing, print the number of products in the file.
2. Create the listing using the BMS message building facility.

Figure 6-21 Specifications for the product listing program (SEND TEXT, printer) (part 1 of 3)

printed. So always code PRINT on each SEND TEXT or SEND MAP command you use to build a message that's intended for a printer.

The NLEOM option   The NLEOM option tells BMS to use new-line and end-of-message printer orders in the data it sends to the printer. Since that can use the printer's buffer more efficiently, I recommend you always specify NLEOM when directing output to a printer.

The FORMFEED option   The FORMFEED option tells BMS to insert a form-feed printer order in the first position of the printer buffer. As you would expect, this causes the printer to advance to the top of the next page. The form-feed order prints as a space in the first column of the first line.

A sample program

In the last topic, you saw two versions of a program that lists the records of a product file at a display terminal using a logical message: one using the SEND TEXT command, the other using the SEND MAP command. Now, I'll present another version of the product listing program. This time, a logical message is created and sent directly to a printer. For this program to work, it must be invoked by an interval control START command (probably issued by a menu program as a result of an operator selection) that attaches the program directly to a printer terminal.

Figure 6-21 gives the specifications for this program. The structure chart is shown in figure 6-22, and figure 6-23 gives the complete program listing. Since you've already seen two versions of this program, you should be familiar with its operation, so I'll just point out the highlights.

Notice that the SEND TEXT commands don't specify the HEADER and TRAILER options. That's because, as I've already mentioned, overflow processing doesn't work as you'd expect for direct printer

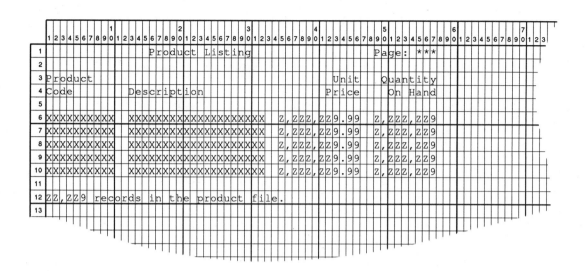

Figure 6-21 Specifications for the product listing program (SEND TEXT, printer) (part 2 of 3)

The PRODUCT copy member

```
01    PRODUCT-MASTER-RECORD.
*
      05    PRM-PRODUCT-CODE              PIC X(10).
      05    PRM-PRODUCT-DESCRIPTION       PIC X(20).
      05    PRM-UNIT-PRICE                PIC S9(7)V99    COMP-3.
      05    PRM-QUANTITY-ON-HAND          PIC S9(7)       COMP-3.
*
```

The ERRPARM copy member

```
01    ERROR-PARAMETERS.
*
      05    ERR-RESP         PIC S9(8)    COMP.
      05    ERR-RESP2        PIC S9(8)    COMP.
      05    ERR-TRNID        PIC X(4).
      05    ERR-RSRCE        PIC X(8).
*
```

Figure 6-21 Specifications for the product listing program (SEND TEXT, printer) (part 3 of 3)

output. Instead of detecting an overflow situation when a printed page is full, BMS detects overflow when the page buffer is full. If I had used the HEADER and TRAILER options in this program, headers and

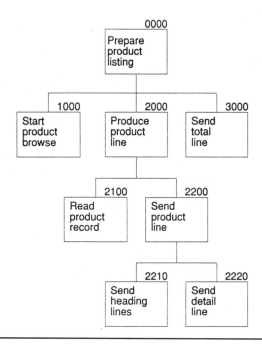

Figure 6-22 Structure chart for the product listing program (SEND TEXT, printer)

trailers would print every 11 lines instead of at the top and bottom of each 66-line page.

Rather than use BMS overflow processing, I count lines as they're added to the message. When enough lines have been added, I issue a SEND TEXT command to send heading lines. Notice that this SEND TEXT command specifies the FORMFEED option. So, before the heading lines are printed, the printer advances to the top of the next page. Remember that the form-feed order prints as a space in column 1. Thus, the first printable position on the first heading line is in column 2.

The SEND TEXT command for the product detail line is this:

```
EXEC CICS
    SEND TEXT FROM(PRODUCT-LINE)
              ACCUM
              ERASE
              PRINT
              NLEOM
END-EXEC.
```

Notice here that I omit the PAGING option. That way, the message is built with terminal disposition so it's sent directly to the printer instead of stored in temporary storage. The ACCUM option is still necessary, though, so an entire page buffer is accumulated before data is sent to the printer. The PRINT option causes the printer to print the data that's sent, and the NLEOM option tells BMS to format data using new-line and end-of-message printer orders.

```
      IDENTIFICATION DIVISION.
*
      PROGRAM-ID. PROLST3.
*
      ENVIRONMENT DIVISION.
*
      DATA DIVISION.
*
      WORKING-STORAGE SECTION.
*
      01  SWITCHES.
*
          05   PRODUCT-EOF-SW  PIC X          VALUE 'N'.
               88   PRODUCT-EOF                VALUE 'Y'.
*
      01  PRINT-FIELDS.
*
          05   LINE-COUNT      PIC S999       VALUE 50    COMP-3.
          05   LINES-ON-PAGE   PIC S999       VALUE 50    COMP-3.
          05   PAGE-NO         PIC S999       VALUE 1     COMP-3.
*
      01  WORK-FIELDS.
*
          05   RECORD-COUNT    PIC S9(5)      VALUE ZERO  COMP-3.
*
      01  RESPONSE-CODE        PIC S9(8)      COMP.
*
      01  HEADER-AREA.
*
          05   HEADER-LINE-1.
               10   FILLER        PIC X(20)   VALUE '            Produc'.
               10   FILLER        PIC X(20)   VALUE 't Listing           '.
               10   FILLER        PIC X(14)   VALUE '         Page: '.
               10   HA1-PAGE-NO   PIC ZZ9.
               10   HA1-NL        PIC XX      VALUE X'1515'.
          05   HEADER-LINE-2.
               10   FILLER        PIC X(20)   VALUE 'Product             '.
               10   FILLER        PIC X(20)   VALUE SPACE.
               10   FILLER        PIC X(17)   VALUE ' Unit    Quantity'.
               10   HA2-NL        PIC X       VALUE X'15'.
          05   HEADER-LINE-3.
               10   FILLER        PIC X(20)   VALUE 'Code          Descript'.
               10   FILLER        PIC X(20)   VALUE 'ion                 '.
               10   FILLER        PIC X(17)   VALUE ' Price    On Hand'.
               10   HA3-NL        PIC XX      VALUE X'1515'.
*
      01  PRODUCT-LINE.
*
          05   PL-PRODUCT-CODE  PIC X(10).
          05   FILLER           PIC XX         VALUE SPACE.
          05   PL-DESCRIPTION   PIC X(20).
          05   FILLER           PIC XX         VALUE SPACE.
          05   PL-UNIT-PRICE    PIC Z,ZZZ,ZZZ.99.
          05   FILLER           PIC XX         VALUE SPACE.
          05   PL-QUANTITY      PIC Z,ZZZ,ZZ9.
          05   PL-NL            PIC X          VALUE X'15'.
```

Figure 6-23 Source listing for the product listing program (SEND TEXT, printer) (part 1 of 3)

```
/
 01   TOTAL-LINE.
*
     05   TL-NL              PIC X         VALUE X'15'.
     05   TL-RECORD-COUNT    PIC ZZ,ZZ9.
     05   FILLER             PIC X(15)  VALUE ' records in the'.
     05   FILLER             PIC X(15)  VALUE ' product file. '.
*
 COPY PRODUCT.
*
 COPY ERRPARM.
*
 PROCEDURE DIVISION.
*
 0000-PRODUCE-PRODUCT-LISTING.
*
     PERFORM 1000-START-PRODUCT-BROWSE.
     PERFORM 2000-PRODUCE-PRODUCT-LINE
         UNTIL PRODUCT-EOF.
     PERFORM 3000-SEND-TOTAL-LINE.
     EXEC CICS
         SEND PAGE
     END-EXEC.
     EXEC CICS
         RETURN
     END-EXEC.
*
 1000-START-PRODUCT-BROWSE.
*
     MOVE LOW-VALUE TO PRM-PRODUCT-CODE.
     EXEC CICS
         STARTBR DATASET('PRODUCT')
                 RIDFLD(PRM-PRODUCT-CODE)
                 GTEQ
                 RESP(RESPONSE-CODE)
     END-EXEC.
     IF RESPONSE-CODE = DFHRESP(NOTFND)
         MOVE 'Y' TO PRODUCT-EOF-SW
     ELSE IF RESPONSE-CODE NOT = DFHRESP(NORMAL)
         GO TO 9999-TERMINATE-PROGRAM.
*
 2000-PRODUCE-PRODUCT-LINE.
*
     PERFORM 2100-READ-PRODUCT-RECORD.
     IF NOT PRODUCT-EOF
         PERFORM 2200-SEND-PRODUCT-LINE.
*
 2100-READ-PRODUCT-RECORD.
*
     EXEC CICS
         READNEXT DATASET('PRODUCT')
                  RIDFLD(PRM-PRODUCT-CODE)
                  INTO(PRODUCT-MASTER-RECORD)
                  RESP(RESPONSE-CODE)
     END-EXEC.
     IF RESPONSE-CODE = DFHRESP(NORMAL)
         ADD 1 TO RECORD-COUNT
     ELSE IF RESPONSE-CODE = DFHRESP(ENDFILE)
         MOVE 'Y' TO PRODUCT-EOF-SW
     ELSE
         GO TO 9999-TERMINATE-PROGRAM.
```

Figure 6-23 Source listing for the product listing program (SEND TEXT, printer) (part 2 of 3)

```
/
 2200-SEND-PRODUCT-LINE.
*
     IF LINE-COUNT = LINES-ON-PAGE
         PERFORM 2210-SEND-HEADING-LINES.
     PERFORM 2220-SEND-DETAIL-LINE.
*
 2210-SEND-HEADING-LINES.
*
     MOVE PAGE-NO TO HA1-PAGE-NO.
     EXEC CICS
         SEND TEXT FROM(HEADER-AREA)
                   ACCUM
                   ERASE
                   PRINT
                   NLEOM
                   FORMFEED
     END-EXEC.
     MOVE ZERO TO LINE-COUNT.
     ADD 1 TO PAGE-NO.
*
 2220-SEND-DETAIL-LINE.
*
     MOVE PRM-PRODUCT-CODE        TO PL-PRODUCT-CODE.
     MOVE PRM-PRODUCT-DESCRIPTION TO PL-DESCRIPTION.
     MOVE PRM-UNIT-PRICE          TO PL-UNIT-PRICE.
     MOVE PRM-QUANTITY-ON-HAND    TO PL-QUANTITY.
     EXEC CICS
         SEND TEXT FROM(PRODUCT-LINE)
                   ACCUM
                   ERASE
                   PRINT
                   NLEOM
     END-EXEC.
     ADD 1 TO LINE-COUNT.
*
 3000-SEND-TOTAL-LINE.
*
     MOVE RECORD-COUNT TO TL-RECORD-COUNT.
     EXEC CICS
         SEND TEXT FROM(TOTAL-LINE)
                   ACCUM
                   ERASE
                   PRINT
                   NLEOM
     END-EXEC.
*
 9999-TERMINATE-PROGRAM.
*
     MOVE EIBRESP  TO ERR-RESP.
     MOVE EIBTRNID TO ERR-TRNID.
     MOVE EIBRSRCE TO ERR-RSRCE.
     EXEC CICS
         XCTL PROGRAM('SYSERR')
              COMMAREA(ERROR-PARAMETERS)
     END-EXEC.
```

Figure 6-23 Source listing for the product listing program (SEND TEXT, printer) (part 3 of 3)

When you build a logical message for a printer, you must still use a SEND PAGE command to force out the last page of the message. Note, however, that I omitted the OPERPURGE option from the SEND PAGE command in module 0000. That option isn't necessary; because the message is never placed in temporary storage, there's no need to delete it.

Message routing

A second way to direct output to a printer is to use a BMS feature called *message routing*. Quite simply, message routing lets you direct a logical message to a terminal other than the one your program is attached to. Using message routing, an operator can invoke a program that routes a message to a printer. It's not necessary to use an interval control START command to attach the message building task to the printer.

Although you can use message routing to direct a logical message to another display terminal, it's more common to route a message to one or more printers. To do that, you use the SEND TEXT and SEND MAP printer options you've already learned: PRINT and NLEOM. Since the routed message must be stored in temporary storage before it's routed to other terminals, you must also specify the PAGING option on the SEND TEXT or SEND MAP commands that build the message. And, you must issue a ROUTE command to tell BMS what terminals will receive the message.

The ROUTE command

Figure 6-24 gives the format of the ROUTE command. Its options name the terminals where a logical message is sent (LIST) and indicate when the message should be delivered (INTERVAL or TIME). Note also that the NLEOM option is required on a ROUTE command if you want the message to include new-line and end-of-message printer orders.

The LIST option   The LIST option specifies the data name for a working-storage table called a *route list*. The route list identifies the terminals you want your message routed to. Figure 6-25 shows a typical route list that sets up two routed printers: one named L1P1, the other named L2P5. As you can see, the route list consists of one or more 16-byte entries, each identifying one terminal. The entire list is ended by a binary halfword field (PIC S9(4) COMP) that's initialized to -1.

The format of each route list entry is simple: The first four bytes supply the terminal-id of the terminal where your message is routed; the other 12 bytes are FILLER data initialized to spaces. Actually, you can put other identifying information in the FILLER area, but it's used only when you're sending messages to specific terminal operators or unusual devices. For routing a message to a 3270 printer, you don't need to use this area.

The ROUTE command

```
EXEC CICS
    ROUTE   LIST(data-name)
           {INTERVAL(hhmmss)}
           {TIME(hhmmss)    }
          [ NLEOM ]
END-EXEC
```

Explanation

LIST   Specifies a list of terminals where the logical message should be routed.

INTERVAL   Specifies a time interval that must elapse before the message is delivered.

TIME   Specifies that the message should be delivered at the specified time of day.

NLEOM   Specifies that BMS should use NL and EM printer orders as it builds the logical
                    message.

Figure 6-24 The ROUTE command

The INTERVAL and TIME options   You use the ROUTE command's INTERVAL and TIME options to indicate when a message should be delivered. INTERVAL says to deliver the message after a certain period of time has passed, and TIME says to deliver the message at a specific time of day.

You specify the time or interval value in the form *hhmmss*, where *hh* is hours, *mm* is minutes, and *ss* is seconds. So, to deliver a message in twenty minutes, you code this ROUTE command:

```
EXEC CICS
    ROUTE LIST(ROUTE-LIST)
          INTERVAL(002000)
END-EXEC
```

And to deliver a message at 5:30 p.m., you code this ROUTE command:

```
EXEC CICS
    ROUTE LIST(ROUTE-LIST)
          TIME(173000)
END-EXEC
```

Note that you specify the time using a 24-hour clock, so 5:30 p.m. is 173000 rather than 053000.

If you omit INTERVAL and TIME or specify INTERVAL(0), the message is delivered as soon as the printer is ready for it. If yours is the only message that's been sent to the printer, it's printed immediately. But if other messages have been sent before yours, your message waits its turn.

```
 01   ROUTE-LIST.
 *
     05   LIST-ENTRY-1.
          10   LE1-TERMINAL-ID        PIC  X(4)      VALUE  'L1P1'.
          10   FILLER                 PIC  X(12)     VALUE  SPACE.
     05   LIST-ENTRY-2.
          10   LE2-TERMINAL-ID        PIC  X(4)      VALUE  'L2P5'.
          10   FILLER                 PIC  X(12)     VALUE  SPACE.
     05   FILLER                      PIC  S9(4)     VALUE  -1      COMP.
```

Figure 6-25 COBOL coding for a two-entry route list

A sample program

Figure 6-26 gives a skeleton of the coding required to send the product listing to a printer using message routing. The parts of this program that are omitted are identical to the corresponding parts of figure 6-23. As you can see, I coded the PAGING option on the SEND TEXT commands. The only other difference is the ROUTE command in module 0000 and the route list defined in the Working-Storage Section.

Discussion   In this topic, I've presented just a brief introduction to the BMS facilities for printer output. I didn't cover many of the print options you can use instead of NLEOM, and I didn't explain the complications involved when you use the SEND MAP command with non-standard forms. I've made this presentation brief because there are usually better ways to prepare printed reports under CICS, like using transient data destinations, which I'll describe in chapter 9. In any event, if you're asked to write a CICS program that prepares a logical message for a printer, this topic should be enough to get you started.

Terms

buffer   carriage-return order
printer order   CR order
form-feed order   end-of-message order
FF order   EM order
new-line order   message routing
NL order   route list

Objective

Given a programming problem that requires you to print a logical message, code an acceptable program for its solution. You may either attach the message building task directly to the printer or use message routing.

```
IDENTIFICATION DIVISION.
*
PROGRAM-ID. PROLST4.
*
ENVIRONMENT DIVISION.
*
DATA DIVISION.
*
WORKING-STORAGE SECTION.
*
        .
        .
        .
*
01  ROUTE-LIST.
*
    05  LIST-ENTRY-1.
        10  LE1-TERMINAL-ID      PIC X(4)     VALUE 'L86P'.
        10  FILLER              PIC X(12)    VALUE SPACE.
    05  FILLER                  PIC S9(4)    VALUE -1  COMP.
*
PROCEDURE DIVISION.
*
0000-PRODUCE-PRODUCT-LISTING.
*
    EXEC CICS
        ROUTE LIST(ROUTE-LIST)
            NLEOM
    END-EXEC.
    PERFORM 1000-START-PRODUCT-BROWSE.
    PERFORM 2000-PRODUCE-PRODUCT-LINE
        UNTIL PRODUCT-EOF.
    PERFORM 3000-SEND-TOTAL-LINE.
    EXEC CICS
        SEND PAGE
    END-EXEC.
    EXEC CICS
        RETURN
    END-EXEC.
*
        .
        .
        .
*
2000-PRODUCE-PRODUCT-LINE.
*
    PERFORM 2100-READ-PRODUCT-RECORD.
    IF NOT PRODUCT-EOF
        PERFORM 2200-SEND-PRODUCT-LINE.
*
```

Figure 6-26 Partial source listing for the product listing program (ROUTE) (part 1 of 2)

```
            .
            .
            .
*
 2200-SEND-PRODUCT-LINE.
*
     IF LINE-COUNT = LINES-ON-PAGE
         PERFORM 2210-SEND-HEADING-LINES.
     PERFORM 2220-SEND-DETAIL-LINE.
*
 2210-SEND-HEADING-LINES.
*
     MOVE PAGE-NO TO HA1-PAGE-NO.
     EXEC CICS
         SEND TEXT FROM(HEADER-AREA)
                   ACCUM
                   PAGING
                   ERASE
                   PRINT
                   NLEOM
                   FORMFEED
     END-EXEC.
     MOVE ZERO TO LINE-COUNT.
     ADD 1 TO PAGE-NO.
*
 2220-SEND-DETAIL-LINE.
*
     MOVE PRM-PRODUCT-CODE        TO PL-PRODUCT-CODE.
     MOVE PRM-PRODUCT-DESCRIPTION TO PL-DESCRIPTION.
     MOVE PRM-UNIT-PRICE          TO PL-UNIT-PRICE.
     MOVE PRM-QUANTITY-ON-HAND    TO PL-QUANTITY.
     EXEC CICS
         SEND TEXT FROM(PRODUCT-LINE)
                   ACCUM
                   PAGING
                   ERASE
                   PRINT
                   NLEOM
     END-EXEC.
     ADD 1 TO LINE-COUNT.
*
 3000-SEND-TOTAL-LINE.
*
     MOVE RECORD-COUNT TO TL-RECORD-COUNT.
     EXEC CICS
         SEND TEXT FROM(TOTAL-LINE)
                   ACCUM
                   PAGING
                   ERASE
                   PRINT
                   NLEOM
     END-EXEC.
*
            .
            .
            .
```

Figure 6-26 Partial source listing for the product listing program (ROUTE) (part 2 of 2)

Chapter 7

Terminal control

In *Part 1: An Introductory Course* and in chapter 6 of this book, you learned how to use Basic Mapping Support (BMS) facilities to communicate with 3270 terminals. As you know, BMS is actually an interface between your application program and CICS *terminal control*, which handles all terminal I/O. In this chapter, you'll learn how to use terminal control commands to process terminal input and output directly, without using BMS as an interface.

Before I go on, a word of caution is in order. The programming requirements for terminal control are complicated. It's unreasonable to use terminal control for a full-screen interactive program; that's what BMS is for. Even so, there are times when it's appropriate to use terminal control directly for simple programs. But because terminal control programming is so complicated, I'll present just a small subset of it in this chapter.

To illustrate how terminal control works, this chapter presents two programming examples. The first is a simple inquiry program that accepts terminal input from an operator and displays the results of the inquiry on the terminal's screen. The second is a more complicated program: It retrieves records stored in a transient data queue and prints them on a 3270 printer. (In chapter 9, you'll learn how transient data queues work and see a program that writes records to the queue processed by the print program presented here.)

A customer inquiry program

As you already know, a user can start a program by typing a transaction identifier and pressing an attention key. What you may not realize is that the user can also pass data to the program by typing additional information following the trans-id. To access this data, the program must use terminal control commands rather than BMS commands.

Figure 7-1 shows the operation of a simple inquiry program that receives data from the command line that invokes it. In part 1, the user enters this line:

```
INQ4 400001
```

Here, the trans-id is INQ4. The data that follows the trans-id, 400001, is a customer number. In part 2, you can see that the program retrieves the record for customer 400001 and displays it. Then, the program ends.

To display data for another customer, the user must clear the screen and enter another command line. As a result, this program is *not* pseudo-conversational: The operator must explicitly invoke the program to display each customer's record.

Figure 7-2 shows the complete specifications for this program, and figure 7-3 presents the structure chart. As you can see, the program has a simple structure. Module 0000 is the main control module. It first invokes module 1000 to receive the data entered by the operator—that is, the command line that contains the customer number. Then, module 0000 invokes module 2000 to read the customer's record. Assuming the customer record is found, module 0000 invokes module 3000 to send the customer's data to the terminal. If the record isn't found, module 4000 is invoked to display an error message. Module 4000 is also invoked if the operator doesn't enter a customer number or enters too much data on the command line.

Figure 7-4 gives the complete source listing for the customer inquiry program. In a moment, I'll explain some of the coding in the Data Division. For now, I want to draw your attention to the three Procedure Division commands that are shaded. The RECEIVE command (in module 1000) is similar to the RECEIVE MAP command, except no BMS mapset is used. Likewise, the SEND commands (in modules 3000 and 4000) are like the SEND MAP and SEND TEXT commands, but no BMS facilities are involved.

The RECEIVE command

Figure 7-5 gives the format of the RECEIVE command. It's coded in module 1000 of the customer inquiry program like this:

```
EXEC CICS
    RECEIVE INTO(COMMAND-LINE)
            LENGTH(COMMAND-LENGTH)
            RESP(RESPONSE-CODE)
END-EXEC.
```

Part 1

The user enters a transaction
identifier and a customer
number.

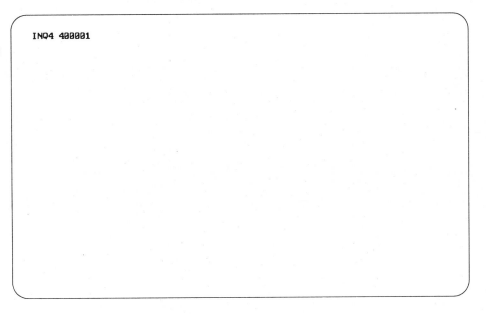

```
INQ4 400001
```

Part 2

The program retrieves the
customer's record and
displays it.

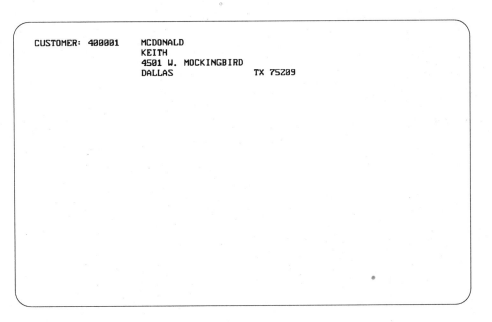

```
CUSTOMER: 400001    MCDONALD
                    KEITH
                    4501 W. MOCKINGBIRD
                    DALLAS              TX 75209
```

Figure 7-1 Operation of the customer inquiry program

Program   CUSTINQ4

Overview   Reads and displays a customer record.

Input/output specifications   CUSTMAS   Customer master file

Processing specifications

1. The user starts the inquiry program by entering the trans-id INQ4, followed by a single space and a customer number.

2. The program responds by retrieving the customer record and displaying it.

3. If the user enters too much data, doesn't enter a customer number, or enters a customer number that doesn't exist in the file, display an appropriate error message.

Figure 7-2   Specifications for the customer inquiry program (part 1 of 3)

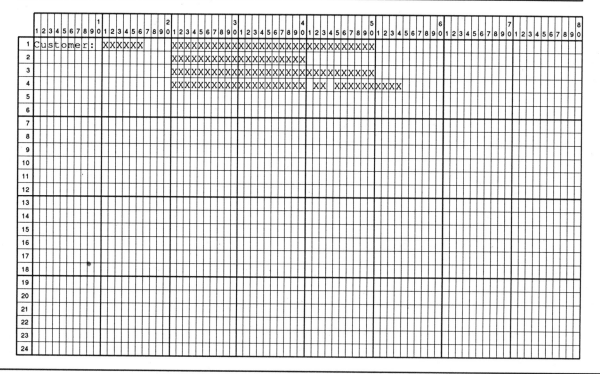

Figure 7-2   Specifications for the customer inquiry program (part 2 of 3)

The CUSTMAS copy member

```
01  CUSTOMER-MASTER-RECORD.
*
    05  CM-CUSTOMER-NUMBER      PIC X(6).
    05  CM-FIRST-NAME           PIC X(20).
    05  CM-LAST-NAME            PIC X(30).
    05  CM-ADDRESS              PIC X(30).
    05  CM-CITY                 PIC X(20).
    05  CM-STATE                PIC X(2).
    05  CM-ZIP-CODE             PIC X(10).
*
```

The ERRPARM copy member

```
01  ERROR-PARAMETERS.
*
    05  ERR-RESP        PIC S9(8)    COMP.
    05  ERR-RESP2       PIC S9(8)    COMP.
    05  ERR-TRNID       PIC X(4).
    05  ERR-RSRCE       PIC X(8).
*
```

Figure 7-2   Specifications for the customer inquiry program (part 3 of 3)

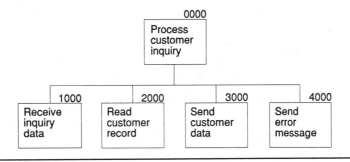

Figure 7-3   Structure chart for the customer inquiry program

The INTO option names the area where the input data is copied, in this case, COMMAND-LINE. Initially, the LENGTH field contains the length of this input area. However, after the RECEIVE command finishes, the length field contains the actual length of the received data. You should define the length field, in this case, COMMAND-LENGTH, as a halfword binary item: PIC S9(4) COMP.

The input area contains the input exactly as it's entered by the operator, including the transaction identifier that invokes the program. So if the operator enters

```
INQ4 400001
```

```
       IDENTIFICATION DIVISION.
     *
       PROGRAM-ID.  CUSTINQ4.
     *
       ENVIRONMENT DIVISION.
     *
       DATA DIVISION.
     *
       WORKING-STORAGE SECTION.
     *
       01   SWITCHES.
     *
           05   VALID-DATA-SW           PIC X        VALUE 'Y'.
                88   VALID-DATA                       VALUE 'Y'.
           05   CUSTOMER-FOUND-SW        PIC X        VALUE 'Y'.
                88   CUSTOMER-FOUND                   VALUE 'Y'.
     *
       01   RESPONSE-CODE               PIC S9(8)    COMP.
     *
       01   COMMAND-LINE.
     *
           05   CL-TRANS-ID             PIC X(4).
           05   FILLER                  PIC X.
           05   CL-CUSTOMER-NUMBER      PIC X(6).
     *
       01   COMMAND-LENGTH              PIC S9(4)    VALUE 11      COMP.
     *
       01   CUSTOMER-DATA-LINES.
     *
           05   CUSTOMER-LINE-1.
                10   FILLER             PIC X(10)    VALUE 'Customer: '.
                10   CDL-CUSTOMER-NUMBER PIC X(6).
                10   FILLER             PIC X(4)     VALUE SPACE.
                10   CDL-LAST-NAME      PIC X(30).
                10   FILLER             PIC X(30)    VALUE SPACE.
           05   CUSTOMER-LINE-2.
                10   FILLER             PIC X(20)    VALUE SPACE.
                10   CDL-FIRST-NAME     PIC X(20).
                10   FILLER             PIC X(40)    VALUE SPACE.
           05   CUSTOMER-LINE-3.
                10   FILLER             PIC X(20)    VALUE SPACE.
                10   CDL-ADDRESS        PIC X(30).
                10   FILLER             PIC X(30)    VALUE SPACE.
           05   CUSTOMER-LINE-4.
                10   FILLER             PIC X(20)    VALUE SPACE.
                10   CDL-CITY           PIC X(20).
                10   FILLER             PIC X        VALUE SPACE.
                10   CDL-STATE          PIC XX.
                10   FILLER             PIC X        VALUE SPACE.
                10   CDL-ZIP-CODE       PIC X(10).
                10   FILLER             PIC X(26)    VALUE SPACE.
     *
       01   ERROR-LINE.
     *
           05   FILLER                  PIC X        VALUE SPACE.
           05   ERROR-MESSAGE           PIC X(79).
     *
       COPY CUSTMAS.
     *
       COPY ERRPARM.
```

Figure 7-4   Source listing for the customer inquiry program (part 1 of 3)

```
/
 PROCEDURE DIVISION.
*
 0000-PROCESS-CUSTOMER-INQUIRY.
*
     PERFORM 1000-RECEIVE-INQUIRY-DATA.
     IF VALID-DATA
         PERFORM 2000-READ-CUSTOMER-RECORD
         IF CUSTOMER-FOUND
             PERFORM 3000-SEND-CUSTOMER-DATA.
     IF NOT VALID-DATA
         PERFORM 4000-SEND-ERROR-MESSAGE.
     EXEC CICS
         RETURN
     END-EXEC.
*
 1000-RECEIVE-INQUIRY-DATA.
*
     EXEC CICS
         RECEIVE INTO(COMMAND-LINE)
                 LENGTH(COMMAND-LENGTH)
                 RESP(RESPONSE-CODE)
     END-EXEC.
     IF RESPONSE-CODE = DFHRESP(NORMAL)
         IF CL-CUSTOMER-NUMBER = SPACE OR LOW-VALUE
             MOVE 'N' TO VALID-DATA-SW
             MOVE 'You must enter a customer number.'
                 TO ERROR-MESSAGE
         END-IF
     ELSE IF RESPONSE-CODE = DFHRESP(LENGERR)
         MOVE 'N' TO VALID-DATA-SW
         MOVE 'Too much data entered.' TO ERROR-MESSAGE
     ELSE
         GO TO 9999-TERMINATE-PROGRAM.
*
 2000-READ-CUSTOMER-RECORD.
*
     EXEC CICS
         READ DATASET('CUSTMAS')
              INTO(CUSTOMER-MASTER-RECORD)
              RIDFLD(CL-CUSTOMER-NUMBER)
              RESP(RESPONSE-CODE)
     END-EXEC.
     IF RESPONSE-CODE = DFHRESP(NOTFND)
         MOVE 'N' TO CUSTOMER-FOUND-SW
                     VALID-DATA-SW
         MOVE 'Customer not found.' TO ERROR-MESSAGE
     ELSE IF RESPONSE-CODE NOT = DFHRESP(NORMAL)
         GO TO 9999-TERMINATE-PROGRAM.
*
 3000-SEND-CUSTOMER-DATA.
*
     MOVE CM-CUSTOMER-NUMBER TO CDL-CUSTOMER-NUMBER.
     MOVE CM-LAST-NAME       TO CDL-LAST-NAME.
     MOVE CM-FIRST-NAME      TO CDL-FIRST-NAME.
     MOVE CM-ADDRESS         TO CDL-ADDRESS.
     MOVE CM-CITY            TO CDL-CITY.
     MOVE CM-STATE           TO CDL-STATE.
     MOVE CM-ZIP-CODE        TO CDL-ZIP-CODE.
     EXEC CICS
         SEND FROM(CUSTOMER-DATA-LINES)
              ERASE
     END-EXEC.
```

Figure 7-4   Source listing for the customer inquiry program (part 2 of 3)

```
/
 4000-SEND-ERROR-MESSAGE.
*
    EXEC CICS
        SEND FROM(ERROR-LINE)
    END-EXEC.
*
 9999-TERMINATE-PROGRAM.
*
    MOVE EIBRESP  TO ERR-RESP.
    MOVE EIBRESP2 TO ERR-RESP2.
    MOVE EIBTRNID TO ERR-TRNID.
    MOVE EIBRSRCE TO ERR-RSRCE.
    EXEC CICS
        XCTL PROGRAM('SYSERR')
             COMMAREA(ERROR-PARAMETERS)
    END-EXEC.
```

Figure 7-4   Source listing for the customer inquiry program (part 3 of 3)

that's exactly what's placed in COMMAND-LINE. If you line up the fields subordinate to COMMAND-LINE with the operator's entry, you'll see that CL-CUSTOMER-NUMBER contains 400001. The program uses this field to read the correct customer record.

The LENGERR condition   The LENGERR condition occurs whenever the operator enters more input data than will fit in your input area (as indicated by the LENGTH field). In the customer inquiry program, I provide an 11-byte input area. If the operator enters more than 11 bytes, the LENGERR condition is raised when the RECEIVE command executes.

If the LENGERR condition is detected in module 1000, the inquiry program formats an error message and sets VALID-DATA-SW to N. Then, the error message is sent by module 4000. Depending on your application's requirements, you could ignore the LENGERR condition and try to process the data that was entered. For this program, though, I consider the LENGERR condition to be an error and handle it as such.

How to detect PF keys   Like the RECEIVE MAP command, the RECEIVE command provides two methods for detecting the use of PF keys. One is to issue a HANDLE AID command before the RECEIVE command. The other is to test EIBAID, which is updated each time a RECEIVE command is executed. In general, I prefer to use the EIBAID technique.

For example, if I had wanted to ensure that the user pressed the Enter key when invoking the inquiry program, I could have added a statement like this to module 1000:

```
IF EIBAID NOT = DFHENTER
    MOVE 'N' TO VALID-DATA-SW
    MOVE 'Invalid key pressed.' TO ERROR-MESSAGE.
```

The RECEIVE command

```
EXEC CICS
    RECEIVE   INTO(data-area)
           [ LENGTH(data-area) ]
END-EXEC
```

Explanation

INTO   Specifies the area that will contain the data read from the terminal.

LENGTH   Initially, the specified field must contain the length of the input area. After the RECEIVE
                        command executes, this field contains the length of the data actually received. Must be
                        a binary halfword (PIC S9(4) COMP).

Figure 7-5   The RECEIVE command

I didn't do that, however, because it detracts from the program's usefulness. After all, if the user enters INQ4 and a valid customer number, then presses a PF key instead of the Enter key, why not just process the inquiry rather than display an error message and make the user type the command line again?

Incidentally, you should realize that a program that isn't pseudo-conversational doesn't need to test for the Clear key or the PA keys. That's because these keys don't transmit any data. So, if you enter a trans-id and press the Clear key or a PA key, the trans-id isn't sent to CICS. As a result, the program never starts.

The SEND command Figure 7-6 shows the format of the SEND command. You use it to transmit output data to a terminal. In module 3000 of the customer inquiry program, I code this SEND command:

```
EXEC CICS
    SEND FROM(CUSTOMER-DATA-LINES)
         ERASE
END-EXEC.
```

As a result, the contents of CUSTOMER-DATA-LINES are sent to the terminal, and the previous contents of the screen are erased. (If you're using the OS/VS COBOL compiler, you must also specify the length of the FROM area using the LENGTH option.)

If you'll look at the definition of CUSTOMER-DATA-LINES in the Working-Storage Section, you'll see that four display lines are defined. Notice that I padded each line with FILLER items so that it's 80-bytes long. That way, each fills an entire screen line. Although it's also possible to use control characters (called *orders*) to format output data like this, I recommend you don't. If your screen's format is complicated

The SEND command

```
EXEC CICS
    SEND    FROM(data-name)
         [ LENGTH(data-value) ]
         [ CTLCHAR(data-name) ]
         [ ERASE ]
END-EXEC
```

Explanation

FROM

Specifies the area that contains the data to be sent to the terminal.

LENGTH

Specifies the length of the FROM field. If you use a data name, it must be a binary halfword (PIC S9(4) COMP).

CTLCHAR

Specifies a one-byte alphanumeric field that contains a write control character. The recommended value for printer terminals is H.

ERASE

Specifies that the terminal's buffer should be erased.

Figure 7-6   The SEND command

---

enough to require orders, you should use BMS instead. For 3270 printers, however, orders aren't that difficult to use. You'll see an example of a printer program that uses orders in a moment.

If you don't specify the ERASE option on a SEND command, the previous screen data isn't erased and the new output data is placed at the current position of the cursor. That's what the SEND command in module 4000 of the customer inquiry program does. For example, suppose the operator enters this line:

```
INQ4 999999
```

Assuming that customer 999999 doesn't exist, module 4000 is invoked to send an error message. Since the SEND command in module 4000 does *not* specify the ERASE option, the error message is positioned at the current cursor location—that is, after the data entered by the operator. In the working-storage definition of ERROR-LINE, notice the FILLER item that defines a space in the first byte. That's included to place a space between the operator's entry and the error message. So after the error message is sent, the screen looks like this:

```
INQ4 999999 CUSTOMER NOT FOUND
```

You use the CTLCHAR option of the SEND command to supply a *write control character* (or WCC) that the 3270 uses to control output operations. For display devices, you can omit the CTLCHAR option. Later in this chapter, you'll see how to specify a write control character for a printer.

There are no exceptional conditions that are likely to occur when you issue a SEND command. As a result, I didn't code the RESP option on the SEND command in module 3000 or 4000.

The transient data print program

In chapter 9, you'll see a program that prepares a report that lists one line for each record in a product file. The product listing program directs this report to a printer by writing records to a *transient data queue* named L86P. Now, I'll present a program that reads records from the L86P queue, formats them in a 1920-byte buffer area, and sends them to a printer using a terminal control SEND command. (You may recall from chapter 6 that 1920 is the size of the buffer in most 3270 printers.)

You'll learn what transient data queues are and how they work in chapter 9. For now, you need to know that a transient data queue is a special type of sequential file. To read records sequentially from the queue, you use the READQ TD command. Records are deleted as they are read, so each record can be read only once.

In addition, you need to know that a transient data queue can be defined so that whenever a record is written to it, a task is automatically started. This feature, called *Automatic transaction initiation* or *ATI*, is the key to the transient data print program's usefulness. Whenever a report preparation program such as the product listing program presented in chapter 9 writes a report to the transient data queue, the print program is automatically started to print the records in the queue.

Figure 7-7 gives the specifications for the transient data print program. As you can see, each record in the transient data queue includes a standard ASA carriage control character in position 1 to indicate printer spacing. If the program encounters a character in position 1 other than one of those shown in figure 7-7, it assumes single spacing.

Figure 7-8 gives the structure chart for the transient data print program, and figure 7-9 gives the program's source listing. For efficiency reasons, the transient data print program formats as many print lines as possible in a 1920-byte buffer area before it issues a SEND command. Unfortunately, the processing required to do that can be confusing. So expect to spend more than a few moments studying the transient data print program if you want to understand it completely.

In the Working-Storage Section, there are three things I want you to notice. First, notice how I defined the transient data queue's input record:

```
01   PRINT-QUEUE-RECORD.
 *
     05   PRINT-CC              PIC X.
     05   PRINT-CHAR           OCCURS 132
                               INDEXED BY PRINT-INDEX
                               PIC X.
```

Program	PRTASA1
Overview	Reads records from a transient data queue and sends them to a printer.
Input/output specifications	Printer queue (transient data queue named using EIBTRMID)
Process specifications	1. This program is started automatically as an ATI task whenever a record is written to the associated transient data queue.
	2. Read and print records from the queue until the queue is empty. Then return without a trans-id.
	3. Use ASA standard control characters in the first byte of each queue record to control printer spacing. The control characters are:

blank	Skip one line before printing
0	Skip two lines before printing
-	Skip three lines before printing
1	Skip to the top of the next page before printing

Figure 7-7 Specifications for the transient data print program

After the one-byte field used for the ASA control character (for clarity, I omitted the 88-level condition names subordinate to PRINT-CC), I define a table consisting of 132 occurrences of a one-byte field named PRINT-CHAR. That way, the program can process the print data one character at a time using PRINT-INDEX as an index. The definition for the buffer area is similar. It consists of 1920 occurrences of a one-byte field named BUFFER-CHAR. So the program can process the buffer area one character at a time using BUFFER-INDEX as an index.

The second thing I want you to notice in the Working-Storage Section is the 01-level item named PRINT-ORDERS. This group contains definitions of three printer orders. The NL-ORDER (hex 15) defines a new-line order (or just NL). That causes the printer to start printing on a new line. The FF-ORDER (hex 0C) defines a form-feed order (or FF); it causes the printer to advance to the top of the next page. And the CR-ORDER (hex 0D) defines a carriage-return order (or CR); it causes the printer to return the carriage to position 1 of the current line.

The transient data print program uses printer orders to implement the spacing indicated by the ASA control character in each print record. For example, if a print record contains a 0 in column 1, the program adds two new-line orders to the buffer area. That way, the printer skips two lines before printing. Since I described printer orders in more detail in topic 3 of chapter 6, you can review that unit if you need a refresher.

The third thing I want you to notice in the Working-Storage Section is the 01-level item named WRITE-CONTROL-CHARACTER.

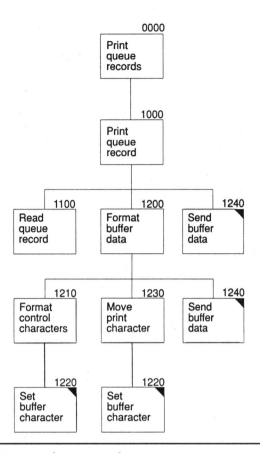

Figure 7-8   Structure chart for the transient data print program

Whenever you issue a SEND command for a printer, you must supply a write control character in the CTLCHAR option to provide control information for the printer. Normally, the write control character's value should be the letter H. That causes the printer's printing mechanism to print the buffer data you send. Incidentally, the value H has no special significance here. It just happens that the bit settings required to activate the printer correspond to that letter.

In the Procedure Division, module 0000 repeatedly invokes module 1000 to process transient data records. Module 1000, in turn, invokes module 1100 to read a queue record and module 1200 to format the record's print data into the buffer. Normally, module 1200 causes buffer data to be sent to the printer whenever necessary. When the end of the queue is reached, however, the buffer may contain data that hasn't yet been sent. In that case, module 1000 invokes module 1240 to send the buffer data.

```
        IDENTIFICATION DIVISION.
       *
        PROGRAM-ID.  PRTASA1.
       *
        ENVIRONMENT DIVISION.
       *
        DATA DIVISION.
       *
        WORKING-STORAGE SECTION.
       *
        01  SWITCHES.
       *
            05  PRINT-QUEUE-EOF-SW      PIC X        VALUE 'N'.
                88  PRINT-QUEUE-EOF                  VALUE 'Y'.
       *
        01  WORK-FIELDS.
       *
            05  BLANK-COUNT            PIC 9.
            05  SET-CHAR              PIC X.
       *
        01  RESPONSE-CODE             PIC S9(8)   COMP.
       *
        01  PRINT-QUEUE-RECORD.
       *
            05  PRINT-CC              PIC X.
                88  FORM-FEED                       VALUE '1'.
                88  SINGLE-SPACE                    VALUE ' '.
                88  DOUBLE-SPACE                    VALUE '0'.
                88  TRIPLE-SPACE                    VALUE '-'.
            05  PRINT-CHAR           OCCURS 132
                                    INDEXED BY PRINT-INDEX
                                    PIC X.
       *
        01  PRINT-RECORD-LENGTH      PIC S9(4)   COMP.
       *
        01  BUFFER-AREA.
       *
            05  BUFFER-CHAR          OCCURS 1920
                                    INDEXED BY BUFFER-INDEX
                                    PIC X.
       *
        01  PRINT-ORDERS.
       *
            05  NL-ORDER             PIC X        VALUE X'15'.
            05  FF-ORDER             PIC X        VALUE X'0C'.
            05  CR-ORDER             PIC X        VALUE X'0D'.
       *
        01  WRITE-CONTROL-CHARACTER  PIC X        VALUE 'H'.
       *
        COPY ERRPARM.
       *
        PROCEDURE DIVISION.
       *
        0000-PRINT-QUEUE-RECORDS.
       *
            MOVE LOW-VALUE TO BUFFER-AREA.
            SET BUFFER-INDEX TO 1.
            PERFORM 1000-PRINT-QUEUE-RECORD
                UNTIL PRINT-QUEUE-EOF.
            EXEC CICS
                RETURN
            END-EXEC.
```

Figure 7-9   Source listing for the transient data print program (part 1 of 3)

```
/
 1000-PRINT-QUEUE-RECORD.
*
     PERFORM 1100-READ-QUEUE-RECORD.
     IF PRINT-QUEUE-EOF
         PERFORM 1240-SEND-BUFFER-DATA
     ELSE
         PERFORM 1200-FORMAT-BUFFER-DATA.
*
 1100-READ-QUEUE-RECORD.
*
     MOVE 133 TO PRINT-RECORD-LENGTH.
     EXEC CICS
         READQ TD QUEUE(EIBTRMID)
                   INTO(PRINT-QUEUE-RECORD)
                   LENGTH(PRINT-RECORD-LENGTH)
                   RESP(RESPONSE-CODE)
     END-EXEC.
     IF RESPONSE-CODE = DFHRESP(NORMAL)
         SET PRINT-INDEX TO 1
     ELSE IF RESPONSE-CODE = DFHRESP(QZERO)
         MOVE 'Y' TO PRINT-QUEUE-EOF-SW
     ELSE
         GO TO 9999-TERMINATE-PROGRAM.
*
 1200-FORMAT-BUFFER-DATA.
*
     IF BUFFER-INDEX + PRINT-RECORD-LENGTH > 1916
         PERFORM 1240-SEND-BUFFER-DATA
         MOVE LOW-VALUE TO BUFFER-AREA
         SET BUFFER-INDEX TO 1.
     PERFORM 1210-FORMAT-CONTROL-CHARACTERS.
     PERFORM 1230-MOVE-PRINT-CHARACTER
         VARYING PRINT-INDEX FROM 1 BY 1
         UNTIL PRINT-INDEX > PRINT-RECORD-LENGTH.
*
 1210-FORMAT-CONTROL-CHARACTERS.
*
     IF NOT (    FORM-FEED
             OR SINGLE-SPACE
             OR DOUBLE-SPACE
             OR TRIPLE-SPACE)
         MOVE ' ' TO PRINT-CC.
     EVALUATE TRUE
         WHEN FORM-FEED
             MOVE CR-ORDER TO SET-CHAR
             PERFORM 1220-SET-BUFFER-CHARACTER
             MOVE FF-ORDER TO SET-CHAR
             PERFORM 1220-SET-BUFFER-CHARACTER
             MOVE CR-ORDER TO SET-CHAR
             PERFORM 1220-SET-BUFFER-CHARACTER
         WHEN SINGLE-SPACE
             MOVE 0 TO BLANK-COUNT
         WHEN DOUBLE-SPACE
             MOVE 1 TO BLANK-COUNT
         WHEN TRIPLE-SPACE
             MOVE 2 TO BLANK-COUNT
     END-EVALUATE.
     IF NOT FORM-FEED
         IF BUFFER-INDEX = 1
             SUBTRACT 1 FROM BLANK-COUNT
         END-IF
         PERFORM BLANK-COUNT TIMES
             MOVE NL-ORDER TO SET-CHAR
             PERFORM 1220-SET-BUFFER-CHARACTER
             MOVE SPACE TO SET-CHAR
             PERFORM 1220-SET-BUFFER-CHARACTER
         END-PERFORM
         MOVE NL-ORDER TO SET-CHAR
         PERFORM 1220-SET-BUFFER-CHARACTER.
```

Figure 7-9   Source listing for the transient data print program (part 2 of 3)

```
/
 1220-SET-BUFFER-CHARACTER.
*
     MOVE SET-CHAR TO BUFFER-CHAR(BUFFER-INDEX).
     SET BUFFER-INDEX UP BY 1.
*
 1230-MOVE-PRINT-CHARACTER.
*
     MOVE PRINT-CHAR(PRINT-INDEX) TO SET-CHAR.
     PERFORM 1220-SET-BUFFER-CHARACTER.
*
 1240-SEND-BUFFER-DATA.
*
     EXEC CICS
         SEND FROM(BUFFER-AREA)
              LENGTH(1920)
              CTLCHAR(WRITE-CONTROL-CHARACTER)
              ERASE
     END-EXEC.
*
 9999-TERMINATE-PROGRAM.
*
     MOVE EIBRESP  TO ERR-RESP.
     MOVE EIBRESP2 TO ERR-RESP2.
     MOVE EIBTRNID TO ERR-TRNID.
     MOVE EIBRSRCE TO ERR-RSRCE.
     EXEC CICS
         XCTL PROGRAM('SYSERR')
              COMMAREA(ERROR-PARAMETERS)
     END-EXEC.
```

Figure 7-9   Source listing for the transient data print program (part 3 of 3)

Module 1200 begins with an IF statement:

```
IF BUFFER-INDEX + PRINT-RECORD-LENGTH > 1916
     PERFORM 1240-SEND-BUFFER-DATA
     MOVE LOW-VALUE TO BUFFER-AREA
     SET BUFFER-INDEX TO 1.
```

Here, module 1240 is invoked to send data to the printer when there's not enough space left in the buffer area for the record just read. So, if the next available buffer position, indicated by BUFFER-INDEX, plus the length of the next record, indicated by PRINT-RECORD-LENGTH, is greater than 1916, module 1200 invokes module 1240 to send the buffer data. (I use 1916 here rather than 1920 to allow for the maximum number of printer orders the record can require.) Then, it clears the buffer area and resets the buffer index to 1.

Next, module 1200 invokes module 1210 to place the correct printer orders for the record just read in the buffer area. Then, module 1230 is invoked repeatedly to move characters one at a time from the queue record to the buffer area.

Because modules 1210 and 1230 both use module 1220, I want to describe it first. It moves the character stored in SET-CHAR to the current buffer position indicated by BUFFER-INDEX. Then, it increases the value of BUFFER-INDEX by one.

Now look at module 1210. The first statement in this module checks to see if the space control character in the print record (PRINT-CC) is valid. If it's not, module 1210 moves a space to PRINT-CC so single spacing is assumed. Next, an EVALUATE statement processes each ASA control character. For a form feed (1), these statements are executed:

```
MOVE CR-ORDER TO SET-CHAR
PERFORM 1220-SET-BUFFER-CHARACTER
MOVE FF-ORDER TO SET-CHAR
PERFORM 1220-SET-BUFFER-CHARACTER
MOVE CR-ORDER TO SET-CHAR
PERFORM 1220-SET-BUFFER-CHARACTER
```

Here, module 1220 is invoked three times: first to move a CR order to the buffer, then to move an FF order to the buffer, and finally to move another CR order to the buffer. The resulting combination of printer orders (CR, FF, and CR) positions the printer to the first print position of the next page.

Here's why three orders are required to do a form-feed operation. First, a CR order is required to return the print carriage to the start of the line. That's because the next order, FF, must always appear at the beginning of a line. When the FF order is processed, the printer advances to the next page and prints a space in the first position of line 1, leaving the carriage at position 2. To reclaim the lost print position, another CR order returns the carriage to the start of line 1.

The other WHEN clauses in the EVALUATE statement set BLANK-COUNT to the number of blank lines to be printed. For single spacing, no blank lines are required. For double spacing, one blank line is printed. And for triple spacing, two blank lines are printed.

After the EVALUATE statement, an IF statement sets up the control characters required for single, double, or triple spacing. First, one is subtracted from BLANK-COUNT if the current buffer position is one. That's because the printer automatically starts each buffer on a new line. Next, the blank lines are formatted using an in-line PERFORM statement:

```
PERFORM BLANK-COUNT TIMES
    MOVE NL-ORDER TO SET-CHAR
    PERFORM 1220-SET-BUFFER-CHARACTER
    MOVE SPACE TO SET-CHAR
    PERFORM 1220-SET-BUFFER-CHARACTER
END-PERFORM
```

For each blank line to be printed, two characters are moved to the buffer: an NL order and a space. The space is required because 3270 printers ignore blank lines. Thus, if you move adjacent NL orders to the buffer, all but the last will be ignored.

Finally, another NL order is moved to the buffer. A following space is not required here because the data from the print record will be moved to the buffer immediately after this NL order.

Compared with module 1210, the operation of module 1230 is simple. It contains just two lines:

```
MOVE PRINT-CHAR(PRINT-INDEX) TO SET-CHAR.
PERFORM 1220-SET-BUFFER-CHARACTER.
```

If you look back to module 1200, you'll see that PRINT-INDEX is varied as module 1230 is invoked. As a result, each character in the print record is moved to the buffer area.

Module 1240 contains the SEND command that sends the buffer data to the printer. Although the command specifies that all 1920 bytes of BUFFER-AREA are to be sent, unused positions aren't transmitted because they contain LOW-VALUE. The CTLCHAR option specifies the write control character required to start the printer. And the ERASE option causes the printer's buffer to be erased before data is transmitted. That way, there won't be any data left over from the previous SEND command in the printer's buffer.

Discussion

I hope you now appreciate the complexity involved when you use terminal control facilities directly. The commands themselves present no difficulty—the problem is formatting and interpreting buffer data that contains control characters. For printer output, the processing requirements are complicated but manageable. For display terminal input and output, though, the processing requirements are unreasonably complex for all but the simplest applications. That's why you'll normally use BMS commands rather than terminal control commands for interactive programs.

Terms

terminal control
order
write control character
WCC

Objective

Given a programming problem requiring the terminal control facilities presented in this chapter, code an acceptable solution.

Section 4

Other advanced CICS features

The chapters in this section present a variety of CICS features you might need to use on occasion. In chapter 8, you'll learn how to use temporary storage to store and retrieve data. In chapter 9, you'll learn how to create and retrieve transient data. In chapter 10, you'll learn about some other CICS control features: interval control, task control, program control, and storage control. In chapter 11, you'll learn about three aspects of error processing under CICS: abend processing, recovery processing, and journal control. And finally, in chapter 12, you'll learn how to use distributed processing facilities.

Chapter 8

Temporary storage control

Many CICS programs have to be able to process data outside their Working-Storage Sections. For example, pseudo-conversational programs often need to save data between executions during a single terminal session. The storage area where you place data like that is sometimes called a *scratchpad*. You already know one way to implement a scratchpad: using the communication area. Now, you'll learn how *temporary storage control* provides a more sophisticated scratchpad facility than the communication area.

After I present the temporary storage concepts you need to know, I'll show you three temporary storage commands that let you read, write, and delete temporary storage data. Then, I'll present a sample program that shows you how to use temporary storage.

Queues and queue names

Temporary storage is just what it says: a place CICS provides that programs can use to store data temporarily. Temporary storage is divided into *temporary storage queues*, or just *TS queues*. Each TS queue contains one or more *records*, sometimes called *items*, that contain data stored by application programs. Although TS queues contain records, don't think of those records in file processing terms. Usually, a TS queue consists of just one record, and the data elements in that record aren't necessarily related in the way data elements in a file record are.

A temporary storage queue is identified by a unique one- to eight-character *queue name* (sometimes called a *data-id*). You don't have to define TS queue names in a CICS table. Instead, queues are created dynamically. When an application program tries to write a record using a queue name that doesn't exist, temporary storage control creates a new TS queue.

I want you to realize that CICS does provide a *Temporary Storage Table* (or *TST*) where you can define TS queue names. But the only reason you use the TST is to specify which TS queues CICS should make recoverable. Since it's unusual to require a recoverable TS queue, you probably don't need to worry about the TST.

Because many users can create temporary storage queues at once, it's important to use a unique name when you create a TS queue. To ensure that TS queue names are unique, you can use the value in the Execute Interface Block's terminal identification field, EIBTRMID, as part of the queue name. Since each terminal within a CICS system has a unique term-id, queue names based on EIBTRMID are also unique. However, if your shop has other standards that dictate how queues should be named, by all means follow them.

Items and item numbers

Within a queue, each record is assigned an *item number*. The first record written to a queue is item 1, the second is item 2, and so on. CICS automatically assigns an item number to each record you add to a queue, so you only need to specify an item number when you retrieve or update a record. Unlike the record key of a VSAM key-sequenced file, a temporary storage item number is *not* a part of the record it's associated with.

Although you can store many records in a TS queue, it's uncommon to store more than one. In most applications, you'll usually store a single record that the next execution of your pseudo-conversational program can retrieve.

An application program can retrieve records from a temporary storage queue in two ways: sequentially and randomly. For sequential retrieval, records are retrieved in item number sequence. For random retrieval, you specify the item number of the TS queue record you want to retrieve. Because most scratchpad applications need only one record, you'll typically use random retrieval, specifying item 1.

An application program can also rewrite a record in a TS queue. For scratchpad applications, that's a common requirement. Usually, a pseudo-conversational program writes one record to a TS queue when the operator invokes the program for the first time. Then, on subsequent executions of the program during the same terminal session, the program rewrites the existing TS record—it doesn't add records.

How temporary storage queues are stored

Normally, temporary storage control maintains TS queues in a single VSAM entry-sequenced data set called the *temporary storage file*, or *DFHTEMP*. For pseudo-conversational programs, that's an efficient way to store data between program executions. In fact, that's one of the advantages temporary storage has over the communication area: It makes better use of your system's resources by not tying up main storage for long periods of time.

In cases where you want to store and retrieve a temporary storage record within a single task execution, however, the additional overhead of disk processing can be a drawback. So temporary storage control lets you choose between disk storage and main storage. If you specify main storage rather than disk, temporary storage saves your records in main storage. That results in faster processing, but bear in mind that main storage is a critical resource in a CICS system. For a routine scratchpad application (that is, where a TS queue exists between task executions), you should place the queue on disk rather than in main storage.

The WRITEQ TS command

Figure 8-1 gives the format of the WRITEQ TS command. Depending on how you code it, the WRITEQ TS command either adds a new record to a TS queue or updates an existing record in a queue.

How to add a record to a queue   To add a record to a temporary storage queue, you code the WRITEQ TS command like this:

```
EXEC CICS
    WRITEQ TS QUEUE(TS-QUEUE-NAME)
              FROM(TS-QUEUE-RECORD)
              LENGTH(TS-QUEUE-LENGTH)
END-EXEC
```

Here, the contents of TS-QUEUE-RECORD, whose length is specified by TS-QUEUE-LENGTH, are written to a queue whose name is in TS-QUEUE-NAME. You should define the LENGTH field as a binary halfword (PIC S9(4) COMP).

If a TS queue with the name you specify already exists, your record is added to the end of that queue. If no queue with that name exists, CICS automatically creates a queue, then adds your record as the queue's first record. As a result, no special processing is required to create a temporary storage queue.

You indicate whether the queue is stored in main storage or on disk by coding AUXILIARY or MAIN. If you code AUXILIARY (or let it default), the queue is stored in the temporary storage file. If you code MAIN, the queue is kept in main storage.

There aren't any errors that are likely to occur when you issue a WRITEQ TS command to add a record to a TS queue. So you don't need to use the RESP option.

The WRITEQ TS command

```
EXEC CICS
    WRITEQ TS    QUEUE(name)
                 FROM(data-area)
                 LENGTH(data-value)
               [ ITEM(data-area) REWRITE ]
               [{MAIN     }]
               [{AUXILIARY }]
END-EXEC
```

Explanation

QUEUE
Specifies the one- to eight-character name of the temporary storage queue where data is written.

FROM
Specifies the data area that contains the record to be written.

LENGTH
Specifies the length of the FROM area. Must be numeric. If you use a data name, it must be a binary halfword (PIC S9(4) COMP). (Optional under VS COBOL II.)

ITEM
Specifies the item number of the record to be updated. Must be a binary halfword (PIC S9(4) COMP).

REWRITE
Specifies that an existing record in the TS queue should be updated.

MAIN
Specifies that the temporary storage queue will reside in main storage.

AUXILIARY
Specifies that the temporary storage queue will reside on disk in the temporary storage file (DFHTEMP).

Figure 8-1   The WRITEQ TS command

How to update an existing record   If you code the REWRITE option on a WRITEQ TS command, an existing record in the TS queue is replaced. In that case, you must specify the ITEM parameter to indicate which record should be updated. For example, suppose the value of TS-ITEM-NUMBER is 1. Then, if you issue the command

```
EXEC CICS
    WRITEQ TS QUEUE(TS-QUEUE-NAME)
              FROM(TS-QUEUE-RECORD)
              LENGTH(TS-QUEUE-LENGTH)
              ITEM(TS-ITEM-NUMBER)
              REWRITE
              RESP(RESPONSE-CODE)
END-EXEC
```

The READQ TS command

```
EXEC CICS
    READQ TS    QUEUE(name)
                INTO(data-area)
                LENGTH(data-area)
               [{ITEM(data-value)}]
               [{NEXT          }]
END-EXEC
```

Explanation

QUEUE   Specifies the one- to eight-character name of the temporary storage queue from which data is read.

INTO   Specifies the data area that will contain the record.

LENGTH   Specifies the length of the INTO area. Must be a binary halfword (PIC S9(4) COMP). (Optional under VS COBOL II.)

ITEM   Specifies the item number of the record to be read. Must be numeric. If you use a data name, it must be a binary halfword (PIC S9(4) COMP).

NEXT   Specifies that the next record in sequence should be read.

Figure 8-2   The READQ TS command

item 1 is replaced by the contents of TS-QUEUE-RECORD. In other words, this command updates the first queue record.

When you update a temporary storage record, one of two exceptional conditions might be raised. If you specify a queue that doesn't exist, the QIDERR condition is raised. And if you specify an item number that doesn't exist within the queue, the ITEMERR condition is raised. Note that the ITEMERR condition is never raised if you're updating item 1. That's because if item 1 doesn't exist, the queue doesn't exist. So the QIDERR condition is raised instead. The default action for both the QIDERR condition and the ITEMERR condition is to terminate your task. So depending on your application's requirements, you may need to provide for one or both of these conditions by coding the RESP option.

The READQ TS command

To retrieve records from a temporary storage queue, you use the READQ TS command, shown in figure 8-2. Typically, you code it like this:

```
EXEC CICS
    READQ TS QUEUE(TS-QUEUE-NAME)
             INTO(TS-QUEUE-RECORD)
             LENGTH(TS-QUEUE-LENGTH)
             ITEM(TS-ITEM-NUMBER)
             RESP(RESPONSE-CODE)
END-EXEC
```

Here, the record whose item number is indicated by TS-ITEM-NUMBER is read. Normally, you'll assign a value of 1 to the item number field to retrieve the first—and only—record in your queue.

If the item you specify doesn't exist, the ITEMERR condition is raised. And if the queue doesn't exist, the QIDERR condition is raised. You may need to provide for one or both of these conditions, depending on your application's requirements. Remember that ITEMERR won't occur when you attempt to read item 1, because a queue doesn't exist until at least one record has been written to it. Instead, the QIDERR condition will occur.

For a READQ TS command, the initial value of the LENGTH field gives the maximum record length your program can process (in other words, the length of the INTO field). If CICS reads a queue record that's longer than this maximum, the LENGERR condition is raised and your task is terminated. You can provide for the LENGERR condition if you wish, but it probably represents a serious error if it occurs. So you may as well let CICS abend your task. Assuming the LENGERR condition doesn't occur, CICS places the actual length of the record that's read in the LENGTH field after the READQ TS command executes.

If you're processing a queue that contains more than one item, you can specify NEXT rather than ITEM to retrieve the queue items in sequence. Quite simply, NEXT means that CICS should retrieve the next record in sequence following the most recently read record. However, you must realize that *any* task in a CICS system can affect the positioning of a READQ TS/NEXT command by issuing a READQ TS command for the same queue. So if your task is reading queue records sequentially while another task is retrieving records from the same queue, your program won't work properly.

Normally, you won't run into contention problems when you process a TS queue. That's because a typical TS queue has a unique name that uses the terminal-id field from the Execute Interface Block. If your application requires that two or more tasks have access to a common TS queue, you'll need to use two CICS commands that let you reserve exclusive access to a CICS resource: ENQ and DEQ. Because it's not common for several tasks to share access to a TS queue, I'm not going to show you how to use the ENQ and DEQ commands in this chapter. But you'll find a complete description of them in chapter 12, so feel free to look ahead to that chapter if you need to.

The DELETEQ TS command

Figure 8-3 gives the format of the DELETEQ TS command. You must issue a DELETEQ TS command to delete a TS queue when you're finished processing it. If you don't, the queue remains indefinitely, wasting valuable disk or main storage space. Note that the DELETEQ TS command deletes an entire TS queue—there's no way to delete a single

The DELETEQ TS command

```
EXEC CICS
    DELETEQ TS QUEUE(name)
END-EXEC
```

Explanation

QUEUE   Specifies the one- to eight-character name of the temporary storage queue to be deleted.

Figure 8-3   The DELETEQ TS command

record. Since most queues contain just one record anyway, that shouldn't be a problem.

If you try to delete a queue that doesn't exist, the QIDERR condition is raised. As a result, you may wish to code the RESP option to provide for this condition. In many cases, your error routine can simply ignore the QIDERR condition. That's because QIDERR means the queue you specify doesn't exist—and your DELETEQ TS command is trying to delete the queue anyway.

A sample program

Figures 8-4 through 8-9 present a program that maintains records in a customer file, allowing additions, deletions, or changes to records in the file. This program is a variation of the maintenance program I presented in chapter 10 of *Part 1: An Introductory Course.* The only difference is how the two programs maintain data integrity across pseudo-conversational executions. The original version of this program in *Part 1* maintained a copy of the customer record in the communication area. Then, it compared this copy with data read from the customer file to see if the record was changed between pseudo-conversations. This version of the maintenance program stores the customer record in temporary storage rather than in the communication area.

Because the specifications, event/response chart, structure chart, BMS mapset, and symbolic map shown in figures 8-4 through 8-8 are identical to those for the original version of the maintenance program, I won't review them here. Instead, I'll focus on the enhancements I made to store the record image in temporary storage rather than in the communication area. Those enhancements are shaded in the source listing in figure 8-9. If you want a detailed description of this program's operation, refer to chapter 10 in *Part 1.*

In the Working-Storage Section, I defined an 01-level item for the fields used to process the temporary storage queue. TS-QUEUE-NAME provides the name of the TS queue. The first four bytes of the name are

Program	CUSTMNT2
Overview	Maintains customer information in the customer master file by allowing the user to enter new customers, change existing customers, or delete existing customers.

Input/output specifications

CUSTMAS	Customer master file
MNTMAP1	Customer maintenance key map
MNTMAP2	Customer maintenance data map

Processing specifications

1. Control is transferred to this program via XCTL from the menu program INVMENU with no communication area. The user can also start the program by entering the trans-id MNT2. In either case, the program should respond by displaying the customer maintenance key map.

2. On the key map, the user selects a processing action (Add, Change, or Delete) and enters a customer number. Both the action field and the customer number field must be entered. If the user selects Add, the customer number entered must not exist in the file. For Change or Delete, the customer number must exist in the file.

3. If the user enters a valid combination of action and customer number, display the customer maintenance data map. For an addition or a change request, all data fields must be entered. For a delete request, all fields should be set to protected so the user cannot enter changes.

4. If the user presses PF3 from either the key map or the data map, return to the menu program INVMENU by issuing an XCTL command. If the user presses PF12 from the key map, return to the menu program. However, if the user presses PF12 from the data map, redisplay the key map without processing any data that was entered.

5. For a change or deletion, maintain an image of the customer record in a temporary storage queue between program executions. If the record is changed in any way between program executions, notify the user and abort the change or delete operation.

Figure 8-4   Specifications for a maintenance program (part 1 of 3)

the terminal-id extracted from the Execute Interface Block. The second four bytes of the name are MNT2, indicating which transaction uses the queue. Next, TS-ITEM-NUMBER identifies which queue record is processed. Because this queue always contains just one record, I gave TS-ITEM-NUMBER a value of 1. The program won't change that value as it executes. TS-CUSTOMER-RECORD will contain the record that's read from the queue. It's 118 bytes long, as indicated by the last field: TS-RECORD-LENGTH.

The second statement in the Procedure Division is:

```
MOVE EIBTRMID TO TS-TERMINAL-ID.
```

That moves the terminal-id field from the Execute Interface Block to the queue name field. That way, the queue name is unique for each operator

Map name ___MNTMAP1_____ Date ___07/01/92_____

Program name _CUSTMNT2_____ Designer _Doug Lowe_____

```
     1         1         2         3         4         5         6         7         8
     1234567890123456789012345678901234567890123456789012345678901234567890123456789 0
 1   MNTMAP1             Customer Maintenance
 2
 3   Type a customer number.  Then select an action and press Enter.
 4
 5   Customer number. . . . . XXXXXX
 6
 7   Action . . . . . . . . . X 1. Add a new customer
 8                               2. Change an existing customer
 9                               3. Delete an existing customer
10
11
12
13
14
15
16
17
18
19
20
21
22
23   XXXXXXXXXXXXXXXXXXXXXXXXXXXXXXXXXXXXXXXXXXXXXXXXXXXXXXXXXXXXXXXXXXXXXXXXXXXXXXXXX
24   F3=Exit    F12=Cancel                                                          X
```

Map name ___MNTMAP2_____ Date ___07/01/92_____

Program name _CUSTMNT2_____ Designer _Doug Lowe_____

```
     1         1         2         3         4         5         6         7         8
     1234567890123456789012345678901234567890123456789012345678901234567890123456789 0
 1   MNTMAP2             Customer Maintenance
 2
 3   XXXXXXXXXXXXXXXXXXXXXXXXXXXXXXXXXXXXXXXXXXXXXXXXXXXXXXXXXXXXXXXXXXXXXXXXXXXXXXXXX
 4
 5   Customer number. . . . : XXXXXX
 6
 7   Last name. . . . . . . XXXXXXXXXXXXXXXXXXXXXXXXXXXXXX
 8   First name . . . . . . XXXXXXXXXXXXXXXXXXXXX
 9   Address. . . . . . . . XXXXXXXXXXXXXXXXXXXXXXXXXXXXXX
10   City . . . . . . . . . XXXXXXXXXXXXXXXXXXXX
11   State. . . . . . . . . XX
12   Zip Code . . . . . . . XXXXXXXXXX
13
14
15
16
17
18
19
20
21
22
23   XXXXXXXXXXXXXXXXXXXXXXXXXXXXXXXXXXXXXXXXXXXXXXXXXXXXXXXXXXXXXXXXXXXXXXXXXXXXXXXXX
24   F3=Exit    F12=Cancel                                                          X
```

Figure 8-4   Specifications for a maintenance program (part 2 of 3)

The CUSTMAS copy member

```
01  CUSTOMER-MASTER-RECORD.
*
    05  CM-CUSTOMER-NUMBER    PIC X(6).
    05  CM-FIRST-NAME         PIC X(20).
    05  CM-LAST-NAME          PIC X(30).
    05  CM-ADDRESS            PIC X(30).
    05  CM-CITY               PIC X(20).
    05  CM-STATE              PIC X(2).
    05  CM-ZIP-CODE           PIC X(10).
*
```

The ERRPARM copy member

```
01  ERROR-PARAMETERS.
*
    05  ERR-RESP      PIC S9(8)   COMP.
    05  ERR-RESP2     PIC S9(8)   COMP.
    05  ERR-TRNID     PIC X(4).
    05  ERR-RSRCE     PIC X(8).
*
```

Figure 8-4   Specifications for a maintenance program (part 3 of 3)

who uses this program. For example, if the terminal name is V123, the queue name will be V123MNT2.

When the user starts the program for the first time, the program moves LOW-VALUE to TS-CUSTOMER-RECORD and issues this CICS command:

```
EXEC CICS
    WRITEQ TS QUEUE(TS-QUEUE-NAME)
              FROM(TS-CUSTOMER-RECORD)
END-EXEC
```

That creates the queue with one record. Subsequent temporary storage commands will retrieve and update that record.

When the user ends the program by pressing PF3, the program deletes the queue with this command:

```
EXEC CICS
    DELETEQ TS QUEUE(TS-QUEUE-NAME)
END-EXEC
```

The same command is also issued if the user ends the program by pressing PF12 while the key map is displayed.

The rest of the shaded elements in figure 8-9 show how the program saves and retrieves the customer record in the temporary storage queue. In module 1300, a WRITEQ TS command writes the customer record to the queue. Here, I specified the ITEM and REWRITE options so that the customer record will always be written to the first record in the queue.

Event	Context	Response	New context
Start the program	n/a	Display the key map.	Get key
PF3	All	Transfer control to the menu program.	n/a
PF12	Get key	Transfer control to the menu program.	n/a
	Add customer Change customer Delete customer	Cancel the operation and display the key map.	Get key
Enter	Get key	Edit input data. If valid read the customer record display the data map else display an error message.	Add customer, Change customer, or Delete customer Get key
	Add customer	Edit input data. If valid add the customer record display the key map else display an error message.	Get key Add customer
	Change customer	Edit input data. If valid change the customer record display the key map else display an error message.	Get key Change customer
	Delete customer	Delete the customer record. Display the key map.	Get key
Clear	All	Redisplay the current map.	Unchanged
PA1, PA2, or PA3	All	Ignore the key.	Unchanged
Any other key	All	Display an appropriate error message.	Unchanged

Figure 8-5   An event/response chart for the maintenance program

Modules 3000 and 4000 both issue READQ TS commands to retrieve the saved customer record from the queue after they've read the customer record from the file. If the current customer record is different from the customer record saved in the queue, an error message is displayed and the operation is aborted.

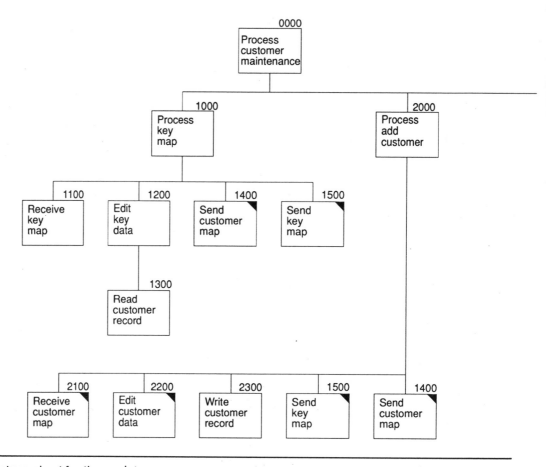

Figure 8-6 Structure chart for the maintenance program

Discussion I mentioned at the start of this chapter that you'll often use temporary storage rather than the communication area to save data between executions of a pseudo-conversational program. Now that you know how to process a temporary storage queue, you may be wondering how to decide whether to use temporary storage or the communication area. In general, I recommend you use temporary storage unless the amount of data you want to save is small—say, 50 bytes or less. When the amount of data is that small, you're probably better off using the communication area because a temporary storage record on disk requires almost that much main storage as overhead.

Terms

scratchpad
temporary storage control
temporary storage queue
TS queue

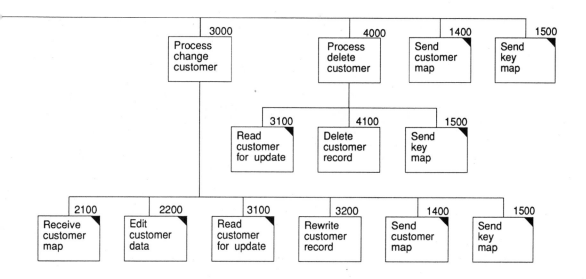

record
item
queue name
data-id
Temporary Storage Table
TST
item number
temporary storage file
DFHTEMP

Objective

Given a programming problem requiring the use of a temporary storage queue, code a program for its solution using the features this chapter presents.

```
          PRINT NOGEN
MNTSET1   DFHMSD TYPE=&SYSPARM,                                              X
                 LANG=COBOL,                                                 X
                 MODE=INOUT,                                                 X
                 TERM=3270-2,                                                X
                 CTRL=FREEKB,                                                X
                 STORAGE=AUTO,                                               X
                 DSATTS=(COLOR,HILIGHT),                                     X
                 MAPATTS=(COLOR,HILIGHT),                                    X
                 TIOAPFX=YES
*********************************************************************
MNTMAP1   DFHMDI SIZE=(24,80),                                              X
                 LINE=1,                                                     X
                 COLUMN=1
*********************************************************************
          DFHMDF POS=(1,1),                                                 X
                 LENGTH=7,                                                   X
                 ATTRB=(NORM,PROT),                                         X
                 COLOR=BLUE,                                                 X
                 INITIAL='MNTMAP1'
          DFHMDF POS=(1,20),                                                X
                 LENGTH=20,                                                  X
                 ATTRB=(NORM,PROT),                                         X
                 COLOR=BLUE,                                                 X
                 INITIAL='Customer Maintenance'
*********************************************************************
          DFHMDF POS=(3,1),                                                 X
                 LENGTH=63,                                                  X
                 ATTRB=(NORM,PROT),                                         X
                 COLOR=GREEN,                                                X
                 INITIAL='Type a customer number.  Then select an action X
                 and press Enter.'
          DFHMDF POS=(5,1),                                                 X
                 LENGTH=24,                                                  X
                 ATTRB=(NORM,PROT),                                         X
                 COLOR=GREEN,                                                X
                 INITIAL='Customer number. . . . .'
CUSTNO1   DFHMDF POS=(5,26),                                                X
                 LENGTH=6,                                                   X
                 ATTRB=(NORM,UNPROT,FSET,IC),                               X
                 COLOR=TURQUOISE,                                           X
                 INITIAL='_____'
          DFHMDF POS=(5,33),                                                X
                 LENGTH=1,                                                   X
                 ATTRB=ASKIP
          DFHMDF POS=(7,1),                                                 X
                 LENGTH=24,                                                  X
                 ATTRB=(NORM,PROT),                                         X
                 COLOR=GREEN,                                                X
                 INITIAL='Action . . . . . . . . .'
ACTION    DFHMDF POS=(7,26),                                                X
                 LENGTH=1,                                                   X
                 ATTRB=(NORM,UNPROT,FSET),                                  X
                 COLOR=TURQUOISE,                                           X
                 INITIAL='_'
          DFHMDF POS=(7,28),                                                X
                 LENGTH=21,                                                  X
                 ATTRB=(NORM,ASKIP),                                        X
                 COLOR=NEUTRAL,                                             X
                 INITIAL='1. Add a new customer'
          DFHMDF POS=(8,28),                                                X
                 LENGTH=30,                                                  X
                 ATTRB=(NORM,ASKIP),                                        X
                 COLOR=NEUTRAL,                                             X
                 INITIAL='2. Change an existing customer'
          DFHMDF POS=(9,28),                                                X
                 LENGTH=21,                                                  X
                 ATTRB=(NORM,ASKIP),                                        X
                 COLOR=NEUTRAL,                                             X
                 INITIAL='3. Delete an existing customer'
```

Figure 8-7   Mapset listing for the maintenance program (part 1 of 3)

```
MSG1        DFHMDF POS=(23,1),                                           X
                   LENGTH=79,                                            X
                   ATTRB=(BRT,PROT),                                     X
                   COLOR=YELLOW
            DFHMDF POS=(24,1),                                           X
                   LENGTH=20,                                            X
                   ATTRB=(NORM,PROT),                                    X
                   COLOR=BLUE,                                           X
                   INITIAL='F3=Exit     F12=Cancel'
DUMMY1      DFHMDF POS=(24,79),                                          X
                   LENGTH=1,                                             X
                   ATTRB=(DRK,PROT,FSET),                                X
                   INITIAL=' '
*******************************************************************
MNTMAP2     DFHMDI SIZE=(24,80),                                         X
                   LINE=1,                                               X
                   COLUMN=1
*******************************************************************
            DFHMDF POS=(1,1),                                           X
                   LENGTH=7,                                             X
                   ATTRB=(NORM,PROT),                                    X
                   COLOR=BLUE,                                           X
                   INITIAL='MNTMAP2'
            DFHMDF POS=(1,20),                                          X
                   LENGTH=20,                                            X
                   ATTRB=(NORM,PROT),                                    X
                   COLOR=BLUE,                                           X
                   INITIAL='Customer Maintenance'
*******************************************************************
INSTR2      DFHMDF POS=(3,1),                                           X
                   LENGTH=79,                                            X
                   ATTRB=(NORM,PROT),                                    X
                   COLOR=GREEN
            DFHMDF POS=(5,1),                                           X
                   LENGTH=24,                                            X
                   ATTRB=(NORM,PROT),                                    X
                   COLOR=GREEN,                                          X
                   INITIAL='Customer number. . . . :'
CUSTNO2     DFHMDF POS=(5,26),                                          X
                   LENGTH=6,                                             X
                   ATTRB=(NORM,PROT,FSET,IC),                            X
                   COLOR=TURQUOISE
*******************************************************************
            DFHMDF POS=(7,1),                                           X
                   LENGTH=24,                                            X
                   ATTRB=(NORM,PROT),                                    X
                   COLOR=GREEN,                                          X
                   INITIAL='Last name. . . . . . . .'
LNAME       DFHMDF POS=(7,26),                                          X
                   LENGTH=30,                                            X
                   ATTRB=(NORM,UNPROT,FSET),                             X
                   COLOR=TURQUOISE
            DFHMDF POS=(7,57),                                          X
                   LENGTH=1,                                             X
                   ATTRB=ASKIP
*******************************************************************
            DFHMDF POS=(8,1),                                           X
                   LENGTH=24,                                            X
                   ATTRB=(NORM,PROT),                                    X
                   COLOR=GREEN,                                          X
                   INITIAL='First name . . . . . . .'
FNAME       DFHMDF POS=(8,26),                                          X
                   LENGTH=20,                                            X
                   ATTRB=(NORM,UNPROT,FSET),                             X
                   COLOR=TURQUOISE
            DFHMDF POS=(8,47),                                          X
                   LENGTH=1,                                             X
                   ATTRB=ASKIP
```

Figure 8-7   Mapset listing for the maintenance program (part 2 of 3)

```
****************************************************************
          DFHMDF POS=(9,1),                                    X
                 LENGTH=24,                                    X
                 ATTRB=(NORM,PROT),                            X
                 COLOR=GREEN,                                  X
                 INITIAL='Address. . . . . . . . .'
ADDR      DFHMDF POS=(9,26),                                   X
                 LENGTH=30,                                    X
                 ATTRB=(NORM,UNPROT,FSET),                     X
                 COLOR=TURQUOISE
          DFHMDF POS=(9,57),                                   X
                 LENGTH=1,                                     X
                 ATTRB=ASKIP
****************************************************************
          DFHMDF POS=(10,1),                                   X
                 LENGTH=24,                                    X
                 ATTRB=(NORM,PROT),                            X
                 COLOR=GREEN,                                  X
                 INITIAL='City . . . . . . . . . .'
CITY      DFHMDF POS=(10,26),                                  X
                 LENGTH=20,                                    X
                 ATTRB=(NORM,UNPROT,FSET),                     X
                 COLOR=TURQUOISE
          DFHMDF POS=(10,47),                                  X
                 LENGTH=1,                                     X
                 ATTRB=ASKIP
****************************************************************
          DFHMDF POS=(11,1),                                   X
                 LENGTH=24,                                    X
                 ATTRB=(NORM,PROT),                            X
                 COLOR=GREEN,                                  X
                 INITIAL='State. . . . . . . . .'
STATE     DFHMDF POS=(11,26),                                  X
                 LENGTH=2,                                     X
                 ATTRB=(NORM,UNPROT,FSET),                     X
                 COLOR=TURQUOISE
          DFHMDF POS=(11,29),                                  X
                 LENGTH=1,                                     X
                 ATTRB=ASKIP
****************************************************************
          DFHMDF POS=(12,1),                                   X
                 LENGTH=24,                                    X
                 ATTRB=(NORM,PROT),                            X
                 COLOR=GREEN,                                  X
                 INITIAL='Zip Code . . . . . . . .'
ZIPCODE   DFHMDF POS=(12,26),                                  X
                 LENGTH=10,                                    X
                 ATTRB=(NORM,UNPROT,FSET),                     X
                 COLOR=TURQUOISE
          DFHMDF POS=(12,37),                                  X
                 LENGTH=1,                                     X
                 ATTRB=ASKIP
****************************************************************
MSG2      DFHMDF POS=(23,1),                                   X
                 LENGTH=79,                                    X
                 ATTRB=(BRT,PROT),                             X
                 COLOR=YELLOW
          DFHMDF POS=(24,1),                                   X
                 LENGTH=20,                                    X
                 ATTRB=(NORM,PROT),                            X
                 COLOR=BLUE,                                   X
                 INITIAL='F3=Exit    F12=Cancel'
DUMMY2    DFHMDF POS=(24,79),                                  X
                 LENGTH=1,                                     X
                 ATTRB=(DRK,PROT,FSET),                        X
                 INITIAL=' '
****************************************************************
          DFHMSD TYPE=FINAL
          END
```

Figure 8-7   Mapset listing for the maintenance program (part 3 of 3)

```
01   MNTMAP1I.
     02   FILLER      PIC X(12).
     02   CUSTNO1L    PIC S9(4) COMP.
     02   CUSTNO1F    PIC X.
     02   FILLER REDEFINES CUSTNO1F.
      03  CUSTNO1A    PIC X.
     02   FILLER      PIC X(0002).
     02   CUSTNO1I    PIC X(0006).
     02   ACTIONL     PIC S9(4) COMP.
     02   ACTIONF     PIC X.
     02   FILLER REDEFINES ACTIONF.
      03  ACTIONA     PIC X.
     02   FILLER      PIC X(0002).
     02   ACTIONI     PIC X(0001).
     02   MSG1L       PIC S9(4) COMP.
     02   MSG1F       PIC X.
     02   FILLER REDEFINES MSG1F.
      03  MSG1A       PIC X.
     02   FILLER      PIC X(0002).
     02   MSG1I       PIC X(0079).
     02   DUMMY1L     PIC S9(4) COMP.
     02   DUMMY1F     PIC X.
     02   FILLER REDEFINES DUMMY1F.
      03  DUMMY1A     PIC X.
     02   FILLER      PIC X(0002).
     02   DUMMY1I     PIC X(0001).
01   MNTMAP1O REDEFINES MNTMAP1I.
     02   FILLER      PIC X(12).
     02   FILLER      PIC X(3).
     02   CUSTNO1C    PIC X.
     02   CUSTNO1H    PIC X.
     02   CUSTNO1O    PIC X(0006).
     02   FILLER      PIC X(3).
     02   ACTIONC     PIC X.
     02   ACTIONH     PIC X.
     02   ACTIONO     PIC X(0001).
     02   FILLER      PIC X(3).
     02   MSG1C       PIC X.
     02   MSG1H       PIC X.
     02   MSG1O       PIC X(0079).
     02   FILLER      PIC X(3).
     02   DUMMY1C     PIC X.
     02   DUMMY1H     PIC X.
     02   DUMMY1O     PIC X(0001).
01   MNTMAP2I.
     02   FILLER      PIC X(12).
     02   INSTR2L     PIC S9(4) COMP.
     02   INSTR2F     PIC X.
     02   FILLER REDEFINES INSTR2F.
      03  INSTR2A     PIC X.
     02   FILLER      PIC X(0002).
     02   INSTR2I     PIC X(0079).
     02   CUSTNO2L    PIC S9(4) COMP.
     02   CUSTNO2F    PIC X.
     02   FILLER REDEFINES CUSTNO2F.
      03  CUSTNO2A    PIC X.
     02   FILLER      PIC X(0002).
     02   CUSTNO2I    PIC X(0006).
     02   LNAMEL      PIC S9(4) COMP.
     02   LNAMEF      PIC X.
     02   FILLER REDEFINES LNAMEF.
      03  LNAMEA      PIC X.
     02   FILLER      PIC X(0002).
     02   LNAMEI      PIC X(0030).
```

Figure 8-8   BMS-generated symbolic map for the maintenance program (part 1 of 3)

```
         02    FNAMEL     PIC S9(4) COMP.
         02    FNAMEF     PIC X.
         02    FILLER  REDEFINES FNAMEF.
          03   FNAMEA     PIC X.
         02    FILLER     PIC X(0002).
         02    FNAMEI     PIC X(0020).
         02    ADDRL      PIC S9(4) COMP.
         02    ADDRF      PIC X.
         02    FILLER  REDEFINES ADDRF.
          03   ADDRA      PIC X.
         02    FILLER     PIC X(0002).
         02    ADDRI      PIC X(0030).
         02    CITYL      PIC S9(4) COMP.
         02    CITYF      PIC X.
         02    FILLER  REDEFINES CITYF.
          03   CITYA      PIC X.
         02    FILLER     PIC X(0002).
         02    CITYI      PIC X(0020).
         02    STATEL     PIC S9(4) COMP.
         02    STATEF     PIC X.
         02    FILLER  REDEFINES STATEF.
          03   STATEA     PIC X.
         02    FILLER     PIC X(0002).
         02    STATEI     PIC X(0002).
         02    ZIPCODEL   PIC S9(4) COMP.
         02    ZIPCODEF   PIC X.
         02    FILLER  REDEFINES ZIPCODEF.
          03   ZIPCODEA   PIC X.
         02    FILLER     PIC X(0002).
         02    ZIPCODEI   PIC X(0010).
         02    MSG2L      PIC S9(4) COMP.
         02    MSG2F      PIC X.
         02    FILLER  REDEFINES MSG2F.
          03   MSG2A      PIC X.
         02    FILLER     PIC X(0002).
         02    MSG2I      PIC X(0079).
         02    DUMMY2L    PIC S9(4) COMP.
         02    DUMMY2F    PIC X.
         02    FILLER  REDEFINES DUMMY2F.
          03   DUMMY2A    PIC X.
         02    FILLER     PIC X(0002).
         02    DUMMY2I    PIC X(0001).
   01    MNTMAP2O REDEFINES MNTMAP2I.
         02    FILLER     PIC X(12).
         02    FILLER     PIC X(3).
         02    INSTR2C    PIC X.
         02    INSTR2H    PIC X.
         02    INSTR2O    PIC X(0079).
         02    FILLER     PIC X(3).
         02    CUSTNO2C   PIC X.
         02    CUSTNO2H   PIC X.
         02    CUSTNO2O   PIC X(0006).
         02    FILLER     PIC X(3).
         02    LNAMEC     PIC X.
         02    LNAMEH     PIC X.
         02    LNAMEO     PIC X(0030).
         02    FILLER     PIC X(3).
         02    FNAMEC     PIC X.
         02    FNAMEH     PIC X.
         02    FNAMEO     PIC X(0020).
         02    FILLER     PIC X(3).
         02    ADDRC      PIC X.
         02    ADDRH      PIC X.
         02    ADDRO      PIC X(0030).
```

Figure 8-8   BMS-generated symbolic map for the maintenance program (part 2 of 3)

```
02    FILLER     PIC X(3).
02    CITYC      PIC X.
02    CITYH      PIC X.
02    CITYO      PIC X(0020).
02    FILLER     PIC X(3).
02    STATEC     PIC X.
02    STATEH     PIC X.
02    STATEO     PIC X(0002).
02    FILLER     PIC X(3).
02    ZIPCODEC   PIC X.
02    ZIPCODEH   PIC X.
02    ZIPCODEO   PIC X(0010).
02    FILLER     PIC X(3).
02    MSG2C      PIC X.
02    MSG2H      PIC X.
02    MSG2O      PIC X(0079).
02    FILLER     PIC X(3).
02    DUMMY2C    PIC X.
02    DUMMY2H    PIC X.
02    DUMMY2O    PIC X(0001).
```

Figure 8-8   BMS-generated symbolic map for the maintenance program (part 3 of 3)

```
       IDENTIFICATION DIVISION.
      *
       PROGRAM-ID.  CUSTMNT2.
      *
       ENVIRONMENT DIVISION.
      *
       DATA DIVISION.
      *
       WORKING-STORAGE SECTION.
      *
       01  SWITCHES.
      *
           05  VALID-DATA-SW              PIC X  VALUE 'Y'.
               88  VALID-DATA                    VALUE 'Y'.
      *
       01  FLAGS.
      *
           05  SEND-FLAG                  PIC X.
               88  SEND-ERASE                    VALUE '1'.
               88  SEND-ERASE-ALARM              VALUE '2'.
               88  SEND-DATAONLY                 VALUE '3'.
               88  SEND-DATAONLY-ALARM           VALUE '4'.
      *
       01  WORK-FIELDS.
      *
           05  RESPONSE-CODE              PIC S9(8) COMP.
      *
       01  COMMUNICATION-AREA.
      *
           05  CA-CONTEXT-FLAG            PIC X.
               88  PROCESS-KEY-MAP               VALUE '1'.
               88  PROCESS-ADD-CUSTOMER          VALUE '2'.
               88  PROCESS-CHANGE-CUSTOMER       VALUE '3'.
               88  PROCESS-DELETE-CUSTOMER       VALUE '4'.
      *
       01  TEMPORARY-STORAGE-FIELDS.
      *
           05  TS-QUEUE-NAME.
               10  TS-TERMINAL-ID        PIC X(4).
               10  FILLER                PIC X(4)   VALUE 'MNT2'.
           05  TS-ITEM-NUMBER            PIC S9(4) COMP   VALUE +1.
           05  TS-CUSTOMER-RECORD.
               10  TS-CUSTOMER-NUMBER    PIC X(6).
               10  FILLER                PIC X(112).
           05  TS-RECORD-LENGTH          PIC S9(4) COMP   VALUE 118.
      *
       COPY CUSTMAS.
      *
       COPY MNTSET1.
      *
       COPY DFHAID.
      *
       COPY ATTR.
      *
       COPY ERRPARM.
      *
       LINKAGE SECTION.
      *
       01  DFHCOMMAREA               PIC X.
```

Figure 8-9   Source listing for the maintenance program (part 1 of 9)

```
/
 PROCEDURE DIVISION.
*
 0000-PROCESS-CUSTOMER-MAINT.
*
     MOVE DFHCOMMAREA TO COMMUNICATION-AREA.
     MOVE EIBTRMID     TO TS-TERMINAL-ID.

     EVALUATE TRUE

         WHEN EIBCALEN = ZERO
             MOVE LOW-VALUE TO TS-CUSTOMER-RECORD
             EXEC CICS
                 WRITEQ TS QUEUE(TS-QUEUE-NAME)
                           FROM(TS-CUSTOMER-RECORD)
             END-EXEC
             MOVE LOW-VALUE TO MNTMAP1O
             MOVE -1 TO CUSTNO1L
             SET SEND-ERASE TO TRUE
             PERFORM 1500-SEND-KEY-MAP
             SET PROCESS-KEY-MAP TO TRUE

         WHEN EIBAID = DFHPF3
             EXEC CICS
                 DELETEQ TS QUEUE(TS-QUEUE-NAME)
             END-EXEC
             EXEC CICS
                 XCTL PROGRAM('INVMENU')
             END-EXEC

         WHEN EIBAID = DFHPF12
             IF PROCESS-KEY-MAP
                 EXEC CICS
                     DELETEQ TS QUEUE(TS-QUEUE-NAME)
                 END-EXEC
                 EXEC CICS
                     XCTL PROGRAM('INVMENU')
                 END-EXEC
             ELSE
                 MOVE LOW-VALUE TO MNTMAP1O
                 MOVE -1 TO CUSTNO1L
                 SET SEND-ERASE TO TRUE
                 PERFORM 1500-SEND-KEY-MAP
                 SET PROCESS-KEY-MAP TO TRUE

         WHEN EIBAID = DFHCLEAR
             IF PROCESS-KEY-MAP
                 MOVE LOW-VALUE TO MNTMAP1O
                 MOVE -1 TO CUSTNO1L
                 SET SEND-ERASE TO TRUE
                 PERFORM 1500-SEND-KEY-MAP
             ELSE
                 MOVE LOW-VALUE TO MNTMAP2O
                 MOVE -1 TO CUSTNO2L
                 SET SEND-ERASE TO TRUE
                 PERFORM 1400-SEND-CUSTOMER-MAP

         WHEN EIBAID = DFHPA1 OR DFHPA2 OR DFHPA3
             CONTINUE

         WHEN EIBAID = DFHENTER
             IF PROCESS-KEY-MAP
                 PERFORM 1000-PROCESS-KEY-MAP
             ELSE IF PROCESS-ADD-CUSTOMER
                 PERFORM 2000-PROCESS-ADD-CUSTOMER
             ELSE IF PROCESS-CHANGE-CUSTOMER
                 PERFORM 3000-PROCESS-CHANGE-CUSTOMER
             ELSE IF PROCESS-DELETE-CUSTOMER
                 PERFORM 4000-PROCESS-DELETE-CUSTOMER
```

Figure 8-9   Source listing for the maintenance program (part 2 of 9)

```
/              WHEN OTHER
                   IF PROCESS-KEY-MAP
                       MOVE LOW-VALUE TO MNTMAP1O
                       MOVE -1 TO CUSTNO1L
                       MOVE 'That key is unassigned.' TO MSG1O
                       SET SEND-DATAONLY-ALARM TO TRUE
                       PERFORM 1500-SEND-KEY-MAP
                   ELSE
                       MOVE LOW-VALUE TO MNTMAP2O
                       MOVE -1 TO CUSTNO2L
                       MOVE 'That key is unassigned.' TO MSG2O
                       SET SEND-DATAONLY-ALARM TO TRUE
                       PERFORM 1400-SEND-CUSTOMER-MAP

           END-EVALUATE.

           EXEC CICS
               RETURN TRANSID('MNT2')
                      COMMAREA(COMMUNICATION-AREA)
           END-EXEC.
*
 1000-PROCESS-KEY-MAP.
*
       PERFORM 1100-RECEIVE-KEY-MAP.
       PERFORM 1200-EDIT-KEY-DATA.
       IF VALID-DATA
           INSPECT CUSTOMER-MASTER-RECORD
               REPLACING ALL SPACE BY '_'
           MOVE CUSTNO1I        TO CUSTNO2O
           MOVE CM-LAST-NAME    TO LNAMEO
           MOVE CM-FIRST-NAME   TO FNAMEO
           MOVE CM-ADDRESS      TO ADDRO
           MOVE CM-CITY         TO CITYO
           MOVE CM-STATE        TO STATEO
           MOVE CM-ZIP-CODE     TO ZIPCODEO
           MOVE -1              TO LNAMEL
           SET SEND-ERASE TO TRUE
           PERFORM 1400-SEND-CUSTOMER-MAP
       ELSE
           MOVE LOW-VALUE TO CUSTNO1O
                             ACTIONO
           SET SEND-DATAONLY-ALARM TO TRUE
           PERFORM 1500-SEND-KEY-MAP.
*
 1100-RECEIVE-KEY-MAP.
*
       EXEC CICS
           RECEIVE MAP('MNTMAP1')
                   MAPSET('MNTSET1')
                   INTO(MNTMAP1I)
       END-EXEC.
       INSPECT MNTMAP1I
           REPLACING ALL '_' BY SPACE.

*
 1200-EDIT-KEY-DATA.
*
       MOVE ATTR-NO-HIGHLIGHT TO ACTIONH
                                 CUSTNO1H.

       IF ACTIONI NOT = '1' AND '2' AND '3'
           MOVE ATTR-REVERSE TO ACTIONH
           MOVE -1 TO ACTIONL
           MOVE 'Action must be 1, 2, or 3.' TO MSG1O
           MOVE 'N' TO VALID-DATA-SW.
```

Figure 8-9   Source listing for the maintenance program (part 3 of 9)

```
/        IF        CUSTNO1L = ZERO
             OR CUSTNO1I = SPACE
           MOVE ATTR-REVERSE TO CUSTNO1H
           MOVE -1 TO CUSTNO1L
           MOVE 'You must enter a customer number.' TO MSG10
           MOVE 'N' TO VALID-DATA-SW.

         IF VALID-DATA
             EVALUATE ACTIONI
                 WHEN '1'
                     PERFORM 1300-READ-CUSTOMER-RECORD
                     IF RESPONSE-CODE = DFHRESP(NOTFND)
                         MOVE 'Type information for new customer.  The
                              'n Press Enter.' TO INSTR20
                         SET PROCESS-ADD-CUSTOMER TO TRUE
                         MOVE SPACE TO CUSTOMER-MASTER-RECORD
                     ELSE
                         MOVE 'That customer already exists.'
                             TO MSG10
                         MOVE 'N' TO VALID-DATA-SW
                 WHEN '2'
                     PERFORM 1300-READ-CUSTOMER-RECORD
                     IF RESPONSE-CODE = DFHRESP(NORMAL)
                         MOVE 'Type changes.  Then press Enter.'
                             TO INSTR20
                         SET PROCESS-CHANGE-CUSTOMER TO TRUE
                     ELSE
                         MOVE 'That customer does not exist.' TO MSG10
                         MOVE 'N' TO VALID-DATA-SW
                 WHEN '3'
                     PERFORM 1300-READ-CUSTOMER-RECORD
                     IF RESPONSE-CODE = DFHRESP(NORMAL)
                         MOVE 'Press Enter to delete this customer or
                              'press F12 to cancel.' TO INSTR20
                         SET PROCESS-DELETE-CUSTOMER TO TRUE
                         MOVE ATTR-PROT TO LNAMEA
                                          FNAMEA
                                          ADDRA
                                          CITYA
                                          STATEA
                                          ZIPCODEA
                     ELSE
                         MOVE 'That customer does not exist.' TO MSG10
                         MOVE 'N' TO VALID-DATA-SW
             END-EVALUATE.
     *
      1300-READ-CUSTOMER-RECORD.
     *
         EXEC CICS
             READ DATASET('CUSTMAS')
                 INTO(CUSTOMER-MASTER-RECORD)
                 RIDFLD(CUSTNO1I)
                 RESP(RESPONSE-CODE)
         END-EXEC.
         IF        RESPONSE-CODE NOT = DFHRESP(NORMAL)
               AND RESPONSE-CODE NOT = DFHRESP(NOTFND)
             GO TO 9999-TERMINATE-PROGRAM.
         IF RESPONSE-CODE = DFHRESP(NORMAL)
             MOVE CUSTOMER-MASTER-RECORD TO TS-CUSTOMER-RECORD
             EXEC CICS
                 WRITEQ TS QUEUE(TS-QUEUE-NAME)
                            FROM(TS-CUSTOMER-RECORD)
                            ITEM(TS-ITEM-NUMBER)
                            REWRITE
             END-EXEC.
```

Figure 8-9   Source listing for the maintenance program (part 4 of 9)

```
/
 1400-SEND-CUSTOMER-MAP.
 *
      EVALUATE TRUE
          WHEN SEND-ERASE
              EXEC CICS
                  SEND MAP('MNTMAP2')
                       MAPSET('MNTSET1')
                       FROM(MNTMAP2O)
                       ERASE
                       CURSOR
              END-EXEC
          WHEN SEND-DATAONLY-ALARM
              EXEC CICS
                  SEND MAP('MNTMAP2')
                       MAPSET('MNTSET1')
                       FROM(MNTMAP2O)
                       DATAONLY
                       ALARM
                       CURSOR
              END-EXEC
      END-EVALUATE.
 *
 1500-SEND-KEY-MAP.
 *
      EVALUATE TRUE
          WHEN SEND-ERASE
              EXEC CICS
                  SEND MAP('MNTMAP1')
                       MAPSET('MNTSET1')
                       FROM(MNTMAP1O)
                       ERASE
                       CURSOR
              END-EXEC
          WHEN SEND-ERASE-ALARM
              EXEC CICS
                  SEND MAP('MNTMAP1')
                       MAPSET('MNTSET1')
                       FROM(MNTMAP1O)
                       ERASE
                       ALARM
                       CURSOR
              END-EXEC
          WHEN SEND-DATAONLY-ALARM
              EXEC CICS
                  SEND MAP('MNTMAP1')
                       MAPSET('MNTSET1')
                       FROM(MNTMAP1O)
                       DATAONLY
                       ALARM
                       CURSOR
              END-EXEC
      END-EVALUATE.
```

Figure 8-9   Source listing for the maintenance program (part 5 of 9)

```
/
 2000-PROCESS-ADD-CUSTOMER.
*
     PERFORM 2100-RECEIVE-CUSTOMER-MAP.
     PERFORM 2200-EDIT-CUSTOMER-DATA.
     IF VALID-DATA
         PERFORM 2300-WRITE-CUSTOMER-RECORD
         IF RESPONSE-CODE = DFHRESP(NORMAL)
             MOVE 'Customer record added.' TO MSG10
             SET SEND-ERASE TO TRUE
         ELSE
             MOVE 'Another user has added a record with that custo
                  'mer number.' TO MSG10
             SET SEND-ERASE-ALARM TO TRUE
         END-IF
         PERFORM 1500-SEND-KEY-MAP
         SET PROCESS-KEY-MAP TO TRUE
     ELSE
         MOVE LOW-VALUE TO LNAMEO
                           FNAMEO
                           ADDRO
                           CITYO
                           STATEO
                           ZIPCODEO
         SET SEND-DATAONLY-ALARM TO TRUE
         PERFORM 1400-SEND-CUSTOMER-MAP.
*
 2100-RECEIVE-CUSTOMER-MAP.
*
     EXEC CICS
         RECEIVE MAP('MNTMAP2')
                 MAPSET('MNTSET1')
                 INTO(MNTMAP2I)
     END-EXEC.
     INSPECT MNTMAP2I
         REPLACING ALL '_' BY SPACE.
*
 2200-EDIT-CUSTOMER-DATA.
*
     MOVE ATTR-NO-HIGHLIGHT TO ZIPCODEH
                              STATEH
                              CITYH
                              ADDRH
                              FNAMEH
                              LNAMEH.

     IF      ZIPCODEI = SPACE
          OR ZIPCODEL = ZERO
         MOVE ATTR-REVERSE TO ZIPCODEH
         MOVE -1 TO ZIPCODEL
         MOVE 'You must enter a zip code.' TO MSG20
         MOVE 'N' TO VALID-DATA-SW.

     IF      STATEI = SPACE
          OR STATEL = ZERO
         MOVE ATTR-REVERSE TO STATEH
         MOVE -1 TO STATEL
         MOVE 'You must enter a state.' TO MSG20
         MOVE 'N' TO VALID-DATA-SW.
```

Figure 8-9   Source listing for the maintenance program (part 6 of 9)

```
/
      IF        CITYI = SPACE
          OR CITYL = ZERO
         MOVE ATTR-REVERSE TO CITYH
         MOVE -1 TO CITYL
         MOVE 'You must enter a city.' TO MSG20
         MOVE 'N' TO VALID-DATA-SW.

      IF        ADDRI = SPACE
          OR ADDRL = ZERO
         MOVE ATTR-REVERSE TO ADDRH
         MOVE -1 TO ADDRL
         MOVE 'You must enter an address.' TO MSG20
         MOVE 'N' TO VALID-DATA-SW.

      IF        FNAMEI = SPACE
          OR FNAMEL = ZERO
         MOVE ATTR-REVERSE TO FNAMEH
         MOVE -1 TO FNAMEL
         MOVE 'You must enter a first name.' TO MSG20
         MOVE 'N' TO VALID-DATA-SW.

      IF        LNAMEI = SPACE
          OR LNAMEL = ZERO
         MOVE ATTR-REVERSE TO LNAMEH
         MOVE -1 TO LNAMEL
         MOVE 'You must enter a last name.' TO MSG20
         MOVE 'N' TO VALID-DATA-SW.
*
  2300-WRITE-CUSTOMER-RECORD.
*
      MOVE CUSTNO2I TO CM-CUSTOMER-NUMBER.
      MOVE LNAMEI   TO CM-LAST-NAME.
      MOVE FNAMEI   TO CM-FIRST-NAME.
      MOVE ADDRI    TO CM-ADDRESS.
      MOVE CITYI    TO CM-CITY.
      MOVE STATEI   TO CM-STATE.
      MOVE ZIPCODEI TO CM-ZIP-CODE.
      EXEC CICS
          WRITE DATASET('CUSTMAS')
                FROM(CUSTOMER-MASTER-RECORD)
                RIDFLD(CM-CUSTOMER-NUMBER)
                RESP(RESPONSE-CODE)
      END-EXEC.
      IF        RESPONSE-CODE NOT = DFHRESP(NORMAL)
          AND RESPONSE-CODE NOT = DFHRESP(DUPREC)
         GO TO 9999-TERMINATE-PROGRAM.
```

Figure 8-9   Source listing for the maintenance program (part 7 of 9)

```
/
 3000-PROCESS-CHANGE-CUSTOMER.
*
     PERFORM 2100-RECEIVE-CUSTOMER-MAP.
     PERFORM 2200-EDIT-CUSTOMER-DATA.
     IF VALID-DATA
         MOVE CUSTNO2I TO CM-CUSTOMER-NUMBER
         PERFORM 3100-READ-CUSTOMER-FOR-UPDATE
         IF RESPONSE-CODE = DFHRESP(NORMAL)
             EXEC CICS
                 READQ TS QUEUE(TS-QUEUE-NAME)
                          INTO(TS-CUSTOMER-RECORD)
                          LENGTH(TS-RECORD-LENGTH)
                          ITEM(TS-ITEM-NUMBER)
             END-EXEC
             IF CUSTOMER-MASTER-RECORD = TS-CUSTOMER-RECORD
                 PERFORM 3200-REWRITE-CUSTOMER-RECORD
                 MOVE 'Customer record updated.' TO MSG10
                 SET SEND-ERASE TO TRUE
             ELSE
                 MOVE 'Another user has updated the record.  Try a
                      'gain.' TO MSG10
                 SET SEND-ERASE-ALARM TO TRUE
         ELSE
             MOVE 'Another user has deleted the record.' TO MSG10
             SET SEND-ERASE-ALARM TO TRUE
         END-IF
         PERFORM 1500-SEND-KEY-MAP
         SET PROCESS-KEY-MAP TO TRUE
     ELSE
         SET SEND-DATAONLY-ALARM TO TRUE
         PERFORM 1400-SEND-CUSTOMER-MAP.
*
 3100-READ-CUSTOMER-FOR-UPDATE.
*
     EXEC CICS
         READ DATASET('CUSTMAS')
              INTO(CUSTOMER-MASTER-RECORD)
              RIDFLD(CM-CUSTOMER-NUMBER)
              UPDATE
              RESP(RESPONSE-CODE)
     END-EXEC.
     IF       RESPONSE-CODE NOT = DFHRESP(NORMAL)
         AND  RESPONSE-CODE NOT = DFHRESP(NOTFND)
         GO TO 9999-TERMINATE-PROGRAM.
*
 3200-REWRITE-CUSTOMER-RECORD.
*
     MOVE LNAMEI    TO CM-LAST-NAME.
     MOVE FNAMEI    TO CM-FIRST-NAME.
     MOVE ADDRI     TO CM-ADDRESS.
     MOVE CITYI     TO CM-CITY.
     MOVE STATEI    TO CM-STATE.
     MOVE ZIPCODEI  TO CM-ZIP-CODE.
     EXEC CICS
         REWRITE DATASET('CUSTMAS')
                 FROM(CUSTOMER-MASTER-RECORD)
                 RESP(RESPONSE-CODE)
     END-EXEC.
     IF RESPONSE-CODE NOT = DFHRESP(NORMAL)
         GO TO 9999-TERMINATE-PROGRAM.
```

Figure 8-9   Source listing for the maintenance program (part 8 of 9)

```
/
 4000-PROCESS-DELETE-CUSTOMER.
*
     EXEC CICS
         READQ TS QUEUE(TS-QUEUE-NAME)
                  INTO(TS-CUSTOMER-RECORD)
                  LENGTH(TS-RECORD-LENGTH)
                  ITEM(TS-ITEM-NUMBER)
     END-EXEC.
     MOVE TS-CUSTOMER-NUMBER TO CM-CUSTOMER-NUMBER.
     PERFORM 3100-READ-CUSTOMER-FOR-UPDATE.
     IF RESPONSE-CODE = DFHRESP(NORMAL)
         IF CUSTOMER-MASTER-RECORD = TS-CUSTOMER-RECORD
             PERFORM 4100-DELETE-CUSTOMER-RECORD
             MOVE 'Customer deleted.' TO MSG10
             SET SEND-ERASE TO TRUE
         ELSE
             MOVE 'Another user has updated the record.  Try again
             '.' TO MSG10
             SET SEND-ERASE-ALARM TO TRUE
     ELSE
         MOVE 'Another user has deleted the record.' TO MSG10
         SET SEND-ERASE-ALARM TO TRUE.
     PERFORM 1500-SEND-KEY-MAP.
     SET PROCESS-KEY-MAP TO TRUE.
*
 4100-DELETE-CUSTOMER-RECORD.
*
     EXEC CICS
         DELETE DATASET('CUSTMAS')
                RESP(RESPONSE-CODE)
     END-EXEC.
     IF RESPONSE-CODE NOT = DFHRESP(NORMAL)
         GO TO 9999-TERMINATE-PROGRAM.
*
 9999-TERMINATE-PROGRAM.
*
     MOVE EIBRESP  TO ERR-RESP.
     MOVE EIBRESP2 TO ERR-RESP2.
     MOVE EIBTRNID TO ERR-TRNID.
     MOVE EIBRSRCE TO ERR-RSRCE.
     EXEC CICS
         XCTL PROGRAM('SYSERR')
              COMMAREA(ERROR-PARAMETERS)
     END-EXEC.
```

Figure 8-9   Source listing for the maintenance program (part 9 of 9)

Chapter 9

Transient data control

The *transient data control* module of CICS provides a convenient way to do simple sequential processing. With it, you can store data sequentially and retrieve it later in the same sequence that it was stored. Although you can implement that kind of processing using VSAM entry-sequenced files, transient data control is often a better choice for reasons you'll learn in this chapter.

One of the most common uses of transient data control is for programs that produce output on 3270 printers. Using transient data control, those programs can store print data that's eventually directed to a printer. The advantage of using transient data control for printing is that you don't have to worry about the complex formatting required by 3270 printers. You'll see a printing application that uses transient data control in this chapter.

Before you learn how to process transient data, you need to learn some important concepts. After I present those concepts, I'll show you the commands you use to process transient data. Then, I'll present a sample program that shows you how to use transient data for a typical printing application.

Transient data concepts

Transient means "passing especially quickly into and out of existence." That aptly describes the nature of a *transient data queue*, or *TD queue*. A record passes into a transient data queue when you write it to the queue. That record passes out of the queue—and out of existence—when you read it. As a result, data in a transient data queue is truly transient.

You process records in a transient data queue sequentially. Each record you write is placed at the end of the queue. And when you perform a read operation for the queue, the first record in the queue is retrieved and deleted. Because a record is deleted as it's read, you can't read the same record twice. Nor can you update a record. So all you can do with a transient data queue is write records to it and read records from it. Although that may seem like a limitation, it's really one of the advantages of transient data: You don't have to worry about deleting data that's already been processed. In contrast, you must explicitly delete records from a VSAM file when they're no longer needed.

Transient data queues are often called *destinations*. In fact, you can use the terms interchangeably. Unlike temporary storage queues, transient data queues must be defined in the *Destination Control Table*, or *DCT*. Each DCT entry defines a queue's name, or *destination-id*, along with the queue's characteristics. The systems programmer normally maintains the DCT, so you don't need to worry about the format of DCT entries. But you do need to know a queue's destination-id and characteristics to use it effectively.

Extrapartition and intrapartition transient data queues

Transient data control provides two types of transient data queues: extrapartition and intrapartition. An *extrapartition transient data queue* can be accessed not only from within CICS, but by batch programs running outside of CICS as well. (That's why they're called *extra*partition transient data queues.) In contrast, *intrapartition transient data queues* can be accessed only from within CICS.

Extrapartition destinations are used mostly to collect data that's entered on-line but processed later by a batch program. For example, an order entry program might write order records to an extrapartition destination on disk or tape. Then, on a nightly basis, the orders can be processed by a standard batch COBOL program.

Extrapartition transient data queues are sequential files that are managed by the host system's sequential access method (SAM for VSE, QSAM for MVS). An extrapartition destination doesn't have to be a disk file; it can reside on any device that's valid for SAM or QSAM, such as a tape drive, a printer, or even a card reader or punch.

Because of efficiency problems that can be associated with extra-partition transient data, it's usually better to collect batches of data in standard VSAM entry-sequenced files. Because extrapartition transient data queues aren't frequently used, the rest of this chapter applies just to intrapartition destinations. You shouldn't have any problems learning how to process an extrapartition destination should the need arise, however, because you use the same commands for both types of destinations.

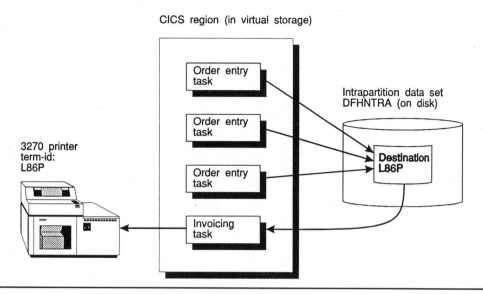

Figure 9-1 An order entry program writes records to an intrapartition destination for subsequent processing by an invoicing program

Intrapartition transient data queues are used more commonly than extrapartition destinations. For example, figure 9-1 shows how an order entry application might use an intrapartition destination to store order data entered by terminal operators. Here, several operators run an order entry program that writes records to an intrapartition transient data queue. And an invoicing program reads records from the queue to print invoices.

As figure 9-1 indicates, CICS stores an intrapartition TD queue in a VSAM file named *DFHNTRA*. Regardless of how many intrapartition transient data queues are in use at one time, they're all stored in DFHNTRA. So you don't have to create a new file to create a new TD queue. But remember that each transient data queue you use must be defined in the DCT.

Automatic transaction initiation

One of the most useful features of intrapartition transient data queues is *automatic transaction initiation*, or *ATI*. ATI provides a convenient way to start a task automatically. To use ATI, you assign a transaction identifier and a *trigger level* to a transient data queue (a destination) by making appropriate entries in the DCT. When the number of records in the queue reaches the trigger level, the specified transaction is automatically started. Because the presence of data in a transient data queue triggers the task, an ATI transaction is often called a *data-driven transaction*.

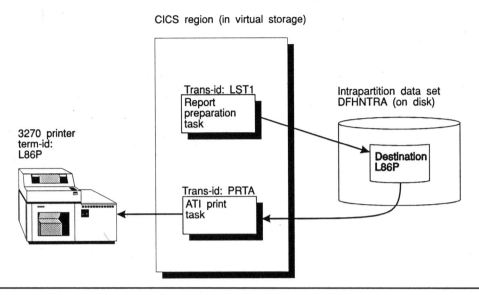

Figure 9-2   A typical generalized printing facility that uses an intrapartition destination to store print lines

To illustrate, figure 9-2 shows how an intrapartition destination is used in a typical printing application. Here, a user-initiated reporting program (trans-id LST1) prepares a report by writing records to an intrapartition destination named L86P. Figure 9-3 shows the DCT entry for the L86P destination. Because the entry specifies a trigger level of 1, a special print program—identified by the trans-id PRTA—is automatically started when a record is written to the destination. The print task reads records from the destination, formats the print data for a 3270 printer, and sends the formatted data to its attached terminal: a 3270 printer whose terminal-id is L86P. (By default, the started task is associated with a terminal whose name is the same as the destination's name. If the systems programmer wants to associate the started task with a different terminal, he or she can specify a terminal-id in the DCT entry for the destination.) Although you probably won't have to code DCT entries, this example should help you understand how an intrapartition destination can be used for a printing application.

Indirect destinations

An *indirect destination* lets a single transient data queue be identified by more than one destination-id. The DCT entry for an indirect destination simply specifies the name of a destination defined elsewhere in the DCT. The name specified for the indirect destination may itself be an indirect destination, but ultimately, each indirect destination must lead to an intrapartition or extrapartition destination.

```
DFHDCT TYPE=INTRA,                                          X
       DESTID=L86P,                                         X
       TRANSID=PRTA,                                        X
       TRIGLEV=1
```

Figure 9-3 Destination Control Table entry for the L86P destination

```
DFHDCT TYPE=INDIRECT,                                       X
       DESTID=PRT1,                                         X
       INDDEST=L86P
```

Figure 9-4 Destination Control Table entry for the indirect destination PRT1

One common reason for using indirect destinations is to shelter application programs from actual destination-ids. By using an indirect destination, you can change a destination-id without having to change and recompile every application program that refers to that destination. That's a valuable feature when a destination is associated with a terminal, because terminal configurations are likely to change.

Figure 9-4 shows the DCT entry for an indirect destination (TYPE=INDIRECT) named PRT1. The INDDEST parameter relates PRT1 to L86P (the destination defined in figure 9-3). As a result, output written to destination PRT1 will be processed through destination L86P by a task running at terminal L86P. If you want to route the output to a different terminal, you just change the DCT entries—not the application program. Because of the indirect destination, programs that write data to PRT1 don't have to know what the final destination is.

Reserving a destination for exclusive use

One minor drawback of transient data is that CICS doesn't automatically ensure that only one task writes records to a destination at one time. So, if two users simultaneously execute a program that writes records to a common destination, those records will be mixed. Although that's not always a problem, it is in a printing application.

Fortunately, CICS provides a facility that lets you reserve—or *enqueue*—a resource for exclusive use: the ENQ and DEQ commands. I'll present the basics of using ENQ and DEQ with transient data queues later in this chapter. And you'll learn more about these commands in chapter 10. For now, I want you to realize that when you write more than one record to a transient data queue, you may need to

The WRITEQ TD command

```
EXEC CICS
    WRITEQ TD    QUEUE(name)
                 FROM(data-area)
               [ LENGTH(data-value) ]
END-EXEC
```

Explanation

QUEUE	Specifies the one- to eight-character name of the transient data queue where data is written.
FROM	Specifies the data area that contains the record to be written.
LENGTH	Specifies the length of the FROM area. Must be numeric. If you use a data name, it must be a binary halfword (PIC S9(4) COMP). (Optional under VS COBOL II.)

Figure 9-5   The WRITEQ TD command

use the ENQ and DEQ commands to make sure another user doesn't mix records with the ones you write.

CICS commands for transient data queues

To process a transient data queue, you use three CICS commands. You use the WRITEQ TD command to add a record to a transient data queue. You use the READQ TD command to retrieve a record from a TD queue. And you use the DELETEQ TD command to delete a TD queue. In addition, you use two other commands—ENQ and DEQ—when you need exclusive access to a destination.

The WRITEQ TD command

You normally code the WRITEQ TD command, whose format is given in figure 9-5, like this:

```
EXEC CICS
    WRITEQ TD QUEUE('L86P')
              FROM(PRINT-AREA)
END-EXEC
```

Here, the contents of the field named PRINT-AREA are written to a transient data queue named L86P.

You use the LENGTH option to specify the length of the record to be written to the destination. When you're using the VS COBOL II compiler, you can omit the LENGTH option if you want to write the entire contents of the FROM field to the destination. Under OS/VS COBOL, the LENGTH option is always required.

The READQ TD command

```
EXEC CICS
    READQ TD   QUEUE(name)
               INTO(data-area)
           [ LENGTH(data-area) ]
END-EXEC
```

Explanation

QUEUE	Specifies the one- to eight-character name of the transient data queue from which data is read.
INTO	Specifies the data area that will contain the record.
LENGTH	Specifies the length of the INTO area. Must be a binary halfword (PIC 9(4) COMP). (Optional under VS COBOL II.)

Figure 9-6   The READQ TD command

Although several exceptional conditions might be raised when your program executes a WRITEQ TD command, all of them represent serious error conditions—like hardware errors—that your program probably can't correct. As a result, I don't recommend you specify the RESP option on WRITEQ TD commands unless your shop has a standard that says otherwise.

The READQ TD command

Figure 9-6 gives the format of the READQ TD command. You usually code it like this:

```
EXEC CICS
    READQ TD QUEUE('L86P')
             INTO(PRINT-AREA)
             LENGTH(PRINT-AREA-LENGTH)
             RESP(RESPONSE-CODE)
END-EXEC
```

Notice that for a READQ TD command, you specify a data name in the LENGTH option. The initial value of the LENGTH field indicates the length of the largest record your program will accept (in other words, the length of the INTO field). After the READQ TD command completes, the LENGTH field is updated to indicate the actual length of the record that was read. You should define the LENGTH field as a binary halfword field (PIC S9(4) COMP).

Although you can omit the LENGTH option entirely under VS COBOL II, you'll usually code it. Since most destinations contain records of varying length, you may need to examine the value returned

The DELETEQ TD command

```
EXEC CICS
    DELETEQ TD QUEUE(name)
END-EXEC
```

Explanation

QUEUE   Specifies the one- to eight-character name of the transient data queue to be deleted.

Figure 9-7   The DELETEQ TD command

into the LENGTH field to determine the length of each record your program reads.

If your program reads a record that's longer than the maximum length you specify, the LENGERR condition is raised. Depending on your application's requirements, you might want to provide for this condition with response code testing. However, when the LENGERR condition occurs, as much of the input data as will fit is placed in the INTO field. As a result, your program can process at least some of the data.

Another exceptional condition that might be raised when your program executes a READQ TD command is QZERO. It occurs when you issue a READQ TD command for a queue that has no records. As a result, you should always provide for the QZERO condition when you use a READQ TD command.

The DELETEQ TD command

When you read a record from a transient data queue, that record is deleted. However, depending on how the DCT entry for the destination is coded, the disk space occupied by that record may still be reserved, even though the record itself is unavailable. As a result, you may need to reclaim that disk space. In other cases, you may need to delete all the records remaining in a destination because of an error condition or some other application requirement.

The DELETEQ TD command, shown in figure 9-7, reclaims unused space and deletes all remaining records in a queue. You issue the DELETEQ TD command like this:

```
EXEC CICS
    DELETEQ TD QUEUE('L86P')
END-EXEC
```

Here, all disk space allocated to the records in the queue named L86P, whether they've been read or not, is released.

The ENQ command

```
EXEC CICS
    ENQ   RESOURCE(data-area)
        [ LENGTH(data-value) ]
END-EXEC
```

Explanation

RESOURCE   Specifies a 1- to 255-byte character string that identifies the resource to be reserved.

LENGTH   Specifies the length of the RESOURCE field. Must be numeric. If you use a data name, it must be a binary halfword (PIC S9(4) COMP). (Optional under VS COBOL II.)

Figure 9-8   The ENQ command

Note that a DELETEQ TD command doesn't remove the queue's DCT entry or disable the queue. It just removes all the queue's records and returns the space they occupied to the system. So, you can still add records to the queue by issuing a WRITEQ TD command. Also note that the DELETEQ TD command isn't valid for extrapartition destinations. If you issue a DELETEQ TD command for an extrapartition destination, the INVREQ condition will be raised.

The ENQ and DEQ commands

Strictly speaking, the ENQ and DEQ commands aren't transient data control commands. Nevertheless, you'll use them often when you process a transient data queue, so I'll describe them briefly here. You'll find a more detailed description of how these commands work in chapter 10.

Figures 9-8 and 9-9 give the formats of the ENQ and DEQ commands. If your program writes more than one record to a destination, you should issue an ENQ command to enqueue the destination. That way, other tasks won't be able to write records to it as long as you have it enqueued.

DEQ releases an enqueued resource. If you don't issue a DEQ command before your task ends, CICS releases the enqueued resource automatically. Still, it's a good idea to issue a DEQ command as soon as possible after you're finished processing the destination. Otherwise, you'll tie up the destination longer than necessary.

In the RESOURCE option of the ENQ and DEQ commands, you provide the name of a field that contains a 1- to 255-character *resource name*. The resource name identifies the resource—in this case a transient data queue—that you want to enqueue. Usually, you just supply the

The DEQ command

```
EXEC CICS
    DEQ     RESOURCE(data-area)
        [ LENGTH(data-value) ]
END-EXEC
```

Explanation

RESOURCE   Specifies a 1- to 255-byte character string that identifies the resource to be released.

LENGTH   Specifies the length of the RESOURCE field. Must be numeric. If you use a data name, it must be a binary halfword (PIC S9(4) COMP). (Optional under VS COBOL II.)

Figure 9-9   The DEQ command

destination-id of the queue you want to enqueue. But your shop may have other standards for forming resource names.

A sample program   Figure 9-10 gives the specifications for a program that lists the contents of a file of product records. For each product record, four fields are printed: product code, description, unit price, and quantity on hand. After all the product records have been listed, a total line showing the number of records in the file is printed.

The product listing program doesn't create its output directly on a printer. Instead, it uses the generalized printing facility in figure 9-2 that lets you write print records to a transient data destination. The destination has a trigger level of one and is associated with a printer terminal and an ATI task. When the product listing program writes records to the destination, the ATI task reads and prints them.

As the specifications indicate, the generalized printing facility I describe here uses a subset of standard ASA control characters to control printer spacing. The product listing program places one of these control characters in the first byte of each output record it writes to the transient data destination. You should realize that this printing facility is by no means a standard facility. Each installation creates its own printing facility, and not all of them use the standard ASA control characters in figure 9-10. I know of one installation that uses an F to skip to the top of a new form and a digit (1-9) to skip one to nine lines before printing data. The point is this: If your installation implements a printing facility using transient data, you'll have to find out how it works.

Figure 9-11 gives the structure chart for the product listing program. This structure is similar to what you'd use for a standard batch report preparation program. Module 1000 starts a browse operation for the

Program	PROLST5

Overview	Lists the contents of a file of product records.

Input/output specifications	PRODUCT Product file

Process specifications

1. Control is transferred to this program via XCTL from the menu program INVMENU with no communication area. The user can also start the program by entering the trans-id LST1.

2. For each record in the product file, list the product code, description, unit price, and quantity on hand. At the end of the listing, list the number of products in the file.

3. Use a transient data destination to route the output data to a printer. An installation-developed utility program will be responsible for reading data from the destination and writing it to the printer.

4. Use ASA standard control characters in the first byte of each destination record to control printer spacing. The control characters are:

blank	Skip one line before printing
0	Skip two lines before printing
-	Skip three lines before printing
1	Skip to the top of the next page before printing

Figure 9-10 Specifications for the product listing program (TD destination) (part 1 of 3)

product file. Then, module 2000 is executed once for each record in the file. It invokes module 2100 to read a product record and module 2200 to print the record. Module 2200, in turn, invokes module 2210 to print heading lines when necessary and module 2220 to write a record to the transient data destination. Because module 2210 needs to write records to the destination as well, it also invokes module 2220. Finally, after all records in the product file have been processed, module 3000 is performed to print the total line. Don't let the word "print" in the module names confuse you. This program writes all of its print output to a transient data destination—not directly to a printer.

Figure 9-12 gives the complete source listing for this program. I don't think you'll have any trouble understanding how it works. In fact, there are only three points I want you to notice. First, each of the print lines defined in the Working-Storage Section (HEADING-LINE-1, HEADING-LINE-2, HEADING-LINE-3, PRODUCT-LINE, and TOTAL-LINE) includes a print control character in the first position. That way, proper printer spacing is ensured for each print line written to the queue.

Second, notice the ENQ and DEQ commands in module 0000. They prevent other tasks from writing to the L86P queue while the product listing program is executing.

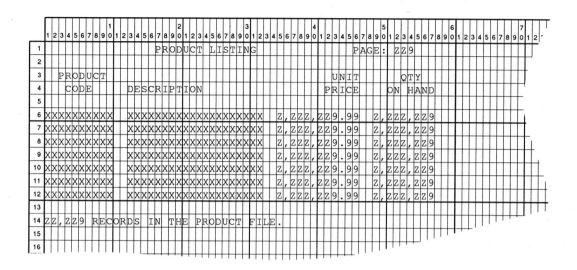

Figure 9-10 Specifications for the product listing program (TD destination) (part 2 of 3)

The PRODUCT copy member

```
01   PRODUCT-MASTER-RECORD.
*
     05   PRM-PRODUCT-CODE           PIC X(10).
     05   PRM-PRODUCT-DESCRIPTION    PIC X(20).
     05   PRM-UNIT-PRICE             PIC S9(7)V99   COMP-3.
     05   PRM-QUANTITY-ON-HAND       PIC S9(7)      COMP-3.
*
```

The ERRPARM copy member

```
01   ERROR-PARAMETERS.
*
     05   ERR-RESP      PIC S9(8)   COMP.
     05   ERR-RESP2     PIC S9(8)   COMP.
     05   ERR-TRNID     PIC X(4).
     05   ERR-RSRCE     PIC X(8).
*
```

Figure 9-10 Specifications for the product listing program (TD destination) (part 3 of 3)

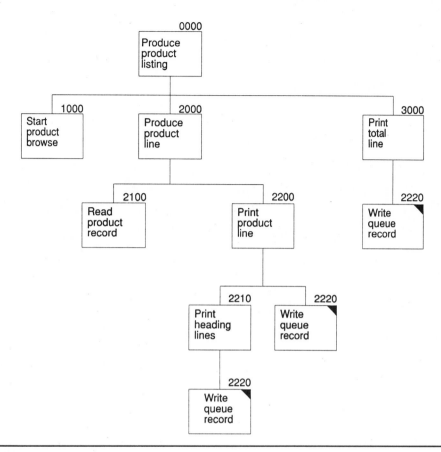

Figure 9-11 Structure chart for the product listing program

Third, notice the two MOVE statements I coded before each PERFORM statement that invokes module 2220. They format two working-storage fields: PRINT-AREA and LINE-LENGTH. For example, I code these statements in module 2210 to print the third heading line:

```
MOVE HEADING-LINE-3 TO PRINT-AREA.
MOVE LENGTH OF HEADING-LINE-3 TO LINE-LENGTH.
PERFORM 2220-WRITE-QUEUE-RECORD.
```

Here, HEADING-LINE-3 is moved to PRINT-AREA and its length is moved to LINE-LENGTH. Then, module 2220 is performed. If you'll look at module 2220, you'll see that the WRITEQ TD command specifies PRINT-AREA in the FROM option and LINE-LENGTH in the LENGTH option. By coding the WRITEQ TD command in this way, I can use it for each print line that's written to the queue, even though they're not all the same length.

Incidentally, if you're using the OS/VS COBOL compiler, you can't specify LENGTH OF to determine the length of a data field. So you'll

```
      IDENTIFICATION DIVISION.
     *
      PROGRAM-ID. PROLST5.
     *
      ENVIRONMENT DIVISION.
     *
      DATA DIVISION.
     *
      WORKING-STORAGE SECTION.
     *
      01  SWITCHES.
     *
          05   PRODUCT-EOF-SW  PIC X         VALUE 'N'.
               88   PRODUCT-EOF              VALUE 'Y'.
     *
      01  WORK-FIELDS.
     *
          05   RECORD-COUNT    PIC S9(5)     VALUE ZERO  COMP-3.
     *
      01  PRINT-FIELDS.
     *
          05   LINE-COUNT      PIC S99       VALUE 99    COMP-3.
          05   LINES-ON-PAGE   PIC S99       VALUE 50    COMP-3.
          05   PAGE-NO         PIC S999      VALUE 1     COMP-3.
          05   PRINT-AREA      PIC X(133).
          05   LINE-LENGTH     PIC S9(4)                 COMP.
     *
      01  RESPONSE-CODE        PIC S9(8)  COMP.
     *
      01  HEADING-LINE-1.
     *
          05   HL1-CC          PIC X         VALUE '1'.
          05   FILLER          PIC X(20)     VALUE '                    PR'.
          05   FILLER          PIC X(20)     VALUE 'ODUCT LISTING       '.
          05   FILLER          PIC X(14)     VALUE '      PAGE: '.
          05   HL1-PAGE-NO     PIC ZZ9.
     *
      01  HEADING-LINE-2.
     *
          05   HL2-CC          PIC X         VALUE '0'.
          05   FILLER          PIC X(20)     VALUE '   PRODUCT          '.
          05   FILLER          PIC X(20)     VALUE SPACE.
          05   FILLER          PIC X(15)     VALUE '  UNIT      QTY'.
     *
      01  HEADING-LINE-3.
     *
          05   HL3-CC          PIC X         VALUE ' '.
          05   FILLER          PIC X(20)     VALUE '    CODE      DESCRIPT'.
          05   FILLER          PIC X(20)     VALUE 'ION                 '.
          05   FILLER          PIC X(17)     VALUE ' PRICE    ON HAND'.
     *
      01  PRODUCT-LINE.
     *
          05   PL-CC           PIC X         VALUE ' '.
          05   PL-PRODUCT-CODE PIC X(10).
          05   FILLER          PIC XX        VALUE SPACE.
          05   PL-DESCRIPTION  PIC X(20).
          05   FILLER          PIC XX        VALUE SPACE.
          05   PL-UNIT-PRICE   PIC Z,ZZZ,ZZZ.99.
          05   FILLER          PIC XX        VALUE SPACE.
          05   PL-QUANTITY     PIC Z,ZZZ,ZZ9.
```

Figure 9-12   Source listing for the product listing program (TD destination) (part 1 of 4)

```
/
 01   TOTAL-LINE.
 *
      05   TL-CC                PIC X        VALUE '-'.
      05   TL-RECORD-COUNT      PIC ZZ,ZZ9.
      05   FILLER               PIC X(15)    VALUE ' RECORDS IN THE'.
      05   FILLER               PIC X(15)    VALUE ' PRODUCT FILE. '.
 *
 01   COMPLETION-MESSAGE.
 *
      05   FILLER               PIC X(15)    VALUE 'Inventory listi'.
      05   FILLER               PIC X(11)    VALUE 'ng printed.'.
 *
 01   DESTINATION-ID           PIC X(4)     VALUE 'L86P'.
 *
 COPY PRODUCT.
 *
 COPY ERRPARM.
 *
 PROCEDURE DIVISION.
 *
 0000-PRODUCE-PRODUCT-LISTING.
 *
      PERFORM 1000-START-PRODUCT-BROWSE.
      EXEC CICS
          ENQ RESOURCE(DESTINATION-ID)
      END-EXEC.
      PERFORM 2000-PRODUCE-PRODUCT-LINE
          UNTIL PRODUCT-EOF.
      PERFORM 3000-PRINT-TOTAL-LINE.
      EXEC CICS
          DEQ RESOURCE(DESTINATION-ID)
      END-EXEC.
      EXEC CICS
          SEND TEXT FROM(COMPLETION-MESSAGE)
                    ERASE
                    FREEKB
      END-EXEC.
      EXEC CICS
          XCTL PROGRAM('INVMENU')
      END-EXEC.
 *
 1000-START-PRODUCT-BROWSE.
 *
      MOVE LOW-VALUE TO PRM-PRODUCT-CODE.
      EXEC CICS
          STARTBR DATASET('PRODUCT')
                  RIDFLD(PRM-PRODUCT-CODE)
                  GTEQ
                  RESP(RESPONSE-CODE)
      END-EXEC.
      IF RESPONSE-CODE = DFHRESP(NOTFND)
          MOVE 'Y' TO PRODUCT-EOF-SW
      ELSE IF RESPONSE-CODE NOT = DFHRESP(NORMAL)
          GO TO 9999-TERMINATE-PROGRAM.
```

Figure 9-12 Source listing for the product listing program (TD destination) (part 2 of 4)

```
/
 2000-PRODUCE-PRODUCT-LINE.
*
     PERFORM 2100-READ-PRODUCT-RECORD.
     IF NOT PRODUCT-EOF
         PERFORM 2200-PRINT-PRODUCT-LINE.
*
 2100-READ-PRODUCT-RECORD.
*
     EXEC CICS
         READNEXT DATASET('PRODUCT')
                  RIDFLD(PRM-PRODUCT-CODE)
                  INTO(PRODUCT-MASTER-RECORD)
                  RESP(RESPONSE-CODE)
     END-EXEC.
     IF RESPONSE-CODE = DFHRESP(ENDFILE)
         MOVE 'Y' TO PRODUCT-EOF-SW
     ELSE IF RESPONSE-CODE = DFHRESP(NORMAL)
         ADD 1 TO RECORD-COUNT
     ELSE
         GO TO 9999-TERMINATE-PROGRAM.
*
 2200-PRINT-PRODUCT-LINE.
*
     IF LINE-COUNT > LINES-ON-PAGE
         PERFORM 2210-PRINT-HEADING-LINES.
     MOVE PRM-PRODUCT-CODE        TO PL-PRODUCT-CODE.
     MOVE PRM-PRODUCT-DESCRIPTION TO PL-DESCRIPTION.
     MOVE PRM-UNIT-PRICE          TO PL-UNIT-PRICE.
     MOVE PRM-QUANTITY-ON-HAND    TO PL-QUANTITY.
     MOVE PRODUCT-LINE TO PRINT-AREA.
     MOVE LENGTH OF PRODUCT-LINE TO LINE-LENGTH.
     PERFORM 2220-WRITE-QUEUE-RECORD.
     ADD 1 TO LINE-COUNT.
     MOVE SPACE TO PL-CC.
*
 2210-PRINT-HEADING-LINES.
*
     MOVE PAGE-NO TO HL1-PAGE-NO.
     MOVE HEADING-LINE-1 TO PRINT-AREA.
     MOVE LENGTH OF HEADING-LINE-1 TO LINE-LENGTH.
     PERFORM 2220-WRITE-QUEUE-RECORD.
     ADD 1 TO PAGE-NO.
     MOVE HEADING-LINE-2 TO PRINT-AREA.
     MOVE LENGTH OF HEADING-LINE-2 TO LINE-LENGTH.
     PERFORM 2220-WRITE-QUEUE-RECORD.
     MOVE HEADING-LINE-3 TO PRINT-AREA.
     MOVE LENGTH OF HEADING-LINE-3 TO LINE-LENGTH.
     PERFORM 2220-WRITE-QUEUE-RECORD.
     MOVE '0' TO PL-CC.
     MOVE ZERO TO LINE-COUNT.
*
 2220-WRITE-QUEUE-RECORD.
*
     EXEC CICS
         WRITEQ TD QUEUE(DESTINATION-ID)
                FROM(PRINT-AREA)
                LENGTH(LINE-LENGTH)
     END-EXEC.
```

Figure 9-12 Source listing for the product listing program (TD destination) (part 3 of 4)

```
/
 3000-PRINT-TOTAL-LINE.
*
     MOVE RECORD-COUNT TO TL-RECORD-COUNT.
     MOVE TOTAL-LINE TO PRINT-AREA.
     MOVE LENGTH OF TOTAL-LINE TO LINE-LENGTH.
     PERFORM 2220-WRITE-QUEUE-RECORD.
*
 9999-TERMINATE-PROGRAM.
*
     MOVE EIBRESP  TO ERR-RESP.
     MOVE EIBRESP2 TO ERR-RESP2.
     MOVE EIBTRNID TO ERR-TRNID.
     MOVE EIBRSRCE TO ERR-RSRCE.
     EXEC CICS
         XCTL PROGRAM('SYSERR')
              COMMAREA(ERROR-PARAMETERS)
     END-EXEC.
```

Figure 9-12 Source listing for the product listing program (TD destination) (part 4 of 4)

have to count up the length of each print record manually and move an appropriate numeric literal to the LINE-LENGTH field.

Discussion I hope by now you appreciate the value of transient data as a generalized queuing facility, especially for printing applications. There are other ways to implement printing applications, as you've already seen in the variations of the product listing program presented earlier in this book. But remember that printing applications are usually implemented using the transient data control elements this chapter presents.

Because you're more likely to develop a program that writes records to a destination than one that reads records from a destination, that's what the program in this chapter shows you how to do. If you want to see a program that reads records from a transient data queue, look back to chapter 7. There, you'll see the program that uses the READQ TD command to read print records from the L86P queue and print them on a 3270 printer. Because the format of the READQ TD command is simple, you shouldn't have any problem understanding how it's used in the program.

Terms

transient data control
transient data queue
TD queue
destination
Destination Control Table
DCT
destination-id

extrapartition transient data queue
intrapartition transient data queue
DFHNTRA
automatic transaction initiation
ATI
trigger level
data-driven transaction
indirect destination
enqueue
resource name

Objective

Given a programming problem that requires reading or writing transient data records, code an acceptable program for its solution.

Chapter 10

Other CICS control features

The four topics in this chapter present CICS commands related to the interval control, task control, program control, and storage control facilities of CICS. Frankly, most CICS programs don't require these commands. But because some programs do, it's good to know about them. Just keep in mind that the material in this chapter is extra: You've already learned the most important elements of CICS.

Interval control

CICS *interval control* provides a variety of time-related features. In this chapter, I'll cover two of those features. The first, provided by the ASKTIME and FORMATTIME commands, lets you obtain the current time and date in a variety of useful formats. The second, provided by the START, RETRIEVE, and CANCEL commands, lets you perform functions related to starting a task.

Formatting the time and date

As you know, you can obtain the current time and date from the Execute Interface Block fields EIBTIME and EIBDATE. EIBTIME is a packed-decimal field that contains the time in the form *hhmmss*, and EIBDATE is a packed-decimal field that contains the date in the form *yyddd*. Although these time and date formats are useful for some purposes, many applications require better control over the format of the time and date. For these applications, you can use the interval control commands ASKTIME and FORMATTIME.

The ASKTIME command, shown in figure 10-1, places the *absolute time* in a 15-digit packed-decimal field (PIC S9(15) COMP-3). This absolute time represents the number of milliseconds that have elapsed since the turn of the century (that is, 0000 hours on January 1, 1900).

Although you can use the absolute time value directly, you're more likely to convert it to a more useful format with the FORMATTIME command. Figure 10-2 shows the FORMATTIME command. As you can see, you supply an absolute time value in the ABSTIME option. Then, you code one or more options that return the converted time or date value.

To illustrate, figure 10-3 shows a sequence of ABSTIME and FORMATTIME commands that obtain an absolute time value and convert it into usable date and time formats. When I tested these statements at 1:53 p.m. on June 1, 1992, the ASKTIME command returned the value 2,916,395,604,090 for the absolute time. Then, the FORMATTIME command returned the value 13:53:24 in the TIME field and 06/01/92 in the DATE field.

Notice in figure 10-3 that I coded the DATESEP and TIMESEP options on the FORMATTIME command. These options cause FORMATTIME to insert separators between the components of a time or date. The default separator for time values is a colon; for dates, the

The ASKTIME command

```
EXEC CICS
    ASKTIME [ ABSTIME(data-area) ]
END-EXEC
```

Explanation

ABSTIME   Specifies a 15-digit packed-decimal field (PIC S9(15) COMP-3) where CICS places an
                           absolute time value representing the number of milliseconds that have elapsed since
                           midnight, January 1, 1900.

Figure 10-1 The ASKTIME command

default separator is a slash. You can force FORMATTIME to use a
different separator by coding a literal, like this:

```
EXEC CICS
    FORMATTIME ABSTIME(ABSOLUTE-TIME)
               DATE(WS-DATE)
               DATESEP('-')
END-EXEC
```

In this case, FORMATTIME would return a value like 06-01-92 in
WS-DATE. If you omit the TIMESEP or DATESEP options altogether,
FORMATTIME doesn't use any separators. Thus, the date value would
be returned as 060192.

When you use the DATE option, CICS returns the date in an
installation-wide default format that's specified by the systems
programmer. In most U.S. installations, this date format is MMDDYY. If
you want to use a specific date format rather than the installation
default, you can use one of the explicit date options (MMDDYY,
DDMMYY, YYMMDD, YYDDMM, or YYDDD).

The DATEFORM option returns a value that corresponds to the
default date format. For example, if your system's default date format is
mmddyy, the DATEFORM option will return the value MMDDYY. You
probably won't use this option in an application program, but you
might use it in the command-level interpreter (CECI) to determine your
installation's default date format.

Five of the date options return a binary fullword value rather than a
character string: DAYCOUNT, DAYOFMONTH, DAYOFWEEK,
MONTHOFYEAR, and YEAR. Although there is no DAYOFYEAR
option, you can obtain the day of the current year by using the YYDDD
option.

The FORMATTIME command

```
EXEC CICS
    FORMATTIME    ABSTIME(data-area)

              [ DATE(data-area)
                  [ DATEFORM(data-area) ] ]
              [ MMDDYY(data-area) ]
              [ DDMMYY(data-area) ]
              [ YYMMDD(data-area) ]
              [ YYDDMM(data-area) ]
              [ YYDDD(data-area) ]
              [ DATESEP[(data-value)] ]

              [ DAYCOUNT(data-area) ]
              [ DAYOFWEEK(data-area) ]
              [ DAYOFMONTH(data-area) ]
              [ MONTHOFYEAR(data-area) ]
              [ YEAR(data-area) ]

              [ TIME(data-area) ]
              [ TIMESEP[(data-value)] ]

END-EXEC
```

Explanation

ABSTIME	Specifies a 15-digit packed-decimal field (PIC S9(15) COMP-3) where CICS places an absolute time value representing the number of milliseconds that have elapsed since midnight, January 1, 1900. Usually, this value is obtained with an ASKTIME command.
DATE	Specifies an eight-byte field where CICS places the date formatted according to the installation default.
DATEFORM	Specifies a six-byte field where CICS returns YYMMDD, DDMMYY, or MMDDYY to indicate the installation's default date format.
MMDDYY	Specifies an eight-byte field where CICS places the month, day, and year in the form *mmddyy*. If DATESEP is also coded, the month, day, and year components will be separated using the specified separator character.
DDMMYY	Specifies an eight-byte field where CICS places the day, month, and year in the form *ddmmyy*. If DATESEP is also coded, the day, month, and year components will be separated using the specified separator character.
YYMMDD	Specifies an eight-byte field where CICS places the year, month, and day in the form *yymmdd*. If DATESEP is also coded, the year, month, and day components will be separated using the specified separator character.
YYDDMM	Specifies an eight-byte field where CICS places the year, day, and month in the form *yyddmm*. If DATESEP is also coded, the year, day, and month components will be separated using the specified separator character.

Figure 10-2 The FORMATTIME command (part 1 of 2)

YYDDD	Specifies a six-byte field where CICS places the year and day within the year in the form *yyddd*. If DATESEP is also coded, the year and day components will be separated using the specified separator character.
DATESEP	Specifies a single character value to be used as a separator between the month, day, and year components of a date value. If you omit DATESEP, no separator is used; if you specify DATESEP but don't provide a value, a slash (/) is used.
DAYCOUNT	Specifies a binary fullword (PIC S9(8) COMP) where CICS places the number of days that have passed since January 1, 1900. (January 1, 1900 is day 0.)
DAYOFWEEK	Specifies a binary fullword (PIC S9(8) COMP) where CICS places a number that corresponds to the day of the week. Sunday is 0, Monday is 1, and so on.
DAYOFMONTH	Specifies a binary fullword (PIC S9(8) COMP) where CICS places the day within the current month.
MONTHOFYEAR	Specifies a binary fullword (PIC S9(8) COMP) where CICS places a number that corresponds to the current month; January is 1, February is 2, and so on.
YEAR	Specifies a binary fullword (PIC S9(8) COMP) where CICS places the full year (that is, 1993 instead of just 93).
TIME	Specifies an eight-byte field where CICS places the time in the form *hhmmss*. If TIMESEP is also coded, the hours, minutes, and seconds components are separated using the specified separator character.
TIMESEP	Specifies a single character value to be used as a separator between the hours, minutes, and seconds components of a time value. If you omit TIMESEP, no separator is used; if you specify TIMESEP but don't provide a value, a colon (:) is used.

Figure 10-2 The FORMATTIME command (part 2 of 2)

Automatic time-ordered transaction initiation	The rest of the interval control commands I'll present in this chapter let you use a CICS facility called *Automatic time-ordered transaction initiation*, or *time-ordered ATI*. Simply put, this facility lets you start a new task by issuing a START command. You can also pass data to the task from the START command. If you do, the started task can then retrieve that data by issuing a RETRIEVE command. And you can cancel a request to start a task by issuing a CANCEL command.

To use time-ordered ATI, you need to understand the difference between starting a task and using program control commands (LINK or XCTL) to invoke a program. Because CICS is a multi-tasking system, it processes more than one task at a time. As a result, a task initiated by a START command can execute simultaneously with the task that issued the START command. In other words, the *starting task* can run at the same time as the *started task*. In contrast, programs invoked by LINK and XCTL commands run one at a time as part of a single task.

```
EXEC CICS
    ASKTIME ABSTIME(ABSOLUTE-TIME)
END-EXEC.
EXEC CICS
    FORMATTIME ABSTIME(ABSOLUTE-TIME)
               DATE(WS-DATE)
               DATESEP
               TIME(WS-TIME)
               TIMESEP
END-EXEC.
```

Figure 10-3 Using the ASKTIME and FORMATTIME commands together to format a date and time

For example, consider how you might use program control and interval control commands in a menu-driven application. When a user selects a data entry program, the menu program issues an XCTL command to transfer control directly to the data entry program. In contrast, suppose the user selects a report preparation function that doesn't require user interaction. If the menu program invokes the report preparation program with an XCTL command, the terminal will be tied up while the report is prepared. If the report takes more than a few seconds to prepare, that could be an inconvenience for the user. But if the menu program uses interval control to start the report preparation program as a separate task, control returns directly to the menu program. As a result, the user can continue with other work while the report is prepared.

When you start a task with time-ordered ATI, you can supply an optional *expiration time* that determines when the task should begin executing. You'll see how to do that when I present the START command. If you don't supply an expiration time, your task starts immediately.

How a task is scheduled   Figure 10-4 shows how interval control schedules a task. As you can see, when a START command is issued, interval control creates a special data area called an *interval control element* (or *ICE*). The ICE contains information about the task to be started, including its transaction-id, terminal-id, and expiration time. Then, if the START command supplied any data to be passed to the started task, interval control invokes temporary storage control to store it. When these steps are complete, interval control returns control to the starting task.

Although interval control uses temporary storage to store data passed between tasks, that's transparent to you. So don't worry if you haven't read about temporary storage in chapter 8. You don't need to know how temporary storage works to use interval control commands. And most of the time, you won't be passing data to a started task anyway.

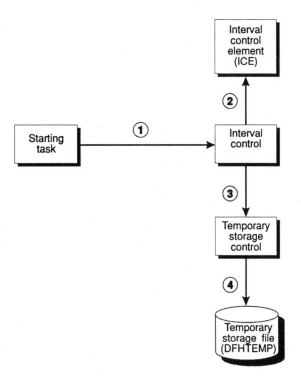

Explanation

1. A user task issues a START command that's processed by interval control.

2. Interval control creates an ICE that indicates the trans-id, expiration time, and terminal-id for the task to be started.

3. Interval control invokes temporary storage control to save data that's passed to the started task.

4. Temporary storage control saves this data in the temporary storage file.

Figure 10-4 How a task is scheduled

How a scheduled task is started   Figure 10-5 shows how a time-ordered ATI task begins execution when its expiration time arrives. A CICS program called *interval control expiration analysis* periodically examines all interval control elements, comparing their expiration times with the system clock. When an ICE has expired, expiration analysis invokes *task control* to start the new task, using the transaction-id and terminal-id saved in the ICE.

Note that the events in figure 10-4 are independent of those in figure 10-5. In other words, once a task issues a START command, it continues execution without regard for the status of the started task. Depending

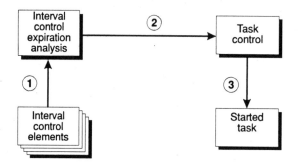

Explanation

1. Interval control expiration analysis compares the current time of day with the expiration time of each ICE.

2. For each expired ICE, expiration analysis invokes task control.

3. Task control starts a task.

Figure 10-5 How a scheduled task is started

on the expiration time in the ICE, the started task may begin immediately or several hours later. Either way, the started task is independent of the starting task.

The START command

Figure 10-6 gives the format of the START command. Usually, you code it like this:

```
EXEC CICS
    START TRANSID('LST5')
END-EXEC
```

Here, a task identified by the transaction identifier LST5 is scheduled for immediate execution. Notice that you specify a transaction-id—*not* a program name—in a START command. That's because CICS requires a trans-id to start a new task.

How to attach a started task to a terminal   In the previous example, LST5 will run without being attached to a terminal. As a result, it can't do terminal I/O directly. If you need to attach a task to a specific terminal, like a printer, you specify the TERMID option on the START command. For example, the command

```
EXEC CICS
    START TRANSID('LST4')
          TERMID('L86P')
END-EXEC
```

The START command

```
EXEC CICS
    START   TRANSID(name)
            INTERVAL(hhmmss)
            TIME(hhmmss)
            AFTER [HOURS(hh)] [MINUTES(mins)] [SECONDS(secs)]
            AT    [HOURS(hh)] [MINUTES(mins)] [SECONDS(secs)]
        [ TERMID(name) ]
        [ FROM(data-area)
             [ LENGTH(data-value) ] ]
        [ RTERMID(name) ]
        [ RTRANSID(name) ]
        [ QUEUE(name) ]
        [ REQID(name) ]
END-EXEC
```

Explanation

TRANSID	Specifies the transaction-identifier that will be used to start the task.
INTERVAL	Specifies an interval in the form *hhmmss*. CICS adds the interval to the current time to determine when the task will start. If specified as a data area, must be a four-byte signed packed-decimal field (PIC S9(7) COMP-3).
TIME	Specifies a time in the form *hhmmss*. If the time is more than 18 hours after the current time, it's considered to have expired already. If specified as a data area, must be a four-byte signed packed-decimal field (PIC S9(7) COMP-3).
AFTER	Specifies that the task should start after the interval specified in the HOURS, MINUTES, and SECONDS options.
AT	Specifies that the task should start at the time specified in the HOURS, MINUTES, and SECONDS options.
HOURS	Must be a number between 0 and 99. If specified as a data area, must be a binary fullword (PIC S9(8) COMP).
MINUTES	If HOURS or SECONDS is also coded, must be a number between 0 and 59. If HOURS and SECONDS are not coded, can be a number between 0 and 5999. If specified as a data area, must be a binary fullword (PIC S9(8) COMP).
SECONDS	If HOURS or MINUTES is also coded, must be a number between 0 and 59. If HOURS and MINUTES are not coded, can be a number between 0 and 359,999. If specified as a data area, must be a binary fullword (PIC S9(8) COMP).
TERMID	Specifies the name of a terminal where the task will run. If omitted, the task will run without a terminal.
FROM	Specifies the name of a field whose value is passed to the started task.

Figure 10-6 The START command (part 1 of 2)

LENGTH	Specifies the length of the FROM field. If you code a data name, it must be a binary halfword (PIC S9(4) COMP). (Optional under VS COBOL II.)
RTERMID	Specifies a four-byte value that's passed to the started task.
RTRANSID	Specifies a four-byte value that's passed to the started task.
QUEUE	Specifies an eight-byte value that's passed to the started task.
REQID	Specifies an eight-byte value that identifies this START command so the started task can be cancelled with a CANCEL command. If omitted, CICS generates a request-id and returns it in EIBREQID.

Figure 10-6 The START command (part 2 of 2)

attaches transaction LST4 to the terminal L86P. In general, you should specify the TERMID option whenever the started task does terminal I/O.

How to specify an expiration time with the TIME and INTERVAL options   If you don't want a started task to begin execution immediately, you can specify an expiration time with the TIME or INTERVAL option. For either option, you code a value in the format *hhmmss* where *hh* is hours, *mm* is minutes, and *ss* is seconds. With the TIME option, you specify a time of day using a 24-hour clock. As a result, 7:30 a.m. is 073000, and 2:00 p.m. is 140000. Midnight is 000000; one second before midnight is 235959. To illustrate, the command

```
EXEC CICS
    START TRANSID('LST4')
          TERMID('L86P')
          TIME(170000)
END-EXEC
```

causes transaction LST4 to start at 5:00 p.m. attached to terminal L86P.

One peculiarity of interval control is that you can't use the TIME option to specify an expiration time that's more than 18 hours from the current time. If you do, interval control assumes that the time you specify has already expired, and the task is started immediately. For example, suppose you issue this command when the current time is 2:00 p.m. (140000):

```
EXEC CICS
    START TRANSID('LST5')
          TIME(104500)
END-EXEC
```

Although the intention of this command may be to start LST5 at 10:45 a.m. *tomorrow*, the effect of the command is that LST5 is started immediately. That's because 10:45 a.m. is more than 18 hours ahead of 2:00 p.m.

The second way to specify an expiration time is to use the INTERVAL option, like this:

```
EXEC CICS
    START TRANSID('LST5')
          INTERVAL(001500)
END-EXEC
```

Here, LST5 will be started in fifteen minutes. CICS adds the INTERVAL value you specify to the current time to determine the correct expiration time.

How to specify an expiration time with the AT and AFTER options
Beginning with CICS version 3.1, you can use the AT and AFTER options as alternatives to the TIME and INTERVAL options. You use both options along with the HOURS, MINUTES, and SECONDS options to specify an expiration time (AT) or an interval (AFTER). The AT and AFTER options were introduced for compatibility with the C language, which doesn't support the packed-decimal data type required by the TIME and INTERVAL options. The HOURS, MINUTES, and SECONDS options all use binary fullword items.

To illustrate how the AT and AFTER options work, suppose you want to schedule a task to execute at 10:45 a.m. To do that, you could use this START command:

```
EXEC CICS
    START TRANSID('LST4')
          TERMID('L86P')
          AT HOURS(10) MINUTES(45)
END-EXEC
```

(Note that you specify the HOURS value using a 24-hour clock, just as you do for the TIME option.) Or, to schedule a task to start in 1 minute and 30 seconds, you could use this START command:

```
EXEC CICS
    START TRANSID('LST4')
          TERMID('L86P')
          AFTER MINUTES(1) SECONDS(30)
END-EXEC
```

The maximum value you can specify for the HOURS option when you use AFTER is 99. The maximum values for the MINUTES and SECONDS options depends on whether you use them alone or in combination with any other AFTER option. If you use them in combination, the maximum value you can specify for MINUTES and SECONDS is 59. If you use MINUTES or SECONDS alone, you can specify larger values. For MINUTES, you can specify a value of up to 5999. That's one minute less than 100 hours. For SECONDS, you can specify a value of up to 359,999. That's one second shy of 100 hours.

How to pass data to a started task   If you specify the FROM option on a START command, the data in the FROM area is passed to the started task. For example, the command

```
EXEC CICS
    START TRANSID('LST6')
          FROM(ITEM-NUMBER)
END-EXEC
```

passes the contents of the field ITEM-NUMBER to transaction LST6. (Under OS/VS COBOL, you must also use the LENGTH option to specify the length of the FROM area.)

Besides the FROM option, the START command provides three other options that pass specific types of data to a started task: RTRANSID (for a transaction-id), RTERMID (for a terminal-id), and QUEUE (for a temporary storage queue name). These options work the same as the FROM option, except that you don't have to specify a length value for them. Both RTRANSID and RTERMID pass a four-byte data field; QUEUE passes an eight-byte data field. You probably won't use these options often.

The RETRIEVE command

To retrieve data passed to it by the starting task, the started task must issue a RETRIEVE command, illustrated in figure 10-7. Then, interval control invokes temporary storage control, which retrieves the correct record from the temporary storage file and returns it to the started task. Interval control keeps track of where the data to be passed to various tasks is stored and insures that it's coordinated with the current interval control elements. As a result, a started task doesn't have to identify what temporary storage queue to retrieve its data from; interval control maintains that information.

For example, the command

```
EXEC CICS
    RETRIEVE INTO(ITEM-NUMBER)
             LENGTH(ITEM-NUMBER-LENGTH)
             RESP(RESPONSE-CODE)
END-EXEC
```

obtains the passed data and places it in ITEM-NUMBER. The initial value of the LENGTH field should be the length of the INTO field. After the RETRIEVE command executes, the LENGTH field contains the actual length of the data retrieved. Although LENGTH is optional under VS COBOL II, you'll probably want to code it so you can check the length of the data retrieved.

Like the START command, the RETRIEVE command provides three options other than INTO for receiving data: RTRANSID, RTERMID, and QUEUE. If the START command that initiated the task specified one or more of those options, you should specify them on the RETRIEVE command as well.

The RETRIEVE command

```
EXEC CICS
    RETRIEVE    INTO(data-area)
              [ LENGTH(data-area) ]
              [ RTRANSID(name) ]
              [ RTERMID(name) ]
              [ QUEUE(name) ]
END-EXEC
```

Explanation

INTO	Specifies the area that will contain the data sent via the FROM option of the START command.
LENGTH	Specifies the length of the INTO area. Must be a binary halfword (PIC S9(4) COMP). (Optional under VS COBOL II.)
RTRANSID	Specifies the area that will contain the data sent via the RTRANSID option of the START command.
RTERMID	Specifies the area that will contain the data sent via the RTERMID option of the START command.
QUEUE	Specifies the area that will contain the data sent via the QUEUE option of the START command.

Figure 10-7 The RETRIEVE command

If a started program issues a RETRIEVE command but no data was passed to it, the NOTFND condition is raised. In most cases, that's probably a serious error condition and you're just as well to let the task abend. However, when passing data to a started task is optional, you can use the NOTFND condition to determine whether or not data was passed.

If the data that's retrieved is longer than your input area, the LENGERR condition is raised. Then, as much of the data as will fit is placed in the INTO area. That way, your program can continue. In most cases, you should treat the LENGERR condition as a serious error.

How one task can fulfill several START requests   When a START command for the same task with the same expiration time is issued more than once, interval control creates an ICE for each START request. If data was passed, a separate temporary storage record is created for each START request.

If the started task is attached to a terminal, a single execution can fulfill all of the pending START requests by issuing RETRIEVE commands repeatedly. Each RETRIEVE command retrieves the data saved by one of the previous START commands, until there's no more data to be retrieved. And, each RETRIEVE command removes the ICE associated with the record that's retrieved, so once you retrieve a record, the START request is completely fulfilled. CICS raises the ENDDATA condition when no more records are available for a RETRIEVE command.

Bear in mind, however, that most START requests do *not* pass data to the started task. And of those that do, few require that multiple data records be passed to a single started task.

The CANCEL command

The CANCEL command, shown in figure 10-8, lets you cancel a task you've scheduled with a START command. In short, the CANCEL command removes the interval control element created by a START command along with any data passed to the started task. Once the task has started, though, you can't use a CANCEL command to cancel it.

On a CANCEL command, you must specify what START request to cancel by supplying a *request-id* in the REQID option. The request-id is an eight-character string that uniquely identifies a START command. For example, the command

```
EXEC CICS
    CANCEL REQID('TRANDEP1')
END-EXEC
```

deletes the ICE created by a START command identified as TRANDEP1.

How do you know the request-id of a particular START command? There are two ways. First, you can let CICS assign a request-id to your START command. Then, you can examine the EIBREQID field in the Execute Interface Block after the START command completes to find out what value CICS assigned.

To illustrate, suppose you code these commands:

```
EXEC CICS
    START TRANSID('LST5')
          INTERVAL(010000)
END-EXEC.
MOVE EIBREQID TO REQUEST-ID.
```

To cancel that START request, you can issue a CANCEL command like this:

```
EXEC CICS
    CANCEL REQID(REQUEST-ID)
END-EXEC
```

Note that you should move EIBREQID to a working-storage field before you issue another CICS command. That's because other CICS commands place request-ids in EIBREQID too.

The CANCEL command

```
EXEC CICS
    CANCEL REQID(name)
END-EXEC
```

Explanation

REQID   Specifies an eight-byte value that identifies the START command to be cancelled.

Figure 10-8 The CANCEL command

The second way to determine a request-id is to assign it yourself using the REQID option of the START command. For example:

```
MOVE 'TRANELOG' TO REQUEST-ID.
EXEC CICS
    START TRANSID('LST5')
          INTERVAL(010000)
          REQID(REQUEST-ID)
END-EXEC.
```

Here, the value of REQUEST-ID (TRANELOG) is used as the request-id for the START command.

Quite frankly, it's uncommon to cancel a task once you've scheduled it. Most tasks are scheduled for immediate execution, so they can't be cancelled. As for a task that's scheduled for future execution, the only reason you might cancel it is if a serious error condition occurs in the starting task *after* it issues the START command. (It's also possible to issue the CANCEL command from a task other than the one that issued the original START command, but that's unlikely.)

Discussion

If you've read chapter 9, you should recall that transactions can also be initiated automatically based on the presence of data in a transient data queue. Now that you've seen how interval control task initiation works and how you use the START, RETRIEVE, and CANCEL commands, look at figure 10-9. Here, I compare the automatic transaction initiation features of transient data control and interval control. As you can see, the main difference is that transient data ATI is data-driven—that is, the ATI task is started based on the presence of data in a transient data queue—while the interval control ATI facility depends on time rather than data.

Although these two ATI facilities are similar, I've found that I use data-driven ATI more than time-ordered ATI. That's because data-

	Data-driven ATI	Time-ordered ATI
What causes the ATI task to begin execution?	The presence of data in a transient data queue.	The arrival of the specified expiration time.
Can the ATI task be attached to a terminal?	Yes.	Yes.
How is data passed to the started task?	Via the transient data queue. Issue a WRITEQ TD command to send the data.	Via temporary storage. Code the FROM option on the START command to send the data.
How does the started task retrieve data?	It issues a READQ TD command.	It issues a RETRIEVE command.
Can you cancel the ATI task before it begins?	No.	No.

Figure 10-9 A comparison of data-driven and time-ordered ATI features

driven ATI lends itself well to printing applications, as you saw in chapter 9.

Terms

interval control
automatic time-ordered transaction initiation
time-ordered ATI
starting task
started task
expiration time
interval control
interval control element
ICE
interval control expiration analysis
task control
request-id

Objective

Given a programming problem involving time-ordered automatic transaction initiation, code an acceptable program for its solution.

Task control

Task control refers to the CICS functions that manage the execution of tasks. One of the major components of task control is the *dispatcher*, which keeps track of all current tasks and decides which of several waiting tasks should be given control of the processor. Although task dispatching is mostly an automatic function, task control provides two facilities that let an application program influence the dispatcher's operation: (1) the SUSPEND command and (2) the ENQ and DEQ commands.

The SUSPEND command

Normally, an application program gives up control whenever it issues a CICS command. For example, when your program issues a READ command, it gives up control while CICS fulfills the read request. In the meantime, the dispatcher gives control to another task. In this way, many tasks can be operating at once. Only one of them is actually executing, though; the rest are either waiting for an I/O operation to complete, or just waiting for their turn to execute.

An important point to note about the way CICS multitasking works is that whenever your program gains control, it continues to execute until it issues a CICS command. For most applications, that's not a long time. But some unusual applications may require a long stretch of CPU processing without an intervening CICS command. An application like that can cause two problems. First, it degrades the performance of other tasks in the system because it monopolizes CPU time. And second, it might exceed the CICS limit for how long a task can run without returning control to CICS. To avoid both problems, you use the SUSPEND command.

The SUSPEND command, shown in figure 10-10, doesn't do anything except temporarily return control to CICS. Because the SUSPEND command has no options, you always code it like this:

```
EXEC CICS
    SUSPEND
END-EXEC
```

When you issue a SUSPEND command, your task is placed at the end of the list of tasks waiting to gain control, and the task at the head of that list takes over. Eventually, control returns to your task. But in the meantime, other tasks have a chance to execute.

The SUSPEND command

```
EXEC CICS
    SUSPEND
END-EXEC
```

Explanation

The SUSPEND command has no options.

Figure 10-10   The SUSPEND command

The ENQ and DEQ commands

The ENQ and DEQ commands, shown in figure 10-11, provide a general queuing facility that's similar to the UPDATE option of the READ command: They let you ensure that two or more tasks don't access a non-sharable resource (like a printer terminal) at the same time. That's called *single-threading* because only one task at a time can access the resource. Any other tasks that try to access that resource must wait their turn.

You use the ENQ command to single-thread a resource, or *enqueue* it. Once you enqueue a resource, any other tasks that try to enqueue the same resource are suspended until you issue a DEQ command to release, or *dequeue*, the resource. (Don't confuse the terms enqueue and dequeue with a transient data or temporary storage queue. There's no relationship at all.)

To understand the ENQ and DEQ commands, you must understand what a *resource* is. In short, a resource is any CICS facility you want to single-thread. Typically, it's a printer terminal, a transient data destination, a temporary storage queue, or an area of main storage, such as a table. When you enqueue a resource, you specify the *resource name*, which may be from 1 to 255 characters long. CICS stores the names of all enqueued resources in a table. Then, any time a task tries to enqueue a resource, CICS checks the table to see if another task has already enqueued a resource with that name. If so, the task must wait.

It's important to know that there's no internal mechanism that relates a resource name to an actual CICS facility. As far as CICS is concerned, resource names are just character strings. Unfortunately, this puts the burden on you to make sure the ENQ and DEQ commands work. So every program that enqueues a specific resource must use the same name for it. And every program that processes the resource must enqueue it. If you don't follow these guidelines, the ENQ/DEQ facility won't work.

Figure 10-12 shows a typical use of the ENQ and DEQ commands. If you've read chapter 9, you'll recognize that figure 10-12 is a portion of the product listing program presented in that chapter. The program

The ENQ command

```
EXEC CICS
    ENQ   RESOURCE(data-area)
        [ LENGTH(data-value) ]
END-EXEC
```

The DEQ command

```
EXEC CICS
    DEQ   RESOURCE(data-area)
        [ LENGTH(data-value) ]
END-EXEC
```

Explanation

RESOURCE   Specifies a 1- to 255-byte character string that identifies the resource to be enqueued or dequeued.

LENGTH   Specifies the length of the RESOURCE field. Must be numeric. If you use a data name, it must be a binary halfword (PIC S9(4) COMP). (Optional under VS COBOL II.)

Figure 10-11 The ENQ and DEQ commands

produces a report by writing records to a transient data destination. To prevent output lines from being mixed, each task that writes records to this destination enqueues it first. That's what the ENQ command at the start of module 0000 does. After the program is finished processing the destination, it issues a DEQ command to release it. Then, other tasks that enqueue the destination can continue.

In the ENQ and DEQ commands, the RESOURCE option specifies the name of a field that contains the resource name. In this case, DESTINATION-ID is a four-character field whose value is L86P. The actual character string you use as a resource name doesn't really matter, as long as every program in your system uses the same name for that resource. Remember, CICS does not associate a resource name with an actual CICS facility. So it's important that you follow shop standards for creating and using resource names.

Terms

task control
dispatcher
single-threading
enqueue
dequeue
resource
resource name

```
WORKING-STORAGE SECTION.
    .
    .
    .
01  DESTINATION-ID          PIC X(4)    VALUE 'L86P'.
    .
    .
    .
PROCEDURE DIVISION.
*
0000-PRODUCE-PRODUCT-LISTING.
*
    PERFORM 1000-START-PRODUCT-BROWSE.
    EXEC CICS
        ENQ RESOURCE(DESTINATION-ID)
    END-EXEC.
    PERFORM 2000-PRODUCE-PRODUCT-LINE
        UNTIL PRODUCT-EOF.
    PERFORM 3000-PRINT-TOTAL-LINE.
    EXEC CICS
        DEQ RESOURCE(DESTINATION-ID)
    END-EXEC.
    .
    .
    .
```

Figure 10-12 A portion of a program that enqueues and dequeues a transient data destination

Objectives

1. Explain when a SUSPEND command should be included in a CICS program.

2. Given a programming problem that requires exclusive access to a shared resource, code a solution using appropriate ENQ and DEQ commands.

Program control

In *Part 1: An Introductory Course*, you learned about three program control commands: RETURN, XCTL, and LINK. You use those commands to manage the execution of programs within a task, passing data via the COMMAREA option. In this topic, you'll first learn another method for passing data between application programs with XCTL and LINK: the INPUTMSG option. Then, you'll learn about a fourth program control command: LOAD.

The INPUTMSG option

As you know, you can use the COMMAREA option on a LINK or XCTL command to pass data to the program you're invoking. The invoked program accesses the data via the DFHCOMMAREA field in its Linkage Section. CICS version 3 introduced a new way to pass data to an invoked program: the INPUTMSG option. When you use the INPUTMSG option on a LINK or XCTL command, CICS passes data to the invoked program as if that data were entered by a terminal user. As a result, the invoked program accesses the passed data by issuing a terminal control RECEIVE command.

You might be wondering why you would use INPUTMSG as an alternative to COMMAREA. The answer is simple: You wouldn't. INPUTMSG isn't intended to be an alternative to COMMAREA. So when you're designing an application in which one program invokes another, the best way to pass data between the programs is still via the communication area.

The INPUTMSG option has a rather specific purpose: It's designed to let you create simple *front-end* programs. Then, these front-end programs can invoke existing application programs that obtain terminal input using the RECEIVE command. For example, consider the simple inquiry program I presented in chapter 7 of this book. To use that program, the user types the trans-id INQ4 followed by a space and a customer number, like this:

```
INQ4 400001
```

Here, the user is asking the inquiry program to retrieve data for customer 400001.

Suppose you want to improve the user interface of this program. Rather than recode the application, you could simply create a front-end program that implements the new interface. Then, the front-end program would invoke the inquiry program directly using an XCTL or

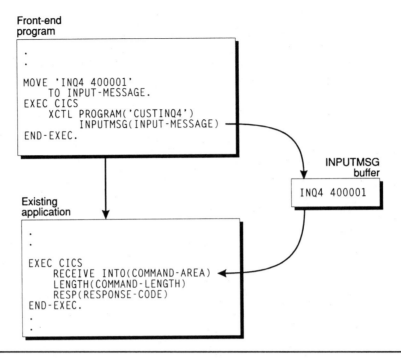

Figure 10-13   Passing data to an application via the INPUTMSG option

LINK command, passing the data entered by the terminal user via the INPUTMSG option. Figure 10-13 shows how this might work. Here, the XCTL command in the front-end program passes an input message to the inquiry program. The inquiry program then retrieves the input message when it issues the RECEIVE command. Because the input message is in the same format as the command line the inquiry program expects to receive from the terminal user, it wasn't necessary to make any changes to the program. In fact, as far as the inquiry program knows, the input message was entered by a terminal user.

Figures 10-14 and 10-15 show the formats of the LINK and XCTL commands with the INPUTMSG option. As you can see, both of these commands also provide an INPUTMSGLEN option, which you can use to specify the length of the INPUTMSG area. INPUTMSGLEN is required only if you're using OS/VS COBOL. Under VS COBOL II, INPUTMSGLEN is optional.

Frankly, the INPUTMSG option by itself isn't powerful enough to create sophisticated front-end programs. That's because it deals only with input messages; it doesn't let you capture terminal output sent by the invoked program. With CICS version 3.3, however, IBM introduced a new CICS facility called the *Front End Programming Interface*, or *FEPI*. FEPI introduces a set of new CICS commands that let you create sophisticated front-end programs that handle both input and output

The LINK command

```
EXEC CICS
    LINK    PROGRAM(name)
          [ COMMAREA(data-area)
              [ LENGTH(data-value) ] ]
          [ INPUTMSG(data-area)
              [ INPUTMSGLEN(data-value) ] ]
END-EXEC
```

Explanation

PROGRAM
Specifies the one- to eight-character name of the program to be invoked. This name must be defined in the Processing Program Table (PPT).

COMMAREA
Specifies a data area that's passed to the invoked program as a communication area. The invoked program accesses the communication area via its DFHCOMMAREA field.

LENGTH
Specifies a binary halfword (PIC S9(4) COMP) or numeric literal that indicates the length of the data area specified in the COMMAREA option. Under OS/VS COBOL, LENGTH is required if you code COMMAREA.

INPUTMSG
Specifies a data area that's passed to the invoked program as an input message. The invoked program accesses the input message by issuing a RECEIVE command.

INPUTMSGLEN
Specifies a binary halfword (PIC S9(4) COMP) or numeric literal that indicates the length of the data area specified in the INPUTMSG option. Under OS/VS COBOL, LENGTH is required if you code INPUTMSG.

Figure 10-14 The LINK command

operations. You can find out more about FEPI by reading the IBM manual, *CICS/ESA Front End Programming Interface User's Guide.*

The LOAD command

The LOAD command, illustrated in figure 10-16, retrieves an object program from disk and loads it into main storage. The program isn't executed; it's just loaded into storage. Why would you load a program but not execute it? Normally, you wouldn't. The one case where you're likely to use the LOAD command is when you're using a *constant table.* A constant table is an area of main storage that contains values for a commonly used table that's not likely to change. For example, a list of the codes for the 50 states (plus Puerto Rico and the District of Columbia) is a good candidate for a constant table because its entries aren't likely to change.

Rather than code the constant table in the Working-Storage Section of each program that needs it, you can code the table as an assembler language program, like the one in figure 10-17. Then, you assemble and

The XCTL command

```
EXEC CICS
    XCTL    PROGRAM(name)
          [ COMMAREA(data-area)
              [ LENGTH(data-value) ] ]
          [ INPUTMSG(data-area)
              [ INPUTMSGLEN(data-value) ] ]
END-EXEC
```

Explanation

PROGRAM   Specifies the one- to eight-character name of the program to be invoked. This name must be defined in the Processing Program Table (PPT).

COMMAREA   Specifies a data area that's passed to the invoked program as a communication area. The invoked program accesses the communication area via its DFHCOMMAREA field.

LENGTH   Specifies a binary halfword (PIC S9(4) COMP) or numeric literal that indicates the length of the data area specified in the COMMAREA option. Under OS/VS COBOL, LENGTH is required if you code COMMAREA.

INPUTMSG   Specifies a data area that's passed to the invoked program as an input message. The invoked program accesses the input message by issuing a RECEIVE command.

INPUTMSGLEN   Specifies a binary halfword (PIC S9(4) COMP) or numeric literal that indicates the length of the data area specified in the INPUTMSG option. Under OS/VS COBOL, LENGTH is required if you code INPUTMSG.

Figure 10-15 The XCTL command

catalog the program. The listing in figure 10-17 isn't a program in the normal sense, because it doesn't have any executable instructions. Still, CICS treats it as a program, so you must define it in the Processing Program Table.

To access a constant table, you define it in your program's Linkage Section. If you're using OS/VS COBOL, you must also include a BLL cell entry for the table so you can establish addressability to it. (I explained how BLL cells work in chapter 4 of this book and in chapter 8 of *CICS for the COBOL Programmer, Part 1*. If you don't understand BLL cells, refer to one of those chapters.) For VS COBOL II, the BLL cell entry isn't required. Once you've made the correct Linkage Section entries, you issue a LOAD command to bring the table into storage and establish addressability to it.

Figure 10-18 shows two versions of a section of code that defines the state table in the Linkage Section and issues a LOAD command. The first version is for VS COBOL II; the second is for OS/VS COBOL. In the VS COBOL II version, I used the ADDRESS OF special register in the LOAD command's SET option to establish addressability to the state

The LOAD command

```
EXEC CICS
    LOAD    PROGRAM(data-value)
            SET(pointer)
        [ HOLD ]
END-EXEC
```

Explanation

PROGRAM   Specifies the one- to eight-character name of the program to be loaded. This name must appear in the Processing Program Table.

SET   Returns the address of the loaded program.

HOLD   Specifies that the program should remain in storage after the task that issues the LOAD command ends.

Figure 10-16 The LOAD command

```
STATABL  CSECT
*********************************************************************
*                                                                 *
*        THIS CONSTANT TABLE CONTAINS 52 TWO-BYTE ENTRIES         *
*        CORRESPONDING TO THE FIFTY STATES PLUS PUERTO RICO       *
*        AND THE DISTRICT OF COLUMBIA                             *
*                                                                 *
*********************************************************************
         DC    CL10'AKALARAZCA'
         DC    CL10'COCTDCDEFL'
         DC    CL10'GAHIIAIDIL'
         DC    CL10'INKSKYLAMA'
         DC    CL10'MDMEMIMNMO'
         DC    CL10'MSMTNCNDNE'
         DC    CL10'NHNJNMNVNY'
         DC    CL10'OHOKORPAPR'
         DC    CL10'RISCSDTNTX'
         DC    CL10'UTVAVTWAWV'
         DC    CL4'WIWY'
         END
```

Figure 10-17 An assembler language constant table

table. In the OS/VS COBOL version, I used the BLL cell entry for the table in the SET option.

The HOLD option of the LOAD command means that the loaded program should stay in storage even after your task ends. If you use the HOLD option, a commonly used table can be loaded into storage once and used repeatedly throughout the day. Since the table is already in main storage, LOAD commands executed by subsequent programs don't reload it from disk. Instead, they just establish addressability to the existing table by returning its address in the SET field.

VS COBOL II version

```
        .
        .
        .
*
  LINKAGE SECTION.
*
  01   STATE-TABLE.
*
      05   STATE-CODE           OCCURS 52   PIC XX.
*
  PROCEDURE DIVISION.
*
      EXEC CICS
          LOAD PROGRAM('STATABL')
              SET(ADDRESS OF STATE-TABLE)
      END-EXEC.
        .
        .
        .
```

OS/VS COBOL version

```
        .
        .
        .
*
  LINKAGE SECTION.
*
  01   BLL-CELLS.
*
      05   FILLER               PIC S9(8)   COMP.
      05   BLL-STATE-TABLE      PIC S9(8)   COMP.
*
  01   STATE-TABLE.
*
      05   STATE-CODE           OCCURS 52   PIC XX.
*
  PROCEDURE DIVISION.
*
      EXEC CICS
          LOAD PROGRAM('STATABL')
              SET(BLL-STATE-TABLE)
      END-EXEC.
      SERVICE RELOAD STATE-TABLE.
        .
        .
        .
```

Figure 10-18 A portion of a program that uses a constant table

Terms

front-end program
Front End Programming Interface
FEPI
constant table

Objectives

1. Given specifications for an existing program that uses a terminal control RECEIVE command to obtain terminal input, code a program that invokes it using an XCTL or LINK command, passing input to the program via the INPUTMSG option.

2. Use the LOAD command to load a constant table into main storage.

Storage control

As you know, there are several ways you can acquire and use main storage. The simplest is through the Working-Storage Section of your program. Any other storage your program requires exists outside your program, so you have to define it in the Linkage Section. You already know several ways to acquire storage outside your program: the communication area, the Common Work Area (CWA) and other system areas, DL/I areas like the UIB and PCB, and areas acquired by the LOAD command. Now, you'll learn how to use *storage control* facilities directly to obtain and release main storage.

Frankly, you usually don't need to use storage control commands. One case where you might is when you use *locate-mode I/O* rather than move-mode I/O. When you use locate-mode I/O, your program processes data while it's still in a CICS buffer. Because move-mode I/O is both safer and easier to use, I recommend you use it instead of locate-mode I/O. However, if you find yourself maintaining a locate-mode I/O program, or if your shop has a standard requiring locate-mode I/O, you'll have to use the GETMAIN storage control command to acquire main storage for I/O areas. And, you may have to use the FREEMAIN command to release the acquired storage. I'll cover both of these commands in this topic.

The GETMAIN command The GETMAIN command, shown in figure 10-19, allocates a specified amount of main storage and returns the address of that storage. For example, suppose you code this command:

```
EXEC CICS
     GETMAIN SET(ADDRESS OF PRODUCT-RECORD)
             LENGTH(32)
END-EXEC
```

When it's executed, CICS allocates a 32-byte storage area and establishes addressability to it via a field named PRODUCT-RECORD defined in the Linkage Section.

If you're using the OS/VS COBOL compiler, you can't use the ADDRESS OF special register. Instead, you have to set up BLL cells to address the Linkage Section fields, then specify the appropriate BLL cell in the GETMAIN command's SET option. (If you don't know how the BLL addressing convention works, refer to chapter 4 of this book or chapter 8 of *CICS for the COBOL Programmer, Part 1*.)

The GETMAIN command

```
EXEC CICS
    GETMAIN   SET(pointer)
             (LENGTH(data-value)              )
             (FLENGTH(data-value) [ BELOW ])
           [ INITIMG(data-value) ]
           [ CICSDATAKEY | USERDATAKEY ]
END-EXEC
```

Explanation

SET	Returns the address of the acquired storage area.
LENGTH	Specifies the number of bytes of main storage to acquire. If you use a data name, it must be a binary halfword (PIC S9(4) COMP).
FLENGTH	Specifies the number of bytes of main storage to acquire using a binary fullword (PIC S9(8) COMP).
BELOW	Specifies that storage is to be acquired from below the 16MB line. Valid only if the FLENGTH option is also specified.
INITIMG	Specifies a one-byte field whose value is used to initialize the storage acquired. If omitted, the storage is *not* initialized.
CICSDATAKEY	Specifies that the storage is acquired from CICS storage.
USERDATAKEY	Specifies that the storage is acquired from user storage.

Figure 10-19   The GETMAIN command

You can also initialize the storage area to any one-byte value by coding the INITIMG option. First, set up a one-byte field like this:

```
01  HEX-00          PIC X   VALUE LOW-VALUE.
```

Then, issue a GETMAIN command like this:

```
EXEC CICS
    GETMAIN SET(ADDRESS OF PRODUCT-RECORD)
            LENGTH(32)
            INITIMG(HEX-00)
END-EXEC
```

Here, a 32-byte area is acquired and initialized to LOW-VALUE.

How to allocate storage above the 16MB line   As you may know, the original System/360 hardware architecture used 24-bit memory addresses, which provides for a maximum of 16MB of virtual storage. In contrast, the extended architecture used on IBM's current mainframes use 31-bit addresses, which allows for up to 2GB of virtual storage. For compatibility reasons, the extended architecture systems allow 24-bit programs to run alongside 31-bit programs. The only restriction is that 24-bit programs are limited to the first 16MB of virtual storage. You control whether a program uses 24- or 31-bit addresses by specifying the AMODE compiler option when you compile the program.

When you use the LENGTH option on a GETMAIN command, CICS allocates an area of storage from the first 16MB of virtual storage—that is, from below the *16MB line*—even if the program is running in 31-bit mode. If you want a 31-bit program to allocate storage from above the 16MB line, you should specify the storage area's length using the FLENGTH option rather than the LENGTH option. For example, to allocate a 4KB storage area from above the 16MB line, you would code a GETMAIN command like this:

```
EXEC CICS
    GETMAIN FLENGTH(4096)
            SET(ADDRESS OF STORAGE-AREA)
END-EXEC
```

Note that if you code the FLENGTH option as a data name, the data name must be defined as a binary fullword field rather than a halfword field.

You can also specify the FLENGTH option in a program that runs in 24-bit mode. But if you do, CICS will allocate the storage from below the 16MB line, just as if you coded the LENGTH option. If you're using a CICS version before 3.1, you should also know that CICS allocates an FLENGTH request for less than 4,096 bytes of storage from below the 16MB line, even if the program is running in 31-bit mode. However, beginning with version 3.1, CICS will allocate FLENGTH requests for programs running in 31-bit mode from above the 16MB line unless you specify the BELOW option.

Storage protection under CICS/ESA 3.3   One of the major weaknesses of CICS is that it doesn't provide *storage protection*...that is, it doesn't prevent one program from accidentally writing over the storage occupied or used by another program. For example, a runaway subscript in one application program might overwrite data in the Working-Storage Section of another application program. Or, worse yet, an addressing error in an application program might overwrite CICS control blocks that are critical to the operation of CICS. When that happens, the entire CICS system can crash.

With CICS/ESA version 3.3, IBM introduced a partial solution to this storage protection problem. If the processor has the necessary hardware options, CICS can protect itself from errant application programs. It does this by using *storage keys* to distinguish between storage owned by CICS and storage owned by applications. Storage used by CICS itself is allocated using *CICS key*. Storage used by application programs is allocated with *user key*.

Every program running under CICS—including CICS itself—runs under an *execution key* that determines what storage it can access. A program running under CICS key can access and modify CICS key or user key storage. However, a program running under user key is not allowed to modify the contents of CICS key storage. As you might guess, CICS system programs run under CICS key, and application programs run under user key. That way, if an application program tries to overwrite CICS key storage, the program is abended.

You might be wondering why I said this is a *partial* solution to the storage protection problem. Unfortunately, CICS 3.3 storage protection doesn't protect application programs from one another. So it's still possible for a runaway subscript to overwrite storage used by another program. However, the most serious problems associated with storage protection are the system failures that occur when an application program overwrites part of CICS. And the new storage protection feature of CICS 3.3 should reduce or eliminate those failures.

I explained all of this only so you'll see why you'll probably never use the CICSDATAKEY and USERDATAKEY options that were introduced on the GETMAIN command with CICS version 3.3. If you code CICSDATAKEY on a GETMAIN command in an application program running under user key, CICS will allocate the storage for you, but won't let you modify it in any way. Obviously, that's not very useful. So you'll want your GETMAIN commands to allocate storage under user key. For an application program running under user key, that's the default. So you shouldn't ever need to code the USERDATAKEY option.

The only time the CICSDATAKEY and USERDATAKEY options are useful is when you're developing an application program that will run under CICS key. To do that, however, you need a more thorough understanding of CICS storage management than I can provide in this book.

The FREEMAIN command

The FREEMAIN command, shown in figure 10-20, releases an area of storage acquired by a GETMAIN command. On the FREEMAIN command, you code either the DATA or the DATAPOINTER option. If you use the DATA option, you specify the name of the Linkage Section field that overlays the area, like this:

```
EXEC CICS
    FREEMAIN DATA(PRODUCT-RECORD)
END-EXEC
```

If you use the DATAPOINTER option, you specify the *address* of the storage to be freed, like this:

```
EXEC CICS
    FREEMAIN DATAPOINTER(ADDRESS OF PRODUCT-RECORD)
END-EXEC
```

The FREEMAIN command

```
EXEC CICS
    FREEMAIN {DATA(data-area)         }
             {DATAPOINTER(pointer)}
END-EXEC
```

Explanation

DATA   Specifies the Linkage Section field for the storage to be released.

DATAPOINTER   Specifies the address of the storage to be released.

Figure 10-20   The FREEMAIN command

(If you're using OS/VS COBOL, you specify the name of the appropriate BLL cell instead of using ADDRESS OF.) In either case, the command releases the storage allocated by the GETMAIN command I showed you earlier.

Normally, any storage acquired for your task—whether by a GETMAIN command or any other means—is released automatically when your task ends. So the only time you need to use the FREEMAIN command is when you want to release an area of storage before your task ends for efficiency reasons.

Terms

storage control
locate-mode I/O
16MB line
storage protection
storage key
CICS key
user key
execution key

Objective

Code a GETMAIN command to allocate a specified amount of main storage and a FREEMAIN command to release the storage.

Chapter 11

Error processing

In this chapter, you'll learn how CICS recovers from error conditions that cause a task—or CICS itself—to terminate abnormally. There are three topics in this chapter. In topic 1, you'll learn how to supplement the standard processing CICS does when an abend occurs. In topic 2, you'll learn about the recovery facilities CICS provides. Finally, in topic 3, you'll learn how to use CICS journal control features.

Abend processing

When a user task develops a problem that CICS, the host operating system (MVS or VSE), or the hardware itself isn't designed to handle, a *transaction abend* occurs. When that happens, CICS produces a *transaction dump* that lists the contents of any main storage associated with the abending task. The transaction dump includes a *trace table* that shows the sequence of events that led to the abend. Using the transaction dump and trace table, you can determine the exact cause of the abend.

In this topic, you'll learn how you can supplement the standard processing CICS does when a task abends. First, you'll learn how to use an abend exit that gets control when an abend occurs. Then, you'll learn how to use the ABEND command to force your program to end abnormally.

Abend exits

An *abend exit* is a segment of code that supplements the standard abend processing CICS provides. Although it can be a paragraph or section within your program, an abend exit is usually a separate program. If an abend exit is active, it's automatically invoked whenever an abend occurs. To activate an abend exit, you issue a HANDLE ABEND command, as you'll see in a moment.

What does an abend exit do? In some cases, an abend exit tries to correct the problem that caused the abend. But that's unusual. More often, an abend exit just records information about the task that's abending. When it's finished, the abend exit ends by issuing an ABEND command, so CICS completes the abend processing and produces a transaction dump. You'll learn how to use the ABEND command later in this topic.

Because they usually need to access information that's not available to command-level programs, abend exits are typically written as macro-level programs, often in assembler language. Fortunately, most shops that use abend exits already have standard programs that are used throughout the system. So you probably won't be asked to write an abend exit yourself. In this topic, then, I'll just show you how to activate an abend exit so if your program abends, the abend exit will be invoked.

The HANDLE ABEND command

```
EXEC CICS
                    (PROGRAM(name)            )
    HANDLE ABEND    {LABEL(procedure-name)    }
                    |CANCEL                    |
                    (RESET                    )
END-EXEC
```

Explanation

PROGRAM   Specifies the one- to eight-character name of a program that should be invoked (via
                 LINK) if the current program abends.

LABEL   Specifies the COBOL paragraph or section name of a routine within the current program
                 that should be invoked (via GO TO) if the program abends.

CANCEL   Specifies that the current abend exit should be cancelled. If no option is coded on the
                 HANDEL ABEND command, CANCEL is assumed.

RESET   Specifies that a previously cancelled abend exit should be reestablished.

Figure 11-1 The HANDLE ABEND command

The HANDLE ABEND command

You use the HANDLE ABEND command to control abend exits in your program. Figure 11-1 presents its format. You'll code it most often like this:

```
EXEC CICS
    HANDLE ABEND PROGRAM('ABEND1')
END-EXEC
```

Here, the program named ABEND1 will be invoked automatically if an abend occurs. The program you specify in a HANDLE ABEND command must be defined in the Processing Program Table, just like any other CICS program.

Usually, you'll code a HANDLE ABEND command at the start of your program. That way, an abend that occurs anywhere in your program causes the abend exit to be invoked. In any event, your shop probably has standards that govern when and how you code the HANDLE ABEND command. So you should find out what they are and follow them.

If you code the LABEL option rather than the PROGRAM option on a HANDLE ABEND command, the paragraph or section name you supply becomes the abend exit. When an abend occurs, CICS branches to that paragraph or section. Because it's easier to provide standard abend processing in a separate program, I recommend you use the PROGRAM option rather than the LABEL option.

On rare occasions, you may need to deactivate an abend exit. That's what the CANCEL and RESET options are for. You deactivate an abend exit like this:

```
EXEC CICS
    HANDLE ABEND CANCEL
END-EXEC
```

Then, a subsequent abend does *not* invoke the abend exit. Later, you can reactivate the abend exit by issuing this command:

```
EXEC CICS
    HANDLE ABEND RESET
END-EXEC
```

This restores the abend exit that was active when you issued the HANDLE ABEND CANCEL command. Keep in mind that you probably won't use these forms of the HANDLE ABEND command often.

Abend exits and logical levels

Usually, the first program executed by a task issues a HANDLE ABEND command to establish an abend exit that's active for the entire task. However, it's possible to issue another HANDLE ABEND command at any time to replace the current abend exit with a new one. If you issue HANDLE ABEND commands at various program levels within a task, you create a hierarchy of abend exits. When an abend occurs, CICS moves up through the hierarchy of program levels until it finds an active abend exit. So the abend exit that's invoked depends on the program level where the abend occurs.

To illustrate, figure 11-2 shows four application programs that run as part of a single task. Program-A begins by issuing a HANDLE ABEND command that makes ABEXIT1 the active abend exit. If an abend occurs in Program-A, ABEXIT1 is invoked. Next, Program-A invokes Program-B with a LINK command. Because Program-B doesn't issue a HANDLE ABEND command, ABEXIT1 is still the active abend exit. Program-B issues a LINK command to invoke Program-C, but Program-C *does* issue a HANDLE ABEND command, so ABEXIT2 becomes the current abend exit. Program-C invokes Program-D with an XCTL command; ABEXIT2 remains the active abend exit during the execution of Program-D. However, when Program-D returns control to Program-B, ABEXIT1 is restored as the active abend exit.

As I said, most tasks have just one abend exit. But if you use the LINK command to invoke programs, be aware that a HANDLE ABEND command you issue in the linked program won't be active in the program that issued the LINK command. That's because CICS looks *up* the hierarchy of program levels to find an active abend exit; it never looks *down*.

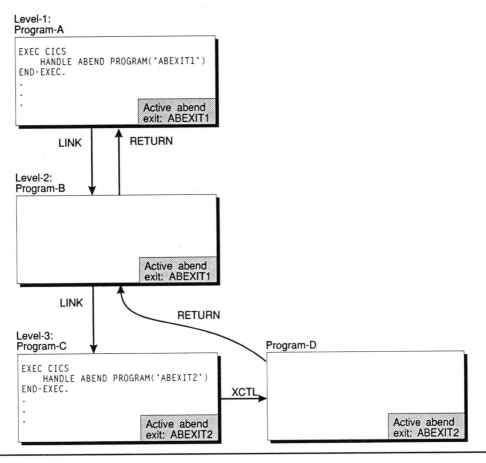

Figure 11-2 Abend exits and logical program levels

The ABEND command

As you probably know, you use the ABEND command to force a task to end abnormally. Figure 11-3 shows the ABEND command's format. You usually code it like this:

```
EXEC CICS
     ABEND ABCODE('X100')
END-EXEC
```

The ABCODE option causes CICS to produce a transaction dump; the value you supply appears in the transaction dump and in the message that's written to the terminal operator. Because the transaction dump is the only way to determine what caused your program to abend, I recommend you always specify the ABCODE option on your ABEND commands.

Even if you don't need a transaction dump when a program abends, you'll probably want to use the ABEND command rather than the RETURN command to terminate the program. That's because the

The ABEND command

```
EXEC CICS
    ABEND [ ABCODE(data-value) ]
          [ CANCEL ]
END-EXEC
```

Explanation

ABCODE   Specifies that a transaction dump should be produced, and the one- to four-character value supplied should be used as the abend code.

CANCEL   Specifies that the active abend exit should be ignored.

Figure 11-3 The ABEND command

ABEND command also invokes the CICS dynamic transaction backout facility to reverse any changes your task made to protected resources. (You'll learn about dynamic transaction backout and protected resources in the next topic.) When your program develops a serious error, you normally want both a transaction dump and dynamic transaction backout.

If your program issues an ABEND command from outside an abend exit and an abend exit is active, the exit is taken just as if CICS initiated the abend. You can bypass the exit by coding the CANCEL option, like this:

```
EXEC CICS
    ABEND ABCODE('X100')
          CANCEL
END-EXEC
```

Here, the active abend exit is ignored.

Terms

transaction abend
transaction dump
trace table
abend exit

Objectives

1. Explain how to activate an abend exit.

2. Code an ABEND command to terminate a task abnormally, with or without a transaction dump.

Recovery processing

In this topic, you'll learn how CICS *recovery* facilities protect data sets and other important resources from a transaction or system abend. To understand CICS recovery facilities, you need to understand four things: logging, dynamic transaction backout, emergency restart, and logical units of work. After I describe these items, I'll show you how to use a CICS command that can make recovery more efficient when it's necessary: SYNCPOINT.

Logging   As a task executes, any changes it makes to protected resources are logged so the changes can be reversed if necessary. A *protected resource* is a file, destination, or temporary storage queue whose resource definition provides for automatic recovery. Figure 11-4 shows how logging works for a protected file. As you can see, each time an application program invokes file control to update the file, file control in turn invokes *journal control* to log the change. Logging for protected destinations and temporary storage queues is similar.

As you can see, CICS records recovery information in two places: the system log and the dynamic log. The *system log* maintains recovery data for an entire CICS system. It can be stored on disk or on tape. As you can imagine, the system log can grow quite large even for a small CICS system.

The *dynamic log* maintains recovery data for a single task. While there's one system log for the entire CICS system, each CICS task has its own dynamic log. If a task ends abnormally, the data in the dynamic log is used to restore protected resources. If a task ends normally, its dynamic log is deleted. For efficiency reasons, the dynamic log is kept in main storage.

The recovery information that's stored in both the system log and the dynamic log consists of *before-images* of each file, destination, or temporary storage record that's added, changed, or deleted. In other words, journal control stores an exact image of each record as it existed before each update occurred. If an abend occurs, those updates can be reversed to restore the resource to its previous condition. This type of recovery is often called *backward recovery*.

An optional CICS product called *CICS VSAM Recovery* (or *CICSVR*) can be used to implement *forward recovery*. With forward recovery, CICS keeps *after-images* of records that are updated. Then, if the file becomes

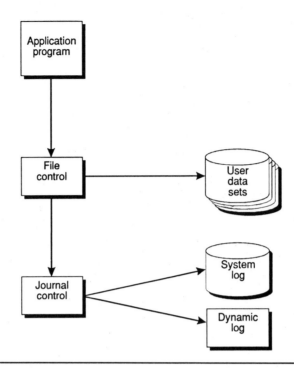

Figure 11-4   How file updates are logged to the system log and the dynamic log

so damaged that backward recovery isn't possible, CICSVR can apply
the after-images to a recent backup copy of the file.

Dynamic transaction backout   When a transaction terminates abnormally, CICS invokes the *dynamic backout program* to perform *dynamic transaction backout* (or *DTB*), as shown in figure 11-5. Dynamic transaction backout processes the before-images stored in the transaction's dynamic log to reverse any changes the transaction made to protected resources. When dynamic transaction backout completes, it's as if the transaction was never started.

Although it's an optional feature, dynamic transaction backout should be specified for all transactions. The dynamic log isn't allocated until a task issues a command that updates a protected resource. So there's no significant loss of performance when you specify DTB for a transaction that doesn't update protected resources.

Emergency restart   When CICS itself terminates abnormally, it must be restarted using a procedure called *emergency restart*. Figure 11-6 shows how CICS recovers protected resources during an emergency restart. First, *recovery control* processes the system log, which contains a record of every update made during the previous CICS execution. Recovery control reads the system

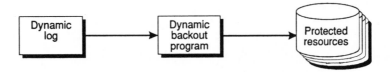

Figure 11-5 The dynamic backout program uses the dynamic log to restore protected resources after a transaction abend

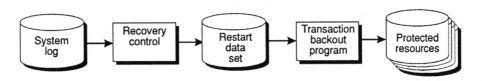

Figure 11-6 Recovery control and the transaction backout program work together during emergency restart to restore protected resources

log backwards, determining which updates were made by *in-flight tasks*—that is, tasks that were active when the uncontrolled shutdown occurred. Each update that was made by an in-flight task is copied to the *restart data set*, which is then processed by the *transaction backout program* to restore the protected resources.

The transaction backout program is similar to the dynamic backout program. The difference is that the transaction backout program restores updates made by many tasks, while the dynamic backout program restores updates made by just one task. Because the transaction and system abend recovery facilities are similar, the programming considerations you'll learn in this topic apply equally to both.

Logical units of work

A *logical unit of work*, or *LUW*, is a collection of updating activity that's treated as a single unit during dynamic transaction backout or emergency restart. Normally, each LUW corresponds to a single task execution. In other words, when a task abends, all updates made by that task are reversed by dynamic transaction backout. And if CICS abends, all updates made by in-flight tasks are reversed during emergency restart.

Sometimes, it's not necessary to reverse all of the updates made by a task. For example, consider a program that reads invoice records stored in a sequential file (a VSAM ESDS) and updates corresponding master records in a customer file, an accounts receivable file, and an inventory file. If the program abends after processing 100 invoice records, DTB

The SYNCPOINT command

```
EXEC CICS
    SYNCPOINT [ ROLLBACK ]
END-EXEC
```

Explanation

ROLLBACK   Specifies that all updates logged since the last SYNCPOINT command (or the
                            beginning of the task) are reversed.

Figure 11-7 The SYNCPOINT command

The SYNCPOINT command

reverses the updates for all 100 records, even though that's probably not necessary: Just the updates for the invoice that was being processed when the abend occurred need to be reversed. To limit the scope of an LUW, you issue a SYNCPOINT command. (The conclusion of an LUW is called a *syncpoint*, whether it's caused by the end of the task or by an explicit SYNCPOINT command.)

The SYNCPOINT command tells CICS that all of the updates made to protected resources so far are final: They shouldn't be backed out even if an abend occurs. In other words, the SYNCPOINT command ends the current logical unit of work and begins a new one. Figure 11-7 shows the format of the SYNCPOINT command. Normally, you'll code it like this:

```
EXEC CICS
    SYNCPOINT
END-EXEC
```

Figure 11-8 shows a typical use of a SYNCPOINT command in a program that reads a file of invoice transaction records and updates related master file records. Module 0000 invokes module 1000 once for each record in the invoice file. After invoking module 1100 to read the invoice record, module 1000 invokes module 1200 to update the master files. Then, it issues a SYNCPOINT command, so all of the updates related to a single invoice record are considered to be a single logical unit of work.

The ROLLBACK option on a SYNCPOINT command causes any changes made during the current LUW to be backed out, as if the task had abended. As you might guess, the SYNCPOINT ROLLBACK command is often used in an abend exit.

```
*
 0000-POST-INVOICE-TRANSACTIONS.
*
        .
        .
        .
      PERFORM 1000-POST-INVOICE-TRANSACTION
          UNTIL INVOICE-EOF.
        .
        .
        .
*
 1000-POST-INVOICE-TRANSACTION.
*
      PERFORM 1100-READ-INVOICE-TRANSACTION.
      IF NOT INVOICE-EOF
          PERFORM 1200-UPDATE-MASTER-FILES
          EXEC CICS
              SYNCPOINT
          END-EXEC.
*
        .
        .
        .
```

Figure 11-8 Using the SYNCPOINT command in a program that posts invoice transactions accumulated in a sequential file

Discussion Obviously, CICS recovery is considerably more involved than I've let on here. Fortunately, systems programmers are responsible for setting up the recovery mechanisms I've described in this topic. As an application programmer, your only responsibility is to be aware of the scope of your programs' logical units of work, and use the SYNCPOINT command when appropriate.

Terms

recovery
protected resource
journal control
system log
dynamic log
before-image
backward recovery
CICS VSAM Recovery
CICSVR
forward recovery
after-image
dynamic backout program

dynamic transaction backout
DTB
emergency restart
recovery control
in-flight task
restart data set
transaction backout program
logical unit of work
LUW
syncpoint

Objectives

1. Describe the recovery facilities provided by dynamic transaction backout and emergency restart.

2. Explain how to use the SYNCPOINT command to limit the scope of a logical unit of work.

Journal control

In the last topic, you learned how journal control automatically logs updates to protected resources in the system log. Actually, the system log is one of 99 *journal files* an installation can use. Journal files, which are simple sequential files on tape or disk, are numbered from 1 to 99. The first journal file—journal 1—is the system log; it's always required. Within a CICS system, every task that updates a protected resource causes recovery information to be logged in journal 1. As a result, the system log maintains complete recovery information for the entire CICS system.

The other journals—called *user journals*—can be used to supplement the standard logging provided by CICS. Many installations use user journals for other purposes as well. For example, you might use a user journal to record audit information. Or, you might use a journal to record transactions that are to be processed later by a batch job.

It's important to realize from the start that as far as your application programs are concerned, journals are output-only files. There's no way a command-level CICS program can process a journal as an input file. Typically, records are written to a user journal during the day and processed by a batch program at night. In many cases, an application like that is better implemented using a simple sequential file (VSAM ESDS).

Before you can learn how to use journal control, you need to know how journal records are formatted and the difference between synchronous and asynchronous journal output. After I present that information, I'll show you how to use the CICS commands to write journal records.

The format of journal records Quite frankly, journal data is stored in a complicated format. It's so complicated, in fact, that the *CICS Customization Guide* spends eight pages just explaining the layout of journal records. Fortunately, you need to understand just the basic format of journal records to create them. The details are important only when you write a program that reads them. If you need to do that, you'll have to refer to the *Customization Guide* for more information.

Figure 11-9 shows how a journal record is organized. As you can see, the record consists of four parts: a *system header*, a *system prefix*, a *user prefix*, and user data. Bear in mind that the record layout in figure 11-9 is simplified. I left out a number of fields, including those that

System header	System prefix				User prefix (optional)	User data
	Task-no	Trans-id	Term-id	Time		

Figure 11-9   Simplified format of a journal record

specify the length of each area; the entire journal record and each of its components is variable-length.

The system header contains information that identifies the journal record type—whether it's a record written automatically by CICS or a user-written record. The system prefix contains the task number, transaction identifier, and terminal identifier for the task that wrote the journal record. In addition, it includes the time of day when the record was written. Both the system header and the system prefix are required. The user prefix, however, is optional. You supply it if you want to provide additional prefix information in a journal record.

Synchronous and asynchronous journal output

When you issue a command to write a journal record, that record isn't immediately written to the journal file. To understand why, look at figure 11-10. Here, an application program running as part of a user's task issues a command that invokes journal control. Journal control, in turn, places the user's output data in a storage area called a *journal buffer*. The actual output operation is performed by a separate system task called a *journal task*. Within a CICS system, there's one journal task for each journal that's used. The job of the journal task is to watch the journal buffer: When it becomes full, the journal task writes the journal buffer to the journal file. To help insure system integrity, the journal task also writes the journal buffer to the journal file at one-second intervals whether the buffer is full or not.

Synchronous journal output means that your program waits until the journal task has written the journal buffer before it continues. Because the journal task automatically writes the buffer at one-second intervals, your program won't have to wait more than one second. If other tasks write records to the journal buffer, the wait will be less.

If your program doesn't need to wait for the journal record to be written, *asynchronous journal output* is used. Here, your program continues execution without waiting for the journal task. Because asynchronous journal output is more efficient than synchronous journal output, you should use it whenever practical.

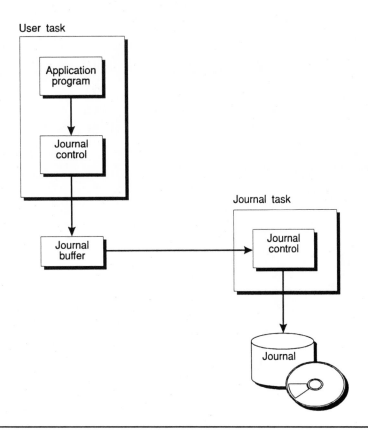

Figure 11-10 Journal output is actually written to journals by a separate task

The WRITE JOURNALNUM and JOURNAL commands

The command you use to write a record to a journal depends on which version of CICS you're using. Earlier versions of CICS used the JOURNAL command to write journal records. With CICS version 2.1, the WRITE JOURNALNUM command was introduced for this purpose. IBM recommends that you use the WRITE JOURNALNUM command rather than the JOURNAL command for all new applications, but the JOURNAL command is still supported so existing programs don't have to be modified.

Figure 11-11 shows the format of both the WRITE JOURNALNUM and the JOURNAL commands. You typically code the WRITE JOURNALNUM command like this:

```
EXEC CICS
    WRITE JOURNALNUM(3)
          JTYPEID('A1')
          FROM(CUSTOMER-MASTER-RECORD)
          WAIT
END-EXEC
```

The WRITE JOURNALNUM command

```
EXEC CICS
    WRITE    JOURNALNUM(data-value)
             JTYPEID(data-value)
             FROM(data-area)
           [ LENGTH(data-value) ]
           [ WAIT ]
           [ REQID(data-area) ]
           [ STARTIO ]
           [ PREFIX(data-area)
               [ PFXLENG(data-value) ] ]
END-EXEC
```

The JOURNAL command

```
EXEC CICS
    JOURNAL  JFILEID(data-value)
             JTYPEID(data-value)
             FROM(data-area)
           [ LENGTH(data-value) ]
           [ WAIT ]
           [ REQID(data-area) ]
           [ STARTIO ]
           [ PREFIX(data-area)
               [ PFXLENG(data-value) ] ]
END-EXEC
```

Explanation

JOURNALNUM	Specifies a value from 1 to 99 that identifies the journal where this record is written. If you use a data name, it must be a binary halfword (PIC S9(4) COMP).
JFILEID	Serves the same function as the JOURNALNUM option when the JOURNAL command is used instead of WRITE JOURNALNUM.

Figure 11-11   The WRITE JOURNALNUM and JOURNAL commands (part 1 of 2)

An equivalent JOURNAL command would look like this:

```
EXEC CICS
    JOURNAL  JFILEID(3)
             JTYPEID('A1')
             FROM(CUSTOMER-MASTER-RECORD)
             WAIT
END-EXEC
```

Both of these commands write the contents of a record named CUSTOMER-MASTER-RECORD to journal number 3. The record type is A1, and WAIT means that this is a synchronous output operation: The program won't resume until the journal task actually writes the journal record.

JTYPEID	Specifies a two-character code that's placed in the journal record to identify the record.
FROM	Specifies the field that contains the data to be written.
LENGTH	Specifies the length of the FROM area. If you use a data name, it must be a binary halfword (PIC S9(4) COMP). (Optional under VS COBOL II.)
WAIT	Says that control should not return to the program until the record has actually been written to the journal file.
REQID	Specifies a data name that will receive a unique identifier that can be used later in a WAIT JOURNALNUM or WAIT JOURNAL command. The data name must be a binary fullword (PIC S9(8) COMP).
STARTIO	Says that the journal buffer should be written to the journal file immediately.
PREFIX	Specifies the field that contains the user prefix that's to be included in the journal record.
PFXLENG	Specifies the length of the PREFIX area. If you use a data name, it must be a binary halfword (PIC S9(4) COMP). (Optional under VS COBOL II.)

Note: The WRITE JOURNALNUM command was introduced with CICS version 2.1 as an intended replacement for the JOURNAL command. Although the JOURNAL command is supported under current CICS releases, the WRITE JOURNALNUM command is preferred.

Figure 11-11 The WRITE JOURNALNUM and JOURNAL commands (part 2 of 2)

The JTYPEID option supplies a two-character field that identifies the type of record written. The value you code here is placed in the system header of the journal record. Because its value depends on how your installation uses the journal file, you'll have to find out how to code the JTYPEID option.

If you want to use asynchronous journal output, omit the WAIT option. Then, your program continues immediately without waiting for the journal record to be written. When you use asynchronous journal output, you may need to resynchronize your task with the journal task. To do that, you issue a WAIT JOURNALNUM or WAIT JOURNAL command, which I'll present in a moment. If you use either of these commands, you need to include the REQID option on the WRITE JOURNALNUM or JOURNAL command. In it, you specify a field where CICS will store a unique value that identifies the journal record to be written. You'll use that value later when you issue the WAIT JOURNALNUM or WAIT JOURNAL command. The data name you supply in the REQID option must be a binary fullword (PIC S9(8) COMP).

If you're writing a record to an infrequently used journal, you might want to code the STARTIO option. It causes the journal task to immediately write out its buffer, even if it isn't full. Use the STARTIO option with care: Although it improves your program's performance, it degrades the performance of other tasks in the system.

If your journal record requires a user prefix to supplement the information provided in the system prefix, you use the PREFIX option to provide that data. And PFXLENG, which is optional under VS COBOL II, provides the length of the field you specify in the PREFIX option. Your installation should have a standard format for the user prefix area of each user journal.

The WAIT JOURNALNUM and WAIT JOURNAL commands

The WAIT JOURNALNUM and WAIT JOURNAL commands, whose formats are given in figure 11-12, suspend your task until the journal record you identify with the REQID option is written to the journal file. Then, your task continues. If you specify STARTIO, the journal buffer is immediately written to disk. If you omit it, your task waits until the journal buffer is filled or one second has elapsed, when the journal task automatically writes the buffer.

IBM introduced the WAIT JOURNALNUM command with CICS version 2.1. IBM recommends that you use the WAIT JOURNALNUM command for all new applications, but supports the older WAIT JOURNAL command for compatibility with existing programs.

The WAIT JOURNALNUM command can sometimes help you improve your program's efficiency by reducing the amount of time your program has to wait if you use synchronous journal output. The idea here is to issue a WRITE JOURNALNUM command *without* the WAIT option, then continue with other work until your program reaches a point where it must be sure the journal record has been written. At that point, you issue a WAIT JOURNALNUM command. If the journal record has already been written, the WAIT JOURNALNUM command simply returns to your program. If not, your program waits until the journal record is written before it continues.

To illustrate, figure 11-13 shows two versions of a routine that writes an image of a customer record to a user journal and deletes the record from a customer master file. In version 1, synchronous journal output is used: The WRITE JOURNALNUM command specifies the WAIT option. In version 2, asynchronous journal output is used: The WRITE JOURNALNUM command doesn't specify WAIT. To ensure that the journal record is written before the program continues, I coded a WAIT JOURNALNUM command after the DELETE command in version 2.

In figure 11-13, version 2 executes more efficiently than version 1. That's because version 2 issues its DELETE command while the journal task writes the journal record. In contrast, version 1 must wait for the journal task to complete before it issues the DELETE command.

The WAIT JOURNALNUM command

```
EXEC CICS
    WAIT    JOURNALNUM(data-value)
            [ REQID(data-area) ]
            [ STARTIO ]
END-EXEC
```

The WAIT JOURNAL command

```
EXEC CICS
    WAIT JOURNAL    JFILEID(data-value)
                    [ REQID(data-area) ]
                    [ STARTIO ]
END-EXEC
```

Explanation

JOURNALNUM   Specifies a value from 1 to 99 that identifies the journal the task should wait for. If you code a data name, it must be a binary halfword (PIC S9(4) COMP).

JFILEID   Serves the same function as the JOURNALNUM option when the WAIT JOURNAL command is used instead of WAIT JOURNALNUM.

REQID   Specifies the value obtained from the REQID option of a WRITE JOURNALNUM or JOURNAL command. Must be a binary fullword (PIC S9(8) COMP).

STARTIO   Says that the journal buffer should be written to the journal file immediately.

Note: The WAIT JOURNALNUM command was introduced with CICS version 2.1 as an intended replacement for the WAIT JOURNAL command. Although the WAIT JOURNAL command is supported under current CICS releases, the WAIT JOURNALNUM command is preferred.

Figure 11-12 The WAIT JOURNALNUM and WAIT JOURNAL commands

Discussion Quite frankly, you probably won't use the CICS commands this topic presents often. Most installations don't use journal control other than for the standard recovery facility provided by the system log.

Terms

journal file
user journal
system header
system prefix
user prefix

journal buffer
journal task
synchronous journal output
asynchronous journal output

Version 1

```
    .
    .
    .
EXEC CICS
    WRITE JOURNALNUM(7)
          JTYPEID('CD')
          FROM(CUSTOMER-MASTER-RECORD)
          WAIT
END-EXEC.
EXEC CICS
    DELETE FILE('CUSTMAS')
           RIDFLD(CM-CUSTOMER-NUMBER)
END-EXEC.
    .
    .
    .
```

Version 2

```
    .
    .
    .
EXEC CICS
    WRITE JOURNALNUM(7)
          JTYPEID('CD')
          FROM(CUSTOMER-MASTER-RECORD)
          REQID(WS-REQID)
END-EXEC.
EXEC CICS
    DELETE FILE('CUSTMAS')
           RIDFLD(CM-CUSTOMER-NUMBER)
END-EXEC.
EXEC CICS
    WAIT JOURNALNUM(7)
         REQID(WS-REQID)
END-EXEC.
    .
    .
    .
```

Figure 11-13   Using synchronous and asynchronous journal output

Objective

Explain how you use journal control commands for both synchronous and asynchronous journal output.

Chapter 12

Distributed processing

CICS provides a variety of *distributed processing* facilities that let two or more CICS systems work together. That means a CICS program running on one CICS system can access resources owned by another CICS system, provided the two systems are properly connected. For example, a terminal user attached to a CICS system in Detroit might run an inquiry program that accesses a file owned by a CICS system in Chicago.

In this chapter, I'll give you a brief overview of the concepts and terms you need to know to use CICS distributed processing. Then, I'll explain the programming considerations for five distributed processing facilities: transaction routing, function shipping, Distributed Program Link, asynchronous processing, and Distributed Transaction Processing.

Distributed processing concepts

In CICS terminology, distributed processing is often called *CICS intercommunication* because it requires CICS systems to communicate with one another. CICS provides two basic communication mechanisms to support distributed processing: *Multi-Region Operation* (or *MRO*) and *Intersystem Communication* (or *ISC*). MRO lets two or more CICS systems within the same host processor communicate. Each system runs independently in its own address space or partition (depending on the host operating system). On the other hand, ISC is designed to let CICS systems on separate processors communicate. For the most part, the programming techniques for distributed processing I'll present in this chapter are the same whether you're using MRO, ISC, or both. Nevertheless, it's helpful to understand the difference.

The systems programmer that sets up MRO can specify one of two mechanisms for transmitting data between MRO systems. The first uses a special *InterRegion Communication Access Method* that's unique to CICS. It depends on supervisor calls that let the InterRegion Communication modules operate in supervisor state while they exchange data between CICS regions. The second mechanism uses *Cross-Memory Services* to exchange data directly between address spaces without the overhead of a supervisor call.

Figure 12-1 shows a typical use of MRO in a production CICS environment. Here, three CICS systems run on a single host processor. All of the terminals are owned by a CICS system called the *Terminal Owning Region*, or *TOR*. All of the application programs are owned by the *Application Owning Region*, or *AOR*. And all of the files are owned by the *File Owning Region*, or *FOR*. This common MRO configuration is completely transparent to the application programs. In other words, an application program running in the AOR is unaware that it is accessing a terminal that's owned by the TOR and files that are owned by the FOR.

You may be wondering why you'd configure an MRO so that the terminals, applications, and files are owned by separate CICS systems. The answer is simple: If one of the systems goes down, it doesn't affect the other systems. So, for example, if the AOR goes down, any files that may have been open in the FOR are unaffected.

To connect CICS systems running on different host processors, ISC must be used. As figure 12-2 shows, ISC lets a local and a remote CICS system communicate by using VTAM as an intermediary. Here, the two host systems are connected by a *host connection*. If the two host systems are close together, the host connection can be a direct channel connection or a single 37x5 communications controller. If the host systems are geographically distant, the host connection includes a telecommunications link with communications controllers on each end. As you might guess, ISC is significantly slower than MRO.

Although it's not apparent from figure 12-2, the CICS systems participating in ISC don't have to be the same CICS version. In fact, they don't even have to run under the same operating system. When I wrote this, ISC could be used to interconnect any of the following CICS systems:

- CICS/ESA 3.3
- CICS/ESA 3.2
- CICS/ESA 3.1
- CICS/MVS 2.1
- CICS/OS/VS 1.7
- CICS/VSE 2.1
- CICS/DOS/VS 1.7
- CICS/VM
- CICS OS/2

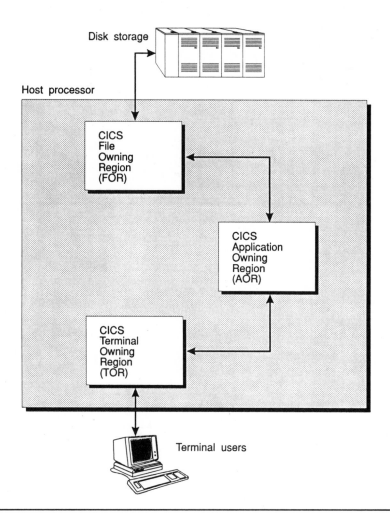

Figure 12-1 Multi-Region Operation (MRO)

And ISC should be available for all future releases of CICS as well. That includes CICS for the AS/400 and CICS for AIX/Unix environments.

You should also realize that MRO and ISC can be used together. For example, consider figure 12-3. Here, three host processors—one in San Diego, one in Houston, and one in Boston—each use MRO to run separate TOR's, AOR's, and FOR's. In addition, the AOR's in Houston and Boston are connected by ISC links to the FOR in San Diego. As a result, transactions run in Boston or Houston can access files that reside in San Diego.

Notice the names I included in parentheses for each CICS system in figure 12-3. In an MRO or ISC environment, every CICS system must have a unique name so that other CICS systems can identify it. This one- to four-character name is called the *system identifier* or *sysid*. As

Local host processor

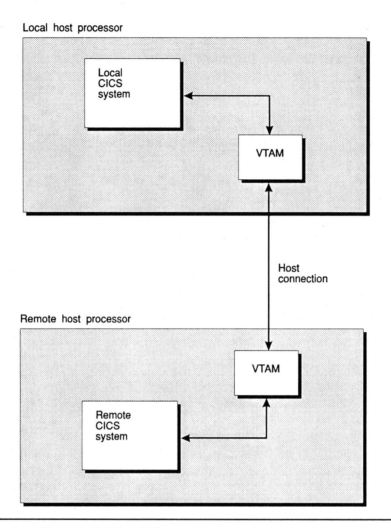

Figure 12-2 Intersystem Communication (ISC)

you'll see in a few moments, the systems programmers use these names to set up the table entries required to implement distributed processing. In addition, many CICS commands let you access a resource that's owned by another CICS system by specifying that system's sysid.

Frankly, the details of setting up and maintaining an MRO/ISC environment are complex. Fortunately, the systems programmers usually set up MRO/ISC so that it is completely transparent to the application programs. So as an application programmer, you don't even need to know that MRO or ISC is in use. From a practical point of view, however, you should have a general understanding of your installation's MRO/ISC configuration, including each system's sysid.

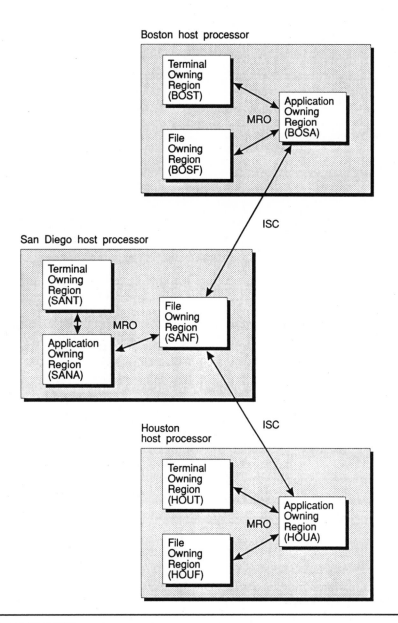

Figure 12-3 A typical MRO/ISC environment

Transaction routing

Transaction routing is a distributed processing facility that lets a terminal owned by one CICS system run a transaction on another CICS system. Transaction routing is what makes it possible to set up separate Terminal Owning Regions and Application Owning Regions. When transaction routing is used, the terminal is owned and managed by the TOR, but the transactions are executed by the AOR.

Figure 12-4 shows the Program Control Table (PCT) entries required to support transaction routing. Here, you can see that two PCT entries

PCT entry in Terminal Owning Region BOST

```
DFHPCT TYPE=REMOTE,                                                    X
       TRANSID=INQ1,                                                   X
       SYSIDNT=BOSA
```

PCT entry in Application Owning Region BOSA

```
DFHPCT TYPE=ENTRY,                                                     X
       TRANSID=INQ1,                                                   X
       PROGRAM=CUSTINQ
```

Figure 12-4 PCT entries for transaction routing

are required: one in the Terminal Owning Region, the other in the Application Owning Region. In the TOR PCT entry, TYPE=REMOTE specifies that the trans-id INQ1 is a remote transaction. In other words, it will be run on the system indicated in the SYSIDNT parameter: BOSA. In the AOR, the PCT defines INQ1 as a local transaction.

Consider what happens when a user at a terminal that's owned by BOST enters the trans-id INQ1. BOST searches its PCT for the INQ1 entry, and finds that it is a remote transaction that resides on BOSA. So it sends a request to the BOSA system to run the INQ1 transaction. BOSA then looks up INQ1 in its PCT, and finds that it is a local transaction. So it executes it, routing any terminal I/O through BOST to the originating terminal.

From an application programming point of view, transaction routing is completely transparent. The only time you even need to be aware of its use is when you need to debug a remote transaction using CEDF. Because CEDF requires your terminal to be owned by the same system that owns the program you're debugging, it won't work with transaction routing. To get around this limitation, IBM supplies a special transaction called the *routing transaction*, or *CRTE*. For it to work, your terminal must be defined to the other CICS system as a remote terminal.

Suppose your terminal is owned by BOST, and you want to debug a program that's owned by BOSA. To do that, you must first initiate a routing session by starting the CRTE transaction, like this:

```
CRTE SYSID=BOSA
```

This connects your terminal to the BOSA system. Once you've started a routing session, you can run CEDF and debug your program. When you're finished, enter this command:

```
CANCEL
```

This ends the routing session.

FCT entry in the Application Owning Region HOUA

```
DFHFCT TYPE=REMOTE,                                                    X
       DATASET=CUSTMAS,                                               X
       SYSIDNT=SANF,                                                  X
       LRECL=118,                                                     X
       KEYLEN=6
```

FCT entry in the File Owning Region SANF

```
DFHFCT TYPE=DATASET,                                                  X
       DATASET=CUSTMAS,                                               X
       ACCMETH=(VSAM,KSDS),                                           X
       SERVREQ=(BROWSE,DELETE,UPDATE),                                X
       RECFORM=(FIXED,BLOCKED)
```

Figure 12-5 FCT entries for function shipping

(Keep in mind that you'll probably use CRTE only to debug a production program. CICS test systems usually don't use MRO, so the CEDF restriction doesn't apply.)

Function shipping

Function shipping lets a CICS program running at one CICS system access a resource that's owned by another CICS system. For example, a transaction running in the AOR in Boston (BOSA) might use MRO to retrieve a record from a file owned by Boston's FOR (BOSF). When the application program in the AOR issues the file control request, BOSA ships the function to BOSF, which reads the record and returns it to BOSA. CICS supports function shipping for VSAM files, transient data destinations, temporary storage queues, and DL/I data bases. (DB2 has its own distributed processing features that CICS programs can use to retrieve data from multiple locations.)

Function shipping is also commonly used in ISC environments to access resources owned by CICS systems at remote locations. For example, suppose an application program running in Houston's AOR wants to access a file owned by San Diego's FOR. In that case, the Houston AOR (HOUA) would function ship the request (via VTAM) to the San Diego FOR (SANF). There, the I/O operation would be performed and the result returned to the application program running at HOUA.

Figure 12-5 shows the table entries that let an application program running in the AOR in Houston access a customer file (CUSTMAS) that's owned by the FOR in San Diego. As you can see, table entries are required for both systems, just as they are for transaction routing. In the AOR, a TYPE=REMOTE entry is required to tell CICS that CUSTMAS is a remote file that resides on a CICS system named SANF. For remote

```
 2100-READ-CUSTOMER-RECORD.
*
     EXEC CICS
         READ DATASET('CUSTMAS')
              INTO(CUSTOMER-MASTER-RECORD)
              RIDFLD(CM-CUSTOMER-NUMBER)
              RESP(RESPONSE-CODE)
     END-EXEC.
     IF RESPONSE-CODE = DFHRESP(NORMAL)
         MOVE 'Y' TO CUSTOMER-FOUND-SW
     ELSE IF RESPONSE-CODE = DFHRESP(NOTFND)
         MOVE 'N' TO CUSTOMER-FOUND-SW
         MOVE 'That customer does not exist.' TO MSGO
     ELSE IF RESPONSE-CODE = DFHRESP(SYSIDERR)
         MOVE 'N' TO CUSTOMER-FOUND-SW
         MOVE 'The remote system is not available.  Try again later.'
             TO MSGO
     ELSE
         EXEC CICS
             ABEND
         END-EXEC.
```

Figure 12-6 A READ module that uses function shipping

VSAM KSDS files, the FCT entry must also supply the record length and the key length. In the FOR, the FCT entry defines CUSTMAS as a local file.

Figure 12-6 shows a typical COBOL paragraph you might use to read a record from the remote CUSTMAS file. As you can see, the CICS READ command doesn't indicate that the file is remote. As a result, the fact that function shipping is used here is nearly transparent to the program. I say *nearly* transparent because although the use of function shipping doesn't affect the way you code CICS commands, it may affect the exceptional condition testing that follows each command. In figure 12-6, you can see that I included a test for the SYSIDERR condition. This condition occurs whenever the connection to the remote CICS system cannot be made. This can happen because of an incorrect sysid, but in a production system, it's more likely to happen because of a failure in the communications link or in the remote CICS system.

When you use function shipping, CICS considers the processing done on the local and remote systems to be a single logical unit of work. It does this by coordinating syncpoints across the systems, and if a failure occurs, by backing out updates made on the local and remote systems together. Unfortunately, there is a slight chance that a failure might occur while CICS is attempting to coordinate syncpoints. When that happens, CICS can't guarantee that data on the local and remote systems is coordinated. The likelihood of that happening is very small, however.

Although you probably shouldn't use it, you should be aware that many CICS commands let you specify the location of a remote resource

The SYSID option

`SYSID(systemname)`   Specifies the one- to four-character name of the remote system that owns the remote resource.

Valid on the following CICS commands

File control	Transient data control	Temporary storage control
DELETE	DELETEQ TD	DELETEQ TS
ENDBR	READQ TD	READQ TS
READ	WRITEQ TD	WRITEQ TS
READNEXT		
READPREV		
RESETBR		
STARTBR		
UNLOCK		
WRITE		

Interval control	Program control
START	LINK (CICS/ESA 3.3 and CICS OS/2 only)
CANCEL	

Figure 12-7 The SYSID option

by using the SYSID option, shown in figure 12-7. For example, you could read a record from the CUSTMAS file at SANF by issuing this command:

```
EXEC CICS
    READ DATASET('CUSTMAS')
        INTO(CUSTOMER-MASTER-RECORD)
        RIDFLD(CM-CUSTOMER-NUMBER)
        SYSID('SANF')
        LENGTH(CUSTMAS-LENGTH)
        KEYLENGTH(6)
        RESP(RESPONSE-CODE)
    END-EXEC
```

Notice that I had to add the LENGTH and KEYLENGTH options on this command. That's because when you use the SYSID option, CICS doesn't look up the local FCT definition for the file, which specifies the record and key length values. So you have to supply those values in the command. (As a matter of fact, when you specify SYSID on a file control command, a local FCT entry isn't even required for the file.)

As I said, you should avoid using the SYSID option. To see why, consider what would happen if the location of the file changed. If you specified the location in the SYSID option, you'd have to change and recompile each program that accesses the file. If you specified the location in the FCT entry instead, all you'd have to do is change the FCT.

Function shipping for transient data destinations and temporary storage queues works much the same as it does for VSAM files. If the systems programmer creates the appropriate table entries, the function shipping is transparent to the application programmer, except for the possibility of the SYSIDERR condition occurring. Alternatively, you can code the SYSID option on a transient data or temporary storage command. For DL/I, function shipping is set up by the database administrator when he or she creates the PSB. Thus, you code the application program as if it were accessing a local database.

Distributed Program Link

Distributed Program Link, or *DPL*, was first introduced in CICS OS/2 and is now available under CICS/ESA 3.3. Simply put, DPL lets a program running in one CICS system issue a LINK command that invokes a program in another CICS system.

Distributed Program Link provides an easy way to implement *client-server applications*. In a client-server application, one program (called the *client*) requests another program (called the *server*) to perform some type of processing. For example, a client program might request a server program to retrieve all the records related to a particular customer. When you use DPL to implement a client-server application, the program that issues the distributed LINK command is the client; the linked-to program is the server.

One common reason for using DPL is to reduce network traffic by avoiding a long sequence of function shipping requests. For example, suppose an application program running in Boston (BOSA) needs to update five records in San Diego (SANF). Figure 12-8 shows how this could be done using function shipping and Distributed Program Link. With function shipping, each file control command requires two network transmissions: one to ship the function request to the remote system, the other to return the results. Since each update operation requires two CICS commands (a READ UPDATE command followed by a REWRITE command), the five updates will require 20 network transmissions.

With DPL, an application program to update the five records can be placed on the SANA system. Then, when the program running at BOSA needs to update the five records, it can use a distributed LINK command to invoke the update program at SANA, passing the data for the updates via the communication area. The result would be two network transmissions rather than 20, resulting in a 10-fold reduction of network traffic. (Of course, the application program running at SANA would function ship the I/O requests to SANF. But that communication would occur at dramatically faster MRO speeds, so it isn't much of a concern.)

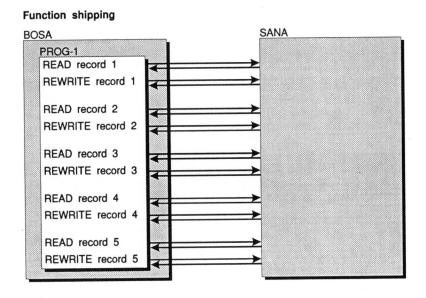

Function shipping

Distributed Program Link

Figure 12-8 Why Distributed Program Link is more efficient than multiple function shipping requests

Figure 12-9 shows the format of the LINK command, including options for Distributed Program Link. As you can see, the SYSID option lets you specify the name of the system where the program exists. The program must be defined in that system's Processing Program Table (PPT). As with function shipping, you probably shouldn't use the SYSID option. Instead, you should let the systems programmer identify the system name in the local system's PPT entry for the program.

The LINK command

```
EXEC CICS
    LINK    PROGRAM(name)
         [ COMMAREA(data-value)
              [ LENGTH(data-value) ] ]
         [ SYSID(systemname) ]
         [ SYNCONRETURN ]
END-EXEC
```

Explanation

PROGRAM   Specifies the one- to eight-character name of the program to be invoked. This name must be defined in the Processing Program Table (PPT).

COMMAREA   Specifies a data area that's passed to the invoked program as a communication area. The invoked program accesses the communication area via its DFHCOMMAREA field.

LENGTH   Specifies a binary halfword (PIC S9(4) COMP) or numeric literal that indicates the length of the data area specified in the COMMAREA option. Under OS/VS COBOL, LENGTH is required if you code COMMAREA.

SYSID   Specifies the one- to four-character name of the system where the program resides.

SYNCONRETURN   Specifies that the linked-to program should perform a syncpoint when it returns control to the linking program. If omitted, the syncpoint is taken when the linking program ends. Valid only for Distributed Program Link.

Figure 12-9 The LINK command

The last option, SYNCONRETURN, tells the remote CICS system to issue a syncpoint when the server program returns control to the client program. If you omit SYNCONRETURN, the local CICS system issues a syncpoint when the client program ends and propagates this syncpoint to the remote system so that any updates performed by the server program are committed. If all of the updates made by the application are done by the server program, you might gain a performance benefit by coding SYNCONRETURN. In most cases, however, you should omit SYNCONRETURN.

Asynchronous processing

Asynchronous processing is the term IBM uses to describe a distributed START command. You may recall from chapter 10 that the START command lets you invoke a transaction that's run as a separate task. When you use asynchronous processing, you issue a START command that includes the SYSID option or that identifies a transaction whose Processing Program Table entry specifies a remote system. Then, CICS sends the START command to the remote system, where the transaction is run.

You can use all of the START command options you learned about in chapter 10 when you use asynchronous processing. Thus, you can use the INTERVAL or TIME options to specify that the task is to start at a particular time. And you can use the FROM option in a distributed START command to pass data to the started task. Then, the started task can retrieve the data using the RETRIEVE command.

Asynchronous processing has one major limitation that you need to be aware of. As far as CICS is concerned, the task that issues the START command and the started task are separate logical units of work. If one task fails, the other is not affected. As a result, it's unwise to use asynchronous processing for applications that update files.

Distributed Transaction Processing

Distributed Transaction Processing, or *DTP,* is the most advanced and most complicated form of distributed processing under CICS. Simply put, it allows two or more programs running on different systems to communicate with one another. This communication is called a *conversation.* The program that initiates the conversation is called the *front end.* As you would expect, the other program is called the *back end.* (These terms mean essentially the same thing as *client* and *server.*)

DTP is the CICS implementation of an IBM standard for interprogram communication called *Advanced Program to Program Communication,* or *APPC.* One of the biggest advantages of DTP is that both of the programs do not have to be CICS programs. In other words, DTP lets a CICS program communicate with any other program that follows the APPC standard. For example, you might create a CICS back-end program that communicates with a front-end program written in standard COBOL running on an AS/400. The two programs can work together because they both use the APPC interface.

Figure 12-10 lists the most important CICS commands used for DTP. Frankly, the details of DTP programming are far beyond the scope of this book. In particular, the details of keeping both ends of the conversation synchronized are tedious. You'll find complete information about developing DTP programs in the IBM manual *CICS/ESA Distributed Transaction Programming Guide.*

You should realize that the Distributed Program Link feature of CICS/ESA 3.3 makes it less compelling to develop APPC applications. Although APPC lets you create distributed processing applications with complicated conversations, most APPC applications have relatively simple conversations: The front end starts the back end and requests some work; the back end does the work and sends the results; and the front end terminates the conversation. In most cases, you're better off implementing this type of application using Distributed Program Link. Then, you don't have to worry about any of the

APPC command	What it does
ALLOCATE	Issued by the front-end transaction to establish a session with the back-end system.
CONNECT PROCESS	Issued by the front-end transaction to initiate the back-end transaction.
SEND	Sends data.
WAIT CONVID	Forces accumulated buffer data to be transmitted.
RECEIVE	Receives data.
CONVERSE	Combines the operation of a SEND, WAIT CONVID, and RECEIVE command.
FREE	Releases the session so it can be used by another application.

Figure 12-10   Basic APPC commands

commands in figure 12-10. Instead, you just code a LINK command and pass data between the programs using the communication area.

Discussion   Just a few years ago, CICS's distributed processing features were considered exotic. Today, however, more and more applications are being built using these features. And as IBM implements CICS for more operating environments (such as AS/400, OS/2, and AIX/Unix), I expect to see these features used even more.

Terms

distributed processing
CICS intercommunication
Multi-Region Operation
MRO
Intersystem Communication
ISC
InterRegion Communications Access Method
Cross-Memory Services
Terminal Owning Region
TOR
Application Owning Region
AOR
File Owning Region
FOR
host connection

system identifier
sysid
transaction routing
routing transaction
CRTE
function shipping
Distributed Program Link
DPL
client-server application
client
server
asynchronous processing
Distributed Transaction Processing
DTP
conversation
front end
back end
Advanced Program to Program Communication
APPC

Objectives

1. Explain what transaction routing is and why it is commonly used.

2. Explain why you should avoid coding the SYSID option on CICS commands for function shipping, and describe the additional error checking you should do whenever you use function shipping.

3. Compare and contrast the features and benefits of Distributed Program Link, asynchronous processing, and Distributed Transaction Processing.

Appendix A

CICS command summary

This appendix summarizes the CICS commands presented in this book and in *Part 1: An Introductory Course*. For each command, you'll find the syntax of the command's options that are covered in the text, as well as a figure and page reference that will help you find more detailed information for the command. You can use this summary as a quick refresher on how to code a particular command or option.

The ABEND command

Figure 6-19 on page 133 of *Part 1*
Figure 11-3 on page 296 of *Part 2*

```
EXEC CICS
    ABEND [ ABCODE(data-value) ]
          [ CANCEL ]
END-EXEC
```

The ADDRESS command

Figure 8-41 on page 214 of *Part 1*

```
EXEC CICS
    ADDRESS [ CWA(pointer) ]
            [ CSA(pointer) ]
            [ TWA(pointer) ]
            [ TCTUA(pointer) ]
END-EXEC
```

The ASKTIME command

Figure 10-1 on page 261 of *Part 2*

```
EXEC CICS
    ASKTIME [ ABSTIME(data-area) ]
END-EXEC
```

The ASSIGN command

Figure 8-20 on page 184 of *Part 1*

```
EXEC CICS
    ASSIGN [ COLOR(data-area) ]
           [ HILIGHT(data-area) ]
           [ SCRNHT(data-area) ]
           [ SCRNWD(data-area) ]
END-EXEC
```

The CANCEL command

Figure 10-8 on page 273 of *Part 2*

```
EXEC CICS
    CANCEL REQID(name)
END-EXEC
```

The DELETE command

Figure 8-7 on page 162 of *Part 1*

```
EXEC CICS
    DELETE   DATASET(filename)
             RIDFLD(data-area)
          [ RRN | RBA ]
END-EXEC
```

The DELETEQ TD command

Figure 9-7 on page 248 of *Part 2*

```
EXEC CICS
    DELETEQ TD QUEUE(name)
END-EXEC
```

The DELETEQ TS command

Figure 8-3 on page 219 of *Part 2*

```
EXEC CICS
    DELETEQ TS QUEUE(name)
END-EXEC
```

The DEQ command

Figure 9-9 on page 250 of *Part 2*
Figure 10-11 on page 277 of *Part 2*

```
EXEC CICS
    DEQ    RESOURCE(data-area)
       [ LENGTH(data-value) ]
END-EXEC
```

The ENDBR command

Figure 1-6 on page 11 of *Part 2*

```
EXEC CICS
    ENDBR DATASET(filename)
END-EXEC
```

The ENQ command

Figure 9-8 on page 249 of *Part 2*
Figure 10-11 on page 277 of *Part 2*

```
EXEC CICS
    ENQ    RESOURCE(data-area)
       [ LENGTH(data-value) ]
END-EXEC
```

The FORMATTIME command

Figure 10-2 on page 262 of *Part 2*

```
EXEC CICS
    FORMATTIME    ABSTIME(data-area)

                  [ DATE(data-area)
                     [ DATEFORM(data-area) ] ]
                  [ MMDDYY(data-area) ]
                  [ DDMMYY(data-area) ]
                  [ YYMMDD(data-area) ]
                  [ YYDDMM(data-area) ]
                  [ YYDDD(data-area) ]
                  [ DATESEP[(data-value)] ]

                  [ DAYCOUNT(data-area) ]
                  [ DAYOFWEEK(data-area) ]
                  [ DAYOFMONTH(data-area) ]
                  [ MONTHOFYEAR(data-area) ]
                  [ YEAR(data-area) ]

                  [ TIME(data-area) ]
                  [ TIMESEP[(data-value)] ]
END-EXEC
```

The FREEMAIN command

Figure 10-20 on page 290 of *Part 2*

```
EXEC CICS
    FREEMAIN {DATA(data-area)          }
             {DATAPOINTER(pointer)}
END-EXEC
```

The GETMAIN command

Figure 10-19 on page 287 of *Part 2*

```
EXEC CICS
    GETMAIN    SET(pointer)
             {LENGTH(data-value)              }
             {FLENGTH(data-value) [ BELOW ]}
           [ INITIMG(data-value) ]
           [ CICSDATAKEY | USERDATAKEY ]
END-EXEC
```

The HANDLE ABEND command

Figure 11-1 on page 293 of *Part 2*

```
EXEC CICS

                       (PROGRAM(name)              )
    HANDLE ABEND {LABEL(procedure-name)}
                       {CANCEL                       }
                       (RESET                        )
END-EXEC
```

The HANDLE AID command

Figure 8-30 on page 196 of *Part 1*

```
EXEC CICS
    HANDLE AID
         option(procedure-name)...
END-EXEC
```

The HANDLE CONDITION command

Figure 8-33 on page 201 of *Part 1*

```
EXEC CICS
    HANDLE CONDITION condition-name(procedure-name)...
END-EXEC
```

The JOURNAL command

Figure 11-11 on page 306 of *Part 2*

```
EXEC CICS
    JOURNAL   JFILEID(data-value)
              JTYPEID(data-value)
              FROM(data-area)
            [ LENGTH(data-value) ]
            [ WAIT ]
            [ REQID(data-area) ]
            [ STARTIO ]
            [ PREFIX(data-area)
                [ PFXLENG(data-value) ] ]
END-EXEC
```

The LINK command

Figure 8-14 on page 171 of *Part 1*
Figure 10-14 on page 281 of *Part 2*
Figure 12-9 on page 322 of *Part 2*

```
EXEC CICS
    LINK  [ PROGRAM(name) ]
          [ COMMAREA(data-area)
             [ LENGTH(data-value) ] ]
          [ INPUTMSG(data-area)
             [ INPUTMSGLEN(data-value ] ]
          [ SYSID(systemname) ]
          [ SYNCONRETURN ]
END-EXEC
```

The LOAD command

Figure 10-16 on page 283 of *Part 2*

```
EXEC CICS
    LOAD   PROGRAM(data-value)
           SET(pointer)
        [ HOLD ]
END-EXEC
```

The READ command

Figure 6-18 on page 132 of *Part 1*
Figure 8-1 on page 157 of *Part 1*

```
EXEC CICS
    READ  DATASET(filename)
          INTO(data-area)
          RIDFLD(data-area)
        [ RRN | RBA ]
        [ LENGTH(data-area) ]
        [ UPDATE ]
END-EXEC
```

The READNEXT command

Figure 1-3 on page 8 of *Part 2*

```
EXEC CICS
    READNEXT   DATASET(filename)
               INTO(data-area)
               RIDFLD(data-area)
             [ RRN | RBA ]
             [ GENERIC ]
             [ KEYLENGTH(data-value) ]
END-EXEC
```

The READPREV command

Figure 1-5 on page 10 of *Part 2*

```
EXEC CICS
    READPREV   DATASET(filename)
               INTO(data-area)
               RIDFLD(data-area)
             [ RRN | RBA ]
             [ GENERIC ]
             [ KEYLENGTH(data-value) ]
END-EXEC
```

The READQ TD command

Figure 9-6 on page 247 of *Part 2*

```
EXEC CICS
    READQ TD   QUEUE(name)
               INTO(data-area)
             [ LENGTH(data-area) ]
END-EXEC
```

The READQ TS command

Figure 8-2 on page 217 of *Part 2*

```
EXEC CICS
    READQ TS   QUEUE(name)
               INTO(data-area)
               LENGTH(data-area)
             [{ITEM(data-value)}]
             [{NEXT           }]
END-EXEC
```

The RECEIVE command

Figure 7-5 on page 201 of *Part 2*

```
EXEC CICS
    RECEIVE    INTO(data-area)
             [ LENGTH(data-area) ]
END-EXEC
```

The RECEIVE MAP command

Figure 6-17 on page 131 of *Part 1*

```
EXEC CICS
    RECEIVE MAP(name)
            MAPSET(name)
            INTO(data-area)
END-EXEC
```

The RESETBR command

Figure 1-7 on page 12 of *Part 2*

```
EXEC CICS
    RESETBR    DATASET(filename)
               RIDFLD(data-area)
             [ RRN | RBA ]
             [ GTEQ | EQUAL ]
             [ GENERIC ]
             [ KEYLENGTH(data-value) ]
END-EXEC
```

The RETRIEVE command

Figure 10-7 on page 271 of *Part 2*

```
EXEC CICS
    RETRIEVE   INTO(data-area)
             [ LENGTH(data-area) ]
             [ RTRANSID(name) ]
             [ RTERMID(name) ]
             [ QUEUE(name) ]
END-EXEC
```

The RETURN command

Figure 6-14 on page 127 of *Part 1*
Figure 8-11 on page 168 of *Part 1*

```
EXEC CICS
    RETURN   [ TRANSID(name) ]
             [ COMMAREA(data-area) ]
             [ LENGTH(data-value) ]
END-EXEC
```

The REWRITE command

Figure 8-5 on page 161 of *Part 1*

```
EXEC CICS
    REWRITE   DATASET(filename)
              FROM(data-area)
          [ LENGTH(data-value) ]
END-EXEC
```

The ROUTE command

Figure 6-24 on page 188 of *Part 2*

```
EXEC CICS
    ROUTE   LIST(data-name)
            INTERVAL(hhmmss)
            TIME(hhmmss)
         [ NLEOM ]
END-EXEC
```

The SEND command

Figure 7-6 on page 202 of *Part 2*

```
EXEC CICS
    SEND   FROM(data-name)
        [ LENGTH(data-value) ]
        [ CTLCHAR(data-name) ]
        [ ERASE ]
END-EXEC
```

The SEND MAP command

Figure 6-16 on page 129 of *Part 1*
Figure 6-17 on page 175 of *Part 2*
Figure 6-20 on page 180 of *Part 2*

```
EXEC CICS
    SEND   MAP(name)
        [ MAPSET(name) ]
        [ FROM(data-area) ]
        [ MAPONLY | DATAONLY ]
        [ ACCUM ]
        [ PAGING ]
        [ ERASE | ERASEAUP ]
        [ CURSOR [(data-value)] ]
        [ PRINT ]
        [ NLEOM ]
        [ FORMFEED ]
END-EXEC
```

The SEND PAGE command

Figure 6-11 on page 163 of *Part 2*

```
EXEC CICS
    SEND PAGE [ OPERPURGE ]
              [ RETAIN | RELEASE ]
END-EXEC
```

The SEND TEXT command

Figure 8-28 on page 194 of *Part 1*
Figure 6-8 on page 158 of *Part 2*
Figure 6-20 on page 180 of *Part 2*

```
EXEC CICS
    SEND TEXT    FROM(data-area)
              [ LENGTH(data-value) ]
              [ ACCUM ]
              [ PAGING ]
              [ ERASE ]
              [ FREEKB ]
              [ HEADER(data-area) ]
              [ TRAILER(data-area) ]
              [ PRINT ]
              [ NLEOM ]
              [ FORMFEED ]
END-EXEC
```

The START command

Figure 10-6 on page 267 of *Part 2*

```
EXEC CICS
    START    TRANSID(name)
            [(INTERVAL(hhmmss)                                                  )]
            [{TIME(hhmmss)                                                      }]
            [{AFTER [HOURS(hh)] [MINUTES(mins)] [SECONDS(secs)]                 }]
            [(AT    [HOURS(hh)] [MINUTES(mins)] [SECONDS(secs)]                 )]
            [ TERMID(name) ]
            [ FROM(data-area)
                [ LENGTH(data-value) ] ]
            [ RTERMID(name) ]
            [ RTRANSID(name) ]
            [ QUEUE(name) ]
            [ REQID(name) ]
END-EXEC
```

The STARTBR command

Figure 1-1 on page 5 of *Part 2*

```
EXEC CICS
    STARTBR    DATASET(filename)
               RIDFLD(data-area)
             [ RRN | RBA ]
             [ GTEQ | EQUAL ]
             [ GENERIC ]
             [ KEYLENGTH(data-value) ]
END-EXEC
```

The SUSPEND command

Figure 10-10 on page 276 of *Part 2*

```
EXEC CICS
    SUSPEND
END-EXEC
```

The SYNCPOINT command

Figure 11-7 on page 300 of *Part 2*

```
EXEC CICS
    SYNCPOINT [ ROLLBACK ]
END-EXEC
```

The UNLOCK command

Figure 8-9 on page 164 of *Part 1*

```
EXEC CICS
    UNLOCK DATASET(filename)
END-EXEC
```

The WAIT JOURNAL command

Figure 11-12 on page 309 of *Part 2*

```
EXEC CICS
    WAIT JOURNAL    JFILEID(data-value)
                  [ REQID(data-area) ]
                  [ STARTIO ]
END-EXEC
```

The WAIT JOURNALNUM command

Figure 11-12 on page 309 of *Part 2*

```
EXEC CICS
    WAIT    JOURNALNUM(data-value)
          [ REQID(data-area) ]
          [ STARTIO ]
END-EXEC
```

The WRITE command

Figure 8-3 on page 159 of *Part 1*

```
EXEC CICS
    WRITE   DATASET(filename)
            FROM(data-area)
            RIDFLD(data-area)
          [ RRN | RBA ]
          [ LENGTH(data-value) ]
END-EXEC
```

The WRITE JOURNALNUM command

Figure 11-11 on page 306 of *Part 2*

```
EXEC CICS
    WRITE    JOURNALNUM(data-value)
             JTYPEID(data-value)
             FROM(data-area)
           [ LENGTH(data-value) ]
           [ WAIT ]
           [ REQID(data-area) ]
           [ STARTIO ]
           [ PREFIX(data-area)
               [ PFXLENG(data-value) ] ]
END-EXEC
```

The WRITEQ TD command

Figure 9-5 on page 246 of *Part 2*

```
EXEC CICS
    WRITEQ TD    QUEUE(name)
                 FROM(data-area)
               [ LENGTH(data-value) ]
END-EXEC
```

The WRITEQ TS command

Figure 8-1 on page 216 of *Part 2*

```
EXEC CICS
    WRITEQ TS    QUEUE(name)
                 FROM(data-area)
                 LENGTH(data-value)
               [ ITEM(data-area) REWRITE ]
               [ {MAIN     } ]
               [ {AUXILIARY} ]
END-EXEC
```

The XCTL command

Figure 6-15 on page 128 of *Part 1*
Figure 8-16 on page 173 of *Part 1*
Figure 10-15 on page 282 of *Part 2*

```
EXEC CICS
    XCTL   [ PROGRAM(name) ]
           [ COMMAREA(data-area)
               [ LENGTH(data-value) ] ]
           [ INPUTMSG(data-area)
               [ INPUTMSGLEN(data-value) ] ]
END-EXEC
```

Appendix B

BMS macro summary

This appendix summarizes the BMS macros presented in this book and in *Part 1: An Introductory Course*. For each macro instruction, you'll find the syntax of the macro's options that are covered in the text, as well as a figure and page reference that will help you find more detailed information for the macro. You can use this summary as a quick refresher on how to code a particular macro.

The DFHMSD macro   Figure 5-8 on pages 73-74 of *Part 1*

Format 1

```
name        DFHMSD      TYPE={&SYSPARM
                              DSECT  },
                              MAP

                        LANG={COBOL
                              ASM   },
                              PLI

                        MODE={IN
                              OUT   },
                              INOUT

                        TERM=terminal-type,

                        CTRL=(option,option...),

                        STORAGE=AUTO,

                        MAPATTS=(COLOR,HILIGHT),

                        DSATTS=(COLOR,HILIGHT),

                        EXTATT={YES
                                NO      },
                                MAPONLY

                        TIOAPFX={YES}
                                 NO
```

Format 2

```
            DFHMSD      TYPE=FINAL
```

Terminal types

ALL
3270
3270-1
3270-2

CTRL options

FREEKB
ALARM

The DFHMDI macro

Figure 5-9 on page 77 of *Part 1*
Figure 6-13 on page 167 of *Part 2*

```
name      DFHMDI    SIZE=(lines,columns),

                    [ LINE={line-number}, ]
                          {NEXT       }

                    [ COLUMN=column-number, ]

                    [ CTRL=(option,option...), ]

                    [ JUSTIFY={FIRST}, ]
                             {LAST }

                    [{HEADER=YES }]
                     {TRAILER=YES}
```

CTRL options

FREEKB
ALARM

The DFHMDF macro

Figure 5-10 on pages 79-80 of *Part 1*

```
name      DFHMDF    POS=(line,column),
                    LENGTH=field-length,
                          (BRT ) (PROT  )
                    ATTRB=({NORM},{ASKIP },NUM,IC,FSET),
                          (DRK ) (UNPROT)
                    INITIAL='literal',
                    COLOR=color,
                    HILIGHT=highlight,
                    PICIN='picture-string',
                    PICOUT='picture-string'
```

COLOR values

BLUE	RED
PINK	GREEN
TURQUOISE	YELLOW
NEUTRAL (white)	DEFAULT

HILIGHT values

BLINK
REVERSE
UNDERLINE
OFF

Index

CICS for the COBOL Programmer

Part 1: An Introductory Course / Second Edition   Doug Lowe

Part 1 of *CICS for the COBOL Programmer* zeroes in on the basic CICS elements you'll use in just about every program you write. You'll learn:

- how to use basic mapping support (BMS) macros to define screens in a CICS program

- pseudo-conversational programming...what it is, why you have to use it, and how it complicates the logic in a COBOL program

- CICS commands for terminal handling, VSAM file handling, and program control

- how to use VS COBOL II features that simplify CICS programming (like the EVALUATE statement, assured LENGTH options, and the ADDRESS register)

- how to *design* a CICS program that's easier to code, test, debug, and maintain...and that

still runs efficiently...using event-driven design

- how to use IBM-supplied transactions like CEMT, CECI, and CEDF to simplify testing and debugging

- how to interpret a transaction dump for a VS COBOL II program

Four complete programs (including screen layouts, mapset listing, symbolic map, program design, and code) are among the many examples that help you learn how to develop CICS programs from start to finish. And the programs are all practical enough that you can use them as models when you start to design and write programs on your own.

CICS, Part 2, 12 chapters, 409 pages, **$31.00**
ISBN 0-911625-60-7

The CICS Programmer's Desk Reference

Second Edition   Doug Lowe

Ever feel buried by IBM manuals?

It seems like you need stacks of them, close at hand, if you want to be an effective CICS programmer. Because frankly, there's just too much you have to know to do your job well; you can't keep it all in your head.

That's why Doug Lowe decided to write *The CICS Programmer's Desk Reference.* In it, he's collected all the information you need to have at your fingertips, and organized it into 12 sections that make it easy for you to find what you're looking for. So there are sections on:

- BMS macro instructions—their formats (with an explanation of each parameter) and coding examples

- CICS commands—their syntax (with an explanation of each parameter), coding examples, and suggestions on how and when to use each one most effectively

- MVS and DOS/VSE JCL for CICS applications

- AMS commands for handling VSAM files

- ISPF editor commands

- complete model programs, including specs, design, and code

- a summary of CICS program design techniques that lead to simple, maintainable, and efficient programs

- guidelines for testing and debugging CICS applications

- and more!

So clear the IBM manuals off your terminal table. Let the *Desk Reference* be your everyday guide to CICS instead.

CICS Desk Reference, 12 sections, 525 pages
ISBN 0-911625-68-2—**Available November 1992**

DB2 for the COBOL Programmer

Part 1: An Introductory Course   **Steve Eckols**

If you're looking for a practical DB2 book that fo-
cuses on application programming, this is the
book for you. Written from the programmer's
point of view, it will quickly teach you what you
need to know to access and process DB2 data in
your COBOL programs using embedded SQL.
You'll learn:

- what DB2 is and how it works, so you'll have
  the background you need to program more
  easily and logically

- how to design and code application programs that retrieve and update DB2 data

- how to use basic error handling and data integrity techniques to protect DB2 data

- how to use joins and unions to combine
  data from two or more tables into a single table

- how to use DB2 column functions to extract
  summary information from a table

- how to use a subquery or subselect when
  one SQL statement depends on the results of
  another

- how to work with variable-length data and
  nulls

- how to develop DB2 programs interactively
  (using DB2I, a TSO facility) or in batch

So if you want to learn how to write DB2 application programs, get a copy of this book today!

DB2, Part 1, 11 chapters, 371 pages, **$32.50**
ISBN 0-911625-59-3

DB2 for the COBOL Programmer

Part 2: An Advanced Course   **Steve Eckols**

Once you've mastered the basics of DB2 programming, there's still plenty to learn. So this book
teaches you all the advanced DB2 features that
will make you a more capable programmer...and
shows you when to use each one. You'll learn:

- how to use advanced data manipulation and
  error handling techniques

- how to use dynamic SQL

- how to work with distributed DB2 data

- how to maximize locking efficiency and con-
  currency to maintain the accuracy of DB2
  data even while a number of programs have
  access to that data

- how to access and process DB2 data in CICS
  programs

- what you need to know about data base ad-
  ministration so you can design and define
  your own tables for program testing (this
  will make you a more productive and professional programmer, even if you never want
  to be a DBA)

- how to use QMF, IBM's Query Management
  Facility, to issue SQL statements interactively and to prepare formatted reports

So don't wait to expand your DB2 skills. Get a
copy of this book TODAY.

DB2, Part 2, 15 chapters, 378 pages, **$32.50**
ISBN 0-911625-64-X

 Call **toll-free**   1-800-221-5528   Weekdays, 8 a.m. to 5 p.m. Pac. Std. Time

IMS for the COBOL Programmer

Part 1: DL/I Data Base Processing   Steve Eckols

This how-to book will have you writing batch DL/I programs in a minimum of time—whether you're working on a VSE or an MVS system. But it doesn't neglect the conceptual background you must have to create programs that work. So you'll learn:

- what a DL/I data base is and how its data elements are organized into a hierarchical structure
- the COBOL elements for creating, accessing, and updating DL/I data bases...including logical data bases and data bases with secondary indexing
- how to use DL/I recovery and restart features

- the basic DL/I considerations for coding interactive programs using IMS/DC or CICS
- how data bases with the 4 common types of DL/I data base organizations are stored (this material will help you program more logically and efficiently for the type of data base you're using)
- and more!

7 complete COBOL programs show you how to process DL/I data bases in various ways. Use them as models for production work in your shop, and you'll save hours of development time.

IMS, Part 1, 16 chapters, 333 pages, **$34.50**
ISBN 0-911625-29-1

IMS for the COBOL Programmer

Part 2: Data Communications and Message Format Service   Steve Eckols

The second part of *IMS for the COBOL Programmer* is for MVS programmers only. It teaches how to develop online programs that access IMS data bases and run under the data communications (DC) component of IMS. So you'll learn:

- why you code message processing programs (MPPs) the way you do (DC programs are called MPPs because they process messages sent from and to user terminals)
- what COBOL elements you use for MPPs
- how to use Message Format Service (MFS), a facility for formatting complex terminal displays so you can enhance the look and operation of your DC programs
- how to develop applications that use more than one screen format or that use physical and logical paging

- how to develop batch message processing (BMP) programs to update IMS data bases in batch even while they're being used by other programs
- how to use Batch Terminal Simulator (BTS) to test DC applications using IMS resources, but without disrupting the everyday IMS processing that's going on
- and more!

8 complete programs—including MFS format sets, program design, and COBOL code—show you how to handle various DC and MFS applications. Use them as models to save yourself hours of coding and debugging.

IMS, Part 2, 16 chapters, 398 pages, **$36.50**
ISBN 0-911625-30-5

 Call **toll-free**   1-800-221-5528   Weekdays, 8 a.m. to 5 p.m. Pac. Std. Time

Structured ANS COBOL

A 2-part course in 1974 and 1985 ANS COBOL   Mike Murach and Paul Noll

This 2-part course teaches how to use 1974 and 1985 standard COBOL the way the top professionals do. The two parts are independent: You can choose either or both, depending on your current level of COBOL skill (if you're learning on your own) or on what you want your programmers to learn (if you're a trainer or manager).

Part 1: A Course for Novices teaches people with no previous programming experience how to design and code COBOL programs that prepare reports. Because report programs often call subprograms, use COPY members, handle one-level tables, and read indexed files, it covers these subjects too. But frankly, this book emphasizes the structure and logic of report programs, instead of covering as many COBOL elements as other introductory texts do. That's because we've found most beginning programmers have more trouble with structure and logic than they do with COBOL itself.

Part 2: An Advanced Course also emphasizes program structure and logic, focusing on edit, update, and maintenance programs. But beyond that, it's a complete guide to the 1974 and 1985 elements that all COBOL programmers should know

how to use (though many don't). To be specific, it teaches how to:

- handle sequential, indexed, and relative files
- use alternate indexing and dynamic processing for indexed files
- code internal sorts and merges
- create and use COPY library members
- create and call subprograms
- handle single- and multi-level tables using indexes as well as subscripts
- use INSPECT, STRING, and UNSTRING for character manipulation
- code 1974 programs that will be easy to convert when you switch to a 1985 compiler

In fact, we recommend you get a copy of *Part 2* no matter how much COBOL experience you've had because it makes such a handy reference to all the COBOL elements you'll ever want to use.

COBOL, Part 1, 13 chapters, 438 pages, **$31.00**
ISBN 0-911625-37-2

COBOL, Part 2, 12 chapters, 498 pages, **$31.00**
ISBN 0-911625-38-0

VS COBOL II: A Guide for Programmers and Managers

Second Edition   Anne Prince

If you work in an MVS COBOL shop, sooner or later you're going to convert to VS COBOL II, IBM's 1985 COBOL compiler. This book will quickly teach you everything you need to know about the compiler:

- how to code the new language elements... and what language elements you can't use anymore
- CICS considerations
- how to use the new debugger
- how the compiler's features can make your programs compile and run more efficiently
- guidelines for converting to VS COBOL II (that includes coverage of the conversion aids IBM supplies)

So if you're in a shop that's already converted to VS COBOL II, you'll learn how to benefit from the new language elements and features the compiler has to offer. If you aren't yet working in VS COBOL II, you'll learn how to write programs now that will be easy to convert later on. And if you're a manager, you'll get some practical ideas on when to convert and how to do it as painlessly as possible.

This second edition covers Release 3 of the compiler, as well as Releases 1 and 2.

VS COBOL II, 7 chapters, 271 pages, **$27.50**
ISBN 0-911625-54-2

VSAM

Access Method Services and Application Programming	Doug Lowe

This is the definitive book on VSAM. As its title suggests, *VSAM: Access Method Services and Application Programming* has two main purposes: (1) to teach you how to use the Access Method Services (AMS) utility to define and manipulate VSAM files; and (2) to teach you how to process VSAM files using various programming languages. To be specific, you'll learn:

- how VSAM data sets and catalogs are organized and used

- how to use AMS commands to define VSAM catalogs, space, clusters, alternate indexes, and paths

- how to set AMS performance options so you make the best possible use of your system's resources

- what recovery and security considerations are important when you use AMS

- how to code MVS and DOS/VSE JCL for VSAM files, and how to allocate VSAM files under TSO and VM/CMS

- how to process VSAM files in COBOL, CICS, and assembler language (the chapter on CO-BOL processing covers both VS COBOL and VS COBOL II)

You'll find the answers to questions like these

- How much primary and secondary space should I allocate to my VSAM files?

- What's an appropriate free space allocation for a KSDS?

- What's the best control interval size for VSAM files that are accessed both sequentially and directly?

- Do I always need to use VERIFY to check the integrity of my files?

- What's the difference between regular VSAM catalogs and the ICF catalog structure?

- When should I...and shouldn't I...use the IMBED and REPLICATE options to improve performance?

- It's easy to find out how many records are in a file's index component. But how do I find out how many of those records are in the sequence set?

- How do I determine the best buffer allocation for my files?

- What's the best way to back up my VSAM files—REPRO, EXPORT, or something else?

So why wait any longer to sharpen your VSAM skills? Get a copy of *VSAM: AMS and Application Programming* TODAY!

VSAM: AMS & Application Programming, 12 chapters, 260 pages, **$27.50**
ISBN 0-911625-33-X

VSAM for the COBOL Programmer

Second Edition	Doug Lowe

If you're looking for a no-frills approach to VSAM that teaches you only what you need to know to code COBOL programs, this is the book for you. You'll learn: the meanings of the critical terms and concepts that apply to VSAM files; the COBOL elements for handling VSAM files; how to handle alternate indexes and dynamic access; why error processing is a must; how to use the Access

Method Services utility (AMS) to create, print, copy, and rename VSAM files; how to code the MVS and VSE JCL to run programs that use VSAM files; and how your COBOL code is affected if you're working under VS COBOL II.

VSAM for COBOL, 6 chapters, 187 pages, **$17.50**
ISBN 0-911625-45-3

DOS/VSE JCL

Second Edition — Steve Eckols

The job control language for a DOS/VSE system can be overwhelming. There are more parameters than you would ever want to know about. And those parameters let you do more things than you would ever want to do. Of course, all those parameters are described in the IBM manuals... somewhere. But who has time to wade through pages and pages of details that don't seem to apply to your situation (although you can't ever be sure because the manuals are so confusing).

Certainly you don't. That's why you need *DOS/VSE JCL*. It doesn't try to teach every nuance of every parameter. Instead, it teaches you how to code the JCL for the applications that occur every day in a VSE shop. You'll learn how to manage job and program execution, how to identify the files a program needs to use, and how to use cataloged procedures. You'll learn how to code POWER JECL statements to manage job scheduling and output

processing and how to use ICCF to manage POWER job processing. You'll learn how to process tape and DASD files. And you'll learn how to use language translators and the linkage-editor, maintain VSE libraries, and use three utility programs: sort/merge, DITTO, and AMS.

Whether you're a novice or an expert, this book will help you use your DOS/VSE system more effectively. If you're new to VSE, this book will get you started right, giving you the confidence you need to take charge of your system. If you're an experienced VSE user, this book will help you understand *why* you've been doing what you've been doing so you can do it better in the future.

DOS/VSE JCL, 18 chapters, 448 pages, **$34.50**
ISBN 0-911625-50-X

DOS/VSE ICCF

Steve Eckols

If you use ICCF on your VSE system, you'll turn to this book time and again for training and reference. It teaches you how to use ICCF's editing and system commands to: enter, change, copy, move, display, and find text in a library member...control keyboard functions, like tabbing, moving the cursor, and using PF keys...use split screens...manage and maintain VSE libraries...handle output directed to your terminal efficiently and easily...and more!

But ICCF is much more than just an editor. So you'll also learn how to use ICCF for VSE job management and interactive partition processing. With the former, you can use the spooling program, POWER, to transfer jobs from ICCF to the batch VSE environment, monitor the progress of

the jobs, and handle their output. With the latter, you can run programs completely within ICCF. That means you'll learn how to use ICCF-supplied procedures for tasks like compiling and running programs, as well as how to write and execute your own procedures. These features are tough to learn by studying the IBM manuals, but this book teaches them in just an hour or two.

So whether you want to learn ICCF for the first time, master the facilities you're not already using, or have an ICCF reference that's quick and easy to use, this is the book for you.

DOS/VSE ICCF, 11 chapters, 372 pages, **$31.00**
ISBN 0-911625-36-4

 Call **toll-free**   1-800-221-5528   Weekdays, 8 a.m. to 5 p.m. Pac. Std. Time

DOS/VSE and MVS Assembler Language

Anne Prince and Kevin McQuillen

"Why learn assembler language?"

That's the question nowadays, when almost no application programs are written in assembler anymore.

But if you've worked in an IBM shop for long, you realize that today, as in the past, all functions on the system eventually get reduced to assembler language. So knowing assembler helps you understand what's happening as your programs...in any language...compile and execute.

In fact, once you know assembler, you'll gain new confidence in your programming skills. When you come up against a tough debugging problem, for example, you'll be able to think through how your programming statements are being broken down into assembler. And that will often point you to the most likely cause of the problem. Knowing something about assembler is also a big help when you have to call assembler subprograms from programs you've written in other languages.

So one purpose of our assembler language book is to teach you the assembler basics that will help your work go more easily, no matter what language you're working in (there are two versions of the book, one for DOS/VSE and one for MVS). The first 3 chapters introduce you to IBM mainframes in general and to VSE or MVS in particular. Then, chapters 4-8 are what I call "the least anyone who uses an IBM system should know about assembler language." When you finish them, you'll understand what's happening as any VSE or MVS program executes. And you'll be able to write and use assembler subprograms.

At that point, if you want to learn more about assembler (because you're interested in systems programming, for example), you can go on to any of the other chapters. They cover: table handling; bit manipulation; translation; floating-point arithmetic; writing macro definitions; handling DASD files; and developing *structured* assembler programs.

So gain the basic knowledge of assembler that's essential for your continued technical growth. Get a copy of our assembler language book today!

DOS/VSE Assembler Language, 19 chapters, 492 pages,
$36.50
ISBN 0-911625-31-3

MVS Assembler Language, 19 chapters, 528 pages,
$36.50
ISBN 0-911625-34-8

 Call **toll-free**   1-800-221-5528   Weekdays, 8 a.m. to 5 p.m. Pac. Std. Time

---

Comment Form

Your opinions count

If you have any comments, criticisms, or suggestions for us, I'm eager to get them. Your opinions today will affect our products of tomorrow. And if you find any errors in this book, typographical or otherwise, please point them out so we can correct them in the next printing.

Thanks for your help.

Mike Murach

Book title: CICS for the COBOL Programmer, Part 2: An Advanced Course (Second Edition)

Dear Mike: _____

_____
_____
_____
_____
_____
_____
_____
_____
_____
_____
_____
_____
_____
_____
_____
_____
_____
_____
_____

Name & Title _____
Company (if company address) _____
Address _____
City, State, Zip _____

Fold where indicated and tape closed.

No postage necessary if mailed in the U.S.

BUSINESS REPLY MAIL

FIRST-CLASS MAIL   PERMIT NO. 3063   FRESNO, CA

POSTAGE WILL BE PAID BY ADDRESSEE

Mike Murach & Associates, Inc.

4697 W JACQUELYN AVE
FRESNO CA 93722-9888

Order Form

Our Unlimited Guarantee

To our customers who order directly from us: You must be satisfied. Our books must work for you, or you can send them back for a full refund...no questions asked.

Name & Title _____

Company (if company address) _____

Street address _____

City, State, Zip _____

Phone number (including area code) _____

Qty	Product code and title	*Price
CICS		
____CC1R	CICS for the COBOL Programmer Part 1 (Second Edition)	$31.00
____CC2R	CICS for the COBOL Programmer Part 2 (Second Edition)	31.00
____CRFR	The CICS Programmer's Desk Reference (Second Edition)	36.50
COBOL Language Elements		
____VC2R	VS COBOL II (Second Edition)	$27.50
____SC1R	Structured ANS COBOL, Part 1	31.00
____SC2R	Structured ANS COBOL, Part 2	31.00
____RW	Report Writer	17.50
VSAM		
____VSMX	VSAM: Access Method Services and Application Programming	$27.50
____VSMR	VSAM for the COBOL Programmer (Second Edition)	17.50

Qty	Product code and title	*Price
Data Base Processing		
____DB21	DB2 for the COBOL Programmer Part 1: An Introductory Course	$32.50
____DB22	DB2 for the COBOL Programmer Part 2: An Advanced Course	32.50
____IMS1	IMS for the COBOL Programmer Part 1: DL/I Data Base Processing	34.50
____IMS2	IMS for the COBOL Programmer Part 2: Data Communications and MFS	36.50
OS/MVS Subjects		
____TSO1	MVS TSO, Part 1: Concepts and ISPF	$31.00
____TSO2	MVS TSO, Part 2: Commands and Procedures	31.00
____MJCL	MVS JCL	34.50
____MBAL	MVS Assembler Language	36.50
____OSUT	OS Utilities	17.50
DOS/VSE Subjects		
____VJLR	DOS/VSE JCL (Second Edition)	$34.50
____ICCF	DOS/VSE ICCF	31.00
____VBAL	DOS/VSE Assembler Language	36.50

☐ Bill the appropriate book prices plus UPS shipping and handling (and sales tax in California) to my ____VISA ____MasterCard:

Card Number _____

Valid thru (month/year) _____

Cardowner's signature _____

☐ Bill me.

☐ Bill my company. P.O. #_____

☐ I want to **save** UPS shipping and handling charges. Here's my check or money order for $_____. California residents, please add sales tax to your total. (Offer valid in the U.S.)

* Prices are subject to change. Please call for current prices.

To order more quickly,

Call **toll-free** 1-800-221-5528

(Weekdays, 8 to 5 Pacific Standard Time)

Fax: 1-209-275-9035

Mike Murach & Associates, Inc.

4697 West Jacquelyn Avenue
Fresno, California 93722-6427
(209) 275-3335

Order Form

Our Unlimited Guarantee

To our customers who order directly from us: You must be satisfied. Our books must work for you, or you can send them back for a full refund...no questions asked.

Name & Title _____

Company (if company address) _____

Street address _____

City, State, Zip _____

Phone number (including area code) _____

Qty	Product code and title	*Price
CICS		
____CC1R	CICS for the COBOL Programmer Part 1 (Second Edition)	$31.00
____CC2R	CICS for the COBOL Programmer Part 2 (Second Edition)	31.00
____CRFR	The CICS Programmer's Desk Reference (Second Edition)	36.50
COBOL Language Elements		
____VC2R	VS COBOL II (Second Edition)	$27.50
____SC1R	Structured ANS COBOL, Part 1	31.00
____SC2R	Structured ANS COBOL, Part 2	31.00
____RW	Report Writer	17.50
VSAM		
____VSMX	VSAM: Access Method Services and Application Programming	$27.50
____VSMR	VSAM for the COBOL Programmer (Second Edition)	17.50

Qty	Product code and title	*Price
Data Base Processing		
____DB21	DB2 for the COBOL Programmer Part 1: An Introductory Course	$32.50
____DB22	DB2 for the COBOL Programmer Part 2: An Advanced Course	32.50
____IMS1	IMS for the COBOL Programmer Part 1: DL/I Data Base Processing	34.50
____IMS2	IMS for the COBOL Programmer Part 2: Data Communications and MFS	36.50
OS/MVS Subjects		
____TSO1	MVS TSO, Part 1: Concepts and ISPF	$31.00
____TSO2	MVS TSO, Part 2: Commands and Procedures	31.00
____MJCL	MVS JCL	34.50
____MBAL	MVS Assembler Language	36.50
____OSUT	OS Utilities	17.50
DOS/VSE Subjects		
____VJLR	DOS/VSE JCL (Second Edition)	$34.50
____ICCF	DOS/VSE ICCF	31.00
____VBAL	DOS/VSE Assembler Language	36.50

☐ Bill the appropriate book prices plus UPS shipping and handling (and sales tax in California) to my ____VISA ____MasterCard:

Card Number _____

Valid thru (month/year)_____

Cardowner's signature_____

☐ Bill me.

☐ Bill my company. P.O. #_____

☐ I want to **save** UPS shipping and handling charges. Here's my check or money order for $_____. California residents, please add sales tax to your total. (Offer valid in the U.S.)

* Prices are subject to change. Please call for current prices.

To order more quickly,

Call **toll-free** 1-800-221-5528

(Weekdays, 8 to 5 Pacific Standard Time)

Fax: 1-209-275-9035

Mike Murach & Associates, Inc.

4697 West Jacquelyn Avenue
Fresno, California 93722-6427
(209) 275-3335

fold

fold

fold

fold

Order Form

Our Unlimited Guarantee

To our customers who order directly from us: You must be satisfied. Our books must work for you, or you can send them back for a full refund...no questions asked.

Name & Title _____

Company (if company address) _____

Street address _____

City, State, Zip _____

Phone number (including area code) _____

Qty	Product code and title	*Price
CICS		
____CC1R	CICS for the COBOL Programmer Part 1 (Second Edition)	$31.00
____CC2R	CICS for the COBOL Programmer Part 2 (Second Edition)	31.00
____CRFR	The CICS Programmer's Desk Reference (Second Edition)	36.50
COBOL Language Elements		
____VC2R	VS COBOL II (Second Edition)	$27.50
____SC1R	Structured ANS COBOL, Part 1	31.00
____SC2R	Structured ANS COBOL, Part 2	31.00
____RW	Report Writer	17.50
VSAM		
____VSMX	VSAM: Access Method Services and Application Programming	$27.50
____VSMR	VSAM for the COBOL Programmer (Second Edition)	17.50

Qty	Product code and title	*Price
Data Base Processing		
____DB21	DB2 for the COBOL Programmer Part 1: An Introductory Course	$32.50
____DB22	DB2 for the COBOL Programmer Part 2: An Advanced Course	32.50
____IMS1	IMS for the COBOL Programmer Part 1: DL/I Data Base Processing	34.50
____IMS2	IMS for the COBOL Programmer Part 2: Data Communications and MFS	36.50
OS/MVS Subjects		
____TSO1	MVS TSO, Part 1: Concepts and ISPF	$31.00
____TSO2	MVS TSO, Part 2: Commands and Procedures	31.00
____MJCL	MVS JCL	34.50
____MBAL	MVS Assembler Language	36.50
____OSUT	OS Utilities	17.50
DOS/VSE Subjects		
____VJLR	DOS/VSE JCL (Second Edition)	$34.50
____ICCF	DOS/VSE ICCF	31.00
____VBAL	DOS/VSE Assembler Language	36.50

☐ Bill the appropriate book prices plus UPS shipping and handling (and sales tax in California) to my ____VISA ____MasterCard:

Card Number _____

Valid thru (month/year)_____

Cardowner's signature_____

☐ Bill me.

☐ Bill my company. P.O. #_____

☐ I want to **save** UPS shipping and handling charges. Here's my check or money order for $_____. California residents, please add sales tax to your total. (Offer valid in the U.S.)

* Prices are subject to change. Please call for current prices.

To order more quickly,

Call **toll-free** 1-800-221-5528

(Weekdays, 8 to 5 Pacific Standard Time)

Fax: 1-209-275-9035

Mike Murach & Associates, Inc.

4697 West Jacquelyn Avenue
Fresno, California 93722-6427
(209) 275-3335

fold

fold

BUSINESS REPLY MAIL

FIRST-CLASS MAIL   PERMIT NO. 3063   FRESNO, CA

POSTAGE WILL BE PAID BY ADDRESSEE

Mike Murach & Associates, Inc.

4697 W JACQUELYN AVE
FRESNO CA 93722-9888

fold

fold